DATE DUE

JE 9 04			
JE 7 06			

DEMCO 38-296

THE INDONESIAN ECONOMY IN THE NINETEENTH AND TWENTIETH CENTURIES

A MODERN ECONOMIC HISTORY OF SOUTHEAST ASIA

General Editors: Anthony Reid (Chair), Professor of Southeast Asian History, the Research School of Pacific and Asian Studies, The Australian National University, Canberra; **Anne Booth**, Professor of Economics, School of Oriental and African Studies (SOAS), London; **Malcolm Falkus**, Professor of Economic History, University of New England, Armidale, Australia; and **Graeme Snooks**, Coghlan Professor of Economic History, Research School of the Social Sciences, The Australian National University, Canberra.

The Australian National University is preparing a multivolume economic history of Southeast Asia, which will for the first time place the remarkable economic changes of the late twentieth century within a broader historical framework. This series is at once a work of pioneering scholarship, since nothing remotely comparable has previously been attempted, and a work of synthesis, since hitherto discrete literatures in several disciplines and on ten countries must be integrated. The series will include several volumes on the economic history of the principal countries of Southeast Asia over the past one hundred and fifty years, and a larger number of volumes integrating the whole region in terms of major themes in economic history. Each volume will be accessible to students and specialists alike, aiming to make coherent a history which has been fragmented or ignored.

The Economic History of Southeast Asia Project has been supported by the Research School of Pacific and Asian Studies of The Australian National University, and by the Henry Luce Foundation.

Other titles in the series include:

R. E. Elson
THE END OF THE PEASANTRY IN SOUTHEAST ASIA

J. Thomas Lindblad
FOREIGN INVESTMENT IN SOUTHEAST ASIA IN THE TWENTIETH CENTURY

R

The Indonesian Economy in the Nineteenth and Twentieth Centuries

A History of Missed Opportunities

Anne Booth
Professor of Economics
School of Oriental and African Studies
University of London

in association with
THE AUSTRALIAN NATIONAL UNIVERSITY
CANBERRA

21 6XS and London
Companies and representatives throughout the world

A catalogue record for this book is available from the British Library.

ISBN 0–333–55309–8 hardcover
ISBN 0–333–55310–1 paperback

First published in the United States of America 1998 by
ST. MARTIN'S PRESS, INC.,
Scholarly and Reference Division,
175 Fifth Avenue, New York, N.Y. 10010

ISBN 0–312–17749–6

Library of Congress Cataloging-in-Publication Data
Booth, Anne.
The Indonesian economy in the nineteenth and twentieth centuries :
a history of missed opportunities / Anne Booth.
p. cm. — (Modern economic history of Southeast Asia)
Includes bibliographical references and index.
ISBN 0–312–17749–6 (cloth)
1. Indonesia—Economic conditions. I. Title. II. Series.
HC447.B675 1997
330.9598—dc21   97–38378
                                                                   CIP

This book is printed on paper suitable for recycling and made from fully managed and
sustained forest sources.

10   9   8   7   6   5   4   3   2   1
07   06   05   04   03   02   01   00   99   98

Printed and bound in Great Britain by
Antony Rowe Ltd, Chippenham, Wiltshire

In memory of my parents

Contents

List of Figures

List of Tables

Preface

These are exciting times to be working on Indonesian economic history. Over the past twenty-five years, the study of the subject has been completely transformed. A paper which appeared in an influential symposium on Indonesian historiography published in 1965 stressed the lack of contemporary research on economic history in Indonesia, and pointed out that what was needed was a new 'hybrid breed' of scholar who was comfortable both with historical research and with economic theory (Tan 1965: 401). But as O'Malley (1990: 1) pointed out, until at least the early 1980s, it was social historians and social anthropologists who dominated the study of economic history in Indonesia; these scholars found that 'they needed to understand the economic side of things better if they were to see more clearly the social changes they were intent on studying'. That they produced much useful work cannot be denied, but inevitably their approach was 'micro' rather than 'macro' and they did not address directly the grand themes of economic growth and structural change which increasingly concerned economic historians in the developed world, and in other parts of Asia, Africa and Latin America. Certainly they appreciated, as Tan (1965: 396–7) stressed, that Indonesian economic history is an international history, and that international economic forces have, over the centuries, determined the evolution of the economies of the far-flung chain of islands which today we know as Indonesia. But they lacked the motivation, and often the analytical tools, to examine the macroeconomic impact of these forces.

The main development which triggered a change in analytical approach over the 1980s was the production and dissemination of the volumes in the Changing Economy of Indonesia series. These volumes (numbering fifteen by 1994) made available a large number of statistical series on agricultural and industrial production, prices, international trade and the balance of payments, money supply, investment, government revenues and expenditures and population growth. They provide not just an invaluable source of data for the quantitative study of Indonesian economic history, but also excellent bibliographic guides to statistical sources and to the secondary literature. Already they have been mined by students writing doctoral dissertations and by scholars not only of Indonesia's economic past but of the economic history of other parts of Asia as well. Increasingly, Indonesia appears in comparative work on Asian economic history, as more scholars seek to discover the secrets of the economic past of what is now the most dynamic part of the global economy.

This book is thus intended to present a stocktaking of what has become a fast-growing field of study. But it also tries to provide at least a tentative answer to what is surely the main question any economic historian of Indonesia must ask: why at the close of the twentieth century is the country still relatively poor and economically undeveloped? What were the major policy errors of both colonial and post-colonial governments which have produced this state of affairs? Were these errors of commission or of omission? What, in short, does a study of Indonesia's economic past teach us about the larger question of persistent poverty in so much of Asia, Africa and Latin America? I have posed these ambitious questions in the Indonesian context out of a conviction that it is only through a detailed study of a country's economic past that we can understand its contemporary problems. In Indonesia it is especially difficult to view economic issues in a longterm perspective because the two great political upheavals of 1945 and 1965 have encouraged many observers to see economic development as a very recent policy concern, and sustained economic growth as a very recent policy achievement. If it does nothing else, I hope that this book will provide a corrective to this view.

This book has been in process for over a decade, and during that time I have built up many debts. The book was begun during my tenure as a Senior Research Fellow at the Australian National University, and I am especially grateful to Tony Reid, the Director of the Project on the Modern Economic History of South East Asia for his help and support. The workshop which the Project held on a draft of the manuscript in April 1995 was of enormous value and I am very grateful to Heinz Arndt, Howard Dick, Pierre van der Eng, Hal Hill, Chris Manning, Ross McCleod, and Peter Warr for their detailed comments. At SOAS I have benefited greatly from interaction with many colleagues whose interests span the length and breadth of Asia and Africa. I am also very indebted to Gregg Huff of the University of Glasgow, and Thomas Lindblad of Leiden University who both gave me valuable comments on parts of the manuscript. Needless to say, I am solely responsible for remaining deficiencies.

Thanks are due to Prentice Hall, Singapore for permission to reproduce material from my chapter in B. K. Kapur, Euston Quah and Hoon Hian Teck, *Development, Trade, and the Asia-Pacific:*

Essays in Honour of Professor Lim Chong Yah (1996), and thanks are also due to Thomas Lindblad for permission to reproduce a chapter in the volume edited by him and published by North Holland in 1996. I am also grateful to John Harriss, Janet Hunter and Colin M. Lewis for permission to use material originally published in the book edited by them, *The New Institutional Economics and Third World Development*, published by Routledge in 1995.

ANNE BOOTH
London

1 Introduction

THE FORMATION OF AN 'INDONESIAN' ECONOMY

After the breakup of the former Soviet Union in the early 1990s, Indonesia became the fourth most populous country in the world. Yet many features of its history, economy and society remain poorly understood, not just by the outside world but also by the great majority of Indonesians. How did this vast and heterogeneous collection of tropical islands become a unified nation state? As Legge (1990: 127) has pointed out, the national motto, 'Unity in Diversity' suggests 'a sense almost of proud surprise' that Indonesia should exist at all. Few serious scholars would deny that Indonesia in its present form is an artifact of Western colonial rule. Yet in 1995 the nation celebrated the fiftieth anniversary of the declaration of independence promulgated by Soekarno and Hatta as Japanese rule was collapsing in August, 1945. Indonesia in the mid-1990s appeared to the outside world as a successful and rapidly developing economy, confidently taking its place among other industrial powers in the dynamic Asia-Pacific region. Certainly it might be true that 'its geographical spread, archipelagic character, ethnic complexity, and economic diversity hardly made it a natural candidate for independent nationhood' (Legge 1990: 127). But against all odds, it had survived as an independent nation for half a century, and few in 1995 would have been prepared to argue that Indonesia would not endure for the foreseeable future.

Thus the mid-1990s appears an opportune time to reassess Indonesian economic history, not just in the period since independence, but in a rather longer time perspective. The first question which anyone writing such an economic history must confront is at what stage does it become possible to talk about an 'Indonesian economy'? The origins of the term 'Indonesia' itself is the subject of scholarly debate, but certainly the term only began to be used in the middle decades of the nineteenth century. It was adopted by the nationalists studying in the Netherlands in the 1920s, but the first time it was ever officially used by the Dutch was after the Japanese occupation, in 1942 (Jones 1994: 280–1). It seems fairly obvious that before the mid-nineteenth century few regarded the sprawling archipelago as a political, administrative or economic entity, so there was no need for a term to encompass it. Until the latter part of the nineteenth century, the

1

Dutch presence outside Java was extremely thin, and apart from Ambon, Minahasa, and West Sumatra, no attempt was made to extend the Javanese policy of forced cultivation of export crops to other parts of the archipelago. A Dutch historian has argued that in the nineteenth century, the term 'Dutch East Indies' actually meant Java, 'a fact which everyone at that time was very much aware of' (Wesseling 1978: 5). Thus it was no accident that three of the best-known books written by non-Dutch authors in the years from 1860 to 1905 in fact referred only to Java (Money 1861; Chailly-Bert 1900; Day 1904).

But if nineteenth-century writings on Indonesia were inevitably 'Java-centric', many scholars writing in the latter part of the twentieth century have tried to correct the balance. Numerous historians have described how the Dutch gradually brought all the diverse territories of the Outer Islands under their rule during the nineteenth century, and have analysed the impact of this incorporation on the indigenous populations. Ricklefs (1993:131) has pointed out that the motives for Dutch territorial acquisitions were mixed and often more strategic than economic:

> Two general considerations applied everywhere. First, to protect the security of the areas they already held, the Dutch felt compelled to subdue other regions which might support or inspire resistance movements. Second, as the European scramble for colonies reached its height in the later nineteenth century, the Dutch felt obliged to establish their claims to the outer islands of the archipelago in order to prevent some other Western power from intervening there, even where the Dutch initially had no great interest themselves (Ricklefs 1993: 131).

Locher-Scholten (1994: 94–5) argues that the Dutch never had a grand strategy of territorial acquisition for the whole archipelago and it is probably reasonable to view Dutch colonial policy in the nine-teenth century as essentially concerned with asserting more effective control over regions which had been broadly considered as within the 'Dutch sphere of influence' since the Treaty of London in 1824 (Wesseling 1988: 66). Locher-Scholten suggests that it was usually impulses from the periphery which provoked the government in Batavia to send military force to subdue particular regions; she also acknowledges that fear of foreign intrusion was always an important factor in Dutch behaviour. For the most part, the Dutch and the British continued to abide by the territorial divisions struck in

London in 1824 for the rest of the century, although the Sumatra Treaty of 1871 effectively ceded all British interests in Aceh to the Dutch in return for Dutch undertakings that British citizens would enjoy the same rights as Dutch in conducting business and trade in North Sumatra (Reid 1969: Chapter 2). The Dutch continued to be wary not just of British intentions but also of those of the Germans, the Portuguese and indeed the increasingly assertive Australian colonies. It was probably Australian requests for grants of land in New Guinea in the 1880s which forced the Dutch to strengthen their presence in 'their half' of that huge and remote island, buttressed by moralistic notions of a civilising mission to the indigenous populations (Locher-Scholten 1994: 105).

How strong were economic motivations in this increasing assertion of Dutch control? Locher-Scholten (1994: 102) points out that 'almost never were economic reasons cited as the main justification for military actions' in the official documents, but this of course hardly means that they were insignificant. Private capitalists became more active in Sumatra and Kalimantan in the last decades of the nineteenth century, and their increasing involvement in export production underpinned what Lindblad (1989: 16) has termed the 'macroeconomics of expansion' outside Java. Almost always, the economic development of the diverse regions outside Java was closely linked to the fortunes of a few key commodities. East Sumatra was transformed in a few decades because of world demand for tobacco and then rubber; oil, and to a lesser extent coal, were certainly major reasons for Dutch intervention in Central Sumatra and Southeast Kalimantan at the close of the nineteenth century; gold was a powerful magnet for foreigners in West Kalimantan and Central Sulawesi, while coffee and then copra were the key crops in North Sulawesi (Lindblad 1989; Schouten 1995).

Other motivations for Dutch actions outside Java included the search for new revenue sources. The punitive expedition against the Raja of Bone in 1905 was motivated in part by irritation at his refusal to cede customs revenues to the colonial government. The pressing need to increase budgetary revenues also explains the Dutch preoccupation with curbing trading links with Singapore, and other regional ports outside the Dutch sphere of influence. As early as the 1820s, Dutch officials tried to 'ring-fence' the Minangkabau lands of West Sumatra, and cut off their trade with both Singapore and Penang by establishing customs posts at the headwaters of rivers flowing down to the east coast (Dobbin 1983: 218–19). The desire to divert trade from Singapore also lay behind the concession of free port status to

Makassar in 1847, although this plan produced unforeseen consequences which in turn led to its withdrawal in 1905 (Poelinggomang
1993: 66–70). In several parts of the archipelago which were free of
direct Dutch control, trading links with Singapore and Penang continued to flourish for much of the nineteenth century. Bulbeck *et al.*
(forthcoming, Table 3.8 to 3.11) describe the steady (albeit fluctuating) growth in pepper trade from the independent states in Northern
Sumatra to Malaysia between 1780 and 1890, while van der Kraan
(1993) discusses the rice trade from Bali and Lombok to Singapore in
the middle decades of the century. Dutch suspicion of the consequences of these flourishing links were certainly important factors
in the military interventions in Bali in 1848 (van der Kraan 1994: 90)
and Aceh after 1870 (Reid 1969: 17–24).

Wesseling (1988: 68) has argued that 1900 witnessed the transition
from 'old to new colonialism' in Indonesia. This new colonialism was
'characterised by a systematic *mise en valeur* and an active role on the
part of the state'. As the new century dawned, strategic, administrative and economic factors all conspired to integrate the disparate
collection of islands over which some form of Dutch control had
been established into something considerably more than just a loosely
integrated free trade area. The colonial authorities could no longer
tolerate a situation where a 'multitude of currencies were used next to
one another' and forceful measures were adopted to make the Indies
guilder the only legal tender in areas such as the east coast of Sumatra
(Lindblad 1989: 21). The impact of more uniform fiscal, monetary,
exchange rate and tariff policies thus began to affect all parts of the
archipelago, and both foreign and domestic investment was increasingly drawn into the exploitation of resources in the more remote
islands. Trade between independent states such as Aceh and Bali
and the rest of the world might have declined after their integration
into the Netherlands Indies, but new exports emerged from other
parts of Sumatra as well as from Kalimantan and Sulawesi, sometimes
at extraordinary speed, to replace the old. By the 1920s the 'outer
islands' accounted for more than half of Indonesian exports, and
exports from Java only began to grow again relative to those from
the rest of the country with the emergence of export-oriented manufacturing industries in Java in the 1980s.

Indeed, it is possible to argue that the single greatest achievement of
the last century of Dutch rule was to create at least the framework for
an integrated economy and nation state out of numerous regions
whose commercial links with one another had hitherto often been

negligible. But the economic costs of a policy of coercive integration were considerable. The impulses transmitted to Sumatra, Kalimantan and Sulawesi by world market forces might have been tugging the trade of these regions in the direction of Singapore, and of other regional ports, but considerations of Dutch imperial 'nation-building' wrenched it towards Java. It is undeniable that tighter economic links with Java were often achieved through the use of blunt regulatory instruments which not infrequently forced the trade of the archipelago to 'flow uphill' through trans-shipment in Java ports (Dick 1996: 37). As Java was transformed into the hub of a vast archipelagic economy, its infrastructure developed rapidly, so that by the 1920s Java had one of the densest road and rail networks outside Europe, several thriving port cities and growing industrial and commercial sectors. By contrast, much of the rest of the archipelago remained relatively undeveloped with modern infrastructure confined to export enclaves.

But in spite of the very visible signs of economic development in Java by the early twentieth century, the island's population remained poor. After the famous speech from the throne in 1901, Java's poverty became a major preoccupation of Dutch colonial economic policy and remained so up to 1942. The reason for this lay in the rather special character of Dutch colonialism. Unlike the major European colonial powers, Great Britain and France, the Dutch had no pretensions to great power status and did not view their enormous colonial possession in Southeast Asia as a platform either for gaining more territory elsewhere in Asia or Africa, or for nationalistic self-assertion in Europe. But, as Wesseling (1988: 69) points out, they did want 'to keep what they had, which was a great deal'. Indeed, after 1900 they wanted their Indonesian possessions to 'belong' to the Netherlands not just in an economic but in a cultural sense as well. And if the islands of Indonesia were truly to become part of Dutch society the gap in living standards would have to be narrowed. Having already acquired the territory, the Dutch thus began to fashion a rhetoric of imperialism to go with it (Schoffer 1978: 80ff). This rhetoric put far more emphasis on material improvement than was the case with British or French imperialism, because this was what an increasingly prosperous Dutch bourgeoisie demanded in order to justify their government's colonial activities in a string of exotic tropical islands on the other side of the world.

There can be no doubt that the gap between Dutch and Indonesian per capita GDP had widened through the nineteenth century, and by 1900 Indonesian GDP per capita was little more than 20 per cent of that in the Netherlands (Table 1.1). By 1950, the per capita GDP gap between Indonesia and the Netherlands had grown even greater. To many Indonesian nationalists, the widening gap was the result of systematic Dutch exploitation of the colonial economy; the wealth of the Indies had been drained away to promote the economic development of the Netherlands. But after independence, although the rate of GDP growth accelerated, the gap between Indonesia and the Netherlands scarcely altered, and Indonesia fell well behind other fast-growing East Asian economies such as Japan and South Korea. Thus, although the origins of Indonesia's relative backwardness are to be found in the colonial era, in the post-independence era, Indonesia has been, at best, only partially successful in catching up.

Table 1.1 GDP per capita in 1990 international dollars

Year	Indonesia	Netherlands	Japan	South Korea
1820	614	1 561	704	
1870	657	2 640	741	
1900	745	3 533	1 135	850
1913	917	3 950	1 334	948
1950	874	5 850	1 873	876
1973	1 538	12 763	11 017	2 840
1992	2 749	16 898	19 425	10 010
Average annual growth rates:				
1820–1900	0.2	1.0	0.6	
1900–50	0.3	1.0	1.0	0.1
1950–92	2.8	2.6	5.7	6.0

Source: Maddison (1995), pp. 23–4

CONTINUITY AND CHANGE IN INDONESIAN ECONOMIC PERFORMANCE

In spite of the fact that the Indonesian archipelago had been the chief colonial possession of one of the most advanced and wealthy countries in Western Europe, and in spite of the fact that, in the last four decades of their rule, the Dutch made what was certainly the most thorough attempt by any European colonial government to implement the kind of policies which today we would think of as 'developmental', Indonesia emerged into independence as a very poor country. It is one of the great ironies of European colonialism that the Dutch were determined to retain their colonial possessions in Indonesia after 1945 because they were certain that their loss would mean the economic devastation of the Netherlands. Yet the two decades following the final surrender of Dutch control in 1949 were ones of rapid economic growth and increasing prosperity in the Netherlands. In Indonesia matters turned out very differently. The nationalists blamed Indonesia's poverty on three centuries of Dutch colonialism, a phrase that conveniently ignored the fact that much of the archipelago had been under effective Dutch control for only a few decades. It was assumed that as soon as Indonesians were masters in their own house, living standards would improve rapidly. Very few Indonesians grasped the fact that the root causes of their poverty went far deeper than Dutch exploitation, and could not be remedied by nationalistic rhetoric and populist policies. There was also a reluctance on the part of the nationalist movement to comprehend that the Dutch achievement in consolidating the country into a single administrative unit was not accompanied by an emergence of national consciousness on the part of the great mass of the population (Nasution 1992: 263).

In common with other newly independent nations in Asia, the Indonesian government during the 1950s sought and obtained the advice of a number of foreign economic advisers. In addition, some of their most promising students were sent abroad for further training in economics, mainly in American universities. Ambitious development plans were drawn up, and specialised bureaucracies established to implement them. But by the mid-1960s Indonesia was viewed by both foreign and Indonesian economists as a development catastrophe. One prominent development economist called Indonesia 'the chronic dropout', and claimed that the country 'must surely be accounted the number one economic failure among the major underdeveloped countries' (Higgins 1968: 678). Higgins then went on to list a catalogue of problems: food production was falling behind population growth, making the country more dependent on imports at a time when export earnings were declining, and successive budget deficits were fuelling runaway inflation. Infrastructure was deteriorating, and real per capita income was almost certainly lower than it had been in the late 1930s, and probably lower than it had been in 1913. The national economy was disintegrating, and resource-rich parts of the country were trading independently with neighbouring countries.

While acknowledging that the policies of successive post-independence governments had been far from helpful, Higgins was inclined to blame much of Indonesia's economic failure on the Dutch colonial regime. In fact, he argued that 'had it not been for the delaying action of three and one-half centuries of colonial rule, an Indonesian "take-off" might have occurred long ago' (Higgins 1968: 683). He quoted a number of historical sources to support his argument that 'when the Portuguese arrived in Indonesia at the end of the fifteenth century, they showed no marked superiority to the Indonesians in technology, labour and managerial skills, or entrepreneurial activities'. Higgins stressed that shipbuilding and navigational technologies in Southeast Asia were not obviously inferior to those of the European maritime powers in the fifteenth and sixteenth centuries, and emphasised the considerable involvement of the various coastal kingdoms in trade and commerce. The open and urbanised nature of the pre-colonial economy of the Indonesian archipelago has also been emphasised by other students of pre-colonial Indonesian economic history (Reid 1993: Chapter 2).

Of course the Indonesian archipelago was hardly unique in being, at the beginning of the age of European overseas expansion, not obviously inferior in technological and commercial development to the European power which was ultimately to become its coloniser. Students of Indian and Chinese economic history have also argued that, in what European historians refer to as the 'dark ages', these countries were in both the cultural and the technological sense more 'developed' than those in Northern Europe who would by the end of the nineteenth century control the trade and commerce of virtually the entire Asian continent. But European military and economic technology, commercial skills and legal infrastructure all developed rapidly after 1600, while those of the Asian states stagnated or declined. In the Indonesian context, the seventeenth century saw the gradual demise of the powerful indigenous kingdoms and the assertion of the commercial hegemony of the Netherlands East India Company which continued through the eighteenth century, until it was replaced by a Dutch administration centred in Java in 1800.

The economic legacy of Dutch colonialism to independent Indonesia was, and remains, an issue which has attracted more emotional rhetoric than dispassionate analysis, and one purpose of this book will be to examine more closely the economic achievements and failures of the last century or so of Dutch rule. It will be argued in the next chapter that gross domestic product, or the real amount of goods and services produced in the economy, almost certainly grew faster than the population in the years between 1830 and 1940. But a number of factors prevented this growth from leading to a process of sustained economic development, such as happened in most parts of Western Europe, including the Netherlands, in the nineteenth and twentieth centuries, and in Japan after 1870. Even less did the growth of output lead to a sustained improvement in living standards for the great majority of the indigenous population. But in spite of these failures, the colonial economy underwent substantial structural change, to the point where the country, and the economy, which the Dutch were forced to surrender to Japan in 1942, would scarcely have been recognisable to Daendels, Raffles or van den Bosch.

Central to the changes which occurred in the nineteenth and early twentieth century was a considerable diversification of economic activity, much of it in response to the growth of population, to changing production technologies and to the emergence of new markets for tropical produce in the industrialising countries of Europe and North America. But a growth strategy based on increased integration with the international economy brought risks, chief among them being fluctuations in prices of key export staples, and sudden exclusion from foreign export markets. Indeed, there is a sense in which the entire economic history of Indonesia from the latter part of the nineteenth century to the present day can be viewed as a series of responses on the part of a series of governments to external economic instability, much of it generated by fluctuations in world prices of key export staples. In the severe world depression of the 1930s, falling export prices and growing protectionism forced the colonial government into a series of policy changes which had important consequences not just for economic performance in the final years of the Dutch colonial era, but also for economic development after 1950.

The four decades from the mid-1920s to the mid-1960s are often seen as ones of economic stagnation, and even of decline, partly because of unfavourable external conditions, and partly because of domestic political upheavals. The decades since 1965, on the contrary, are usually viewed as characterised by economic growth quite unprecedented in the country's historical experience (van der Eng 1992: 353; Boomgaard 1993: 210). Certainly the statistical evidence supports such a view. Between 1969 and 1993 real GDP grew at a trend rate of almost 7 per cent per annum. Not only was this economic growth remarkable in comparison with what had gone before, but it was also much better than that of most other developing countries. The growth acceleration after 1969 coincided with the dramatic improvement in the country's terms of trade, due mainly to the improvement in the world price of oil, and created the impression that the two events were causally linked. But Indonesia's growth performance in the years of high world oil prices was in fact substantially better than that of several other 'populated petroleum economies', such as Iran or Nigeria.

Even after world oil prices began to fall in the early 1980s, the Indonesian government continued to attract favourable comment from the international development agencies such as the World Bank for its implementation of appropriate and well-timed stabilisation and adjustment policies. But at the same time doubts were expressed about how much had really changed in the Indonesian economy. Indeed, some scholars saw the oil boom years as just a brief interruption in the long-term record of slow growth and stagnant living standards. In his survey of economic growth in the third world from 1850 to 1980, Reynolds (1985: 357) concluded that modern economic growth only started in Indonesia after 1965, 'and the impressive GDP figures since that time are heavily weighted with oil exports. The longer-range future is still uncertain'. A survey in the *Economist* in August 1987 referred to Indonesia as Asia's 'underachiever'. This image of Indonesia as a vast and resource-rich country which stubbornly refuses to realise its development potential continues to be widespread among observers of international affairs in many parts of the world.

To what extent does this image accord with the reality of Indonesian economic performance over the past 150 years? It is easy to dismiss at least some of the opinions quoted above as snap reactions on the part of outsiders to temporary phases in Indonesian economic development, which in turn reflect the vicissitudes of the international economic environment. The same point, indeed, can be made about the more recent inclusion of Indonesia in a group of Asian economies categorised by the World Bank in 1993 as 'high performers', who seem to 'have done almost everything right' (Bruno 1994:10). To many observers of Indonesia since 1965, such an assertion is surprising, especially as the World Bank in 1993 still classified Indonesia as a 'low-income economy', considerably poorer, in fact, than most of its East Asian neighbours.

Certainly there are plausible reasons for claiming that the growth and structural change which has occurred in Indonesia since the late 1960s is in some important aspects 'different' from the economic changes of earlier times. For one thing, the export economy has become far more diversified, and less reliant on a few primary staples whose prices on world markets are prone to massive and unpredictable fluctuations. By the early 1990s a substantial and growing part of total export revenues comprised manufactured goods, and services such as tourism. The ratio of investment to GDP increased considerably between 1970 and 1990, and the consequences of this investment in the form of greatly improved infrastructure, and new factories and offices are visible everywhere, not just in the largest cities but in towns and villages throughout the archipelago. Access to education has improved and, perhaps most important of all, the institutions of a market economy are developing rapidly, and becoming more familiar to the mass of the population.

Do these changes represent a dramatic break with the past, or a continuation of a much longer cyclical process of economic and social change, whose roots go back at least to the nineteenth century and perhaps further? Will the phase of accelerated economic growth since 1965 prove to be just another in a long series of missed opportunities, leading not to accelerated economic development, but rather to another period of stagnation? A striking aspect of much of the recent literature on Indonesian economic development is that these questions are seldom raised. Indeed, most studies of Indonesia's rapid growth over the past twenty-five years have generally been reluctant to make any longer-term comparisons. Many focus on limited topics, covering the years since 1970, or later. Historical studies also concentrate on particular periods, and few venture beyond 1940. While this episodic approach has produced a number of excellent studies of specific issues, it has tended to reinforce the impression that each phase of Indonesian economic history is a self-contained entity with few linkages to what has gone before, or to what has come after. This view has been particularly strong among students of post-independence economic developments, who have, almost without exception, been averse to any investigation of the colonial period. Among Indonesian, and indeed some foreign, scholars this aversion is sometimes reinforced by rather simplistic views of how the colonial economy operated, and of the impact of political independence on the economic policy-making process.

One result of this piecemeal approach to the study of economic change in Indonesia is that policy makers in general have been reluctant to learn from past experience. Indeed, they can hardly be expected to draw lessons from the past when they possess such a poor understanding of it. Needless to say, this is even truer of the large numbers of foreigners from a host of international organisations and bilateral aid agencies who have participated in the economic policy-making process in Indonesia since the late 1960s. Thus the World Bank and other important lending agencies have praised Indonesia for its fiscal and monetary restraint, its market-oriented exchange rate policies, and its open-door policies to foreign investment since the late 1960s. As far as macro-economic policy is concerned, Indonesia has indeed been a prominent exponent of what has come to be called the 'Washington consensus' (Williamson 1994: 26–8). But precisely these same policies were consistently pursued by the colonial regime for at least six decades from 1870 to 1930. If they did not usher in a process of sustained economic development then, why should they now?

A central argument of this book is that a much better understanding of Indonesia's economic past is essential for formulating policies for future change. History casts a long shadow over the present, in economic matters as much as in other aspects of human affairs. As North (1990:112) has pointed out,

> Path dependence is the key to an analytical understanding of long-run economic change . . . Path dependence comes from the increasing returns mechanisms that reinforce the direction once on a given path. Alterations in the path come from unanticipated consequences of choices, external effects, and sometimes forces exogenous to the analytical framework. Reversals of paths (from stagnation to growth and vice versa) may come from the above described sources of path alteration, but will typically occur through changes in the polity.

In this book I will argue that Dutch colonial policies between 1815 and 1942 placed the Indonesian economy on a trajectory from which it has only partially departed. While I do not wish to deny the important economic changes which have occurred since independence, and especially since 1965, I will try to highlight the underlying continuities in policy-making and the implications of these continuities for Indonesian economic development in the longer term. In the fifty years since independence the rhetoric of nationalism has replaced the rhetoric of imperialism in the economic sphere as elsewhere. But there were, and continue to be, more similarities in the economic goals of the Dutch colonialists and the Indonesian nationalists than has yet been acknowledged. These similarities are in turn due to the persistence of many underlying problems. The Dutch in 1900 were alarmed at Javanese poverty and at the size of the gap between incomes and living standards in the Netherlands and in the colonial territories. Since independence, however, the gap in per capita income between

Indonesia and the Netherlands has scarcely altered. Between Indonesia and the dynamic economies of Northeast Asia such as Japan and South Korea it has greatly increased. And within Indonesia, the economic development process is reinforcing regional inequalities which originated in the colonial era. I begin, therefore, with an examination of the process of economic growth and its distributional outcomes over the past two centuries.

2 Output Growth and Structural Change: 1820–1990

PHASES OF GROWTH: AN INTRODUCTION

Fortunately for students of Indonesian economic growth in the last twelve decades of Dutch colonial rule, there is an abundance of evidence on growth of output of key commodities, as well as on imports and exports, government revenues and expenditures, and the volume of money in circulation. During the early and middle decades of the nineteenth century, much of the available quantitative information is for Java only, although as more work is done on other parts of the archipelago, it is increasingly possible to place the Javanese story in a broader perspective. This becomes easier after 1870, as more production and trade data for the entire area of the Netherlands Indies are available in official sources. Following the work of Leff (1982), van Laanen (1989) used the evidence on growth of the real money supply between 1850 and 1940 to estimate growth of output. More recently, van der Eng (1992) has compiled a time series of real GDP from 1880 to 1989. Although both these exercises are flawed for reasons which will be discussed in more detail below, they both offer valuable insights into the nature of the growth process in Indonesia in the nineteenth and twentieth centuries.

Both these studies demonstrate that per capita GDP did grow in real terms over the last century or so of Dutch colonial rule, albeit with considerable fluctuations. But, as van Laanen stresses, the growth was not rapid; he suggests a growth of per capita national income over the ninety years from 1850 to 1940 of only 0.5 per cent per annum. Van der Eng's estimates indicate a rather higher growth in per capita GDP over the years from 1880 to 1940 of around 0.9 per cent per annum. This was higher than the growth achieved in other Asian economies such as India or Thailand over the same period, although much lower than what was achieved after independence. It was also lower than per capita GDP growth in most parts of Western

Europe, the USA, and Japan in the latter part of the nineteenth and the early twentieth centuries.

It would thus appear that Indonesia entered what one economic historian has termed 'the phase of intensive growth', characterised by increasing per capita output, around the middle of the nineteenth century (Reynolds 1985: 8). Indeed, as will be argued below, Java's GDP probably grew in per capita terms from the late 1820s, or even from the latter part of the eighteenth century. Of course, GDP data tell us nothing about the ultimate destination of the goods and services produced. How much was consumed, or invested, within Indonesia, how much used to finance imports of goods and services and how much remitted abroad in the form of unrequited export surpluses? To what extent were domestic resources supplemented by external borrowing? How did fluctuations in the terms of trade affect the real value of domestic output? To what extent, in short, was the growth in the real value of output reflected in growth in real national income, corrected for fluctuations in the terms of trade?

In this and following chapters, I try to answer some of these questions. This chapter focuses on the quantification of output growth, and structural change. It examines in detail annual time series data for a range of variables and indexes. But before embarking on such an examination, it is important to establish markers for periods, or phases, of growth in the nineteenth and twentieth centuries. Boomgaard (1993: 210) has argued that between 1800 and 1990 six such phases can be identified:

1800–1835: stagnation
1835–1875: growth
1875–1895: stagnation
1895–1925: growth
1925–1965: decline/stagnation
1965–1990: growth

While Boomgaard argues that, taken as a whole, these two centuries were characterised by growth and development, according to his schema ten decades out of the nineteen being considered were in fact ones of stagnation or decline. In what follows I will suggest a rather different approach to the problem of periodicity. First, in the nineteenth century it is essential to separate out evidence relating to Java from the (admittedly more meagre) evidence relating to the rest of the archipelago. It cannot simply be assumed that trends in Java were mirrored elsewhere. Second, several of the periods put forward by

Boomgaard are too long, in that they embrace a diverse range of political and economic events which affected output growth in different ways. This is especially true of the 'long depression' from the late 1920s to the late 1960s. While there can be no doubt that per capita GDP in 1970 was little different from that in 1930, these four decades were marked by a series of momentous events, beginning with the world slump of the early 1930s and ending with the violent political upheavals of the 1960s. Thus in what follows, rather shorter time periods will be examined, and trends in output growth will be linked both to changes in domestic economic policies, which frequently reflected changes in political priorities, and to world market trends.

ECONOMIC GROWTH IN JAVA: 1800–70

Although Java had been important as a producer of export crops (pepper, rice and sugar) in the sixteenth and seventeenth centuries and the ports along the north coast had developed as important centres of entrepot trade, Java could hardly be said to have dominated the trade of the archipelago, as the standard histories by Meilink-Roelofsz (1962) and Glamann (1958) make clear. But for the first seven decades of the nineteenth century, Javanese export trade is often treated as synonymous with Indonesian export trade, and many discussions of the causes and consequences of export growth in Indonesia in this period concern themselves almost entirely with Java. This is obviously misleading; as was pointed out in the last chapter, several parts of the archipelago which were not under Dutch control in the early nineteenth century developed quite important export markets. But because so much more data are available for Java, it is useful to discuss the Javanese case first before looking at the evidence for other regions. This section focuses especially on the consequences of the *cultuurstelsel* (CS) for growth in output in Java for the years from the late 1820s to the early 1870s. As Fasseur (1992:7) has pointed out, no other topic in Dutch colonial historiography has generated so much discussion, and no attempt is made to summarise the large and still growing literature on the CS in its entirety. I focus here on the impact which the CS had on growth of output.

When we read the descriptions of Java in the first decade of the nineteenth century left by Raffles (1817) and Crawfurd (1820), we are struck by the impression of land abundance and low population densities which both writers convey. In a famous passage, Raffles

(1817: Vol. 1: 108) claimed that 'over far the greater part, seven-eights of the island, the soil is either entirely neglected or badly cultivated and the population scanty', while Crawfurd (1820: Vol 3: 54–5) noted that an 'extraordinary quantity of good land is still unoccupied' and emphasised the 'high price of labour, and the extraordinary demand for cultivators'. To Raffles, Java was a land of fertile soils and a benign climate, where 'subsistence is procured without difficulty' and where the bulk of the population had little difficulty in obtaining sufficient surplus income for such other comforts as their limited wants and needs might require. These observations might appear to indicate that most of the agricultural production was for subsistence, with little or no cultivation of cashcrops. Certainly there can be little doubt that the volume of cashcrop production (mainly sugar and coffee) being produced in Java in the last decade of the eighteenth century was quite small, about 5,500 tons of coffee and 5,000 tons of sugar (Boomgaard 1989a: 119). On the other hand, a wide variety of foodcrops was cultivated, of which rice appeared to Raffles and Crawfurd to be the most important, although both stress the importance of maize in some areas. Boomgaard and van Zanden (CEI Vol 10: 51) estimated that the per capita production of all foodstuffs, including coconuts, fish and meat amounted to 1,917 calories per day in 1815, of which 86 per cent came from rice and *palawija* (corn, rootcrops and pulses) crops. In addition, cotton was widely cultivated, mainly for use by the cultivating household. The spinning of yarn and weaving of cloth was an important activity, especially for women, who in many parts of Java devoted a considerable amount of time to the task (van der Kraan 1996: 37–8; Fernando 1996: 85).

By the end of the 1820s, exports of sugar and coffee had grown to more than 25,000 tons, which suggests an annual average rate of growth of about three per cent for these two export staples in the first three decades of the nineteenth century. But this growth pales into insignificance compared with what was achieved in the decade of the 1830s, when the *cultuurstelsel* got underway. Volume of exports of the principal staples (sugar, coffee, indigo, and rice) grew by an average of 13.5 per cent per annum between 1830 and 1840 (Table 2.1), which implies more than a threefold increase in ten years. But this remarkable expansion cannot be interpreted as the response either of foreign entrepreneurs or of indigenous smallholders to the challenge offered by growing foreign markets. As van Niel (1992: 207–8) has pointed out,

European capital, the only capital available at the time, had had varied experiences with colonial agrarian enterprises, and was not attracted to investment in Java because of the high risks...The Javanese village was totally outside the realm of capital economic involvement, and showed no interest in the area of cultivation for export. Left to its own devices, it focused on its own subsistence, producing rice, cotton, indigo, and other products for daily use...Experience between 1815 and 1830 had shown that where export cultivations, such as coffee gardens, had been turned over to village control they were neglected or abandoned.

Table 2.1 Annual average growth* in major economic aggregates 1830–1990

Period	Export volume†	Export prices†	Income terms of trade	Per capita GDP	Real money supply	Real government expenditure
Culture System:						
1830–40	13.5	5.0	20.4	n.a	n.a	8.5
1840–48	1.5	−4.5	−2.4	n.a	n.a	** ..
1849–73	1.5	1.5	3.8	n.a	6.3	2.6
Liberal period:						
1874–1900	3.1	−1.9	4.2	** ..	2.7	2.3
(1885–1900	3.9	−2.0	4.1	** ..	1.6	2.2)
Ethical period:						
1901–28	5.8	17.4	5.3	1.7	3.6	4.1
(1920–28	7.7	−7.1	6.8	2.3	4.8	1.6)
1928–34	−3.9	−19.7	−6.9	−3.4	−2.2	0.4
1934–40	2.2	7.8	2.2	2.5	3.8	3.4
Old order:						
1950–65	0.8	−2.1	0.1	1.0	7.3	1.8
(1950–57	1.3	−3.6	2.5	3.4	11.3	2.7)
New order:						
1966–90	5.4	11.6	15.8	4.4	9.3	10.6
(1974–81	2.5	16.1	19.5	5.0	10.6	11.4)
(1982–90	4.3	−8.6	1.7	3.0	7.1	5.9)

* Calculated by fitting an exponential curve to the data for the years indicated.
† Up to 1873 data refer only to Java.
** very low.
Sources: Export volume and prices: Up to 1940 the Laspeyres index of export volume and prices calculated by van Ark (1986: 44–6), was used. Between 1950 and 1967 the indexes calculated by Rosendale (1975: 73–8), were used. After 1967 the export volume and price indices published in the monthly International Monetary Fund publication, *International Financial Statistics* were used.

(*Cont'd*)

(*Cont'd*)

Income terms of trade: Up to 1940 the income terms of trade have been obtained by deflating the index of nominal export values by the import price index given in CEI, Vol. 15, Appendix A. Between 1950 and 1967 the income terms of trade index computed by Rosendale (1975: 80) was used. From 1967 to 1990 the income terms of trade were computed from data in the *International Financial Statistics*.

Real money supply: Up to 1940 data on money supply and deflator were taken from van Laanen (1989), Table 1. After 1950 data on money supply from Nugroho (1967: 476) and *Indonesian Financial Statistics* were deflated by the GDP deflator.

Real government expenditure: Up to 1913 data on government expenditure from CEI Vol. 2, Table 3, 4 and 5 was deflated by the deflator used by van Laanen (1989). Between 1913 and 1940 the deflator used was the Batavia retail price index as reported in Central Bureau of Statistics (1938), Table X. After 1950 data on public expenditure obtained from *Statistical Pocketbook of Indonesia, 1968–9*, p. 317, and *Indonesian Financial Statistics* were deflated by the GDP deflator.

Real national income: Between 1880 and 1941 data taken from van der Eng (1992), Table A4. Between 1950 and 1959 a real domestic product series was estimated from data in World Bank *World Tables, 1976*, pp. 122–3, and in United Nations *Yearbook of National Accounts, 1960*, p. 114. After 1960 successive publications of the *National Income of Indonesia* from the Central Bureau of Statistics have been used.

Faced with these obstacles to the private cultivation of export crops, and 'desperate for profit from the colony' the Dutch king was persuaded by van den Bosch to try a quite different mechanism for increasing export crop production, which involved the imposition by government of obligations to grow crops on individual villages (van Niel 1992: 137 ff). At least in theory, only one-fifth of village land would be set aside for the cultivation of export crops stipulated by the government, which the farmer 'would have to cultivate, harvest and deliver to the state warehouses' (van Baardewijk: CEI Vol 14: 12). This would, in fact, have lightened the tax burden on the peasantry compared with the land tax imposed by Raffles, which amounted to 40 per cent of the rice harvest. But the labour demands placed on the peasants were considerable; by 1834 it was estimated that 658,000 labourers were involved in the cultivation of coffee, sugar and indigo, and by 1840 this had increased to more than 870,000 labourers or an estimated 12 per cent of the total population of Java (CEI Vol 14: 190). The increase in labour devoted to crop cultivation meant that less was available for other activities such as household handicraft production, although the growth of cloth imports from Britain and Belgium in the 1820s had led to a decline in the domestic weaving sector even before the CS really began (van der Kraan 1996: 60).

The extraordinary success of the CS in its first decade in increasing both volume and value of exports from Java can be attributed to several factors. First, international market conditions were propitious; the price index for the five major staples increased at 5 per cent per annum over the decade, and this combined with the high volume growth of exports to produce an increase in the income terms of trade of over 20 per cent per annum (Table 2.1). Second, as we have already noted, contemporary observers were agreed that there were abundant reserves of unutilised land suitable for the cultivation of crops, if only the necessary labour could be mobilised. Given that the CS was successful, at least in the short run, in breaking the labour bottleneck, the resulting rapid growth can be said to have justified Dutch expectations. Third, and probably most important of all, the CS was so successful in alleviating the extremely serious budgetary problems of the Netherlands that its critics were rapidly silenced. In his study of Dutch industrial retardation in the 1830s and 1840s, Griffiths (1979: 47 ff.) has discussed these fiscal problems in some detail and points out that it was only after 1835

> that the situation was relieved as the fruits of the Culture System, particularly the revenue from the sale of colonial produce ... flowed into government coffers which enabled it to reduce taxation slightly and balance its books at the same time ... The colonial surplus was to prove the crucial variable in the delicate equation of government solvency.

Fasseur (1992: 62) has argued that 'the Indies surpluses in the period 1832–1850 amounted to around 19 per cent of total Dutch public revenues'. After 1850, this proportion rose to over 30 per cent. Certainly the continued large remittances from the Indies were a major reason why the Dutch government delayed the imposition of an income tax, a point which was hardly lost on Dutch liberals (Fasseur 1978: 155–6). Indeed, van Zanden (1993: 149) points out that the increase in revenues from Java in the 1850s permitted the Dutch government to abolish a number of excises, which stimulated economic growth in the Dutch economy. Obviously effects of this magnitude must have served to justify the CS in the eyes of many doubters, especially as a part of these payments were described in Dutch budgetary documents as interest payments on a largely ficticious colonial debt incurred in the VOC period, which was 'useful as an expedient for putting Dutch bad consciences to sleep' (Fasseur 1992: 61).

But after 1840, at least on the production side, things began to go wrong. Prices of tropical products began to decline on European markets, with adverse consequences for the income terms of trade facing Java (Table 2.1). In addition, the colonial income accruing to the Dutch government began to decline. The colonial authorities might have been expected to react to export price declines by forcing further increases in output in order to stabilise real revenues. But this did not happen; the amount of labour devoted to export crop cultivations reached a peak in 1840, and then fell throughout the decade (CEI, Vol 14: 190–1). It could be argued that growth of export output had, by 1840, largely absorbed such surplus labour time as the Javanese peasant farmer might have had, so that after 1840 labour force growth set a limit to further growth in export production. The problem of labour availability was aggravated by the growth in demands on the peasantry for corvée labour for public works, and more importantly, for a range of projects determined by indigenous officialdom. As Elson (1994: 123–6) has argued, the success of the government-imposed system of forced cultivations encouraged many local and village officials to add demands of their own for both labour and output. Given these demands, together with the requirements of subsistence food production, further rapid growth in export output was impossible.

Indeed, there was much official concern during the latter part of the 1840s about the impact of the CS on indigenous foodcrop production. According to the official figures, rice production growth was slow and erratic for Java as a whole during the 1840s, and in some residencies there were marked declines between years, especially in the later part of the decade (CEI, Vol 10: 112). The official production series for this period cannot be considered very accurate, and the extreme annual fluctuations in some residencies probably reflect changes in the way the data were collected rather than actual rises or falls in production (Knight 1985). But there can be little doubt that severe famines were experienced in some residencies towards the end of the decade (Elson 1994: 100–8). These famines were not directly caused by the land and labour demands of the CS, which had, in fact, changed very little over the decade. But some colonial officials felt concerned that the cumulative impact of two decades of exactions by both Dutch and indigenous authorities had slowly eroded the peasants' ability to accumulate agricultural surpluses to tide them over bad years. Thus, pressures for reform of the CS began to mount.

From the 1850s onwards we have more complete data on growth of government revenues and expenditures, money supply and imports, all of which give some indication of rates of growth of output in the economy. Although export volume growth between 1849 and 1873 was no faster than in the 1840s, export prices did improve, compared with the decline of the 1840s. Import prices fell, and the income terms of trade increased at about four per cent per annum over the whole period from 1851 to 1873, reflecting a considerable improvement in the international purchasing power of Indonesian exports (Table 2.1). But there is little evidence that slower growth of export crop production led to more rapid growth of foodcrops. Rice production growth was slower in the decade from 1856 to 1865 than in the 1840s, and no faster than it had been in the era of rapid export growth. It was only in the period from 1866 to the late 1870s that rice production growth accelerated sharply, and this apparent increase was at least partly due to improved reporting of crop harvests (Table 2.2).

Table 2.2   Annual average rates of growth[*] in foodcrop and agricultural production in Java 1841–1940

Years	Rice[†]	All foodcrops[**]	All agriculture
1841–55	1.3	n.a.	n.a.
1856–65	0.9	n.a.	n.a.
1866–79	4.0	n.a.	n.a.
1880–1900	0.9	0.9	1.2
1901–15	2.3	2.8	2.5
1916–30	0.7	0.8	2.0
1931–40	2.4	2.5	2.1

[*] Derived by fitting an exponential curve to the annual data.
[†] Padi sawah and padi gogo. Up to 1915 data exclude native states and private lands.
[**] Padi sawah, padi gogo, corn, cassava, sweet potatoes, soyabeans and groundnuts.
Source: CEI, Vol. 10, Table 9A, 9B, Table 10. Van der Eng (1993: Table A.1.2)

There were some signs of accelerated growth in that part of the economy which was monetised. Because a substantial part of total budgetary revenues were earned in Holland from the sale of products, while most expenditures were made within the colony, the large overall fiscal surplus was accompanied in most years by a substantial domestic budget deficit (CEI Vol 2: Table 3). This in turn was probably one reason for the rapid growth of coins and notes circulating within the colony, and might explain the rather faster rate of growth of domestic prices, as proxied by the rice price in Java, than international prices. Over the entire period from 1850 to 1873, the currency stock grew more rapidly than domestic inflation as measured by the simple average of rice, export and import prices; the deflated annual average growth rate was over 6 per cent (Table 2.1).

Following the model devised by Leff for Brazil (1982: 30), we can use this growth rate to form an estimate of real output growth in the monetised economy by subtracting the assumed decline in the velocity of circulation. Most authorities tend to assume with Gurley and Shaw (1960: 130) that 'the ratio of money to national income rises during the early stages of growth and then eventually levels off' i.e. velocity falls. In the Brazilian case, Leff (1982: 32–3) assumed a decline in velocity of around 1 per cent per annum. Given the fact that the ratio of currency stock to output must have been quite low in Java in the 1840s and probably rose rapidly for several decades thereafter, this is probably a conservative estimate for Indonesia. If, for example, the decline in velocity between 1850 and 1873 was as high as 2 per cent per annum, which assumes a rather rapid rate of monetisation from a low base, then the real growth in output would have been around 3.5 per cent per annum over these years. Assuming a rate of population growth of around 1.5 per cent per annum, then per capita output in the monetised part of the economy could have been rising at about 2 per cent per annum over this period.

These results are obviously very rough, but they do indicate that the decades of the 1850s and 1860s saw some real per capita output growth in the monetised sector of the Javanese economy. This in turn serves to emphasise the complex nature of the interaction between population growth, growth in output of foodcrops, and growth in output of the export-oriented sector at this stage of Java's integration into the world economy. Although in some regions there can be little doubt that cultivation of export crops did interfere with food cultivation for subsistence, such interference was much less pronounced after the 1850s than before, simply because export volume growth was so much slower. In fact, it was little faster than population growth. To a considerable extent the foodcrop economy had developed a momentum of its own, which was primarily a function of population growth. The export economy was primarily driven by labour availability. External demand for tropical crops was a less important determinant of export growth than if export cultivation had been in private hands, because the payments received by cultivators did not necessarily reflect international prices, and cultivators were in any case hardly free to choose what crops to plant in what quantities. Were it not for the labour constraint, falling export prices might well have induced colonial officials to accelerate output volume in order to maintain the real value of export revenues.

By 1840, at the end of the phase of very rapid export expansion from Java, the export sector must have been quite large relative to the rest of the economy. In the five years from 1838 to 1842, for example, gross value of rice production, valued at Semarang prices, was 58.2 million guilders, compared with total exports of 63.5 million guilders. If we assume that rice production was underestimated by a factor of 25 per cent, and constituted 15 per cent of total output value in Java, which is probably a conservative estimate, then export production must have accounted for about 12 per cent of total output, and a higher proportion of value added. On the other hand, the non-export economy was certainly developing a dynamism of its own in Java as the century progressed. The fact that the growth of the monetised economy was almost certainly faster than export volume growth after 1850 indicates that other sectors of the domestic economy such as manufacturing, construction, transport and trade must have been growing also, helped along by a modest but steady increase in real government expenditures in the colony (Table 2.1).

Throughout the first seven decades of the nineteenth century, labour and capital, rather than land, were the constraints on economic growth in Java, and indeed elsewhere in the archipelago. The labour constraint was broken through the brutal but effective means of forced labour; the result was, as van Niel (1992: 225) has argued, 'that the symbiotic relationship between cheap labour and the provision of life's basic subsistence grew ever stronger, while the concept of working for a wage on which one could survive was never generated among Java's poorer peasantry'. The capital constraint was gradually overcome through the investment of savings from within Java itself, on the part of those private entrepreneurs who were benefiting from the government-induced growth of the export economy. As the century wore on, and world transport networks and trade developed, there may have been, as van Niel argues, a growing awareness among at least some private businessmen in the colony that they could accelerate exports more rapidly than the 'cumbersome, patronage-ridden government system of forced cultivation' (van Niel 1992:224).

Both private entrepreneurs and officials must have appreciated that the very constraint that necessitated this system in the first place, the acute shortage of labour, was slowly vanishing with the inexorable growth of population (Blusse 1984: 111). Although, as Fasseur (1978: 156) has argued, the bourgeoisie within the Netherlands were hardly enthusiastic about losing the colonial contribution to the budget, as they knew this would inevitably lead to the introduction of an income tax, the rising tide of liberal opinion in the Netherlands after 1859 swept these objections before it. But the changes of the 1870s were essentially changes in means, while the overall end of colonial policy remained the same. According to Furnivall (1944: 174–5):

> The Liberals, no less than van den Bosch, regarded the colony as a *bedrif*, a business concern, and in this matter they differed from him merely in admitting more shareholders; their new contribution to economic policy, however, was their contention that no plan was necessary, that, if all restrictions on enterprise and commerce were removed, the development of Java and the promotion of Dutch interests might be left to the play of market forces.

ECONOMIC GROWTH OUTSIDE JAVA: 1800–70

The Java-centric nature of much historical writing on Indonesia in the nineteenth century has already been noted. But over the past three decades a number of studies have been published on Sumatra, Kalimantan and Sulawesi which permit us to make at least informed speculations on trends in output growth in regions such as Aceh, West Sumatra and both North and South Sulawesi in the nineteenth century. We can also contrast developments in Aceh, whose trade and commercial links remained almost wholly outside Dutch control until at least the 1870s, with West Sumatra where Dutch military and economic intervention began much earlier in the century. In both West Sumatra and North Sulawesi, forced cultivation of coffee was implemented, while in South Sulawesi the Dutch tried to build the deep-water port of Makassar into a rival to Singapore. As might be expected, such different policies produced rather different outcomes.

The case of Aceh is in some ways the most interesting, as a dynamic export economy was developing rapidly there in the late eighteenth and early nineteenth centuries, wholly outside the Dutch sphere of influence. Indeed, by the 1820s, Aceh was producing half the world's pepper output, and in the second decade of the nineteenth century pepper was still the single most valuable export from Southeast Asia, although it was soon to be overtaken by coffee and sugar (Reid 1969: 14ff; Bulbeck *et al.*: forthcoming). Part of the Acehnese output crossed the Malacca straits in small native craft, and a part was carried in American craft to the USA. Pepper prices fell on world markets after the early 1820s, and Reid observed that 'production fluctuated widely in response to the unstable prices in Europe'. But the pepper trade continued to develop, and new pepper gardens were opened up as the soil in the older ones became exhausted. Reid's series on Penang's trade from 1829 onwards shows that imports from Sumatra (mainly Aceh) increased from 1.3 million guilders in 1829 to over 9 million guilders in 1873. Exports from Penang to Sumatra also showed considerable growth (Table 2.3).

Table 2.3   Exports and imports from Java, Sumatra and Makassar, 1829–73 (millions of guilders)

Year	Java exports	Penang imports from Sumatra	Makassar exports
1829	16.58	1.27	n.a.
1830	16.57	n.a.	0.64
1837	45.71	2.38	n.a.
1845	69.12	1.26	0.27
1854	77.73	2.00	3.43
1858	120.60	3.90	4.02
1862	114.96	2.63	5.33
1866	133.23	2.08	6.57
1873	155.88	9.24	11.81

Year	Java imports	Penang exports to Sumatra	Makassar imports
1829	18.39	1.54	n.a.
1830	19.56	n.a.	0.90
1837	29.26	1.91	n.a.
1845	37.90	1.86	1.39
1854	63.78	2.39	4.09
1858	65.77	4.84	4.20
1862	67.45	3.86	6.19
1866	69.39	5.79	7.02
1873	111.43	7.72	11.86

Sources: Java exports and imports: CEI, Vol 12a, Tables 1A and 2A (Line 1). Penang–Sumatra trade: Reid (1969: 292–4) (Data in dollars converted into pounds sterling using the exchange rate $1=£0.2125, and then converted into guilders using the exchange rate given in CEI Vol 6, Table 8). Makassar exports and imports: Poelinggomang (1993: 72–3)

One can only speculate on what might have happened to the Acehnese economy had it never been absorbed into the Netherlands Indies, and been left to develop its export economy independently in the late nineteenth and twentieth centuries. There can be little doubt that the trading links with Penang and Singapore would have continued to develop, while those with the rest of the Indonesian archipelago, and indeed with much of the rest of Sumatra, would have probably been negligible. Such an outcome was unacceptable to the Dutch, and after 1870 Aceh was forcibly incorporated into the Dutch empire. West Sumatra had undergone a similar experience in the 1830s, and during the 1840s the Dutch experimented with systems of forced deliveries of coffee, similar to those from Java. The results were not encouraging. Coffee exports from Padang, which had increased almost ten-fold between 1819 and 1831 to over 40,000 pikul, and more than doubled again to over 100,000 pikul by 1843, crashed to just over 56,000 pikul by 1848 (Dobbin 1983: 248). The modified system of forced deliveries which was implemented after 1847 did lead to a rapid expansion in exports, which reached 191,000 pikul in 1857. But in spite of the considerable government coercion, coffee production and exports fell more or less continually thereafter, and after 1885 exports never exceed 100,000 pikuls. In spite of the mounting evidence that coffee was no longer a profitable crop, the system of forced deliveries of coffee was only terminated in 1908 (Dobbin 1983: 236).

The other region where forced coffee cultivation was implemented was Minahasa, in North Sulawesi. Schouten (1995: 5–10) points out that there the CS was actually in place earlier than in Java, although coffee deliveries from Minahasa were much smaller than those from either Java or West Sumatra, and only exceeded 30,000 pikuls in three years. As in West Sumatra and Java, production declined quite rapidly after 1870, as other crops such as copra and tobacco became more lucrative. Schouten argues that there is little evidence that the people of Minahasa derived much benefit from coffee cultivation even in its heyday in the 1860s and 1870s, and they became increasingly resentful at the large difference between the official procurement price and the free market price. As in West Sumatra, there can be little doubt that, had market forces been allowed free reign, more coffee would have been produced, and the profits accruing to cultivators would have been larger. This in turn would have meant that the multiplier effects of export cultivation on the domestic economy would also have been greater.

The forced cultivation of export crops imposed by the Dutch on an unwilling population in Minahasa and in West Sumatra contrasts sharply with policies pursued in South Sulawesi, and especially in the port city of Makassar in the nineteenth century. Makassar and its hinterland had been under effective Dutch control since the seventeenth century, but enterprising Makassar–Buginese traders continued to flourish not just in Eastern Indonesia but in other parts of the Malay-Indonesian archipelago. They were quick to avail themselves of new opportunities presented by the foundation of Singapore as a 'free port' and by the early 1830s Makassar's trade with Singapore had grown to a considerable size (Poelinggomang 1993: 71). Makassar also became known as a centre of smuggling; according to Poelinggomang as much as two-thirds of the goods being traded in Makassar in the 1830s were illegal imports. Many of these then found their way to Java and to other islands. The Dutch responded to this situation by making Makassar a free port in 1847, and indeed by fostering the development of the port city as a rival to Singapore. This policy was in many respects extremely successful. Exports and imports increased rapidly, although this was partly due to the statistical effect of the elimination of smuggling. Many entrepreneurs, both indigenous and from Singapore, invested in trading and other businesses in Makassar, and by 1873 the value of the city's export and import trade had reached almost 24 million guilders which was around 9 per cent of the value of Java's trade (Table 2.3).

But the Dutch became increasingly unhappy with the orientation of trade to other parts of the region rather than to Java. Although opposition from local traders meant that the city's free port status was only abolished in 1906, the Dutch authorities used a variety of regulatory devices and subsidies to divert trade to Dutch ships operating from Java (Poelinggomang 1993: 68–9). This 'strategic' use of shipping contracts to strengthen Javanese hegemony over the archipelago was to continue until the termination of Dutch rule and beyond. After 1873, the value of Makassar's exports and imports declined, and by 1908 amounted to only 17.4 million guilders. Java's trade by contrast had surged ahead, and by 1908 the value of Java's exports and imports was 526 million guilders. An even more telling comparison is between Makassar and Singapore. In 1873, when Makassar's exports peaked at 11.8 million guilders, Singapore's exports amounted to 89.9 million guilders (Huff 1994: Table A1; data converted using the exchange rates in CEI Vol 6, Table 8). But by 1908 the guilder value of Singapore's exports had soared to 253.5 million while those of Makassar were only 10.9 million. Singapore continued to forge ahead as a free port and regional entrepot, but Makassar became a stagnant backwater. A similar fate befell Lombok after its incorporation into the Dutch empire at the end of the nineteenth century. The island had developed a considerable external trade in rice from 1830 onwards, which had important consequences for the domestic economy (van der Kraan 1993). But in the twentieth century, these links were subordinated to the requirements first of the Dutch colonial economy and then of the independent national economy, and by the 1970s Lombok had become one of the poorest parts of the country.

What do we learn from these contrasting stories of economic growth and decline in the regions outside Java in the nineteenth century? The most important lesson is that several of these regions had, by the middle of the nineteenth century, demonstrated considerable potential for rapid export expansion in an open market environment. Certainly there is no evidence at all to support the argument that Aceh, West Sumatra, Lombok or Sulawesi were inward-looking subsistence economies whose populations had to be coerced into participating in international trade. Indigenous entrepreneurs were there in abundance to respond to the signals transmitted from world centres of commerce via regional entrepots such as Penang and Singapore. Indigenous cultivators were prepared to grow new crops if they could sell them at prices which they considered to be profitable. Government intervention, when it occurred, was usually damaging and certainly the evidence lends no support to the theory that coercion was necessary to promote the growth of export crops. But such coercion as was applied, in Java and elsewhere, had other damaging consequences which are explored in more detail in later chapters.

POLICY REFORM AND SLOW GROWTH: 1870–1900

The decade of the 1860s witnessed mounting debate over 'the colonial question' in the Dutch parliament. Fasseur (1991: 35) has argued that three main interests were at stake; those of the Dutch treasury, Western agricultural enterprises in Java, and lastly the indigenous populations of Java. In the Government Regulation (*Indisch*

Regeringsreglement) of 1854 which served as an 'Indies constitution', the CS was seen only as a transitional step towards a more liberal, market-driven economy in which the government would have no direct involvement in the Javanese export economy. But the problem for the Dutch parliament was how to move to a system of export cultivation based on private enterprise without depriving the Dutch budget of an important source of revenue. Between 1862 and 1870, 'no fewer than four bills were introduced in the Dutch parliament with the aim of presenting Western agricultural enterprises with more opportunities for expansion without disproportionately damaging the interests of the treasury or of the native population' (Fasseur 1991: 36). The fourth was finally successful. It became the so-called Agrarian Law of 1870 which, together with the Sugar Law passed a few months later, is often considered as signalling the demise of the CS, at least in Java.

Some recent scholars have argued that this legislation produced no dramatic change in Java's economy. Fasseur (1991: 42) stresses that 1870 was hardly the watershed that liberal historians have claimed, and there was 'absolutely no question of private entrepreneurs taking Java by storm after that year'. But there is evidence that the liberal legislation had an impact on export growth over the longer term. Export volume growth in the last twenty-five years of the nineteenth century was much more rapid than was achieved in the years from 1850 to 1873 (Table 2.1). After 1873, export data were collected for the whole of Indonesia, and export production outside Java grew rapidly from the 1870s onwards, although from a small base, so that exports from Java still accounted for over 70 per cent of the total value of exports in 1899 (CEI Vol 12a, Table 2B). Volume growth of export crops accelerated markedly in the decade up to 1884 compared with the earlier period mainly because of growth in sugar production, which occurred entirely on Java. Coffee production more than held its own, and tobacco output grew rapidly (CEI Vol 1, Table 5). This expansion in turn could be attributed, at least in part, to the Agrarian Law of 1870 which facilitated the leasing of land by private estate companies. Land under long leases (*erfpacht*) arrangements in Java increased from 7,000 hectares in 1874 to 185,000 hectares in 1885, by which year agricultural concessions outside Java totalled almost 160,000 hectares. By 1900, 435,000 hectares of land were leased out to large estates in Java and a further 372,000 hectares outside Java; in addition, almost 480,000 hectares of land outside Java were under various types of agricultural concessions (CEI Vol 1, Table 6).

However, other indicators suggest that the growth in volume of exports was not reflected in a similar growth in output in the domestic economy. Real money supply growth slowed somewhat in the decade or so from 1874 to 1885, which indicates some slowdown in output growth in the monetised economy (Table 2.1). Certainly, as Furnivall (1944: 196) has stressed, the period after 1874 saw a steep decline in prices for all the major export staples, led by coffee, whose price more than halved between 1874 and 1882. The aggregate index of export prices in the years from 1874 to 1900 declined at almost two per cent per annum (Table 2.1). But the last three decades of the nineteenth century were characterised by declining prices internationally, and the import price index for Indonesia fell more sharply between 1874 and 1900 than export prices, indicating an improvement in the net barter terms of trade (CEI Vol 15, Appendix A). Combined with the acceleration in export volume growth, this meant that the income terms of trade grew at more than four per cent per annum in the last quarter of the nineteenth century (Table 2.1). The real value of imports grew at almost 5 per cent per annum between 1874 and 1900, compared with less than 4 per cent between 1849 and 1873 (Table 2.4).

Table 2.4   Annual average growth in real volume of imports, 1830–1941

1830–40	13.2
1840–48	−0.2
1849–73	3.7
187–1900	4.8
1901–28	3.9
1928–34	−10.4
1934–41	3.6

Source: Import data from CEI, Vol 12a were deflated by the import price index contained in CEI, Vol 15, Appendix A

Given the evidence of a sustained improvement in the income terms of trade, and sustained growth in export volume, real imports, real money supply and real government expenditures over the years from 1874 to 1900, it is perhaps surprising that the last quarter of the nineteenth century was often depicted as a period of economic stagnation. Creutzberg (1972: xvii) points to a period of 'export stagnation' from the latter part of the 1880s to the end of the century, but the data do not bear this out. Export volume growth was, in fact, quite rapid over these years (Table 2.1). Neither does his characterisation of the period from 1885 to 1900 as one of 'long depression' seem justified by the evidence (Creutzberg 1972: xxxii). Certainly there can be little doubt that the banking crisis of 1884 reduced the supply of credit to the private (primarily the large estate) sector. Furnivall (1944: 197–8) and van Laanen (1990: 254–6) have described the dubious banking practices adopted by the Culture Banks in their lending to the estate companies, and the rescue measures adopted by the Java Bank and the Netherlands Trading Company (NHM) after the international sugar price fell in 1884. These measures resulted in much closer control of the entire banking system by financial institutions based in the Netherlands who imposed their own prudential standards on the colonial institutions. Real money supply growth did drop in the years from 1885 to 1900, compared with the decade from 1874 to 1884, and was little faster than population growth. This suggests that per capita output growth in the monetised part of the economy between 1885 and 1900 was probably very slow, although it hardly indicates a sustained fall in output.

The most important factor colouring judgements of economic performance from 1880 to 1900 was the poor performance of the food-crop economy, which, according to the value added series constructed by van der Eng, grew by less than 1 per cent per annum over these two decades (Table 2.2). The apparently sharp decline in the rate of growth in rice production after 1885 contributed to slower growth of agricultural output. Creutzberg (1972: xxxi: Table facing 734) and Scheltema (1936: 12) both draw attention to the steep fall in per capita rice production and consumption which occurred in the 1890s, although neither suggests any convincing explanation. Certainly the slow growth of rice production after 1885 was accompanied by a slow growth in harvested area, which is difficult to explain (van der Eng 1993: Table A7). It was not related to slower population growth; all the evidence indicates an acceleration in population growth in Java after 1850 (CEI Vol 11: 82).

One possible explanation is that the growth in area under rice slowed because of competition from estates for suitable land. This argument is most plausible in the context of sugar. But it is obvious when we look at the figures for the last decade of the century that harvested area of sugar, while almost doubling, could not have made that much difference to the growth of area under rice in Java as the absolute amount of land involved was quite small (Table 2.5). Area under the other major cashcrops competing with rice hardly changed. What did increase was area under non-rice foodcrops, which grew by about 650,000 hectares between 1880 and 1900 (van der Eng 1993: Table A7). This suggests that as population outgrew available rice-land, there was expansion in land under *palawija* crops such as corn and cassava, and production of these crops grew faster than rice. Certainly the foodcrop production estimates made by Boomgaard and van Zanden (CEI Vol 10: Table 15) show that non-rice foodcrop production growth accelerated between 1880 and 1900, especially output of roots and tubers. But these crops contributed much less value added to total foodcrop output than rice, and thus could not compensate for the slow-down in rice output growth.

Table 2.5 Harvested area* of rice, sugar, indigo and other foodcrops, Java
1892–1901 (000 hectares)

	Rice	Palawija	Sugar	Tobacco	Indigo
1892	1967	1469	68	99	19
1896	1958	1458	87	105	22
1901	2053	1797	132	102	18

*Area excludes principalities and private lands.
Sources: *Jaarcijfers*, various issues.

It has been argued that the export sector of late nineteenth century Indonesia, like that of other gold standard countries, was penalised by the appreciation of its currency *vis-à-vis* the silver standard countries (Nugent 1973). Nugent supports this argument with evidence which indicates that export and income growth were relatively faster in the silver standard countries between 1872 and 1894. However, as Hanson (1975) has pointed out, Nugent's argument is unconvincing for several reasons. To begin with, he does not discuss trends in domestic price levels in the two sets of countries; in fact, Indonesia like other gold standard countries experienced a fairly sharp internal deflation after 1874, and both rice and export prices fell. To a considerable extent this deflation offset the nominal appreciation of the guilder relative to the silver currencies. Furthermore, even if there was some real appre-ciation in the value of the guilder, this would only have affected Indonesia, and the other gold countries, to the extent that the silver countries were exporting competitive goods; as Hanson argues, in most cases they were not. But the most serious problem with the exchange rate argument in the Indonesian case is that it fails to explain why the decline in economic activity in the 1880s and 1890s, as measured by the rice production and money supply data, was not apparently related to export volume growth, which in fact was more rapid than in earlier decades (Table 2.1). It seems clear that factors not directly related to export performance must have been at work to explain the deceleration in output growth after 1885, although it is far from clear what they were.

ACCELERATED GROWTH AND ECONOMIC DIVERSIFICATION: 1901–28

Although there is little consensus in the literature on the reasons for the slow growth of output in the last two decades of the nineteenth century, most students of Indonesian economic history in the late colonial period agree that the first three decades of the twentieth century saw a marked acceleration in output growth compared with the preceeding two decades. Certainly all the major economic indicators support this claim. Export volume growth accelerated, and there was an improvement in both export prices and the income terms of trade (Table 2.1). Real money supply (coins, notes and bank deposits) growth also accelerated after 1901; as a larger part of the economy was monetised, increases in real money supply more closely reflected increases in total output. If indeed the decline in velocity was only around 0.5 per cent per annum, then with population growing at about one per cent per annum (CEI Vol 11: 82), per capita real income growth in the monetised sector of the economy could have been around 2 per cent per annum. This is consistent with the data on export volume growth and food production growth, both of which accelerated after 1900 (Tables 2.1 and 2.2). It is also consistent with van der Eng's GDP data which show that real per capita GDP grew by 1.7 per cent per annum between 1901 and 1928 (Table 2.1).

There is other evidence to support the view that the decade or so before 1914 saw considerable acceleration in economic activity throughout the economy. Perhaps the most striking is the data on real imports. Not only did their growth accelerate compared to the last part of the nineteenth century (Table 2.4), but there was also a marked change in their composition. The data assembled by Creutzberg (CEI Vol 3, Table 5) on imports of capital goods show that they grew only slowly through the 1890s (Table 2.6), but after 1896 there was a marked upward trend. By 1913, capital goods accounted for 18 per cent of all imports, compared with only 7 per cent in 1890. While most of this increase was due to the private sector, government imports of capital goods also grew, especially after 1905, when there was an increase in the share of government expenditures going to public works (Booth 1990: Table 10.5).

Table 2.6 Trends in imports of capital goods,[*] 1885–1913

	Value of capital imports (million guilders)	Percentage breakdown Private	Government	Capital goods as a percentage of all imports
1885	7.53	85.5	14.5	6.1
1890	9.97	77.8	22.2	6.8
1895	12.40	86.7	13.3	8.1
1900	26.43	91.7	8.3	14.4
1905	26.75	90.3	9.7	13.1
1910	44.89	89.0	11.0	13.8
1913	72.97	86.7	13.3	17.9

[*]Machines and apparatus, iron, steel and steelgoods and railway materials and rolling stock.
Source: CEI, Vol. 3, Table 5.

The years before the First World War also saw the emergence of several regions outside Java as significant components of the monetised sector of the colonial economy. This was largely due to the growth of export production in Sumatra, Kalimantan and Sulawesi, both by large estate companies and by smallholders. The large estate companies outside Java, at least up to 1913, concentrated on crops such as tobacco and coffee, while the smallholders grew copra, coffee, tea and tobacco as well as a range of spices. By 1913, 35 per cent of Indonesia's earnings from agricultural exports accrued from outside Java: of this, 40 per cent was produced by smallholders. In fact, the growth of smallholder output of non-food crops was much more rapid than the growth of output from estate crops in the years from 1901 to 1914 (Booth 1988: Table 6.1). This growth in smallholder output was particularly remarkable in that it occurred in many places as a spontaneous response on the part of the indigenous population to the new opportunities which international trade offered. The greater range of goods available on international markets no doubt served as inducements for increased involvement in international trade. In addition, both improved infrastructure and greater awareness of the outside world encouraged indigenous cultivators in many parts of the archipelago to produce for the world market.

If the rapid growth in smallholder agriculture outside Java in the years leading up to the First World War can be explained in terms of the vent for surplus model (Booth 1988: 205), another explanation must be sought for the recovery of rice production in Java. It was pointed out above that the very slow rice production growth after 1880 was accompanied by an equally slow growth in planted area; after 1900 rice output accelerated considerably (Table 2.2). This expansion was largely due to the expansion in area of sawah, although some increase in cropping ratios certainly occurred in the better irrigated areas (CEI Vol 10: 74–6). More intensive cropping was in turn the result of the growth of government irrigation expenditures, which increased relative to total government expenditure in the first decade of the new century, although by 1912–14 they still accounted for only 2 per cent of total government expenditures (van der Eng 1993, Table A.8.2; CEI Vol 2, Table 1).

The first two decades of the twentieth century also saw a considerable expansion in, and diversification of, the colony's industrial capacity. As in other colonies, the early phase of industrialisation in Indonesia was driven by the processing requirements of export commodities. In Java during the CS indigo, tea, coffee, tobacco and sugar factories were built in the main areas of cultivation, and supporting industries clustered around the agricultural processing centres. As Boomgaard (1989: 112) has stressed, this led to a very rural pattern of industrialisation, and explains the slow pace of urbanisation in nineteenth century Java. After 1870 the sugar industry continued to grow in Java, both in absolute terms and relative to most other processing industries. By 1900 sugar mills accounted for 90 per cent of steam boiler capacity in Java, and 86 per cent of horsepower capacity. Outside Java, the petroleum industry was almost as dominant (Dick 1993: 140–1). In addition, the growth of the expatriate community, and the emergence of a class of indigenous consumers with Western tastes gave rise to demand for a range of goods which enjoyed considerable natural protection, such as building materials and perishable foodstuffs. Metal, machine and equipment factories and repair shops, as well as dry docks, grew in response to the growth of the export processing industries and their transport needs (Siahaan 1996, Chapter 1). The growth in budgetary expenditures would have served as an additional stimulus to domestic manufacturing.

The industrial sector which evolved under these circumstances provided employment for only a small part of the labour force. Data on the sectoral breakdown of the labour force collected in 1905 indicated that almost 540,000 people were employed in industrial activities in Java, and a further 128,000 elsewhere, accounting for just 3.5 per cent of the total labour force in Java and 3.6 per cent outside Java (CEI, Vol 8: 64–5). In Java over 50 per cent of these were women, and at least 25 per cent were also employed in agricultural occupations which indicates the 'cottage' nature of much of the manufacturing employment not directly linked to export processing. An official survey carried out in 1915 found that only 82,000 people were employed in the 2,578 manufacturing establishments employing five or more workers, excluding estate factories. Of these 62,223 were located in Java (CEI Vol 8: 69). The metal products, machinery and equipment sector employed the largest number of workers (around 27 per cent of the total) followed by chemical industries (mainly petroleum refining) and foodstuffs and tobacco.

Data on industrial output prior to 1913 are too fragmentary to attempt to compile an aggregate index. But it seems plausible to argue that, from 1870 to 1913, the growth of sugar and petroleum production, and their ancillary industries, together with the growth in demand for transport services, and the growth in real government expenditures would all have combined to produce a faster growth of manufacturing output than of total GDP. Certainly van der Eng's finding that manufacturing value added actually declined as a proportion of GDP from 1880 to 1913 (from 10 per cent in 1880 to 9 per cent in 1913) seems difficult to credit (van der Eng 1992: 351). Van der Eng derived his series on manufacturing value added from rather patchy data on employment growth which seems to have led to an understatement of growth rates over these decades. An alternative series on manufacturing value added is developed in the appendix to this chapter: there it is argued that the manufacturing sector comprised under 5 per cent of GDP in 1880, and its share grew to a little over 6 per cent by 1913.

As in many other parts of the colonial world, the First World War, by cutting off supplies of manufactured goods from Europe, gave local industry considerable protection (Shepherd 1941:51). In addition, some industries gained from being able to capture markets formerly dominated by Germany (Dick 1993: 137). This appears to have been especially important for the coconut oil and quinine industries, which experienced rapid growth in output and exports between 1914 and 1920. Segers identifies eight industrial sectors which benefited from wartime import constraints; they included factories producing oxygen, plywood chests, structural clay products, sodium and carbon bisulphite and ink and paint (CEI Vol 8: 21). However, as Segers points out, the export sector remained the main engine driving industrial development in Indonesia even during the period of European hostilities. In 1915 the Governor-General, Idenburg, established a committee to investigate the potential of import-substituting industrialisation in the colony, but as Prince (1993: 168) observed, 'the committee soon shifted its activities from seeking import substitution to obtaining full employment as a leading element in industrial development'. This policy objective in turn gave rise to considerable interdepartmental debate and contention about appropriate means of expanding non-agricultural employment. But after the termination of hostilities in 1918, government interest in fostering import-substituting industrialisation waned and the Idenburg committee was wound up in the mid-1920s, without producing any comprehensive strategy for industrial development (Shepherd 1941: 52). Industrialisation policy only became a matter of government concern again after the onset of the world depression in the 1930s.

There can be little doubt that, by the 1920s, Indonesia's industrial development was in key sectors lagging behind that in other parts of Asia. In contrast to colonies such as British India, Formosa (Taiwan), Indochina and the Philippines, Indonesia in the early twentieth century had no capacity to produce basic industrial goods such as cotton yarn and textiles, pig iron and steel, cement, sulphuric acid, or superphosphates. Bairoch (1991: 10) has shown that in 1910 India was already the largest per capita producer of cotton yarn in Asia after Japan, followed by China, Indochina, and the Philippines. Indochina had a significant cement industry while Formosa was an important producer of superphosphates. Cement production began in Indonesia shortly before the First World War, but little capacity in the cotton textile sector emerged before the 1930s, and development of industries such as chemical fertiliser and iron and steel was delayed until after independence.

The 1920s was a period of rapid growth in export volume; in fact, the annual average growth accelerated to almost 8 per cent per annum between 1920 and 1928, which was higher than that achieved in any period between 1841 and 1913. By the 1920s, exports accounted for well over 20 per cent of GDP, and their accelerated growth in the 1920s was certainly an important factor in GDP growth, which averaged over 2 per cent per annum in per capita terms between 1920 and 1928 (Table 2.1). This export volume growth was higher than that achieved in other parts of Southeast Asia such as Burma, or Thailand

(Booth 1991: Table 4). But previous periods of rapid export growth, such as the 1830s and the decade leading up to the First World War were also periods of rising export prices (Table 2.1). In the 1920s, by contrast, export prices fell away from their post-war peak, although the rise in export volume, and falling import prices, meant that the purchasing power of exports in terms of imports (the income terms of trade) continued to grow at almost 7 per cent per annum (Table 2.1). But this was reflected not in rapid import growth but rather in a marked increase in the surplus on the current account of the balance of payments. This issue is explored in greater depth in Chapter 5.

As in the period from 1900 to 1913, the growth in smallholder export volume was more rapid than the growth in total export volume (Booth 1988: 196). The continued rapid growth in volume of exports up to 1930 was due mainly to the emergence of two important new commodities, rubber and oil. Oil production more than doubled during the decade, while rubber production trebled; by 1930 these two commodities accounted for 30 per cent of total export earnings, even before the collapse of the sugar industry. By the late 1920s, exports accounted for around 25 per cent of GDP, as measured by van der Eng. This high degree of openess made the Indonesian economy very vulnerable to the severe downturn in the world economy of the 1930s.

DEPRESSION AND RECOVERY: 1929–41

What was the effect of the world depression of the 1930s on output growth in the Indonesian economy? In terms of the variables in Table 2.1, the most obvious impact was on export volume, export prices and real money supply. Between 1928 and 1934 export volume fell by almost 4 per cent per annum, export prices by almost 20 per cent per annum and real money supply by more than 2 per cent per annum. Declines of these magnitudes indicate a fall in GDP; the series estimated by van der Eng, in fact, fell by 3.4 per cent per annum over these years. According to Polak's series on real income by region and ethnic group, total income accruing to all ethnic groups except indigenous Javanese fell, with the most severe downturn in real incomes experienced by the Europeans on the one hand and the Indonesian population outside Java on the other (CEI, Vol 5: Table 16.4). To a large extent, this reflected the greater involvement of these two groups in the export economy. Per capita incomes of the indigenous population in Java also declined, although at a slower rate than outside Java.

But rice and total foodcrop production grew much more rapidly over the 1930s than in the preceding decade (Table 2.2). Indeed, growth in total agricultural output showed little perceptible decline in the 1930s, in spite of the collapse of the sugar industry. It is sometimes argued that the contraction of sugar production benefited the local population in the sugar areas, in that it allowed foodcrop cultivation to expand; area planted to rice in Java expanded by over 400,000 hectares between 1929 and 1934 which did in part reflect the decline in area under sugar (CEI Vol 10: 96). This in turn led to accelerated growth in foodcrop production over these years, especially as the land released by the sugar companies was often the best irrigated and could be cropped not just to rice but to a second foodcrop in the dry season. On the other hand, the collapse of the sugar industry meant that by far the most important source of wage employment in rural Java almost entirely vanished over a space of four years. The consequences of this for the wider rural economy were severe, as the multiplier effects of declining wage expenditures were felt on a range of industries and services. The impact of this on rural living standards in Java is examined in the next chapter.

Perhaps the most striking feature of the Indonesian economy in the early 1930s was the magnitude of the deflation experienced, especially in rural areas. The rural Java food price index was only 41 per cent of its 1928 value in 1934; the Batavia cost of living index was only 58 per cent. In the Netherlands, the United Kingdom, British India and the USA, retail prices fell at a much slower rate (Central Bureau of Statistics 1938: 63–4). The adherence of the Netherlands, and thus the Dutch colonies, to the gold standard until 1936 is the reason usually given for the rapid deflation (Maddison 1989: 59). Faced with deteriorating terms of trade on the one hand and a nominal appreciation in the exchange rate on the other, a sharp internal deflation was the only way to bring about the necessary real depreciation of the currency. As we will see in the next chapter, this deflation had important implications for the distribution of income between regions and social classes. But it was not wholly successful in maintaining the real value of the guilder *vis-à-vis* the currency of some of the colony's major trading partners, particularly in the early part of the 1930s. In real terms the guilder appreciated against sterling, and even more against the yen, after 1930. The consequences of this appreciation are discussed in greater detail in Chapter 5.

After 1934, there was a rapid resurgence of growth in the Indonesian economy, and incomes of all groups grew rapidly. In per capita terms, GDP grew by 2.5 per cent per annum between 1934 and 1941 (Table 2.1). According to Polak's estimates, real incomes accruing to ethnic Indonesians grew quite rapidly in per capita terms after 1934, and by 1939 had more than caught up with 1928 levels. His estimates also showed that European and foreign Asiatic incomes recovered rapidly after 1934 (CEI, Vol 5: Table 16.4). To what was the recovery due? Certainly foodcrop agriculture in Java performed well during the latter part of the decade, and export volume picked up quickly after 1934, especially for smallholders. By 1940, smallholder production of rubber had almost caught up with production from large estates (CEI, Vol 1: 94). Export prices improved after 1934, and in spite of the fact that the commodity terms of trade once again deteriorated after 1936, the growth in export volume was sufficiently fast to ensure an improvement in the income terms of trade (Table 2.1). But perhaps the most remarkable feature of the recovery in the latter part of the 1930s was the growth in industrial output.

Using the data on wages and purchases of domestic materials provided by Polak (CEI: Vol 5: Table 8.2) and other evidence from Sitsen (1943: Table XV), van Oorschot (1956: 93) estimated the real value of output in large, small and cottage industry for the years 1928–39. The results show a very rapid growth in real output in the large factory sector between 1931 and 1939 (over 20 per cent per annum) and a slower, although still impressive growth in the small-scale sector. The cottage sector, by contrast, declined over the decade. Overall, output growth was 9 per cent per annum in the years from 1931 and 1939. This estimate is based on the assumption that the ratio of labour costs to value added did not change over the 1930s in the three segments of the industrial sector. Polak's estimates of national income figures by sector of origin showed that the manufacturing sector accounted for over 17 per cent of total incomes accruing to indigenous Indonesians in Java. For the country as a whole, Polak estimated that manufacturing accounted for 14.9 per cent of Indonesian income, where the sector was defined to exclude the processing of both agricultural and mineral products for export (CEI, Vol 5, Table 15.4). Van Oorschot (1956: 97) has further broken down this percentage into the three components of manufacturing industry which the colonial officials used for statistical purposes: large-scale factory industry, either using mechanised techniques or employing more than fifty workers (4.5 per cent), small-scale industries using manual techniques and employing fewer than fifty workers (5.9 per cent) and cottage industry carried on within households (4.4 per cent).

Polak's estimates of total wages in the manufacturing sector, on which van Oorschot's estimates were based have been challenged by Segers, who has produced an alternative series (CEI, Vol 8, Table XI). The Segers estimates are rather lower than those of Polak, especially for the latter part of the 1930s, and as a result show lower real growth over the years from 1931 to 1939. But the growth is still of the order of eight per cent per annum. This is a much higher growth rate than shown by van der Eng's series on value added in the manufacturing sector which was based on a linear extrapolation using labour force data. It is argued in the appendix to this chapter that this procedure does appear to have considerably underestimated the growth of manufacturing output, especially in the 1930s. An inspection of the output data compiled in CEI (Vol 8) confirms that, with the exception of the sugar industry, most manufacturing industries were not greatly affected by the depression of the early 1930s, and showed rapid growth over the decade as a whole. Output of petroleum products and re-milled rubber both grew rapidly, as did output of woven sarongs, cigarettes, cement and beer (Table 2.7). There can be little doubt that the growth of manufacturing value added exceeded that of GDP as a whole over the years from 1931 to 1939, and while Polak's estimate that manufacturing value added accounted for 14.8 per cent of national income in 1939 is probably an overstatement, van der Eng's estimate of 11.1 per cent (compared with 10.8 per cent in 1931) seems too low. An alternative set of estimates is presented in the appendix.

In spite of the fact that much of the manufacturing sector growth occurred in the large-scale factory sector, while the household sector stagnated, the growth in manufacturing employment in the 1930s was substantial. Indeed, van Oorschot (1956: 86) has argued that almost half the estimated increment in the labour force in Indonesia in the 1930s was absorbed in factory and small-scale manufacturing, and that employment in these two sectors accounted for about 12.5 per cent of the labour force in 1940. Given that the population census scheduled for 1940 was never held, it is not possible to check the accuracy of this assertion, but there is little reason to doubt that the percentage of the labour force in all sectors of manufacturing, including household enterprises, increased from the 10.4 per cent recorded in the 1930 census (CEI, Vol 5: 96).

What accounted for the remarkable growth in both industrial output and employment in the latter part of the 1930s? The reasons lie mainly in the changes in government policy towards industrial development which occurred as a result of the impact of the depression on

Table 2.7   Index of manufacturing output growth, 1929–59 (1952 = 100)

	1929	1940	1952	1959
Processed foods				
Cane Sugar	627	351	100	187
Coconut oil	77	121	100	149
Margarine	n.a.	34	100	n.a.
Chocolate	n.a.	20	100	n.a.
Other manufactures				
Beer	n.a.	57	100	n.a.
Cigarettes (white)	92	73	100	163
Cigarettes (kretek)	37	75	100	75
Woven cloth	n.a.	174	100	230
Yarns	n.a.	66	100	194
Soap	n.a.	151	100	n.a.
Paint	18	126	100	98
Phosphate	n.a.	854	100	n.a.
Bulbs	n.a.	31	100	n.a.
Carbonic acid	n.a.	77	100	n.a.
Motor vehicles	n.a.	89	100	n.a.
Bicycles	n.a.	66	100	n.a.
Inner car tyres	n.a.	45	100	n.a.
Outer car tyres	n.a.	64	100	n.a.
Inner cycle tyres	n.a.	80	100	n.a.
Outer cycle tyres	n.a.	76	100	n.a.
Oxygen	n.a.	80	100	n.a.
Cement	108	148	100	289
Oil products				
Diesel	n.a.	54	100	130
Motor/aviation spirits	50	94	100	92
Kerosene	67	88	100	143

Sources: CEI, Vol 8, Tables XII–XVIII; Java Bank (1953), Table 89; Palmer (1972), Tables 14 and 40 (data on yarns and woven cloth); Siahaan (1996), Table 46. 1959 data from Nugroho (1967), p. 348, and *Statistical Pocketbook of Indonesia, 1968–69*, p. 191.

the foreign-owned and dominated sectors of the colonial economy. Although the encouragement of non-agricultural employment had been part of the ethical policy since its inception, little had been done to encourage the development of manufacturing industry by way of direct government assistance before the early 1930s. From 1931 onwards, the colonial government regulated production of the major export industries, beginning with sugar, and once the precedent of government intervention had been established, controls spread to imports. Import restrictions were seen as particularly necessary because of the growth of Japanese imports, especially of textiles which were both displacing European imports and harming domestic production (Shepherd 1941: 54–5). As Barber (1939: 198) pointed out, most of the arguments which were used to justify the adoption of quantitative restrictions on imports were at bottom concerned with the so-called Japanese threat.

But the import restrictions and other powers to regulate domestic industry also achieved another aim, that of encouraging large multinational companies to establish branches in Indonesia. During the 1930s, companies such as Goodyear, National Carbon, Unilever and Bata all built Indonesian plants; in addition, breweries, paper mills, canneries and several large weaving and spinning mills were established. It was this influx of foreign capital and technology into the factory sector which was in part responsible for the very rapid growth rates recorded by van Oorschot. Some, such as the weaving mills, were given import protection, while others were granted exemption from duties on imported inputs (van Eeghen 1937: 131; Boeke 1953: Chapter XXII; Palmer 1972: 28 ff). All factories were legally bound to a licensing system which gave government officials discretion to regulate capacity, and in some cases to fix prices (Boeke 1953: Chapter XXIII). It was indeed no exaggeration to describe the policies pursued between 1933 and 1939 as 'six years of economic planning in Netherlands India' (Barber 1939), although, as Palmer (1972: 33) has argued, some aspects of industrial policy in the latter part of the decade were not well thought out, reflecting differences of opinion within the colonial bureaucracy over which industries should be assisted, and appropriate assistance policies.

In spite of the impressive growth in industrial output in the 1930s, by the end of the decade, mechanised industry was still quite undeveloped. Shepherd (1941:79) draws attention to the very low per capita electricity consumption in Indonesia in 1939, only 6 kwH, which was less than 2 per cent of the figure in the industrially advanced countries. During 1939, the government established a commission to promote the use of electricity for industrial purposes, which lowered the rates at which electricity was supplied to industrial users. After the fall of the Netherlands in 1940, the colonial government emphasised industrial self-reliance as a key element in its defence effort. Shepherd (1941: 85) reported that the government was pushing ahead with new hydro-electric projects, the establishment of a chemical industry, a scrap-iron smelting plant, a blast furnace and a rolling mill and an aluminium smelter using local bauxite. But none of these schemes was to come to fruition before the arrival of the Japanese in 1942.

ECONOMIC GROWTH IN THE COLONIAL ERA: A SUMMING UP

Several conclusions follow from this overview of output growth in Indonesia in the years from 1830 to 1940. First, as has already been stressed, there can be little doubt that real GDP grew in per capita terms. Second, the growth which occurred was slow by more recent standards, and erratic. This was especially the case with that part of the economy oriented to export production, which was subjected to considerable instability from fluctuating world prices. Overall, as van der Eng's series shows, GDP growth in per capita terms was very slow for the last two decades of the century, but accelerated in the years between 1901 and 1928 to close to 2 per cent per annum. The years from 1929 to 1934 saw a sharp fall in per capita GDP, but a rapid recovery took place from 1934 to 1941. By 1941, per capita GDP was back at the peak level achieved in 1928 (van der Eng 1992: 369). If we allow for van der Eng's underestimate of manufacturing growth in the latter part of the 1930s, it is likely that per capita GDP at the time of the Japanese occupation was somewhat above its pre-depression peak.

A third conclusion concerns structural change. As the pioneering work of Clark and Kuznets has shown, sustained economic growth leads over time to a decline in the share of agriculture in GDP, and an increase in the share of industry and services. There seems to be little doubt that this occurred in Indonesia in the last century of Dutch colonial rule. Although with the available evidence it is impossible to produce a definitive series on sectoral output, there can be little doubt that manufacturing industry, construction, transport, wholesale and retail trade and government, financial and other services all grew more rapidly than total GDP, so that over time their share of total output would have increased. Van der Eng's series indicates that between 1880 and 1929 agriculture dropped from nearly 50 per cent of GDP to 35 per cent (van der Eng 1992: Table A4). By 1941 the agricultural share had dropped further to 34 per cent. For reasons discussed in the appendix, the share of manufacturing in GDP prob-ably grew from under five percent in 1880 to about 12 per cent by 1940.

Changes also occurred between the end of the nineteenth century and 1940 in the structure of the labour force and in the pace of urbanisation. In 1870, the great majority of the population in both Java and the rest of the country derived the bulk of their income from agricultural employment, with some recourse to other sources of income in the slack seasons. By 1930, it is clear that a substantial minority of the population in Java derived almost all its income from non-agricultural employment. The data assembled by Mertens (1978: 50) from the 1930 census show that in Java 34 per cent of the male labour force and 41 per cent of the female labour force were in non-agricultural employment. The percentages were lower in other parts of the archipelago, but for the country as a whole over 30 per cent of those gainfully employed were outside agriculture. To an increasing extent the non-agricultural labour force was located in urban areas. The proportion of the population in Java living in towns with more than 20,000 inhabitants increased from 3.4 per cent in 1890 to 6.1 per cent in 1930 (CEI, Vol 11, Table 15.2b). The impact of these changes on living standards, and on other aspects of the colonial economy, will be addressed in later chapters.

Finally, it is essential to bear in mind the increasingly open nature of the Indonesian economy in the nineteenth and twentieth centuries, and the consequences this had for measurement of output growth. The System of National Accounts used by the United Nations distinguishes between GDP (total output produced within an economy), and GNP or GNDI (which is the amount of income actually available for consumption or investment within an economy). In a closed economy the two are identical but in an open one they differ by the sum of net factor payments abroad, and net current transfers (Parkin and King 1991: 574). In Indonesia for much of the period from 1830 to 1941, the balance of payments was in surplus, and the sum of net factor payments and current transfers abroad was positive. This meant that GNDI was less than GDP, often by a considerable margin.

The increasing openness of the Indonesian economy after 1870 meant that it was vulnerable to fluctuations in the terms of trade. Since the 1950s it has become usual for primary-exporting countries to publish estimates of GDP corrected for fluctuations in the terms of trade. As we will see in the next section, several such estimates have been prepared for Indonesia since the 1960s. In the years from 1913 to 1939, the net barter terms of trade deteriorated as export prices declined more steeply than import prices (CEI Vol 15, Appendix A). The very sharp decline in import capacity (the income terms of trade) which occurred in the early 1930s, and which was only partially rectified in the latter part of the decade, meant that per capita GDP corrected for the decline in import capacity was lower in the late 1930s than at its peak in 1927. In fact, corrected per capita GDP in 1939 was still below the level achieved in 1913 (Booth 1995: 358–9). Thus, in spite of the considerable increase in volume of output which occurred between 1913 and 1939, the real resource value of GDP was lower because of the fall in the international purchasing power of Indonesia's exports which had taken place over these years.

THE JAPANESE OCCUPATION AND THE INDONESIAN REVOLUTION: 1942–49

The capitulation of the Dutch colonial government to the invading Japanese army in 1942 marked 'a more permanent break with the past in Indonesia than in other parts of Southeast Asia' (Reid 1980: 18). Dutch colonial rule over the entire archipelago was finally terminated, and indigenous Indonesians were at last able to contemplate a future in which they could be masters in their own land, albeit under the tutelage of imperial Japan. There can be no doubt that, in 1942, most Indonesians did view the Japanese as benevolent liberators, and in many parts of the country the Japanese army was welcomed with open delight. The Dutch had made little attempt to resist the Japanese army with military force, and thus the destruction of infrastructure and productive plant and equipment was modest, with the partial exception of the oil industry, and some other industrial capacity. The Japanese, for their part, appointed many low-ranking Indonesian officials to more responsible posts in the civilian administration, and, in Java at least, the Japanese commanding officer preached the virtues of a pragmatic administrative policy which would give the local people maximum opportunity to better their economic lot (Reid 1980: 19).

The immediate aim of the Japanese armed forces in Indonesia was to secure supplies of the strategic raw materials (rubber, oil, tin and other metals) which had long made the archipelago so attractive to the Japanese government. The assumption was that the regions producing these commodities would continue to do so and would be supplied with imports of food and other basic needs as had been the case under the Dutch. But by the middle of 1943 the acute shortage of shipping meant that this policy was unworkable. Instead, the occupying forces emphasised regional self-sufficiency. Inter-regional trade in food and other basic needs was actively discouraged, and anyway was made increasingly difficult by the breakdown of the transport network. The impact on an economy which by 1942 had achieved a high degree of regional specialisation was devastating. In Java, the military administration tried to procure 1.6 million tons of paddy in 1943, and in spite of widespread resistance on the part of farmers, deliveries totalled 1.49 million tons (Sato 1994: 122). But high procurements combined with falling production meant that there was less food left in the villages, and prices rose sharply. Shortages and price rises were even more pronounced in those parts of the Outer Islands which had relied on rice imports from Java, Thailand or Burma (Reid 1980a: 19–20; van der Eng 1994: 34–41).

By 1945, the effect of Japanese policies on food production in Java was little short of catastrophic. Although it is probable that underreporting of yields became more widespread as Japanese food levies became more onerous, there can be little doubt that rice production declined from 1943 onwards. The production series compiled by van der Eng (1994: Table A1) shows that production of dry stalk paddy fell from almost nine million tons in 1941 to 6.47 million tons in 1945. Production of maize, cassava, soyabean and peanuts also fell. Only sweet potato production increased. It is likely that the production data for rootcrops were understated to an even greater extent than those for grains and pulses, and that many people were existing very largely on cassava, potatoes and other tubers in the final phases of the war. Outside Java there are few data available on food production and consumption during the Japanese period, but there can be little doubt that food availability declined. In those areas which had depended on food imports, the Japanese authorities urged self-sufficiency, and indeed reduced the food rations to those regions deemed to have potential for producing more food. In the Medan area, over 150,000 hectares of tobacco land were made over to foodcrop cultivation, although it was acknowledged that such measures were hardly sufficient to compensate for declining food imports (Nishijima and Kishi 1963: 265–73). In some areas food production probably did increase, but for many the price of the Japanese occupation was hunger and malnutrition. Although the Japanese had ambitious plans for increased rice production in both Java and the Outer Islands, most of these plans were based on little more than an awareness that rice yields in Indonesia were lower than in Japan. Japanese officials, for the most part, showed little understanding of the very different agro-climatic conditions in Indonesia, and anyway had few budgetary resources to devote to improved irrigation or research into higher-yielding varieties (van der Eng 1994: 17–21; Nishijima and Kishi 1963: 265–6).

The non-food agricultural economy suffered even more badly under the Japanese than the food economy. Production of plantation export crops not deemed essential for the war effort was terminated. Most Javanese tea estates were closed down, depriving over two million Javanese workers of an important source of cash income (Nishijima and Kishi 1963: 268). Because sugar production exceeded requirements in the Japanese empire, sugar factories were either told to produce alcohol and butanol, or converted to other purposes (Siahaan 1996: 128–30). Estate production of strategic crops such as rubber and quinine was strictly regulated, and output was procured at a very low price. Smallholder production of cashcrops which did not have a local market became increasingly pointless in most areas as marketing channels became more disrupted; in addition, most farmers had little choice but to devote their labour to foodcrops in order to survive. The dynamic export-oriented smallholder sector which had developed since the 1890s had, by 1945, been reduced to a small rump producing crops such as coffee, tobacco and copra for local markets.

Production in the non-agricultural sectors of the economy declined even more rapidly. The departing Dutch had inflicted considerable damage on petroleum installations, and although the Japanese were desperate to increase crude petroleum production as rapidly as possible, output in 1942 was less than half that reached in 1938 (Hunter 1966: 257). In 1943, production was estimated at 6.5 million tons (almost 90 per cent of the 1938 level) but this fell again rapidly, and in 1945 was only 850,000 tons. In that year the Sumatran installations were subjected to heavy allied bombardment. Other segments of the mining sector, including tin, coal and other metals fared little better. The manufacturing sector also suffered sustained output declines. Factories owned by European and American interests were taken over by the Japanese, but the increasing scarcity of raw materials and spare parts for machines meant that output declined rapidly. (Nishijima and Kishi 1963: 270; Siahaan 1996: 130–3).

Only those industries producing essential war materials received official support under the policy of 'self reliance'. These included chemicals for ammunition and explosives, machine shops for vehicle repair, food processing, cement, shipyards, medicines, textiles and garments. In the textile sector, the Japanese authorities brought 10,000 modern looms from Japan and 150,000 old looms, together with a number of technical experts who were charged with expanding Dutch-owned mills. The looms were distributed across the country, in the expectation that a textile industry could develop in Sumatra and Sulawesi as well as in Java, but in 1945 only a small number were still in use (Siahaan 1996: 115–33). Van Warmelo (1946) estimated that there were 549 industrial enterprises in operation in 1945, of which 184 had been built by the Japanese or converted from other uses. But by 1945 shortage of raw materials and spare parts had reduced production in most of these enterprises to very low levels.

Given the data deficiencies it is impossible to state with certainty by how much output declined in Indonesia in the years from 1941 to 1945. Van der Eng (1992: Table A4) estimates that by 1945 GDP (in 1983 constant prices) was only 43 per cent of its 1941 level, which seems plausible, in spite of the fact that the official foodcrop statistics could overstate the actual production decline. Certainly, the allied armies which entered Indonesia in 1945 were greeted with scenes of hunger, poverty and considerable devastation of infrastructure. The returning Dutch administrators were keen to embark on a programme of post-war reconstruction, but they simply did not appreciate the change in attitude which had taken place in Indonesia in the three years of Japanese occupation. Many Indonesians who had not been supporters of the independence movement in the pre-war years, or who had been 'cooperating nationalists' had become disillusioned by the ignominious Dutch defeat in 1942, and by the brutalities of the Japanese military regime. They realised that no foreign power, either European or Asian, could be relied upon to govern Indonesia in the interests of Indonesians. Those with a more sophisticated understanding of the new world order in the aftermath of the war realised that the Netherlands, devastated by five years of German occupation, was hardly in a position to sustain a long colonial war. And the new world superpowers, the USA and the USSR, both had their own reasons for supporting independence movements in Asia.

In August 1945, Sukarno and Hatta declared Indonesia to be an independent and sovereign state, and a further four years of armed struggle and economic dislocation ensued. In some respects, quantifying the effects of the independence struggle on output is even more difficult than quantifying the effects of the Japanese occupation. Java and many other parts of the country were, in effect, partitioned into those zones controlled by the nationalist forces and those under the control of the Dutch. Official statistics published by the Dutch government could only estimate output in the Dutch-controlled parts of the country. The nationalist forces had more pressing concerns in the areas they controlled than producing accurate output data. What does seem clear is that in most productive sectors, recovery to pre-war levels was a prolonged process. Food production in Java in 1947 was still well below 1940 levels, while output of rubber, tea, coffee, palm oil and sugar from the estate sector was reduced almost to zero. Output of crude petroleum, coal and tin was also much reduced, compared with 1940 (Table 2.8).

Table 2.8   Output of agricultural and mineral products, 1940–54

	1940	1947	1950	1954
Foodcrops (Java) (000 tons)				
Rice	8,969	6,840	7,528	9,263
Corn	1,900	1,328	1,600	2,154
Cassava	8,415	5,776	5,760	6,430
Sweet potatoes	1,418	1,294	942	1,064
Soyabeans	294	188	245	362
Peanuts	197	134	171	204
Livestock (000)				
Cattle	4,599	n.a.	4,261	4,968
Buffalo	3,176	n.a.	2,734	2,921
Pigs & goats	9,108	n.a.	7,777	10,673
Large estates (000 tons)				
Rubber	283	14	178	288
Coffee	39	3	11	14
Tea	82	1	35	47
Palm oil	240	1	126	169
Sugar	1,607	7	277	600
Timber	4,747	750	2,845	3,628
Smallholder crops (000 tons)				
Rubber	266	n.a.	467	517
Coffee	46	16	28	43
Tea	13	0	n.a.	21
Copra	412	181	396	1,202
Mining (000,000 tons)				
Crude petroleum	8	1	6	11
Coal	2	0.3	0.8	0.9
Tin	0.04	0.02	0.03	0.04
Bauxite	0.275	n.a.	0.531	0.173

Sources: van der Eng (1994), Table A1; *Economic Review of Indonesia*, Vol III (1), January–March 1949, p. 15; *Statistical Pocketbook of Indonesia, 1959.*

Destruction of plant and acute shortages of raw materials reduced output to very low levels in most parts of the manufacturing sector. In 1947, the only manufactures where production had returned to 1940 levels were margarine and beer; industries such as weaving, cement, sugar, and refined petroleum products where output had grown rapidly between 1929 and 1940 all suffered considerable devastation (Department of Economic Affairs 1949: 17). Although Dutch officials expressed optimism that the sugar industry could be revived, the problems were formidable (Klasing 1948). Many factories had undergone conversion, or sustained damage at the hands of both the Japanese and the Republican armies, and farmers were far less inclined to be intimidated by the factories into renting out land which they preferred to use for foodcrops. The textile industry faced even more severe problems. Reviewing the situation in 1948, Hardon (1948: 161–2) estimated that the textile industry was operating at about 20 per cent of its 1942 capacity, and that in centres such as Madjalaja in West Java, 80 per cent of plant had been damaged beyond repair:

> the oil factories at Banjoemas are not worth reconstruction, whilst very considerable damage was inflicted on the rice mills, especially in the Karawang and Indramajoe areas. The batik industry, of considerable economic importance to West and Middle Java, was practically at a standstill through the lack of cloth and of dyes. The smithies did not produce tools, the tapioca mills remained idle, and the various cottage industries, including weaving and plaiting, ceased to function (Hardon 1948: 161).

Other key sectors of the economy such as transport, trade, construction, and public services all suffered from the depredations of the Japanese army and the effects of the struggle between the Dutch and Indonesian forces. By 1948, road, rail and coastal shipping services were functioning again, although because of the shortage of rolling stock on the railways and of trucks, the volume of both road and rail freight was well below 1940 levels. Shortage of ships prevented the revival of coastal shipping, while native *prahus* preferred the lucrative smuggling trade to 'legitimate' activities. The government tried to curb smuggling by demanding that money deposits were made at the time of shipment of goods, which were forfeited if the goods were not delivered to the declared destination. But the deposits were high, and officials acknowledged that they were deterring legal transport activities (Department of Economic Affairs 1949: 21).

RECOVERY FROM WAR AND REVOLUTION: 1950–57

In an analysis of the transition to independence in India, Vaidyanathan (1983: 948) stressed that 'along with an impoverished economy, independent India also inherited some useful assets in the
form of a national transport system, an administrative apparatus in
working order, a shelf of concrete development projects and substantial reserves of foreign exchange'. The newly independent Indonesian
republic in 1950 had none of these advantages. Transport infrastructure had not recovered from the devastation of war and revolution,
and far from possessing an 'administrative apparatus in working
order', the new republic was desperately short of trained administrative, professional and managerial workers. Certainly many low-ranking Indonesian officials in both the government and the private
sectors had been promoted into more senior posts by the Japanese,
but the times were hardly propitious for an orderly transfer of
administrative responsibilities. And whereas India had substantial
reserves of foreign exchange in the sterling balances to draw on for
financing development projects, by the end of 1949 Indonesian foreign
reserves were estimated to be $142 million, compared with $458
million in 1945 (Oey 1991: 37). Given that imports in 1950 averaged
$137 million per month, these reserves were quite inadequate. In
addition, when sovereignty was finally transferred to the Republic of
the United States of Indonesia at the end of 1949, the new government
was obliged to take over not just a shattered economy but also a
public debt of 1.56 billion guilders (Oey 1991: 57). Although part of
this debt was incurred after 1945 in the form of credits from the
American, Canadian and Australian governments, over half was a
legacy of the colonial era. Rapid inflation in the post-1945 period
forced the government to devalue the rupiah in September 1949,
thereby increasing the rupiah burden of the debt service obligations.

There can be little doubt that total GDP in Indonesia in 1950 was
still well below that attained in 1940. Muljatno (1960: 184) estimated
that national output only returned to 1937 levels in 1952, a finding
broadly supported by van der Eng (1992: Table A4). Output of rice,
corn, soyabean and groundnuts in Java only returned to 1940 levels in
1954, while production of rootcrops, an important source of calories
for the poor, was still well below that of 1940 (Table 2.8). The Kasimo
Plan, put forward in 1950, was intended to promote food production
through cooperatives and farmer associations, but little progress was
made in disseminating new production technologies, either in rice or

in other foodcrops. The nationalists shared the expectation of colonial officials that transmigration would ease population pressure in Java, and increase food production in Sumatra and Sulawesi, although there was little appreciation of the barriers to rapid expansion of agricultural land outside Java (Thompson 1947: 179). Output from the large estates in 1950 was also still well below that achieved in 1940. The best performance in the agricultural sector was in the smallholder treecrop sector. Production of smallholder rubber and copra increased very rapidly from the late 1940s, and by 1954 smallholder rubber output was twice that of 1940 and copra output three times as high (Table 2.8). Favourable world prices in the early 1950s gave producers an incentive to which they responded keenly. The estates, by contrast, were viewed as colonial legacies, and were subjected to strikes and increasingly strident demands from squatters to hand over land. Output growth continued to be slow for much of the 1950s.

Ministers in successive cabinets in the early 1950s realised the crucial role that industrial development must play in accelerated output growth. The early plans formulated by the republican government in the 1940s followed the thinking of the colonial officials such as Sitsen who stressed the importance of small industries using local raw materials to produce basic consumer goods, although heavy industry was also considered important in the medium term (Thompson 1947: 179). The Economic Planning Committee set up by Hatta in 1947 emphasised the importance of increasing production of basic needs, and considered export industries should be supported only in so far as they paid for essential imports. Public utilities, the rail and tram network, postal and telecommunications services, banks and mining companies should all become state enterprises. Foreign capital would be able to participate in joint ventures and cooperatives, but it would not have the same dominant role as in the colonial era (Anwar 1995: 234–6). This thinking was based on Article 33 of the 1945 constitution, which emphasised the importance of state and cooperative enterprises in the economy. But although this article was repeated in the 1950 constitution, the emphasis of official statements on the economy after the transfer of sovereignty began to change.

In an extensive economic statement made before the parliament in September 1950, Prime Minister Natsir stressed the importance of industries producing basic needs such as textiles, agricultural processing, agricultural equipment and basic consumer goods. But he also emphasised the important role that foreign manpower and capital could play in different parts of the economy (Natsir 1950: 4–6). By now, there was less stress on state enterprises, or on 'self-reliance' in production of basic needs. Instead, official pronouncements were characterised by a sober realisation that the task of economic rehabilitation would be a lengthy one, and it would be some time before ordinary Indonesians could expect any sustained improvement in incomes. The report of the Java Bank published in 1953 emphasised that output in a number of industries was still below that achieved in 1940:

> ... production in the years 1950/1 of margarine, beer, tyres, cigarettes, radio sets and electric lamps exceeded pre-war level, whereas the production of cement, paint, soap, coconut oils, textiles etc., has declined, in some cases considerably. Unfortunately, the group of products of which the output has decreased, forms a considerably larger part in total production than the articles which were produced in 1950/51 in greater quantities (Java Bank 1953: 179).

The Java Bank report stressed the unreliable quality of many industrial production statistics, but there can be little doubt that in industries such as sugar and coconut oil, woven cloth, paint, cement and phosphate fertiliser, output was still below 1940 levels in 1952 (Table 2.7). In the petroleum processing sector, where rehabilitation had been carried out by the foreign oil companies who were permitted to operate almost completely independently of other parts of the domestic economy, output of kerosene and motor spirits was slightly above 1940 levels in 1952 (Table 2.7). Output of diesel oils had almost doubled compared with 1940. The so-called 'let-alone' contracts, negotiated by the Dutch with the oil companies in 1948, which permitted the rapid rehabilitation of oil refineries, were heavily criticised after 1950, although the government was able to ride out this criticism, at least in the short run (Hunter 1966: 259; Oey 1991: 58–63).

National income data available from several sources for the 1950s can be used to examine the growth of production by sector as well as in the aggregate. Between 1950 and 1955, GNP grew at 5.6 per cent per annum, according to World Bank estimates (World Bank 1976: 122). Between 1953 and 1957, United Nations estimates from the 1960 Yearbook of National Accounts (YBNA) show that real net domestic product at factor cost grew by 5 per cent per annum; about half the total real growth which occurred was in the primary sector (agriculture and mining) while the rest was equally divided between manufacturing and 'other', embracing construction, utilities, transport and trade (Table 2.9). Van der Eng's data indicate that over these four

years, over 40 per cent of the growth in GDP was due to the oil sector
alone. This seems to be an overstatement due to his use of 1983 prices,
although there can be little doubt that output of both crude petroleum
and refined products did grow rapidly until the late 1950s. By 1957
crude petroleum production was almost twice that reached in 1940
(Hunter 1966: Table 1). By 1959 output of kerosene and diesel (but
not of motor spirits) was above 1952 levels (Table 2.7).

Table 2.9   Sectoral growth rates, 1953–57

Sector	Annual average growth rate 1953–57	Percentage breakdown of sectoral contribution to total growth
Agriculture	2.8	34
Mining and Quarrying	25.6	13
Manufacturing	13.9	27
Other	4.2	26
GDP (factor cost)	5.0	100
GNP (market prices)	5.6*	
GDP (van der Eng)	2.3	

*1950–55
Sources: GDP data: United Nations, *Yearbook of National Accounts Statistics, 1960*, p. 114. GNP data: World Bank, *World Tables, 1976*, p. 122; van der Eng (1992: 369).

The YBNA figures show a very rapid industrial growth rate between 1953 and 1957; value added grew by 73 per cent over these four years. Did this simply represent rehabilitation, or was it new growth, beyond what had occurred in the industrial sector in the 1930s? Given that the damage and destruction wrought by war and revolution in medium and large-scale manufacturing was greater than in most other parts of the economy, rehabilitation probably proceeded slowly. In addition to problems of rehabilitation, increased labour militancy meant that higher wages had to be paid to workers in some industries, thus adding to costs and making domestic output less competitive with imports. Inadequate provision of electricity and transport infrastructure added to already high production costs. The extent of the manufacturing recovery is very difficult to judge, given the lack of published production data for many industries in the 1950s, although output of coconut oil, refined petroleum products (except motor spirits), textiles, white cigarettes and cement was all higher in 1959 than in 1940 (Table 2.7). This suggests that the quite high manufacturing growth rates of the 1950s involved more than just rehabilitation, and that new capacity was created.

The surveys of manufacturing industry which began to appear in 1954 show that total wages paid by the large factory sector had not caught up, in real terms, with pre-war levels by 1954 (Table 2.10). Employment in the large factory sector (defined in 1940 as any establishment employing more than fifty workers, or employing less than fifty workers but using machinery) was about the same in 1958 as in 1940, although the post-war definition was probably narrower. Total wage costs as a ratio of value added in large-scale manufacturing were lower in 1958 than the estimate given by Sitsen for 1940, and fell sharply thereafter (Table 2.10). The most plausible explanation for this was the overvaluation of the rupiah which encouraged manufacturers rehabilitating existing plant or constructing new factories to use capital-intensive technologies imported from abroad. Negative real interest rates in the formal financial sector would also have contributed to this trend.

Table 2.10   Employment, real wage costs and wage costs per worker in the large factory sector,* 1940–62

Year	Numbers employed	Real wages (million guilder/ rupiahs)	Wage costs as a % of value added	Real wage costs per worker (guilder/ rupiah)
1940	344,177	897.5	44.6	2,608
1954	263,286	741.9	n.a.	2,818
1958	334,792	696.9	18.0	2,082
1959	318,356	488.6	15.2	1,535
1960	330,593	442.9	12.4	1,340
1961	339,674	584.0	12.1	1,719
1962	349,898	381.4	n.a.	1,064

*Data for 1940 refer to the factory sector, which according to Seegers (CEI, Vol. 8: 94) includes industries using considerable mechanical installations, electrical or steam power, and/or conducted in relatively large establishments of fifty or more workers. After 1950 the 'large factory' sector was defined as any establishment employing more than fifty people, or using machinery of more than five hp. The deflator used is the cost of thirty local and imported goods in Jakarta (1953 = 100).

Sources: CEI (Vol 8: 104, 114); Sitsen (c. 1943:44); *Perusahaan Industri* (Manufacturing Industry), Jakarta: Central Bureau of Statistics, 1954; Nugroho (1967: 319–43).

The United Nations estimates of net domestic product at factor cost show that in spite of rapid growth in the 1950s, manufacturing output accounted for only 12 per cent of net domestic product in 1957, and fell below this share thereafter. Paauw (1963: 177) argues that the post-independence data are probably understated, mainly through the omission of the handicraft sector, although there was also substantial under-reporting in the factory sector. Figures produced by ECAFE (1961: 15) for the 1950s show that Indonesia had the lowest share of non-agricultural to total national product of any Asian country except Pakistan. Furthermore, Indonesia was the only Asian country to experience a decline in that share between 1950–52 and 1957–59. The share of manufacturing in GDP in 1957–59 was estimated by ECAFE to be only nine per cent, which was lower than for any Asian country except Ceylon and Cambodia. This could be a slight under-statement, although it is argued in the appendix that by 1960 the manufacturing share of GDP was only 9.4 per cent, and it fell thereafter.

Until 1957, Indonesia's growth of real product was about average by Asian standards; faster than the South Asian countries, but slower than China, Taiwan or Japan (Table 2.11). This was in spite of the fact that, according to ECAFE figures, Indonesia's investment rate was the lowest in Asia; the low investment and high growth outcome thus produced one of the lowest incremental capital–output ratios (ICORS) in Asia. This could presumably be explained by the fact that much of the growth was due to rehabilitation of existing plant and infrastructure, rather than to new investment. Even so, contemporary observers pointed out that the very low investment rates were to some extent an artifact of the undervalued exchange rate, which meant that the rupiah values of capital imports did not take into account the inflation-induced rise in rupiah prices relative to world prices (Paauw 1963: 197). In addition, UN experts claimed in a report prepared in 1964 that private investment was understated, especially in agriculture, small-scale industry and much of the service sector, because of inadequate reporting procedures (United Nations 1964: 213 ff). They computed a new series on investment, both public and private, which in turn yielded a rather higher ratio of investment of GNP; the ratio fluctuated over the years from 1952 to 1957 between 8.3 and 10.7 per cent of GNP (United Nations 1964: 243). On average, according to the UN study, investment accounted for about nine per cent of GNP over these years, a figure rather closer to the median value for the countries shown in Table 2.11, although still on the low side. However, even these adjusted data may still have been too low;

alternative estimates for 1955 published by the World Bank (1976: 122) put the investment ratio at 10 per cent, rather than the 8.3 per cent estimated by the UN study. Given the data problems it is impossible to come up with an accurate figure, although the World Bank figure can be treated as a maximum and the UN figure as a minimum.

The problem of the unrealistic exchange rate which led to undervaluation of capital imports relative to domestic output also bedevilled any attempt to calculate the ratio of exports to national product. Paauw (1963: 183) acknowledged the problem, and computed the ratio of exports in rupiah to constant price GDP to eliminate the effect of domestic inflation. Even with this adjustment, his estimates showed that the ratio of exports to GDP fell between 1952 and 1953, and remained at around 8 per cent until 1957. This was a much lower ratio than the pre-war one. The United Nations study already referred to took exports valued in US dollar terms, deflated by a dollar price index, and converted these at the 1955 exchange rate; the ratio was then computed using GDP data valued at constant 1955 prices. This procedure yielded a slightly higher and more stable ratio,

Table 2.11 Growth in selected Asian countries of real national product, investment, and the incremental capital–output ratio*

Country	Index of real national product in 1957 (1953 = 100)	Investment as % of GDP (annual average, 1950–59)	Incremental capital–output ratio (1950–9)
China	134	n.a.	n.a.
Japan	133	21.6	2.4
Taiwan	130	13.1	1.7
Burma	127	17.1	3.4
Cambodia	125	n.a.	n.a.
Philippines	125	7.0	1.2
Indonesia	123	6.2	1.7
South Korea	119	12.3	2.2
Thailand	115	14.4	2.6
Ceylon	110	11.3	2.9
Pakistan	108	7.8	3.0
India	107	14.9	4.8

*See source document for full details of data and adjustments made.
Source: *Economic Survey of Asia and the Far East* (1961: 10, 24).

although it never exceeded 10 per cent of GDP (United Nations 1964: 208). But the problem with both the Paauw and the UN approaches was that they still relied on the obviously over-valued 1955 exchange rate. If the current US dollar value of exports is converted at the 'free market' rate reported in Pick (1956: 144; 1965: 265) rather than the official rate, then the ratio of exports to national product increases markedly. But as inflation gathered pace and political instability mounted it is likely that the black market rate undervalued the rupiah. An alternative procedure is to adjust the 1938 export/GDP ratio by the ratio of the export volume index computed by Rosendale (1975) to the real GDP index for each year after 1951. This procedure shows that up to 1953 the ratio was even higher than that derived from nominal dollar export values and the black market rate (Table 2.12). This adjusted series also suggests that there was little or no decline in the export/GNP ratio after 1957; this point is discussed in more detail in the next section.

Table 2.12   Growth in real GDP and export volume, 1938–68

	Index of		Exports as % of GDP*
	Real GDP	*Export volume*	
1938	100	100	17.1
1951	90	137	26.1
1952	97	132	23.3
1953	100	131	22.5
1954	107	141	22.6
1955	111	127	19.6
1956	114	133	20.0
1957	123	140	19.5
1958	122	135	19.0
1959	122	136	19.1
1960	123	129	18.0
1961	130	140	18.5
1962	132	148	19.2
1963	129	129	17.1
1964	134	147	18.8
1965	135	151	19.2
1966	139	147	18.1
1967	141	166	20.2
1968	151	184	20.9

*1938 ratio multiplied by export volume index and divided by GDP volume index.
Sources: Real index of GDP: estimated from the series based on World Bank (1976: 122) and United Nations (1960: 114). Export volume index: Rosendale (1975: 73). The ratio of exports to GDP in 1938 is estimated from the export data in CEI, Vol 12a and current price data on GDP in 1938 supplied by van der Eng.

Given the valuation problems caused by the fixed exchange rate, it is clearly impossible to make exact estimates of trends in investment or exports relative to national income; indeed, the various national income estimates themselves can only be considered indicative of broad trends. But the data do allow the following conclusions to be drawn concerning economic performance up to 1957. Indonesia was able to grow quite rapidly in the immediate post-independence years because there was an immense amount of rehabilitation of war-ravaged plant and infrastructure to be carried out. Typically, this type of investment yielded quite high returns from modest outlays. Even after the scope for quick-yielding expenditures was reduced, growth continued at quite high, albeit erratic, rates up to 1957. A GDP series based on data from World Bank (1976) and United Nations (1960) indicated an average annual growth of per capita GDP of 3.4 per cent between 1950 and 1957 (Table 2.1). An important reason for this reasonable growth performance appears to have been quite high investment rates in the private sector; the government sector, including state enterprises, never accounted for more than 36 per cent of total investment until 1957 (United Nations 1960: 114)

However, the problems created by inflation and a severely over-valued exchange rate inevitably began to have some impact on patterns of investment, both in the export sector and in the rest of the economy. After 1954 export volume fluctuated but did not show any significant growth; over the entire period from 1950 to 1957 export volume grew by only 1.3 per cent per annum (Table 2.1). In spite of the fact that early pronouncements by government leaders supported foreign investment, as long as Indonesians were encouraged to participate in management (Natsir 1950: 6), both official and popular attitudes became more overtly hostile as governments changed, and nationalistic sentiment grew. In any event, growing political instability, coupled with the increasingly over-valued exchange rate and controls on capital exports, discouraged foreign firms outside the oil sector from investing in the modern manufacturing or in the service sector.

Issues of ownership and control of the economy lay behind many of the problems of macroeconomic management in Indonesia in the early post-independence years. Although the country was a sovereign nation after 1950, even many moderates felt that political independence had not been accompanied by economic independence and indeed that 'the Indonesian revolution had not yet entered its economic phase' (Glassburner 1962: 80). More than 100,000 Dutch nationals remained in Indonesia after independence, and Dutch firms continued to dominate the export-import trade, banking and shipping. Over 1,000 colonial civil servants were retained in senior positions in the Indonesian bureaucracy in the early 1950s, and, according to one foreign adviser, many used their power to benefit Dutch-owned interests, and in some cases 'to undermine the economic position of the struggling young Republic' (Higgins 1984: 65). This situation was extremely galling to many former liberation fighters, but there was little consensus on how to change matters. On one side, the moderate pragmatists, best represented by Sjafruddin Prawiranegara, who was Minister of Finance in the first two cabinets of Hatta and Natsir, and who became Governor of the Java Bank (subsequently Bank Indonesia) after its nationalisation, argued that changes in the pattern of ownership and control would have to come slowly as an indigenous entrepreneurial class emerged.

Sjafruddin's main sparring partner in the early years of the Republic was Sumitro Djojohadikusomo, who served with him, as Minister of Trade and Industry in the Natsir cabinet, and who became Minister of Finance in the Wilopo cabinet. As cabinet colleagues, they clashed over the so-called 'economic urgency' or 'Benteng' plan which Sumitro designed to promote indigenous participation in the non-agricultural economy, and which Sjafruddin considered too nationalistic (Glassburner 1962: 85). The two debated their differences at considerable length in the press (Sumitro 1953a, Chapter XXIII) but, as Glassburner argues, their differences were, in fact, over details of policy rather than broad goals; 'the orientation of both these men was at least nominally socialist and essentially pragmatic – toward making the system work'. But the influence of both waned after the installation of the first cabinet led by Ali Sastroamidjojo, which was far more nationalistic in character. The Minister of Economic Affairs in this cabinet was Iskaq Tjokroadisurjo, described by Feith (1962: 374) as 'an energetic and tough-willed PNI leader who had been known for some time as an advocate of stronger measures to make the economy effectively "national"'.

Iskaq set about greatly increasing the share of foreign exchange allocations for imports granted to 'national' importers so that, at the end of his tenure, they were receiving almost 90 per cent of the allocation. Similarly, over fifty new private banks were established, and even more new shipping companies, many run by individuals with the right political connections but little business experience (Feith 1962: 375). The fall of the Ali cabinet in August 1955, and the return of Sumitro to the Finance portfolio in the Harahap cabinet, led to a return of confidence which was reflected in a sharp appreciation in the free market value of the rupiah. But this cabinet lasted only a few months, and after the 1955 elections the second Ali cabinet saw a return to blatant buying of political loyalties through the allocation of licences and foreign exchange (Feith, 1962: 479). By the end of 1957, both Sumitro and Sjafruddin, together with two of the Prime Ministers they had served under, had thrown in their lot with the rebels establishing an alternative government in Sumatra.

Much has been written about the reasons for the failure of parliamentary democracy in Indonesia in the years between 1950 and 1958. But there seems to be a consensus of views that the underlying economic reason was, in Glassburner's words 'the continued existence of an entrenched Dutch economic interest, and...the economic impotence of the Indonesian elite in general' (Glassburner 1962). This impotence made it impossible for successive governments to fulfil the revolutionary expectations generated by the independence struggle. The first four cabinets, those of Hatta, Natsir, Sukiman and Harahap, were 'intensely concerned with solving administrative and economic problems, with the strengthening of law and order, administrative regularisation and consolidation, the maximisation of production and planned economic development' (Feith 1962: 556). But the technocrats in these administrations were thwarted by nationalists who resented what they saw as the continuing foreign domination of the economy. Thus the developments of the 1950s led finally to the expulsion of Dutch nationals and the government takeover of Dutch companies. This action, taken after the failure of the Indonesian motion on the future of West Irian to pass through the UN General Assembly in November 1957, was a crossing of the Rubicon for the Indonesian Republic. Economic as well as political policy-making could never be the same again.

PERFORMANCE OF THE GUIDED ECONOMY, 1958–65

In late 1956 and early 1957, President Sukarno made a series of speeches which foreshadowed the demise of parliamentary democracy as it had functioned since the installation of the Hatta cabinet in December 1949, and its replacement with an indigenous version of democratic government based on supposedly Indonesian values and customs. When the second cabinet of Ali Sastroamidjojo finally collapsed in March 1957, it was replaced the next month by an 'extra-parliamentary party of experts', chosen by President Sukarno, and led by the widely respected planning expert, Juanda. The period between April and November was 'marked by a long and many-faceted tug of war between Jakarta and the regionalist-controlled areas', with dissident regional councils establishing themselves in many parts of Sumatra and Sulawesi (Feith 1962: 581). Late in the year, the position worsened when two former prime ministers, Natsir and Harahap, together with the two leading economic managers, Sumitro and Sjafruddin, joined forces in Padang, in West Sumatra. In February 1958, a rival cabinet was established, led by Sjafruddin.

Mackie (1980: 673–4) has argued that an important causal factor behind the regional rebellions was the perception that the centre had lost its ability to administer the national economy, or indeed to prevent its officials, both civilian and military, from exploiting the growing economic dislocation through barter trade and black marketeering. The rebels did not want the regions to secede from Indonesia; rather, they wanted to bring about the collapse of the central government and replace it with one whose policies would be more beneficial to the regions. But they failed. The army, under Major General Nasution, regained control of key locations in Sumatra and Sulawesi with relative ease during 1958–95, and all those connected with the rebellions, both in Sumatra and elsewhere, became discredited. Several leaders went into exile, and others were imprisoned. Political parties in general were increasingly restricted in their activities, and over the next two years President Sukarno strengthened his personal power. In July 1959, the return to the 1945 constitution greatly reduced the power and prestige of parliament, and in March 1960, after all the opposition elements had combined to oppose the draft budget, the president dismissed all members of parliament, and appointed an entirely new body, intended to support his policies. From then on, he exercised close to absolute power in economic as in other matters.

The government takeover of Dutch enterprises in late 1957, together with the state of civil war in some key exporting regions, led to a decline in output in some sectors of the economy in 1958, although there is some disagreement on the extent of the decline. The figures in the UN Yearbook of National Accounts (YBNA) for 1960 indicate a decline in net domestic product of around three per cent in 1958, entirely due to steep output declines in the manufacturing and service sector. The Indonesian National Planning Bureau data cited by Paauw (1963: 193) showed a much more severe decline of 12.9

per cent. Paauw (1963: 194) thought that the YBNA figures under-stated the decline in national product in 1958, although the alternative estimate appears to be exaggerated, given that the main impact of the Dutch withdrawal was borne by the manufacturing and modern services sectors, and that these were both relatively small, so that even the 39 per cent decline in manufacturing value added shown in the figures only translated into a 3.3 per cent decline in net domestic product. A subsequent study which tried to reconcile the two series found the YBNA series to be the more reliable (United Nations 1964: 206). The YBNA figures show a slight recovery in 1959, although net domestic product in 1959 was still two per cent below the 1957 figure.

On the other hand, van der Eng's estimates show that there was no decline in GDP at all between 1957 and 1959, but rather that output grew by almost 9 per cent over these two troubled years. Van der Eng bases this assertion not just on the good performance of the agricul-tural sector, which the YBNA data also show, but also on the con-tinued rapid growth of manufacturing and mining output. He estimates that manufacturing value added grew by 9 per cent between 1957 and 1959. This is highly unlikely, given that the available evi-dence indicates stagnating output in sectors such as large-scale weav-ing and petroleum derivatives in 1958 and 1959 (Palmer 1972: 341; *Statistical Pocketbook of Indonesia* 1961: 87). However, van der Eng correctly draws attention to the continued growth in the petroleum sector over these years; in fact, crude petroleum output grew by over 20 per cent between 1957 and 1959 although growth slowed down thereafter (Nugroho 1967: 354). If the YBNA data are adjusted to indicate growth rather than decline in the mining and petroleum sector, then the fall in output over these years is further modified, although it is probable that some decline did occur.

From 1958 to 1965, GDP growth was positive but low compared to 1950–57; the average annual growth of net national product as esti-mated by the Central Bureau of Statistics was 1.7 per cent per annum, which implies falling per capita income, as population was growing by around 2 per cent per annum in the decades from 1950 to 1970 (Nugroho 1967: 539). This series shows an absolute decline in net domestic product in 1963, due mainly to a drought-induced decline in agricultural output. In 1964 and 1965, growth was positive but low, and there can be little doubt that in 1965 per capita GDP was below the level achieved in 1940. The relatively poor growth performance between 1958 and 1965 was reflected in each of the main sectors of the economy, with the exception of government services, which grew at

The Indonesian Economy

more than twice the growth of GDP (Sundrum 1986: 58). However, the reasons for the poor performance of each of the major sectors were rather different.

In the foodcrop sector, attempts were made to promote the new seed-fertiliser technologies in rice production through the three-year rice production programme inaugurated in 1959 (Palmer 1977: 22). Under this programme, fertiliser imports increased from 250,000 to 450,000 tons, but because of the succession of very poor rainfalls, especially in Java, in 1961, 1963, 1965 and 1967, rice output growth was disappointing (Sie 1968: 120–1). The 1963 rice crop fell by 10 per cent as a result of exceptionally dry conditions; in Java there was a further fall in 1964. Although there was some evidence of yield increases in the areas of Java where fertiliser was applied most intensively, overall yields were stagnant from 1960 to 1967 (Mears 1981: 448). Some authorities (e.g. Mears and Affif, 1968) blamed the disappointing rice production performance, in spite of increased fertiliser use, on the declining effectiveness of the irrigation system, which made crops such as corn more attractive to farmers, especially in the dry season, but it is probable that most of the shift in hectarage from rice to corn in these years was due to poor rainfall, although lack of funds for irrigation maintenance certainly aggravated the situation. The rice procurement system implemented in the early 1960s also discouraged the marketing of surplus rice. As in the Japanese period, those farmers with the potential to produce a surplus often chose to cultivate other crops where marketing was less strictly regulated.

The smallholder cashcrop sector showed some growth from 1958 to 1965, but value added in the large estates sector hardly grew at all (Central Bureau of Statistics 1970: 43). This was partly because the estates sector was largely Dutch-owned, and thus affected by the nationalisation measures, although as Mackie (1961) argued, the effects of nationalisation were not entirely adverse. Labour unrest was modified, and some replanting was undertaken. The smallholders were better able to avoid the disincentive effects of an increasingly over-valued exchange rate by smuggling out their produce to Malaysia and the Philippines, although the smuggled output may not be fully reflected in the production figures. Furthermore, their production technologies were less dependent on increasingly scarce and expensive imported inputs. Value added in the large and medium scale manufacturing sector stagnated in the years from 1961 to 1963, and fell between 1963 and 1965 (Central Bureau of Statistics 1970: 43). To a considerable extent this reflected the acute lack of foreign exchange for inputs and spare parts; in addition, the decline in per capita income reduced demand for industrial goods. The small industry sector appears to have fared only slightly better in the early and mid-1960s than the large sector; as with the smallholder cashcrop sector, it is probable that this sector was less dependent on imported inputs, although this might not have been true for industries such as weaving. Palmer (1972: 341) shows that, although estimated capacity in the small-scale weaving sector doubled between 1957 and 1962, output began to fall away after 1961 as imports of yarn began to decline.

It is probable that the role of small-scale industry in the economy was less important by the early 1960s than it had been in the late colonial era. The most persuasive evidence pointing in this direction concerns changes in female manufacturing employment between the 1930 and 1961 population censuses. A striking feature of the Indonesian labour force as revealed by the 1930 Population Census was the very high female labour force participation rates, particularly in Central and East Java, and in some parts of the Outer Islands. An important reason for these high participation rates was the high female employment in non-agricultural activities, especially in manufacturing where women accounted for 67 per cent of the total labour force in Java (Mertens 1978: Table 1.4). The 1961 population census revealed an absolute decline in the size of the manufacturing labour force in Indonesia, which was entirely due to a decline in female employment from over one million in 1930 to only 500,000 in 1961.

Various interpretations of this apparently steep decline in the female manufacturing labour force are possible. Jones (1966: 55) has suggested that many part-time handicraft workers who were classified as 'industrial' in 1930 were classified as 'agricultural' in 1961, although the actual allocation of their time between farm and handicraft activities may not have changed. A second possibility is that a much more narrow definition of 'economically active' was used in 1961, compared with 1930, and many women engaged in various types of handicraft activity considered 'gainful employment' in 1930 failed to qualify as members of the labour force in 1961. A third possibility is that the handicraft production techniques which had survived in Java in sectors such as textiles, clothing and bamboo working until 1930 could not compete with the advent of large-scale mechanised plants in the 1930s and the 1950s. If the first interpretation were correct, then we would expect that overall activity rates for women would have remained roughly stable between 1930 and 1961, with the relative decline in the industrial share of the female labour force being offset by an increase in the agricultural share. In fact, the regional data show a decline in female participation rates in Java, with particularly marked declines in Central Java and Yogyakarta (Table 2.13).

A decline of this magnitude seems unlikely to have been the result of purely statistical factors, and it does seem plausible that many small-scale and cottage industries employing females disappeared between 1930 and 1961. One reason may have been competition from larger and more efficient enterprises, particularly in the later 1930s.

Table 2.13 Female labour force participation rates,[*] and the percentage of the female labour force employed in manufacturing, 1930–61

Region	Female labour force[*] participation rates		Percentage of the female labour force employed in manufacturing	
	1930	1961	1930	1961
Java	36.6	30.7	27.7	8.7
Jakarta	19.7	23.1		16.5
West Java	21.5	24.0	24.2[†]	9.8
Central Java	45.8	30.1	25.5	10.8
Yogyakarta	59.3	48.8	46.3	14.6
East Java	37.4	35.4	18.2	5.3
Outer Islands	28.3	32.1	12.6	6.1
Indonesia	34.2	31.2	22.5	7.8

[*]1930 figures refer to all indigenous female workers as a percentage of all adult females. 1961 figures refer to all female workers over the age of 15 as a percentage of total population aged 15 and over.
[†]Includes Jakarta.
Sources: 1930 *Population Census*, Vol. VIII, Table 19. 1961 *Population Census*, Series S.P. II.

Certainly, van Oorschot's estimates show that real output in the factory sector was growing rapidly at the same time as that in the household sector was declining during the 1930s (van Oorschot 1956: 93). Another possible explanation more applicable to the post-independence era, and particularly the years from 1958 to 1965, could have been falling real incomes, which meant falling demand for industrial goods of all kinds. It is also likely that changing tastes and greater foreign influence after independence meant that demand for the more homespun products of small-scale industry declined while that for factory products grew, especially if the latter were no more expensive. Of course, if factory goods were cheaper, as well as more modern in appearance, it is hardly surprising that they rapidly displaced the output of small and cottage industries.

When we turn from a discussion of sectoral growth performance to examine the expenditure of national income in the years from 1960 to 1965, it is important to bear in mind that these years saw a very substantial decline in the net barter terms of trade. An index published by Bank Indonesia had declined to almost half its 1960 value by 1965; this is broadly consistent with the index computed by Rosendale (1975: 80) from the commodity trade statistics. This decline must have led either to a reduction in reserves, or to a reduction in real income available to the domestic economy. As with the pre-war national income estimates, it is essential to adjust the GDP figures for terms of trade fluctuations. The estimates prepared by Sundrum (1986: Table 4) show that the terms of trade decline after 1960 was sufficiently sharp to have a marked impact on GDP; once the official CBS series is adjusted for this decline, the average annual growth rate over the years 1960–67 fell from 1.7 per cent to only 0.6 per cent.

Sundrum's calculations show clearly that, as real resources available to the domestic economy fell in per capita terms in the early 1960s, efforts to maintain real consumption levels led to a steady squeezing of expenditures on both government consumption and investment. Whereas in 1960, private consumption expenditure was 78 per cent of adjusted GDP (GDY), by 1965 this percentage had risen to almost 84 per cent, and by 1967 to over 90 per cent. In 1967, investment was only 9.7 per cent of GDY, and 8.8 per cent of GDP, a lower percentage than the ten per cent estimated by the World Bank (1976: 122) for 1955. The years from 1960 to 1966 were also marked by a considerable rise in the ICOR from the low level which had prevailed before 1957. While this was partly due to the fact that the stock of quick-yielding rehabilitation projects was exhausted by 1960, the jump in the ICOR also reflected the fact that an increasing share of government investment resources were channelled into 'prestige' construction projects with low yields.

Given the rapid deterioration in the terms of trade after 1959, and the succession of unusually dry years from 1961 to 1967 in many parts of the country, was the poor real growth performance inevitable, even if more sober political and economic policies had been pursued from 1959 onwards? The answer to this question would seem to be no, for several reasons. First, if a more accommodating foreign policy had been pursued towards the Western powers, more foreign borrowing at concessional rates would have been possible, which in turn could have cushioned the economy from at least some of the adverse effects of the terms of trade decline. In particular, it would have allowed a higher level of real government expenditures to have been maintained without recourse to deficit financing on the scale which in fact occurred. Had these resources been devoted to productive infrastructure development in sectors such as irrigation, it is probable that the adverse effects of the poor weather could have been mitigated. Second, there can be little doubt that the inflation, together with the over-valued exchange rate, distorted incentives in the private sector, so that resources and entrepreneurial skills which could have been devoted to the development of businesses were diverted into various kinds of speculative activity.

Certainly other economies, equally affected by declining terms of trade, had much higher real rates of growth in these years; for example, Malaysian GDP grew by 6 per cent per annum between 1960 and 1967, compared with the Indonesian annual average growth rate of 1.7 per cent. Both the Thai and Philippine economies also grew rapidly over these years (Yoshihara 1994; Table 1.1). Slow economic growth led to a widening gap between key economic indicators in Indonesia and those in other Southeast Asian economies. By 1964, production of cement in Indonesia was lower than in Malaysia, less than half that in Thailand and almost a third of that in the Philippines. Electricity production was also lower in Indonesia than in Malaysia in the early 1960s, in spite of the huge disparity in populations (Nugroho 1967: 554–5).

STRUCTURAL RETROGRESSION IN THE INDONESIAN ECONOMY: 1940–65

It has been argued that the Indonesian economy underwent 'structural retrogression' between the late 1930s and the early post-independence years, in the sense that the share of the labour-intensive or traditional sectors in total output increased while that of the modern, capital-intensive sectors declined. For example, Paauw (1960: 209), on the basis of Polak's pre-war figures and Neumark's rather dubious national income data for 1952, and some rather rough assumptions about labour- and capital-intensities of various sectors, concluded that the share of the labour-intensive sector in total output had increased from 68 per cent to 76 per cent.

> This is tantamount to arguing that the Indonesian economy showed retrogression (in terms of extending the scope of the capital-intensive sector) during the domestic political turmoil which characterised most of the period 1939–52. In the years since independence, Indonesian development activity...has been effective in raising output mainly in the labour-intensive sector of the economy. In the capital-intensive sector the Indonesian government's primary concern has been transferring ownership of enterprise from foreign to Indonesian nationals. On balance, the result of this policy has probably been a net reduction of capital facilities in this sector, at least outside the petroleum industry (Paauw 1960: 209).

In a later paper, Paauw (1969) went on to argue that these trends accelerated in the late 1950s and early 1960s, in contrast to other Southeast Asian countries such as Thailand and the Philippines where the manufacturing sector in particular was far more dynamic. The series on manufacturing value added presented in the appendix confirms Paauw's argument, in that the share of GDP accounted for by the manufacturing sector fell from 12 per cent in 1939, to only 7 per cent in 1965. There can be little doubt that by the 1960s trade and other services were performing the function of 'last resort employers', soaking up the workers who could find employment neither in agriculture, in manufacturing nor in the modern service sector which was dominated by government. The decline in the manufacturing share of the labour force between the 1930 and 1961 population censuses, which has already been commented on, was reflected in a similar increase in the service sector share (Jones 1966, Table 2). The drift of labour into the least productive sectors of the economy in turn led to a very high proportion of the population in many parts of the country living in poverty by 1964–65.

By the mid-1960s, the picture of the Indonesian economy which most reports presented was a sad one. Inflation was accelerating, output was stagnating, poverty and hunger were widespread, and a tiny minority with access to import licences were enriching themselves while incomes of virtually everyone else were declining. Infrastructure was deteriorating, and new public investment was devoted either to defence equipment or to a few showpiece buildings in the capital city. Private investment had almost ceased, except in speculative activities yielding quick returns. And yet it was also clear to more perceptive observers that this was an economy with potential for rapid growth if only the government could be induced to follow prudent fiscal and monetary policies. True, much infrastructure was in need of rehabilitation, but this meant that relatively modest outlays could achieve considerable returns in the form of increased output. Most manufacturing establishments were producing at less than capacity, not because they were constrained by lack of demand, but because they were unable to get the foreign exchange for raw materials and spare parts. While the large estates sector was declining, smallholder producers of cashcrops had demonstrated their resilience in the face of adverse terms of trade, and highly discriminatory government policies. How much better could they perform if they were given incentives to replant and extend their holdings, and adopt improved production and processing technologies. In the rice sector, experiments with extension programmes in some parts of Java were already demonstrating the potential for increasing yields from the new seed-fertiliser technologies. What the farmers needed was extension, and credit to purchase the new inputs. Only through the application of new technologies could enough rice and other basic necessities be produced to alleviate the appalling problem of rural poverty.

The economic legacy of the first fifteen years of independence was not entirely negative. It will be argued in later chapters that progress was made in expanding access to education, in building up an indigenous civil service and professional class, and in increasing the number of indigenous businesspeople. But these achievements were outweighed by the policy failures listed above. A strong government, able to implement appropriate policies, and willing to take assistance from international and bilateral development agencies, could clearly achieve much in a short space of time. But in 1965 there seemed little prospect of such a government emerging in the near future.

GROWTH AND STRUCTURAL CHANGE IN THE NEW ORDER ERA

On the night of September 30, 1965, a coup was staged in Jakarta by a group of officers and soldiers under the command of Lieutenant-Colonel Untung. The motives of this group were, and remain, far from clear. But whether they were in fact acting on behalf of, and with the full knowledge of, the top leadership of the Indonesian Communist Party (PKI), or quite independently, and whether or not they had the approval, open or tacit, of President Sukarno, their coup provided the trigger for the final, bloody resolution of the power struggle between the army and the Communists. Soldiers loyal to the top leadership of the army (six of whom had been murdered in the coup) rallied around General Suharto, the commanding officer of KOSTRAD, and General Umar, the commanding officer of the Jakarta garrison, and rapidly regained control of Jakarta and other major cities. Then began a wave of killings throughout Java, Bali, and many parts of Sumatra. The number killed will never be accurately known, but probably ran to hundreds of thousands. In addition, many members of organisations affiliated to the PKI were taken prisoner. The Communist Party was effectively destroyed, and the power and authority of President Sukarno were gravely compromised. As order was slowly restored to a shattered nation, it became clear that the Indonesian political system, and the role of political parties within it, had undergone a change even more far-reaching in its implications than that which took place in the late 1950s.

Central to this change was the role of the armed forces. It might have been expected that, with the PKI destroyed and Sukarno discredited, power would pass to the commanding officer of the armed forces, General Nasution, who had narrowly escaped assassination on the night of September 30. But by early 1966 it was clear that the new military strongman was the officer who had acted swiftly to restore order in Jakarta in the immediate aftermath of the coup, General Suharto. Together with the Sultan of Yogyakarta and Adam Malik, Suharto wrested effective power from Sukarno in March 1966, and the triumvirate then set out to tackle the grave problems facing the nation. The next few months were, in the words of one contemporary observer, 'a time of awakening in Indonesia, awakening to the country's economic condition, and perhaps the beginning of a new era.... a picture of economic breakdown has been revealed to the Indonesian people and to the world which can have few parallels in a great nation in modern times except in the immediate aftermath of war or revolution' (Arndt 1966:1).

In fact, per capita GDP, while certainly lower than in the late 1950s, had not sunk back to the level of 1945. But even so the economic situation was grim enough. The most pressing problem concerned the balance of payments. Debt service payments were expected to be at least $530 million in 1966; as total export earnings (including oil) were estimated to be only $430 million (Arndt 1966:4), it was clear that substantial rescheduling of foreign debt was inevitable. Indeed, even with rescheduling, it was unlikely that export receipts would be sufficient to pay for imports of foodstuffs, raw materials and capital goods in sufficient quantities to curb inflation and revitalise those productive enterprises working at low capacity because of lack of spare parts and other inputs. In short, massive injections of aid, or loans on very soft terms, would be essential to achieve the twin objectives of lower inflation and faster economic growth. Such aid would, in turn, only be forthcoming if the Western nations were convinced that the new Indonesian government was turning its back on regional military confrontation and giving top priority to economic stabilisation and growth.

In order to establish its legitimacy in the eyes of the international financial community, it was essential that the new rulers enlist the services of people with skills in economics and financial management. The older generation of academic economists, politicians and civil servants with training and experience in these areas had either gone into exile, like Sumitro, or been dismissed from their positions. Some, including Sjafruddin, had been imprisoned. So the government turned to the small group of economists, trained mainly in the USA, who were teaching at the University of Indonesia in Jakarta. This group, which was to assume considerable prominence and power in successive New Order governments, was not slow in expressing its views on what needed to be done. In a collection of essays published at the end of 1965 (LEKNAS 1965), and again at a seminar held at the University of Indonesia in January 1966 (KAMI 1966), they argued for a package of measures to bring down inflation and increase production. Stressing that the 'monetary approach' and the 'production approach' to solving these problems were not alternatives, but essential parts of an integrated strategy, Ali Wardhana emphasised the overwhelming importance of reducing government expenditures, and thus the budget deficit on the one hand, and guaranteeing the supply of 'strategic' producer and consumer goods on the other (LEKNAS 1965: 49–50). He pointed out that if both these goals could be speedily attained, the experience of other countries, such as China in the late 1940s, indicated that monetary stability would be restored within months. Policy-makers could then devote themselves to the longer-run problems of growth and development.

That foreign credits and aid would be essential if these problems were to be solved was acknowledged explicitly by Sadli in his contribution to the KAMI seminar. The most pressing problem was the rescheduling of foreign debt; in addition, Sadli argued that credits of $300 million would be needed in order to import goods which could be sold domestically. The most crucial good was rice; he pointed out that if 1.5 million tons of rice could be procured from overseas, this would allow the government to eliminate Rp3 billion from the expenditure budget which had been earmarked for domestic procurement, thus making a substantial reduction to the expected budget deficit. Sadli conceded that a policy of deliberately soliciting foreign credits conflicted with the principle of 'self-reliance', which was supposedly the cornerstone of Indonesian foreign policy, but at the same time pointed out that the government had, in fact, made strenuous efforts in recent months to procure more foreign credits but was thwarted by its poor credit rating. If the new leadership was criticised for taking the very foreign loans which had been refused Sukarno, then this was only 'sour grapes' on the part of the discredited old leaders. But it was crucial that the foreign credits be used for productive purposes, rather than government consumption (KAMI 1966: 105).

In these and subsequent writings, the University of Indonesia economists established their reputation for pragmatic and realistic analysis which made them indispensible to the new regime as it began the difficult process of convincing foreign creditors and potential aid donors of its bona fides. That the path back to monetary stabilisation and faster growth would be a difficult and painful one was acknowledged by the new leaders (Arndt 1966: 2). Moreover, external circumstances continued to be unfavourable. Although there was some slight improvement in the commodity terms of trade in 1966, they deteriorated again in 1967 (Rosendale 1975: 80). And although a consortium of creditor countries agreed in principle to debt rescheduling in September 1966, and pledged $200 million in aid in 1967, they were clearly reluctant to make long-term commitments to funding Indonesia's recovery programme until they were convinced that the new government was determined to implement tough fiscal and monetary policies (Weinstein 1976: 228–32). Together with the IMF and the World Bank, the donor nations instituted a process of continual monitoring of Indonesia's economic policies which inevitably injured the nationalistic sensibilities of even the more moderate in the civilian and military bureaucracies.

For these and other reasons, the years 1966 and 1967 saw only very modest improvement in the Indonesian economy. Budgetary expenditures stayed at about 10 per cent of GDP, but revenues more than doubled in 1967, partly due to improved tax collection and partly due to aid receipts so that the deficit was almost eliminated. But the budgetary stringency, combined with a severe drought in the latter part of 1967, meant that growth rates stayed at the low levels of the years 1960–65, and per capita GDP continued to stagnate. The government found itself caught in the inevitable dilemma faced by any regime attempting to reduce inflation through reducing monetary demand; it proved impossible to reduce the rate of growth of the money supply through budgetary stringency and curbs on bank lending to the private sector without depressing activity in the productive sectors of the economy. In the early part of 1967, there were many complaints from professional and business associations as well as powerful elements within the military about continuing high levels of excess capacity in manufacturing, and chaotic conditions in the ports and railways which slowed the movement of goods and aggravated domestic shortages (Arndt 1967: 6–8). Popular frustration and disappointment found an outlet in many cities in violent attacks against the Chinese minority.

But the new government, with General Suharto now more firmly in control and officially designated Acting President, survived the crises which followed one another in rapid succession through 1967 and into 1968. Urban public opinion was particularly upset by the sharp increase in rice prices which occurred in the closing months of 1967, and the fourfold increase in the price of petroleum products in April 1968, which was immediately followed by substantial increases in public transport fares, electricity tariffs and a range of other charges (Arndt 1968: 8). But the storm of protest subsided, with no serious political effects, and as 1968 progressed the first real benefits from improving economic performance began to be felt by a population which had suffered steadily declining living standards for over a decade. Most important was the dramatic increase, of more than 12 per cent, in rice production; this combined with higher imports meant that per capita rice availability increased to 98 kg per capita, the highest it had been since 1962 (Mears 1984: Table 2). The agricultural sector was also assisted by an improvement in prices for export crops after almost a decade of continually declining terms of trade. In April 1969, the first of the New Order government's five-year plans (*Repelita*) was inaugurated. Although it was still far from obvious at the time, the economy was now poised for a period of more rapid growth, and greater structural change, than had occurred at any previous period in its history.

The years from the mid-1960s to the early 1980s were remarkable ones in Indonesian economic history for several reasons. First, the average annual rate of growth of GDP accelerated to over 7 per cent per annum, or more than 5 per cent per annum in per capita terms (Table 2.1). From 1968, there was also remarkable stability in the growth rate, which dropped below 6 per cent per annum in only one of the fourteen years from 1968 to 1981 (Sundrum 1986: 42). This was an impressive record compared with what had been achieved in the first fifteen years of independence, when growth had been on average much slower, and more erratic. It was also an impressive record compared with many other developing countries. In the late 1960s, per capita GDP in Indonesia was still among the lowest in the world, but by 1981, the country had moved into the ranks of what the World Bank terms 'lower middle-income countries'. World Bank sources indicated that the Indonesian growth rate in the 1970s was not only better than that of most other Asian countries at similar levels of development, but also better than that of other 'populated petroleum economies' such as Nigeria, Mexico and Venezuela (World Bank 1983: 150–1).

The period of rapid growth from the late 1960s coincided with a dramatic improvement in the country's terms of trade. The net barter terms of trade, as calculated from the national income statistics, more than doubled between 1966 and 1973, even before the OPEC-induced increases in the price of oil. During the years of the oil boom, from 1973 to 1981, the net barter terms of trade trebled again (Sundrum 1986: 44). Thus GDP corrected for the terms of trade improvement grew even more rapidly than GDP in constant prices between 1967 and 1981, at over 10 per cent per annum (Sundrum 1986: Table 4). Export volume growth was also rapid in the years from 1966 to 1973, and the income terms of trade grew at the remarkable rate of over 28 per cent per annum, a faster rate than had ever been experienced before (Table 2.1). After 1973, export volume growth was much more modest, reflecting the slow growth in petroleum exports as OPEC quotas were applied. But the income terms of trade continued to grow at over 19 per cent per annum. As much of the improvement in the terms of trade accrued directly to the government in the form of the oil company tax, and to a lesser extent other export taxes, these years also saw a dramatic growth in real government income and expenditures.

Indonesia's experience of rapid growth from 1966 to 1981 may seem at first sight to support the view that foreign exchange and public revenues were the two important constraints on economic growth in Indonesia in the first fifteen years of independence, and that a relaxation of these constraints, combined with 'sound economic management', especially in the area of fiscal policy, were the main causes of the accelerated growth after 1966. But in order to understand the mechanisms through which the relaxation of these constraints led to rapid growth, we must try to clarify the central role of foreign exchange earnings, especially those accruing from the export of oil. Obviously, we cannot just attribute the post-Sukarno growth to the rapid growth in oil earnings which occurred as a result of the OPEC-induced price rises of 1973–74, as the acceleration in growth had started well before then. But after 1981, when oil revenues began to decline, growth did slow down. This raises important questions. To what extent could the growth rates of the years 1968–81, and especially in the period after 1973, have been achieved with much less foreign exchange? Was the rapid growth simply a phenomenon connected with the post-Sukarno economic stabilisation and rehabilitation and the foreign exchange bonanza of the 1970s? Or could Indonesia have emulated the growth performance of the more successful oil-importing Asian countries such as Thailand? To answer these questions, it is necessary to look at the sectoral composition of the growth which occurred.

If the sectoral growth rates for the period 1967–81 are compared with those for 1960–67, we find that there was an acceleration in growth rates in all sectors, but the fastest growth occurred in the non-agricultural sectors (Sundrum 1986: 58). In the manufacturing and construction sectors the rate of growth increased dramatically, and there were also substantial increases in growth rates in transport and communications, banking, residential accommodation and public administration. When we look at the years 1967–81 in more detail, we see that although the overall growth remained quite steady, there were some significant changes in the growth of individual sectors. For much of the period, agricultural growth rates remained above 4 per cent, except for a slackening in 1973–77. The growth rate of mining and quarrying, by contrast, declined after 1973, as quota restrictions retarded the growth of petroleum output. There was a similar deceleration of growth in the construction and finance sectors. In contrast, there was an acceleration in manufacturing and public utilities.

But an analysis in terms of sectoral growth rates is not particularly helpful in explaining the overall growth of the economy. A sector's contribution to overall growth depends not only on its growth rate, but also on its relative size. Thus even a fast-growing sector may not contribute much to overall growth if it is small. If we examine the sectoral contributions to growth in real GDP over time, we see that between 1967 and 1973, the agricultural sector in fact contributed most to overall growth, followed by the trade sector (Table 2.14). These two sectors accounted for over half the total growth in these years. Between 1973 and 1981, the shares of both agriculture and trade fell, while those of manufacturing and the public sector grew. Other sectors whose share increased in 1973–81 were construction, transport, and ownership of dwellings. All these sectors except for manufacturing were producing non-traded goods and services. In the case of manufacturing, part of the growth occurred in the oil and gas processing sector itself, while much of the rest took place as a result of quantitative import controls so restrictive that domestic prices were largely insulated from world prices.

Table 2.14   Structural change, 1966–91

Sector	% Share of increment in real GDP*			Percentage breakdown of GDP by sector[†]			
	1967–73	1974–81	1982–91	1966	1973	1981	1991
Agriculture	27.4	16.4	11.1	53.3	40.1	23.4	19.6
Mining	12.9	4.4	6.9	1.6	12.3	22.6	13.8
Manufacturing	9.8	23.5	31.3	8.4	9.6	12.1	21.0
Utilities	0.7	1.1	1.2	—	0.5	0.5	0.8
Construction	7.6	8.4	6.3	1.1	3.9	6.0	5.7
Trade	25.9	17.1	17.3	19.0	16.6	15.3	16.2
Transport	4.4	8.1	6.7	1.8	3.8	4.1	6.1
Finance	4.4	3.0	6.6	0.5	1.2	2.7	4.5
Ownership of Dwellings	1.6	3.9	1.8	2.0	2.1	2.6	2.6
Public Administration	3.6	13.2	7.9	5.1	6.0	7.2	6.4
Other Services	1.6	1.0	2.8	7.2	3.9	3.6	3.3
Total	100.0	100.0	100.0	100.0	100.0	100.0	100.0

* 1967–73: 1960 prices
1974–81: 1973 prices
1982–91: 1983 prices
[†] Current price data
Source: Central Bureau of Statistics *National Income of Indonesia 1960–1968*, Jakarta, 1970; Central Bureau of Statistics *National Income of Indonesia (Main Tables)*, various issues; Sundrum (1986), Table 13.

The evidence on sectoral growth rates after 1973 may be taken as lending some support to the neo-classical analysis of resource booms,

or the so-called 'Dutch Disease', which predicts a movement of resources out of tradables and into non-tradables as a result of the real
appreciation effect consequent upon the resource boom. Under a
regime of flexible exchange rates, the real appreciation effect would
have been reflected in an actual appreciation of the exchange rate. In
Indonesia, where the rate against the US dollar was fixed for seven
years, the appreciation occurred through the faster rate of domestic
inflation relative to major trading partners (McCawley 1980; Corden
and Warr 1982). But the government intervened in various ways to
protect many domestic producers of tradable goods from the full
effect of this real appreciation. Many manufacturing industries producing import substitutes were assisted through quantitative controls
on imports, which sometimes amounted to outright import bans. In
the case of those products, such as rice, whose domestic prices the
government wished to stabilise for welfare reasons, prices were partially insulated from both domestic and international supply and
demand fluctuations through government domestic procurement and
stockpile programmes on the one hand, and import monopolies on
the other. In addition, government assistance to particular tradable
sectors was granted through subsidised inputs; the foodcrop sector,
for example, received subsidised fertiliser, irrigation and credit. This
assistance was important in accelerating the growth of foodcrop output after 1979.

In assessing the impact of the oil boom on domestic resource
allocation and sectoral growth rates, we also need to consider its
distributional implications. It is striking that the most rapid acceleration in sectoral growth rates after 1973 occurred in the public administration sector; this reflected the higher remuneration for public sector
employees which was treated in the national accounts as increases in
real output. If we assume that this group had a higher than average
propensity to consume non-food goods and services such as consumer
durables, housing and personal services, their growing income would
have rapidly led to increased demand for them, in turn creating
further employment opportunities for factors used in their production. To the extent that these factors were in elastic supply, real output,
in turn, grew in sectors such as manufacturing and construction.
Where inputs had to be imported, which was particularly true in the
case of some manufacturing industries, the growth in demand rapidly
spilled over into imports. Thus the growth in incomes of those sections of the population with high propensities to spend on import-
intensive goods and services explains both the rapid growth in imports

which occurred, and also the fact that much of this growth was in imports of raw materials and industrial inputs.

The impact of these trends on the structure of the economy is shown in Table 2.14. By 1981, agriculture had fallen to 23 per cent of GDP, compared with over 50 per cent in 1966. The share of the mining sector had grown to over 20 per cent. The share of construction, manufacturing, communications and the government sector also increased while that of trade and services fell slightly. The 'structural retrogression' of the years from 1940 to 1965 had obviously been reversed, and the 1970s witnessed substantial growth of the modern, capital-intensive sectors of the economy. This process of 'structural progression' was accompanied by a marked acceleration in the growth of investment expenditures (Sundrum 1986: 49). In the years from 1967 to 1973, growth in investment as recorded in the national income statistics was extremely rapid, at over 20 per cent per annum. This investment was extremely productive in the sense that the incremental capital–output ratio (ICOR) was very low (Booth 1992: Figure 1.3). Much of the investment in these years was in rehabilitation of rundown infrastructure and in new equipment and spare parts for industry. After 1973, the scope for such quick-yielding investment was much less, and there was some increase in the ICOR, although it was still lower than in the 1960s.

Another factor contributing to the accelerated output growth of the years from 1968 to 1981 was the rapid growth in the supply of labour. This was due not just to population growth, but also to a considerable movement of employed workers from tasks characterised by very low productivity to new jobs where productivity was higher. Part of this growth in employment was due to growth in investment, but a considerable part appears to have been due to technological progress in the sense of a decline in the ICOR in per capita terms (Sundrum 1986: 53–63). The impact of technological progress in this sense was probably most dramatic in foodcrop agriculture, where investment in irrigation rehabilitation, and in complementary inputs such as fertiliser and improved seeds brought about substantial improvements in output per unit of land and permitted increases in both the amount of labour employed and increases in labour productivity.

Compared with many other OPEC economies, Indonesia spent relatively little of the foreign exchange bonanza of the 1970s on consumption imports, and for this reason experienced higher growth rates. But there were several reasons for suspecting that some part of the growth which occurred was a direct consequence of the terms of trade improvement, and could not be sustained if the terms of trade began to deteriorate. Especially after 1973, part of the higher growth rate reflected growth in spending on public administration which was only partially a reflection of improved productivity. Within the context of the balanced budget principle, continued increases in such expenditure could only be maintained through severe cutbacks in other components of government expenditures, including those on productive infrastructure. Furthermore, although very little foreign exchange was used to import consumer goods, much was used to import raw materials and components for consumer durables. To the extent that growth in the manufacturing sector was mainly devoted to the final stages of production of imported raw materials and components, it could not be sustained when the capacity to import declined. It would be necessary to reorient domestic production to goods and services which could be sold on the international market.

After 1981, the rate of GDP growth dropped considerably, and for the five years from 1982 to 1987 averaged only 4 per cent per annum. Only in one year (1984) did the growth rate exceed 6 per cent per annum. While this performance was still better than that in the very disturbed years of the early 1960s, it was obviously disappointing in comparison with the rapid growth of the years from the latter part of the 1960s to 1981. The most obvious explanation for the decline in growth rates was the decline in import capacity due to the deterioration in the country's terms of trade, which was in turn mainly due to a fall in the world price of oil. A second reason for the decline in GDP growth was the imposition of OPEC quotas, to which Indonesia adhered with a greater degree of fidelity than many of her OPEC colleagues. These quotas had the effect of reducing the volume of oil output, so that by 1988 the index of petroleum production stood at 99, compared with 100 in 1975 and 123 in 1981. Petroleum output has a high weight in total real GDP (especially when calculated in 1983 prices), so a decline in output volume in this sector obviously has had an appreciable impact on total GDP. A third reason for the decline was the generally depressed state of the world economy in the early 1980s, which affected both the prices of Indonesia's non-oil export staples, and also inflows of private foreign investment. A fourth reason for the growth slowdown could be framed in terms of government policy responses to the changing economic climate of the 1980s. To the extent that government failed to adjust quickly to the vicissitudes of the international environment, or took inappropriate policy action, their impact on the growth of GDP was unnecessarily severe.

On the face of it, these reasons may seem plausible enough explanations for the fall in growth rate. Certainly most of the other OPEC countries, as well as Indonesia's ASEAN partners, experienced a fall in growth rates in the early part of the 1980s. But, on closer examination, we encounter some difficulties with the first and third explanations in particular. While the net barter terms of trade certainly declined since 1980, the magnitude of the decline was not particularly pronounced until 1986 (Sundrum 1988: 38). In 1986 the deterioration in the terms of trade was quite severe, but the decline in this one year is hardly an explanation for the poor growth performance in the four preceding years. Neither does it seem plausible to argue that the years since 1981 witnessed a catastrophic decline in real foreign exchange receipts from all sources, including government borrowing. In fact, the annual average inflow of foreign exchange in real US dollar terms from all sources was $13.2 billion in 1982–89 compared with $12.4 billion in 1973–81 (Booth 1992: Table 1.2). Certainly there was a fall in oil receipts, and in net private inflows of capital but these declines were offset by increases in receipts from non-oil exports and from borrowing on government account. Thus it would seem that the decline in growth in the 1980s was not a direct consequence of declining foreign resources available to the economy, but rather due to the way these resources were spent.

After 1981, gross domestic capital formation, as reported in the national income statistics, grew much more slowly than in the 1970s, and actually declined in real terms from 1983 to 1985. It is probable that this slowdown in investment affected aggregate demand which also affected the rate of economic growth in these years. In addition the ICOR more than doubled in 1982–86, compared with 1973–81 (Sundrum 1988: 47). To what extent was this increase in the ICOR the cause, and to what extent the result of slower growth? It seems plausible to argue that at least part of the increase in the ICOR was due to more and more investment being channelled away from less capital-intensive sectors such as agriculture, and into capital-intensive industrial and communications enterprises in both the state and the private sector, as well as into commercial buildings and private housing. Continued provision of subsidised credit to both state enterprises and individuals aggravated this trend.

In the 1986–87 budget speech, President Suharto announced the first nominal decline in budgetary expenditures in the history of the New Order, and this led commentators to predict a further slowdown in GDP growth (Glassburner 1986: 18). In the event, budget policy in

1986–87 and 1987–88 was rather less contractionary than appeared from the budget documents (Asher and Booth 1992: 60–4). The modest fiscal stimulus, together with an acceleration in growth in both the agricultural and manufacturing sectors led to some increase in GDP growth in 1986. The policy reforms of 1985–86, culminating in the large devaluation of September 1986, gradually improved the incentive structure for export producers, and non-oil export growth began to accelerate, especially from the manufacturing sector. From 1987 to 1991 non-oil exports grew rapidly, although the slow growth of oil and gas exports meant that total export volume growth in the years from 1982 to 1990 was only 4.3 per cent per annum (Table 2.1).

The less robust economic performance of the mid-1980s, both compared with the 1970s and compared with many other Asian economies, created some pessimism about the medium-term prospects for Indonesian development. The slower growth of GDP, combined with two very large devaluations meant that by 1988 per capita income in dollar terms had fallen below the 1980 level. In 1989 the World Bank reclassified Indonesia as a 'low-income' country (World Bank 1989: 164), a move which inevitably created the impression that many of the economic gains of the 1970s had been eroded in the 1980s. But such an impression was in many ways misleading, especially in the light of the accelerated economic growth after 1987, and the ongoing process of structural change in the economy. After 1987, GDP again began to grow at a sustained average annual rate of between 6 and 7 per cent. Taking the period 1982–91 as a whole, it is clear that the manufacturing sector has become the leading sector in the economy, accounting for almost one-third of the growth in GDP (Table 2.14). By 1991, manufacturing accounted for a higher share of total GDP than agriculture, while the share of sectors producing non-traded goods such as construction and public administration declined compared with 1981.

The shift in the composition of output which occurred between 1982 and 1991 could be interpreted as a shift towards production of internationally traded goods and services which is what would be expected as a result of a substantial real depreciation of the rupiah, and the other reforms to the trade regime. By the early 1990s it was obvious that Indonesia was moving rapidly into the ranks of the 'newly-industrialising' countries, with both manufacturing industry and the modern service sector accounting for a steadily increasing share of national output. Most studies have concentrated on the period since 1965, and thus have exaggerated the structural change which has occurred, in that they do not take into account the retrogression of the years from 1940 to 1965. But there can be little doubt that manufacturing and modern services in 1991 accounted for a larger share of total output than was the case in 1940, or in the late 1950s. The driving forces behind growth and structural change in the Indonesian economy since 1965, and over a longer time perspective, are analysed in greater depth in subsequent chapters.

PHASES OF GROWTH: A SUMMING UP

While there can be little doubt that GDP has grown in per capita terms in Indonesia for much of the period between 1830 and 1990, it is clear that there have been substantial fluctuations in that growth rate, and that there have been some periods of retrogression. In following chapters I examine the extent to which these vicissitudes were policy induced, rather than the inevitable consequence of external economic fluctuations. At this point it may be useful to provide a brief summary of the main phases of growth and retrogression, as follows:

(1) 1830–70

The early part of this period saw very rapid export growth, although it slowed after 1840. Per capita GDP growth was certainly positive over the entire four decades although GNP growth was lower because of the large outward remittances. The period from 1850 to 1870 saw quite rapid monetisation of the economy, albeit from a low base.

(2) 1870–1900

The policy reforms of the 1870s did not usher in a period of accelerated economic growth; these three decades were characterised by sluggish growth, especially in the foodcrop economy. Per capita GDP fluctuated over this period but there was no discernible upward trend between 1880 and 1900.

(3) 1900–30

The ethical policy was introduced in 1901 and its early phase coincided with rapid growth in export prices, although these declined in the 1920s. Real government expenditures grew more rapidly than at any time since the 1830s, with an emphasis on capital works rather than routine administration. Industrial growth accelerated, albeit from a low base, and the share of manufacturing in GDP increased.

(4) 1930–42

The main consequences of the world depression for Indonesia were a contraction in export volume and a decline in the income terms of trade. GDP also contracted; the contraction was more severe if GDP is adjusted for the terms of trade decline. The policy reaction was to regulate export production, place quotas on imports, especially from Japan, and encourage foreign investment in manufacturing industry. The recovery after 1934 was led by manufacturing, which increased to around 12 per cent of GDP by 1939.

(5) 1942–50

The period of the Japanese occupation saw substantial decline in output in most parts of the economy, and post-war rehabilitation proceeded slowly because of the independence struggle. In 1950 total GDP was still below the 1939 level, and the share of manufacturing in GDP had fallen.

(6) 1950–58

In spite of political instability and a lack of continuity in economic policy-making, the seven years of parliamentary democracy did coincide with considerable rehabilitation of the economy and output grew in all sectors. By 1957, per capita GDP had regained its 1942 level.

(7) 1958–66

These years were ones of declining per capita GDP, accelerating inflation, declining investment and structural retrogression. By 1965 the manufacturing sector's share of GDP was lower than in the late 1920s. The share of investment in GDP had declined to only 6–7 per cent by the mid-1960s.

(8) 1966–73

Economic recovery was rapid after 1966, and from 1968 onwards GDP growth was rapid and sustained. The income terms of trade improved rapidly, inflation fell to single figures and investment grew relative to GDP.

(9) 1973–81

The years of the oil boom saw rates of growth sustained at around seven per cent per annum. The share of agriculture in GDP fell sharply, while that of manufacturing and modern services grew.

(10) 1981–90

Growth slowed after 1981 as export prices fell, but a series of policy reforms designed to improve incentives for non-oil export producers led to accelerated output growth after 1987, which continued into the 1990s.

APPENDIX: GROWTH OF MANUFACTURING INDUSTRY: 1880–1970

The series developed here works backwards from the same value for manufacturing value added (MVA) as that estimated by van der Eng for 1970, but uses the following assumptions:

1 The growth rates for 1960–70 are estimated from Central Bureau of Statistics (1970) and from subsequent national accounts data published by the Central Bureau of Statistics.
2 The series for 1960–70 was linked back to 1959 using data from Nugroho (1967: 568) and to 1952 using the data in the United Nations *Yearbook of National Accounts* (1960: 114). The growth of MVA between 1952 and 1953 was estimated to be 3.3 per cent.
3 1952 MVA was assumed to be 90 per cent of the 1939 level.
4 Growth of MVA between 1931 and 1939 was assumed to be 7 per cent, or slightly lower than that estimated by van Oorschot (1956: 93) from wage data. The downward adjustment is based on the revised wage data given in CEI, Vol 8, Table XI.
5 Following van Oorschot, 1928 MVA was assumed to be 3.2 per cent higher than in 1931.

6 The 1928 MVA estimate was then backcast to 1880 using the following assumptions about growth rates:

1880–1900   2.5 per cent per annum
1900–13   4.0 per cent per annum
1913–28   4.5 per cent per annum

These assumptions give the trends in MVA (1970=100) and ratios of MVA to GDP shown in the appendix table. Although some of the assumptions are rough, and could certainly be improved on the basis of further research, especially for the colonial period, they tell a broadly plausible story. A ratio of MVA/GDP of around 5 per cent is reasonable for 1880. The Japanese ratio for 1885 was 6.9 per cent, reaching 11 per cent in 1900 and 17 per cent in 1913 (Ohkawa and Shinohara 1979: Table A12). There are few grounds for assuming that the ratio of MVA to GDP in Indonesia in 1900 was almost as high as in Japan. The slow growth in the ratio between 1900 and 1928 is consistent with the statistical evidence, as is the rapid growth between 1931 and 1939. It was argued in Chapter 2 that the contemporary evidence indicated that MVA had not returned to the level of the late 1930s by 1952, and although there was quite rapid growth in MVA up to 1957 it fell thereafter. By 1965 the ratio of MVA to GDP had fallen to around 7 per cent, although there was a rapid recovery after 1965. This again is far more consistent with the contemporary evidence than the van der Eng series which indicates that the MVA/GDP ratio reached nearly 15 per cent in 1960 and fell to 10.4 per cent by 1970.

Table A2.1   Trends in manufacturing value added, 1880–1970

Year	Manufacturing value added (1970 = 100)		Manufacturing share of GDP	
	Eng	*Booth*	*Eng*	*Booth*
1880	15	7	10.1	5.2
1900	20	12	9.5	5.7
1913	27	19	9.0	6.5
1928	45	37	9.5	8.1
1931	49	36	10.8	8.2
1939	57	62	11.1	12.0
1952	74	56	14.1	11.0
1960	104	64	14.5	9.4
1965	102	70	13.3	7.0
1970	100	100	10.4	10.4

3 Living Standards and the Distribution of Income

EVALUATING TRENDS IN LIVING STANDARDS AND INCOME DISTRIBUTION IN INDONESIA

Given that real GDP has almost certainly been growing faster than population in Indonesia for much of the last two centuries, what does this tell us about changes in living standards? There are several reasons why sustained, if erratic, growth in GDP might not translate into a broadly based improvement in living standards. If we define improving living standards in terms of real growth in household consumption expenditures shared by all classes of society, then we need to examine not the growth of aggregate GDP, but rather the growth in that part of it which is devoted to household consumption, after subtracting both current government expenditures and expenditure on capital formation on the part of both government, and private corporations and individuals. In the case of open economies, such as Indonesia has been for most of the nineteenth and twentieth centuries, we also need to allow for remittances abroad. To the extent that a significant part of gross domestic product has been used to finance overseas remittances, and these remittances have not been offset by inward capital flows, the capacity of the domestic economy to finance either domestic consumption or domestic capital formation is reduced.

It will be argued in this chapter that growing expenditure on both government consumption and capital formation, together with high levels of remittances abroad meant that, for much of the colonial era, private consumption expenditures grew less rapidly on average than GDP. But, in addition, there is evidence that such growth as occurred in average consumption expenditures did not benefit all classes of society equally. There were gainers and losers, and the gainers were often concentrated in particular ethnic groups and regional locations. As in other colonial societies, economic stratification along ethnic lines was pronounced in Indonesia by the early twentieth century, and in spite of the egalitarian rhetoric of the independence struggle, this stratification persisted into the post-1950 period. The growth which has occurred since the 1950s has in turn produced new patterns of differentiation by ethnic group, social class and region.

In the absence of detailed national income accounts broken down by expenditure, how can we estimate trends in household expenditures? And in the absence of reliable household income and expenditure surveys, how can we say anything about inequalities between households, regions or social classes? One method is to examine trends in per capita consumption of basic foodstuffs. The household surveys conducted by the Central Bureau of Statistics in the last phase of the colonial era indicate that most indigenous households in both urban and rural areas were spending a high proportion of their budgets on food (van Niel 1956: 77; Central Bureau of Statistics 1939: Table 39; Weinreb and Ibrahim 1957: Table 14). The income elasticity of demand for food was quite high in the early twentieth century. Van Laanen (1979: 137) used the data collected by Ochse and Terra (1934) to derive an estimate of around 0.6. This implies that a 10 per cent increase in total household expenditures would lead to a 6 per cent increase in expenditures on food, so the use of food availability, in calorie terms, as a proxy for growth in household consumption expenditures is not unreasonable.

There is the complication that Indonesians, like most people, have strong food preferences, and do not regard calories from all sources as equally desirable. In Java and other rice-growing areas, corn and dried cassava (*gaplek*) have been quite widely consumed as a substitute for rice, especially in the dry season, for well over a century. The evidence from household expenditure surveys carried out in the 1960s and 1970s shows that corn and *gaplek* have negative expenditure elasticity of demand, i.e. as household expenditure increases less of these foods are consumed, while rice has a high positive income elasticity of demand, which suggests that as household income and expenditure rise, people substitute rice for corn and dried cassava (Dixon 1984: 78). But these results are averages, and disguise considerable variation by expenditure class. For the bottom half of the expenditure distribution in rural areas in 1976, Dixon (1984: 82) found that the expenditure elasticity of demand for *gaplek* was in fact positive, although for corn it was negative. Fresh cassava has positive income elasticities of demand for all expenditure classes.

Several writers have argued that corn and cassava are not preferred foods but were increasingly cultivated, especially in Central and East Java, as population pressure mounted and more dry land came under cultivation (Boomgaard 1989: 87–9; Napitupulu 1968: 65). While it is undeniably true that most Indonesians prefer to eat rice if it is available at a price they feel they can afford, it cannot automatically be assumed that increased consumption of cassava or corn is a sign of falling income. It could, in fact, signal some improvement in the incomes of the very poorest groups in society. On the other hand, given the high expenditure elasticities of demand for rice which were found for rural households even as late as 1976, it seems clear that increased rice consumption does indicate a broad-based improvement in real incomes.

Some non-food consumption indicators have also been used to evaluate changes in living standards, including availability of cotton cloth and other imported consumer durables such as bicycles. Van der Eng (1994a: Table 2) has argued that a range of indicators such as growth in numbers of postal items, train rides, credit availability and numbers going on the hadj to Mecca can be used as indicators of broadly based economic change in Indonesia. But caution must be exercised in using such indicators to derive conclusions regarding changing living standards on the part of the great majority of the population. In the final phase of the colonial period, and indeed as recently as the 1970s, only a minority of Indonesians were posting letters, using trains and trams regularly, obtaining credit from formal institutions, or going on the hadj. It could indeed be argued that increases in such indicators are evidence of widening income disparities between the top one or two quintiles of the population and the rest.

In the absence of reliable data on income distribution in Indonesia for much of the last two centuries, it is very difficult to draw hard and fast conclusions about the impact of economic growth on living standards of different social groups. Even for the period since 1965 the data are by no means unambiguous. In this chapter, it will be argued that many debates about popular welfare in Indonesia since the early nineteenth century have been based on inadequate evidence, often motivated more by political ideology than by dispassionate enquiry. But some readily available indicators are very revealing, because they refer to items of mass consumption which for the poorer segments of the population have quite high expenditure elasticities of demand. The most important of these indicators is per capita rice consumption; another is cotton cloth. Even cassava falls into this category, although a distinction must be made between the fresh and the dried form. In what follows, trends in these indicators will be used to evaluate arguments about changing living standards since the early nineteenth century.

TRENDS IN LIVING STANDARDS IN THE NINETEENTH CENTURY

One of the most widely held views about Indonesia, and especially Java, in the nineteenth century was that such economic growth as occurred did not benefit the mass of the indigenous population, whose living standards almost certainly declined. Many scholars have drawn attention to the evidence that per capita rice production fell after 1880 as proof that living standards were declining in the last two decades of the century, while others have not hesitated to draw the bolder conclusion that living standards declined almost continually after 1800:

> One theme stands out most prominently in Javanese society during this time: the theme of involution and reaction...Despite the promises of the changing colonial policies to further the individual welfare of the Javanese, conspicuously little was done in this regard. Instead the Javanese farmer became gradually more impoverished throughout the whole of the nineteenth century, with a particularly severe drop in living standards in the second half of the liberal period (1885–1900) (Carey 1979: 10).

If these assertions appear extreme, it is worth recalling that among the harshest critics of the colony's performance in the late nineteenth century were Dutch colonial administrators. Writing in 1900, Assistant-President van Heutz declared that

> During the past century the Netherlands has succeeded in reducing to complete poverty a very diligent and cultured people, which is endowed with a great capacity for development, in a land that may be called an ideal example of tropical fertility. The poverty of the Javanese is so abject that it deserves to become proverbial (van Heutz as translated in Penders 1977: 60).

Before we can assess the validity of these views, we should consider the nature of Javanese society before 1830. A cursory reading of the descriptions of Raffles and Crawfurd might suggest that by and large the Javanese lived in a state of 'subsistence affluence' in a land abundant environment, and that society consisted in the main of relatively isolated, homogeneous village units, within which there was much mutual cooperation for the purposes of agricultural and handicraft production and the construction and maintenance of infrastructure, but which had little contact with higher authorities or the monetised economy. Such a view is obviously an oversimplification. Many historical and anthropological studies have stressed that Javanese society by the early nineteenth century was highly stratified, with the most powerful members of the village often directly linked by a variety of bonds of patronage or outright coercion to supra-village authorities (Van Setten Van Der Meer 1979; Kumar 1980; Breman 1980). Indeed, it was precisely because these linkages already existed in a society that was both authoritarian and hierarchical that the Dutch were so dramatically successful in increasing production of export crops after 1830. Carey (1976: 63ff) has described at length the economic conditions prevailing over much of south-central Java on the eve of the Java War; the picture is one of a peasantry subjected to a heavy burden of taxes in cash and kind exacted by a complex network of officials stretching from village to *kraton*. Raffles's attempts to impose a fixed land tax on the cultivator, based on the productivity of his land, had foundered in the absence of proper cadastral surveys. Instead, the tax was assessed in an arbitrary fashion in addition to, rather than in place of, other imposts and the requirement of cash payments was forcing the cultivators to greater reliance on money-lenders. The situation was made worse in the early 1820s by poor weather and cholera epidemics.

If the economic situation for many Javanese was already so bad in the early 1820s, even before the Java War started, one wonders how they could have become worse in the following decade, after the imposition of the *cultuurstelsel* (CS), and the dramatic growth in volume of exports which occurred in the 1830s (Table 2.1). Given the fragmentary nature of the rice production statistics prior to the 1830s, and continuing debate about the population figures, it is very difficult to draw conclusions about trends in per capita rice production and consumption, at least for the two decades after 1830. Using the official rice production series which began in the late 1830s, Elson (1994, Table 8.2) has argued that there was an increase of 20 per cent in per capita rice production between 1837 and 1845 in the CS residencies, a fairly steady decline between 1845 and 1865 and a considerable improvement between 1865 and 1870, at which date per capita rice production was about the same as it had been in 1850. Boomgaard and van Zanden (CEI, Vol 10: 41) argue that per capita rice production rose between 1836 and 1846 (from 190 kg to 205 kg *padi* per capita), but stress that it was still well below the levels prevailing in 1815 (260 kg *padi* per capita). Boomgaard (1989: Table 4) estimates that per capita food consumption in Java in 1840, corrected for the increase in the number of hours worked, was less than 70 per cent of the 1815 level. These figures lend some support to the argument that the early years of the CS had a disruptive effect on rice cultivation, although some of the decline could have occurred between 1815 and 1829, before the CS was in operation.

By the early 1840s, the Dutch authorities were sufficiently disturbed by reports of food shortages and declining living standards to commission an investigation in the regency of Jepara; this was the first in a series of such investigations whose scope and frequency increased over the last century of Dutch rule in Java (Husken 1994: 214). In 1849–50, severe food shortages in Demark, Grobogan and Semarang attracted the attention of the Dutch press and parliament, and local officials were called upon to explain what was happening. In reviewing the contemporary documentation, modern scholars have argued that although rice production per capita did decline in the famine years, for reasons that were only partly climatic, there are also indications of what Sen (1981) has termed 'entitlement' failures. Essentially this means that the famines were caused not by a decline in food availability, but rather by a decline in purchasing power, especially on the part of those groups in society which depended on earnings from wage labour to buy their food. Elson (1985) in discussing the Demak-Grobogan famine has argued that 'despite drastically lowered rice production from the 1848–9 harvest and the almost total failure of the 1849 second crops, food remained in relatively good supply and prices remained remarkably low'. Much the same argument is made by Hugenholtz (1986: 165), who claims that 'the Semarang famine was thus not so much a deficiency famine as in essence a price famine. It was not the result of a shortage of food but of total absence of money'. The real problem was that large numbers of people had no means to buy the available food. The burden of the land tax and the demands on their time for often unpaid or poorly paid work on the tobacco plantations, together with the decline in cattle numbers which involved, in many cases, the loss of lifetime savings, all meant that even those with access to some land had few reserves to tide them over the bad harvest. Those with only their labour to sell were in an even worse position.

It was argued in the previous chapter that the decades of the 1850s and 1860s saw a gradual improvement in economic conditions in the colony and indeed there was probably some per capita growth in real output. Although export volume growth was very slow, these two decades were characterised by quite rapid growth in real money supply, and in real government expenditure (Table 2.1). In the agricultural economy, Boomgaard and van Zanden estimate that per capita rice output stayed roughly stable between 1846 and 1870, although there was probably some improvement in total calorie intake due to increased dependence on *palawija* crops, and the output of housegardens. Fish and meat production per capita stayed constant throughout the period from 1815 to 1880 (CEI, Vol 10: 51). Until the 1870s Java was a net rice exporter, and per capita rice availability was thus lower than production. The rice availability series estimated by Scheltema indicates some improvement between 1850 and 1880 (Table 3.1).

Table 3.1 Trends in per capita rice consumption and textile imports, 1850–1939 (five-year average centred on the year shown)

Year	Rice (kg per capita)[*]	Real value of net textile imports[†] (guilders per 1,000 people)	
		Java	Outer islands
1850	103	198.2	
1855	101	283.3	
1860	97	355.1	
1865	96	193.8	
1870	100	117.6	
1875	118	708.9	424.4
1880	120	743.8	453.8
1885	119	832.4	618.7
1890	102	872.2	763.9
1895	108	1,017.1	579.8
1900	103	931.4	623.1
1905	100	964.1	680.8
1910	113	1,422.3	1,130.8
1915	117	1,620.6	1,178.7
1920	107	1,319.3	922.1
1925	101	1,679.7	1,253.3
1930	95 (87)[*]	1,507.6	957.3
1935	(82)[*]	1,253.1	844.6
1939	(85)[*]	1,192.7	727.6

[*]Up to 1930, the series on per capita rice consumption prepared by Scheltema (1936: 12) is used. As Scheltema points out, in the earlier years both rice production and population data are understated; he assumes that the understatement is similar for both series, so the per capita data are roughly equal. The series excludes Yogyakarta, Surakarta, Madura and the residency of Batavia. After 1930, the all-Java data on per capita rice availability is shown in brackets, as reported in *Indisch Verslag*, Part 2, various issues.

[†]Up to 1913 the deflator used for textile prices is the series on prices for Dutch madapollams, as reported in CEI, Volume 15, Table 1A, lines 22,25,27. After 1913, the deflator used is the textile component of the Wholesale Price Index, as reported in Central Bureau of Statistics (1938), Table 1.

Sources: CEI, Vol 12a, Tables 5a, 5b; CEI, Vol 15, Table IA; Scheltema (1936: 12).

The demands made on both land and labour by compulsory culti-vation of export crops decreased steadily through the 1850s and 1860s. Van Baardewijk has shown that the proportion of arable land under compulsory cultivation fell from a peak of 22 per cent in the early 1840s to only 12 per cent by 1880, while the proportion of the indigenous population subject to compulsory labour demands fell from 12.5 per cent in 1840 to under 6 per cent by 1880 (CEI, Vol 14: Table A22). But the impact of compulsory labour imposts was still substantial right up to the 1880s. Indeed, it can be argued that the most serious effect which the CS had on the welfare of the indigenous population of Java was to coerce them into sacrificing time which could have been spent on a range of pursuits, from the cultivation of food and hunting to handicraft activity, housebuilding and commu-nity public works. The income and consumer satisfaction which they were forced to forgo was almost certainly not fully compensated by the crop payments. Clarence-Smith (1994: 258–9) has argued with respect to coffee cultivators that they probably would have received higher incomes if they had grown coffee on a voluntary basis and paid the land rent at the official rate. In addition, the government would have saved the considerable budgetary outlays which coerced cultiva-tions entailed, a point which is taken up again in the next chapter.

Some writers have suggested that the rapid growth in so-called 'indigenous imports' (mainly textiles) from 1830 onwards indicate growth in indigenous purchasing power, and by implication living standards. This argument was advanced by Reinsma in his 'revisio-nist' thesis of 1955, and has subsequently been endorsed by Fasseur (1986: 145), and Elson (1994: 315). Certainly the money value of cotton textile imports increased substantially between the 1830s and 1873. If we deflate their value by the Dutch textile price series com-puted by Korthals Altes (CEI Vol 15, Table 1A) we see that their real value did rise considerably in per capita terms from the early 1820s to the early 1840s, fell thereafter, and only returned to the 1840 level in the mid-1850s (Figure 3.1). Between 1855 and 1873 the trend was much more erratic, although this was largely due to disruptions in world trade in cotton goods as a result of the American civil war. However, the increase in the real volume of per capita imports of cotton goods which undoubtedly occurred over the whole period from 1830 to 1870 does not necessarily mean that per capita availability increased, because local production almost certainly fell. Raffles (1978: 85ff) described the attire of the Javanese he was able to observe in some detail and argued that the natives were 'in general better clothed than those of Western India'. But the methods by which they produced cloth were time-consuming and with increased demands for labour for other purposes, and the growth of imports, home cloth production fell in many parts of Java as the nineteenth century progressed (van der Kraan 1996: 60). Boomgaard (1991: 30–1) has argued that even by 1825, 'the opportunity costs of female labour were too high to permit indigenous households to continue to produce expensive cotton cloth when cheaper, although lower quality, cloth became readily available'. If indeed women workers in particular voluntarily chose to reallocate their time to other activities and buy imported cloth, then rising cloth imports would indicate increasing real incomes. But if women were coerced into other activities as a result of the increased labour demands placed on their households, then the growth in use of imported cotton goods cannot be interpreted as evidence of improving living standards.

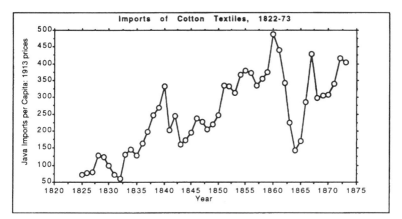

Figure 3.1 *Sources*: Cotton imports: CEI, Vol. 12a, Table 5a; Textile price index constructed from the series on Dutch madapollams in CEI, Vol 15, Table 1A. Population data for Java interpolated from CEI, Vol 11 p. 82.

Should we treat the growth in the indigenous population which undeniably occurred after 1815 as evidence of improving living standards, as some students of the CS have been inclined to do? Such an argument involves an interpretation of the reasons for growing population, and particularly of fertility behaviour, which may not be widely accepted. It implies that couples decided to have more children because they, in some sense, felt 'better off' i.e. they regarded children as consumer durables. It also implies that they were regulating their fertility before, which runs counter to at least some theories of traditional fertility behaviour. In fact, quite another kind of argument has had some currency in the literature; this is the notion that the demands for labour imposed by the CS forced peasant families to have more children by abandoning certain customs such as prolonged breast-feeding which tended to reduce fertility (White 1973; Alexander and Alexander 1979; Boomgaard 1981). To the extent that this idea has any validity it would seem to turn the first argument on its head, as it sees increasing population as the consequence of declining rather than improving economic conditions.

It has also been argued that part of the growth in population in nineteenth century Java was due to declining mortality, in turn the result of the 'Pax Nederlandica' and also public health measures such as vaccination campaigns. But the available evidence indicates that such public health measures as were introduced had little impact on mortality before the twentieth century (Boomgaard 1987: 64–5; Gardner and Oey 1987: 86–7). Still others have argued that increased prosperity, especially after 1850, encouraged an earlier age of marriage, and thus higher fertility. Elson (1994: 288–91) has drawn on estimates of Boomgaard to argue that the marriage rate increased steadily from the 1830s to the 1850s, although these figures also show a sharp decline in the 1860s which is difficult to explain in strictly economic terms. On balance, the demographic data, while giving many tantalising clues to the nature of social change in Java through the nineteenth century, do not tell us much about changes in living standards.

Perhaps we can best sum up the four decades from 1830 to 1870 by saying that the real growth in output which occurred brought few dramatic material benefits to Javanese society, beyond permitting the accommodation of a growing population. A corollary of this argument is, of course, that most of the benefits from the remarkable growth in volume and value of exports which occurred in the 1830s, and the more modest growth which took place in the 1850s and 1860s accrued either directly to the Netherlands or to a small minority of expatriates and the indigenous elite in the colony. Indeed, some scholars of the period do stress that the main beneficiaries within native society were the village chiefs and the supra-village elites, who were gradually turned into Dutch vassals, thereby losing such legitimacy as they had with their own people (Carey 1979: 83–6; van Niel 1992: 153). On the other hand, the evidence assembled by recent scholars in the CEI series and elsewhere gives little support to the theory that the nineteenth century saw increasing impoverishment of the mass of the Javanese population. Per capita rice availability was fairly stable for much of the century and rising imports of cotton cloth compensated for the decline in household handicraft activity, some of which was probably voluntary.

But neither is there much support for the more extreme argument advanced by Elson (1994: 305) that the CS 'promoted a previously unknown level of general prosperity among the peasantry'. The data advanced by Elson himself hardly support this case, and indeed much of his evidence would appear to contradict it. Elson does not disagree with the judgement of Boomgaard that in its early years, when the growth of export volume was so rapid, the CS caused considerable disruption to established patterns of production and consumption in many parts of Java. Rather he points to the evidence of improvements in the middle decades of the century to support his case, as does Fernando (1996: 110) who also argues that the five decades following the introduction of the CS led to increasing prosperity in Java. But nowhere do either of these writers produce any convincing evidence that living standards in the 1850s and 1860s were higher than in the first decade of the century, before the negative effects of both the Java War and the early years of the CS. Neither do they address the issue of the impact on indigenous welfare of decades of coercion, both to produce export crops and to carry out a range of tasks for indigenous rulers and the colonial government. Indeed, it can be argued that the most harmful legacy of the CS for future economic development in Java, and in other parts of the country, was to frustrate the growth of market institutions, and to supplant such markets as did exist with a dirigiste command economy run by powerful bureaucrats very largely in their own interests. This argument is taken up again in Chapter 7.

Outside Java, there is little evidence on living standards before the end of the nineteenth century. Schouten (1995: 6–7) argues that in North Sulawesi, the money earned from the coffee monopoly brought little extra income to the cultivators, in spite of the fact that households often had to work more than 100 days in the coffee gardens, in addition to subsistence food cultivation. The annual head tax of five guilders (minimum) took much of the cash income received. As in Java, the CS in Minahasa was associated with extra demands for corvée labour, especialy to build the roads and bridges necessary to transport the coffee to the ports. Schouten cites several eye-witness reports that poverty in the non-coffee growing areas was considerably less than in the coffee districts.

How much change in living standards came with the new liberal spirit of the 1870s? As was argued in the previous chapter, the last quarter of the nineteenth century did see some acceleration in export growth, although rice production growth decelerated sharply after 1880, and growth in the foodcrop sector was slower than population growth from 1880 to 1900 (Tables 2.1 and 2.2). The real value of imports did accelerate and at least some of this increase would have benefited the indigenous population (Table 2.4). Furnivall (1944: 215) points to the increase in both cotton goods and rice imports as evidence of growing indigenous prosperity in the 1870s; the increasing rice imports added to increasing home production, so that rice availability per capita increased by a remarkable 23 per cent during the decade. Cotton textile imports into Java (1913 prices) also increased in per capita terms between 1875 and 1885 (Table 3.1). By 1880 per capita rice availability had reached 116 kg, a much higher figure than had been achieved since the 1850s. However, it is quite possible that the improvements in the 1870s reflect improved reporting procedures rather than actual output increases (CEI Vol 10: 41) and it would be rash to conclude that the policy changes of the 1860s and 1870s had an immediate positive effect on food production in Java.

Even allowing for the data problems, it would seem that consumption standards did improve for the indigenous population of Java in the 1870s and early 1880s. But the very indicators which were used to demonstrate improving welfare up to 1885 were those seized upon to prove a dramatic decline thereafter. In particular, it was the fall in per capita rice production and availability in Java after 1885 which was most often cited both by contemporary observers and by subsequent scholars to support the argument that native welfare must have been declining (Homan van der Heide, 1901, as cited in Penders, 1977: 56–8; van Deventer, as cited in Furnivall, 1944: 214; Creutzberg, 1972: xxxi: 734–5). The time series compiled by Scheltema shows that rice availability in Java declined after 1885 until 1905 (increasing imports did not compensate for falling domestic production in Java). But the expansion in non-rice foodcrops which took place after 1880 ensured that there was no mass starvation, even though many millions of Javanese must have been forced to change their consumption patterns towards non-preferred food staples. Van der Eng's estimates show that total calorie supply in Java was roughly stable between 1880 and 1905, although there was some decline in the latter part of the 1880s.

The estimated average daily intake of around 1,650 calories was low, even allowing for a high proportion of children in the population, and indicates that chronic malnutrition may have been common in at least some parts of the island (van der Eng 1993a: Figure 4).

The figures on non-food consumption do not lend much support to the declining welfare argument. The value of per capita imports of cotton goods in real terms was considerably higher in Java in 1895 than five years previously. Although there was some decline between 1895 and 1900, cotton imports were still considerably higher in 1900 than twenty years previously (Table 3.1). Another piece of evidence frequently adduced to support the 'declining welfare' case was the decline in money wages and employment opportunities (Furnivall 1944: 214), although here also the figures are not entirely persuasive. The data on coolie wages in the main cities of Java in the last two decades of the century do indicate some decline, though the trends are not very strong. In Batavia, for example, the minimum and maximum daily wages paid to coolies were much the same in 1900 as in 1885; as prices of wage goods such as rice and cloth were also much the same (or slightly lower) in these two years, real wages would seem to have been roughly constant (Booth 1988a, Table 2).

But the authorities in both Java and the Netherlands were sufficiently impressed by the arguments of van Deventer and others to commission a comprehensive enquiry into living standards in Java in the first decade of the new century. Although the purpose of the research was 'to provide an overall analysis of the stagnating rural economy' (Husken 1994: 216), the outcome was rather different. Hasselman in his comprehensive review of the voluminous reports published by the Declining Welfare Enquiry (*Mindere Welvaarts Onderzoek*), came to the conclusion that

> The general impression given by the reports from the districts – taking into account the circumstances under which, after all, the investigation was held – is that economic prosperity has declined in thirteen districts or parts thereof, and that it has increased in thirty-two districts or parts thereof. In the other districts the situation has remained the same (as translated in Penders 1977: 90).

Hasselman was writing this summary some ten years after the research was initiated; in the interim, general economic conditions had improved so much that some observers were probably wondering what all the fuss had been about. Certainly, as Husken (1994: 217) has argued, the final reports of the Enquiry were 'a far cry' from the original intention of providing a sound foundation for the ethical policy. If indeed there had been no general decline in living standards, then was there any need for new policy initiatives to improve indigenous welfare? Part of the problem was that, as van der Eng (1993a: 47) has pointed out, the term '*mindere welwaart*', though in wide currency in the early years of the century, was never very carefully defined, and different people used the term in different ways. No doubt some Dutch officials did sincerely believe in the impoverishment thesis, and argued that living standards among the indigenous population in Java had declined continually through the nineteenth century. But to others, the problem was not so much one of declining living standards as of growing inequalities, both within the colony and between the colony and metropolitan Holland.

It is striking that almost all the discussion about living standards and levels of welfare during the latter part of the nineteenth century was conducted in terms of trends in averages; few, if any, of the participants seemed concerned with disparities between individuals. The general impression conveyed by much of the discussion was that the indigenous population, in particular, could be regarded largely as an undifferentiated mass, and the only important disparities were between ethnic groups. The most obvious, of course, was between the indigenous Indonesians on the one hand and the immigrant Chinese and expatriate Europeans on the other. In fact, it is clear when we look at the available data that divisions within the indigenous economy had become quite marked by the turn of the century. Some indication of the extent of the differentiation within the indigenous population is provided by the data on the size distribution of holdings collected in 1903 as part of the Declining Welfare Surveys, and summarised by Hasselman (1914: Appendix R). These show quite marked disparities in the distribution of land under individual tenure, especially in the Priangan region of West Java, where the Gini coefficient of land-holdings was 0.6 (Booth 1988: Table 3.4). For Java as a whole, 71 per cent of holdings surveyed were under one *bouw* (0.71 ha). Although the average holding size was very small compared with many other parts of Asia, the variation both between and within regions was quite considerable. As land was the main economic asset of the indigenous population, this would suggest that disparities within native society in income and wealth were far from negligible.

We do not have any data set from the nineteenth century as comprehensive as those collected in the Declining Welfare Study, so that it is impossible to detect trends in concentration of land ownership prior to 1900. But the Declining Welfare Study showed clearly that in those residencies where a substantial proportion of the land was still under rotating tenures, their effect in most cases was to reduce inequalities in the distribution of land (Booth 1988, Table 3.10). As the proportion of land under these rotating tenures in Java declined in the late nineteenth and early twentieth century, and as the market for land developed, and land sales accelerated, it seems probable that access to land became more skewed. In his study of Pasuruan residency, Elson (1984: 176–7) argues that by the end of the nineteenth century, 'in those places where social barriers to land alienation were weaker, the play of economic forces and circumstances was beginning to create greater disparities in wealth than had ever before been the case'.

Although agriculture was still the main occupation and primary source of income for the great majority of the labour force in Indonesia at the turn of the century, the labour force data published in 1905 indicate that in Java almost 30 per cent gave their primary occupation as non-agricultural. Of those who gave agriculture as their main occupation, 18 per cent had further sources of income from non-agricultural activities (Booth 1988: Table 2.13). We can, in fact, use the data on the revenues from the tax on incomes from trades and professions, available from the mid-1870s, to determine the extent to which a relatively well-to-do, non-agricultural and non-European merchant and professional class was emerging in Java in the last decades of the nineteenth century, and examine its ethnic composition. This tax was levied on both indigenous Indonesians and foreign orientals in Java on the same basis, although outside Java the method of assessment varied by region and, in some places, by race (Paulus 1909: 123). It was only a minor revenue earner, accounting for little more than 2 per cent of government revenue in 1881, which indicates the smallness of the base, but at that time the bulk of the taxpayers were indigenous.

In 1874, the first year in which comprehensive data concerning the tax were published in the *Koloniaal Verslag*, over 90 per cent of the taxpayers were Indonesian, and the balance foreign Asians, mainly Chinese. Although the distribution of foreign Asian taxpayers was more skewed towards the higher income brackets, a substantially higher absolute number of indigenous taxpayers in Java was in the higher income brackets (Booth 1988a: Table 3). This, in fact, continued to be the case until 1890; however, by 1905, foreign Asian taxpayers accounted for more than half of those with assessable incomes in excess of 2,500 guilders per annum, in spite of the fact that they still comprised less than 10 per cent of all taxpayers, and their numbers had, in fact, been growing less rapidly than those of indigenous taxpayers.

The data on the distribution of taxpayers by assessed income over the three decades up to 1905 show how different was the experience of the non-agricultural indigenous population and the Chinese. Whereas the average taxable incomes of the two groups were not very different in 1874, by 1905 the average foreign Asian taxpayer was earning four times the assessable income of the average Indonesian (Booth 1988a: Table 3). In real terms, the average assessable income of Indonesian taxpayers had almost certainly fallen, while that of the foreign Asian had risen. Given that the bulk of the Indonesian taxpayers would have been small businessmen, artisans and employees in both government and private enterprise, it is possible that real living standards among this class of the indigenous population did fall over the final decades of the nineteenth century. By contrast, those of foreign Asian businessmen improved quite dramatically. In 1901, Sollewijn Gelpke estimated the average annual income of the population of Java to be about 110 guilders (Huender, as quoted in Penders 1977: 92). By 1905 the great majority of the Indonesian taxpayers had an assessable income less than this, while more than half the Chinese and other foreign Asian taxpayers were earning more.

This evidence would suggest that the Chinese business community was quite successful in exploiting such opportunities as were available in late nineteenth century Java while indigenous Indonesians were less successful, in spite of the fact that the Chinese were still a small community. Was this the result of their superior business acumen and entrepreneurial skills, or were they deliberately favoured, and the indigenous business sector deliberately discriminated against, by government? In his discussion of the growing economic role of the Chinese in the later part of the nineteenth century, Furnivall (1944: 213) emphasises that in 1855 they were brought under the European Civil Code in most of their commercial transactions, and this gave them higher social standing, and possibly other advantages as well. They were also granted monopolies over the opium shops, pawnshops and gambling houses, 'so much of the newly created wealth as went to the Javans passed on immediately to the Chinese' (Furnivall 1944: 213). In addition, they increasingly supplied the European demand for 'competent subordinates on low wages' and filled many of the available clerical and sales jobs in European enterprises.

LIVING STANDARDS IN THE FINAL PHASE OF COLONIAL RULE

The ethical period in Dutch colonial policy was remarkable in that it was the first sustained attempt by any European colonial power to implement the kind of policies which today we would think of as 'developmental'. Scholars differ in their evaluation of the policy's main goal; Dick (1985a: 84) has argued that it was mainly intended to restore living standards to 'an adequate subsistence', although others see it as having, from its inception, more ambitious long-term development aims (van der Eng 1993a: 4). The debate is rather an artificial one, in that policy aims changed as the century progressed, and in the inter-war years the colonial government assumed functions which were certainly never envisaged in 1901. To begin with, the main aim of the policy was to raise indigenous living standards through investment in irrigation, dissemination of improved cultivation practices, improved access to education and state-sponsored migration from Java to the less densely settled parts of Sumatra and Sulawesi.

In the first decade of its operation, the policy appeared to be successful. Certainly there is general agreement that there was a marked improvement in living standards in Java in the decade or so before the outbreak of the First World War. Once again, the main indicators used are trends in per capita availability of rice, and trends in imports of consumer goods such as cloth. The time series prepared by Creutzberg (1972: 734–5) shows an increase of 17 per cent in per capita rice availability between 1903–7 and 1913–17, in part due to the growth in domestic production discussed in the previous chapter, and in part due to rapid growth in imports. Boomgaard and van Zanden (CEI, Vol 10: 50) estimate that per capita foodcrop production in calorie terms increased by a remarkable 23 per cent between 1900 and 1916–20, although this result could have been affected by understatement of output in the early years of the century. This improvement in production translated into a rapid improvement in calorie consumption per capita after 1905 (van der Eng 1993a: Figure 4).

After 1900, cotton cloth imports also increased in real per capita terms and, by 1910, they exceeded the levels achieved in the latter part of the nineteenth century in both Java and the Outer Islands (Table 3.1). The rapid growth in imports of such basic consumption staples as rice and cloth, at the same time as per capita GDP was growing, confirms the finding of the previous chapter that growth in per capita indigenous purchasing power in the decade up to 1914 must have been quite rapid. It would also suggest that the income growth was fairly widely shared, given that the lower income groups would have been those with the highest income elasticity of demand for basic staples. If they had experienced little or no income growth, it is unlikely that average consumption of rice and cloth would have increased so rapidly. Other indicators, such as numbers embarking on the *hadj*, also showed impressive growth in the years from 1908 to 1914 (Table 3.2). Although only the wealthier classes of indigenous society would have had the means to undertake the pilgrimage to Mecca, the sharp increase in numbers of pilgrims certainly suggests that their real incomes were growing over these years.

Table 3.2   Numbers of pilgrims going to Mecca, 1878–1994 (annual average for the years shown in thousands)

1878–88	4.8	1930–35	6.1
1888–98	7.0	1935–40	7.7
1898–1908	7.1	1969–74	20.6
1908–14	19.0	1974–79	51.6
1919–24	25.6	1979–84	57.6
1926–30	40.0	1984–89	49.3
		1989–94	89.3

Sources: *Indisch Verslag 1938*, p. 140; *Statistical Pocketbook of Indonesia, 1941*, p. 146; Department of Information (1993: Table XV–3); Department of Information (1995: Table XVI–3).

By 1910, there were almost one million Indonesian non-agricultural income taxpayers in Java, with assessable incomes over 50 guilders. This large increase compared with the 1905 data can be explained by a combination of factors: inflation leading to some 'bracket creep', growing real incomes and better administration. Although the Chinese taxpayers still had an average assessable income well over twice that of the indigenous taxpayers, and were disproportionately concentrated in the higher income brackets, over half the taxpayers in the top 5 per cent of the income distribution (some 25,000) were Indonesians. It was really only in the very highest assessable income bracket, over 1,000 guilders per annum, that Chinese taxpayers dominated. The distribution of assessable income, as shown by the Gini coefficients, was in fact much more unequal for Chinese taxpayers than for Indonesians. Among Chinese taxpayers, a relatively small proportion of taxpayers accounted for a large share of assessed income (Booth

1988a: Table 4). Outside Java, a much higher proportion of taxpayers were Chinese, and they dominated the highest centiles of the income distribution. But this was probably due to the fact that indigenous taxpayers outside Java were brought into the tax net only quite slowly; it was not until the 1920s that their incomes were taxed on the same basis as the Chinese. As we shall see in the next section, the income tax data for the inter-war period offer important clues on trends in the distribution of non-agricultural incomes both within ethnic groups, and between races and regions.

After the end of the 1914–18 war, per capita GDP growth accelerated to over 2 per cent per annum (Table 2.1). The 1920s saw a rapid growth in export production from both large estates and smallholders, and Polak's income estimates show that in real terms per capita income accruing to indigenous Indonesians grew steadily from 1921 to 1928 (CEI, Vol 5, Table 16.4). All this would suggest that living standards should have continued to improve at least at the rate achieved in the decade from 1905 to 1915. But the evidence on food availability in Java does not support this hypothesis; indeed it confirms Kahin's judgement that 'even prior to the depression the general level of economic welfare was declining' (Kahin 1952: 25). Scheltema's series show that by 1930 per capita rice availability had fallen back to 95 kg per annum, compared with 117 kg in 1915 (Table 3.1). The series on per capita food availability computed by van der Eng (1993a: Figure 4) shows a marked decline after the peak reached in 1920. Per capita textile imports into both Java and the Outer Islands fell between 1915 and 1920 and, although they recovered in 1925, they fell thereafter (Table 3.1).

In an influential report published in 1921, Huender argued that the rise in money incomes experienced by peasant families in the immediate post-war era was insufficient to compensate for the rapid inflation, 'so their situation . . . has either remained the same or has deteriorated' (as translated in Penders 1977: 93). Certainly real wages declined in the early 1920s, for both urban and rural workers, as money wages failed to keep up with rising prices (Booth 1988a, Table 6). Huender was disturbed by the fact that tax revenues were not increasing more rapidly (the real value of government revenues declined between 1913 and 1920, and the budget deficit increased with alarming speed after 1915, necessitating heavy borrowing abroad), but was adamant that the tax burden on Indonesians should not be increased. Yet, there can be little doubt that their tax burden did increase during the 1920s and 1930s. Because the revenues accruing from the main taxes falling on indigenous incomes, especially the land tax, were quite inelastic with respect to falling incomes, the ratio of taxes to the income base steadily grew (Booth 1980: Table 6).

But it is far from clear that the increase in the burden of taxation on indigenous incomes was the only, or the most important, reason for the decline in rice consumption per capita which occurred in the 1920s. It has already been noted that rising per capita incomes in the decade before 1914 were accompanied by a rapid increase in rice availability, due at least partly to a rapid growth in imports (Table 3.1). In seeking the reasons for the failure of the ethical policy to continue to raise living standards after the First World War, Wertheim (1956: 87) stressed the high rate of capital outflow through remitted profits after 1920, and the failure to invest in improving production technologies in foodcrop agriculture or in other activities where the Indonesian population earned the bulk of their livelihood. Certainly the balance of payments surpluses increased in the 1920s, which reduced the income available for either consumption or investment within the colonial economy. But this by itself is insufficient to explain the decline in per capita consumption of basic foods including rice which occurred in the 1920s (Table 3.1; see also van der Eng 1993: Figure 4). A further reason appears to have been increasing inequality in the distribution of incomes among the indigenous populations both of Java and the Outer Islands.

A valuable source of information on disparities within the indigenous population in Java is the report on tax burdens compiled by Meijer Ranneft and Huender (1926). They estimate earnings for the main socio-economic groups of the indigenous population in both urban and rural areas (Booth 1988a, Table 7). Their data show that in rural areas over 60 per cent of the indigenous population were either agricultural labourers, coolies, sharecroppers or small farmers, and had average annual incomes of not more than 30 guilders per capita. A much smaller group of village officials, large landowners, civil servants and large traders, comprising slightly over six per cent of the rural population, enjoyed incomes of around 100 guilders per capita, and considerably more in the case of the last two groups. In the towns, there was a sharp divide between coolies who comprised 40 per cent of the population and had per capita incomes of 35 guilders per annum, and civil servants who were nine per cent of the population, earning on average 145 guilders per annum. These figures show that by the 1920s marked disparities existed between different social groups within indigenous society in Java.

Although it is not possible to obtain data on the distribution of Indonesian incomes for later years similar to that provided by Meijer Ranneft and Huender for 1925, some important clues on changes in income distribution in the 1920s and 1930s can be obtained from the income tax data. In 1921, the income tax was reformed and all races were assessed everywhere in the country according to the same scale. The threshold was an annual income of 120 guilders, and indigenous incomes from agriculture continued to be excluded (Fowler 1923: 391–3). By 1930, about 5 per cent of the adult Indonesian population in Java were paying the income tax, and about 22 per cent of the population outside Java (Booth 1988a: Table 9). As the assessed income per capita in 1930 was substantially higher than Polak's estimate of average income per employed Indonesian, it is safe to assume that income taxpayers in Java as a group represented a relatively affluent segment of the Indonesian population. In fact, Kahin (1952: 29–30) has argued that, by the mid-1920s, the great majority were salaried government officials, or private sector employees. It is clear when we compare the changes in average income per Indonesian worker during the 1920s computed from Polak's data with changes in average assessed income per taxpayer that the latter grew rapidly relative to the former, both in Java and in the Outer Islands (Booth 1988a: Table 9). This would suggest that Indonesian taxpayers, already in 1920 a relatively high-income group in Java, although not elsewhere, experienced faster income growth than other workers, thus widening disparities within the indigenous population.

Thus it would appear that the modest growth which took place in real per capita incomes of indigenous Indonesians during the 1920s was offset by a rising burden of taxation and worsening distribution of income as between income taxpayers and the rest, a division which was broadly consistent with business people and non-agricultural salaried workers on the one hand and small-scale artisans, casual labourers and all those employed in agriculture on the other. As a result of this, per capita rice consumption in Java, and indeed total food consumption, fell in the 1920s. We do not have any data on food availability outside Java in these decades; it could be argued that as Indonesian incomes were growing more rapidly outside Java in the 1920s, the decline in living standards was less marked. But on the other hand, the faster population growth probably meant that per capita income growth was slower than in Java. In addition, the estimates made by Gotzen (1933: 473) suggest that the tax burden on indigenous incomes outside Java was considerably higher than on

Java in the early 1930s, at least in part because of the impostion export tax on smallholder rubber (O'Malley 1979: 239: Booth 1980: 105). The fact that the disparity between average income per employed Indonesian and average assessed income per taxpayer grew more rapidly outside Java might indicate that inequality was growing there as well, although taxable incomes were almost certainly underassessed in 1920.

That a group of relatively affluent indigenous Indonesians existed by the 1920s is clear from the growing numbers of hadj pilgrims, who exceeded 50,000 in 1926–27. In this year, Indonesian pilgrims accounted for over 40 per cent of all foreign pilgrims visiting Mecca (*Indisch Verslag* 1931: 130). Over the four years from 1926–27 to 1929–30, numbers going on the hadj averaged 40,000, a figure which was only exceeded during the oil boom of the 1970s (Table 3.2). But given that the average cost of the hadj per pilgrim in 1926 was estimated to be at least 870 guilders, or more than ten times the average income of an indigenous Indonesian as estimated by Polak, these data cannot be considered evidence of a broadly based improvement in indigenous incomes. Rather, a restricted group of large farmers and salaried employees must have spent accumulated savings on the pilgrimage, or sold land and other assets to undertake the trip.

It is sometimes asserted that the depression years saw some improvement in indigenous living standards, especially in Java where the collapse of the sugar industry, although depriving many workers of their wage employment opportunities, also restored over 100,000 hectares of well-irrigated land to foodcrop cultivation. However, this had no immediate impact on foodcrop production, which in fact grew less rapidly between 1930 and 1935 than in the 1920s, although there was a rapid recovery in the second part of the decade. Per capita availabilities of both rice and other foodstuffs also fell after 1930, but the extent of the decline was modest, except for 1934. As Polak pointed out in his pioneering national income study, indigenous incomes in Java were not greatly affected by the depression, although outside Java the fall was greater (CEI, Vol 5: Table 16.4). But the depression years did see a marked increase in the burden of taxation on the Indonesian population; in particular, the land tax assessments in Java did not decline as rapidly as food prices or the real value of foodcrop production, so that the real burden of the tax increased (Booth 1980, Figure 1).

The evidence assembled by Polak, and by van Laanen (1979: 144), useful though it is in indicating trends in average income and expenditures over the 1930s, tells us nothing about distributional changes. Whether the distribution of income among the Indonesian population worsened in the early 1930s, especially in Java, is difficult to establish. Certainly, wage earners fortunate enough to have kept their jobs during the early 1930s appear to have enjoyed a considerable improvement in real wages, as the wage data from the Javanese sugar industry make clear. By 1934, foremen were earning over twice as much per day as they did in 1930 if the rural Java food index is used as a deflator. All male and female workers were, on average, earning 50 per cent more, although numbers employed had declined by more than half (Booth 1988a, Table 10). On the other hand, Ingleson (1988: 309) points out that higher real wages for those workers still in wage employment was accompanied by a deterioration in conditions of work; the working day was lengthened and fringe benefits were reduced. But, even allowing for such changes, income disparities between wage earners and other indigenous social groups must have increased. In his study of the impact of the depression on the indigenous economy, van Laanen (1982: 13) argues that the falling price level meant not only that those who kept their wage employment enjoyed an increase in real income, but also that creditors gained at the expense of debtors. Thus, he concluded that 'the gap between rich and poor, between purchasing agents/money lenders and debtors became irrefutably wider'.

It was noted in the previous chapter that per capita GDP grew at over 2 per cent per annum in the years from 1934 to 1941. Real per capita income of the Indonesian population on Java increased over these years, and the tax burden on Indonesian incomes was somewhat reduced, compared to earlier in the decade. After 1935 Java became a net exporter of rice for the first time since the 1870s; by 1936–40 net exports from Java averaged 94,000 tons (CEI, Vol 4, Table 6). This was the result of government controls on rice imports, which led to a diversion of Javanese rice to the Outer Islands to replace imports. Thus, in the years from 1936 to 1940 per capita rice availability in Java was below per capita production for the first time since 1870. Real expenditure on foodstuffs did recover rapidly after 1935, but much of the growth in food expenditure went on increased cassava consumption in particular, and rice consumption accounted for less than half of total food consumption in calorie terms (Table 3.3). Given that a considerable part of the cassava was eaten in the form of *gaplek*, for which the expenditure elasticity of demand was probably positive for the poorest groups in rural areas, this may indicate some improvement in their incomes and expenditure. In addition, dried cassava prices fell relative to rice prices between 1935 and 1940, no doubt partly as a result of the increased rice exports from Java, and some of the growth in cassava consumption would have been due to price rather than income effects. The real value of imported textiles continued to fall in per capita terms in both Java and the Outer islands throughout the 1930s, although this was at least partly the result of the import substitution policy in the textile sector.

Table 3.3 Changes in food and cloth availability per capita, 1940–60

	Rice	Total food	Cotton cloth	
	(kg per capita)		Imports	Domestic
			(metres per capita)	
Java				
1936/40	86.2	197.7	n.a.	n.a.
1956/60	89.4	178.7	n.a.	n.a.
Indonesia				
1940	n.a.	n.a.	3.9	1.8
1960	97.1	180.9	1.9	3.5

Sources: Statistical Pocketbook of Indonesia, 1961, pp. 124–6, 215; Palmer (1972: Table 36).

Wertheim (1956: 95) argued that, in the last few years of Dutch rule, 'greater social differentiation went hand in hand with impoverishment for many people', although he did not produce any convincing evidence for this assertion. But even if the poorest segments of society did not become poorer in absolute terms, income disparities could well have increased. The most revealing evidence on disparities between indigenous Indonesians in the late 1930s is that collected in the investigations into the living standards of plantation labourers and employees of the Batavia Municipality (van Niel 1956; Central Bureau of Statistics 1939). The calorie and protein consumption data show that the most glaring disparity was between supervisory staff and factory labourers living on the plantation on the one hand, and field and factory labourers living off the plantation, and local farmers, on the other. Even the poorest group of Batavian coolies had calorie or protein intakes well above those of the farmers and field labourers (Booth 1988a: Table 11). Certainly, the disparities within the indigenous population which were already evident in the 1920s were still significant at the end of the 1930s.

But there can be no doubt that it was disparities between rather than within ethnic groups which continued to be most obvious in the late colonial Indonesian economy. Polak's study showed that disparities in income per worker between the ethnic groups widened (CEI, Vol 5: 75). By 1939, an employed European earned on average sixty-one times, and a Chinese worker eight times, what an Indonesian earned. Of course, this simply reflected the fact that the Europeans occupied the highly paid positions in government and business, while the Chinese dominated trade and those sections of industry and commerce not controlled by the Europeans. Polak's estimates show that the share of national income accruing to indigenous Indonesians fell consistently from 1921 to 1939, while that accruing to Europeans and foreign Asians grew (CEI, Vol 5: tables 15.1 and 15.3).

Kahin (1952: 29) has used the income tax data to support the argument that the Indonesian urban middle class was, in the 1930s, extremely small and almost entirely 'non-capitalistic'. Certainly it is true that a very high percentage of income accruing to Indonesians in Java with an income over 900 guilders in 1935 and 1939 was from salaries and wages (Booth 1988a, Table 13). But at least some of these were in large industrial enterprises, run along capitalist lines; in fact, Sitsen (c. 1943: 58) claimed that 25 per cent of managerial positions in private industry were occupied by Indonesians by 1940. Outside Java many more taxpayers were self-employed. It is also important to note that, outside Java, Indonesian taxpayers grew as a percentage of the total in the 1930s, rather than declining as in Java. Even in 1939, they accounted for 40 per cent of taxpayers in the top 5 per cent of the assessable income distribution, compared with less than 6 per cent in Java (Booth 1988a: Table 12). The disparity between Java and the Outer Islands is also apparent from the data on non-wage incomes assessed for the income tax. Of the assessed income accruing from non-wage sources under 900 guilders per annum, almost 85 per cent was earned by Indonesians, of whom the great majority were outside Java (Booth 1988a: Table 14). Most would have been small merchants, traders and artisans.

POVERTY AND INEQUALITY IN THE COLONIAL ERA: A SUMMING UP

In what sense can we say that Indonesians were on average richer, or poorer, when the Japanese arrived in 1942 than when Raffles left in

1815? It seems highly probable that per capita rice consumption in Java was lower; because of deficiencies in both the food production and the population figures we cannot be dogmatic about trends, but there seems to be little doubt that per capita rice availability in Java fell in the latter part of the nineteenth century, rose again in the decade before 1913, and then fell again through the 1920s and 1930s. These developments were not accompanied by recurrent famines, as in South Asia, because calorie intake was maintained, or at least not permitted to fall too drastically, by increased production of corn and cassava which became staple commodities. Should the switch from rice to less preferred staples such as corn and cassava be regarded as evidence of 'declining welfare'? Certainly, the income elasticity of demand for all foods was quite high in Java in the late colonial era, and increased calorie consumption, from whatever source, could be seen as evidence of improved incomes, especially on the part of the poorer classes in rural areas with the highest unsatisfied demand for food. On the other hand, falling calorie consumption, as occurred in the 1920s, is strong evidence for declining real incomes on the part of the poorest groups in society. Outside Java it is impossible to determine trends in per capita food consumption over time because of lack of data. It seems probable that consumption rose in major rice producing areas, such as West and North Sumatra and Aceh more or less in step with population, while in the main smallholder export crop regions, imports would have risen and fallen in step with trends in smallholder incomes.

Of course, it can be argued that other determinants of welfare should be considered besides per capita availability of food. One could, for example, examine the growth in publicly provided services such as irrigation, credit, education and health, increased provision of which could have at least partially compensated for declining consumption of preferred food staples. In addition, the greater provision of transport services led to substantial improvements in mobility, especially in years from 1900 to 1930. More people travelled by train, and more went on the pilgrimage to Mecca. However, the available evidence would suggest that access to these services was largely confined to the top strata of the indigenous population whose living standards almost certainly improved relative to those of the bottom groups. Landowners controlling relatively large parcels of irrigated land (many of whom in Java were village officials), successful cultivators and traders of cash crops, employees of private companies, especially those with some security of tenure, and those with government jobs would all have improved their position relative to the average Indonesian over the last decades of the colonial era. They would have accounted for many of the growing numbers securing loans from formal financial institutions, or undertaking the long and expensive sea voyage to Mecca. But while the absolute numbers of Indonesians earning very large incomes (more than ten times the average) almost certainly grew quite rapidly between 1900 and 1940, they remained a tiny fraction of the total population. In 1913 there were fewer than 1,000 indigenous income tax payers in Java with an assessable income of more than 1,000 guilders; by 1939, when the general price level had returned to roughly that prevailing in 1913, and the average income per employed Indonesian in Java was roughly 80 guilders, there were over 19,000. But they still accounted for only 0.1 per cent of the labour force.

This would suggest that Kahin's assertion concerning the 'minuteness' of the non-agricultural middle and upper classes in the late colonial era was broadly correct. Certainly, there can be no doubt that the highest income groups were almost exclusively European and Chinese, and that in Java the bulk of the Indonesian income tax payers were salary earners, many of them in government service. Outside Java the great majority of the 1.7 million Indonesian income taxpayers in 1939 were not salaried employees, but own account workers. True, most of them were earning little more than the average income for all indigenous workers, and one cannot quarrel with Kahin's conclusion that 'economic position in colonial society was determined along ethnic lines' (Kahin 1952: 36). But certainly an embryonic entrepreneurial class was there, which could respond to the new opportunities provided by political independence.

The distribution of income between ethnic groups and within the Indonesian labour force at the end of the 1930s is summed up in Booth (1988a: Table 15). At the top of the pyramid were European workers, who accounted for 0.4 per cent of the labour force, but who appropriated 12.6 per cent of national income as computed by Polak. They occupied most of the senior and best-paying jobs in both the public and private sectors. The only effective challenge to their economic supremacy was posed by the Chinese in trade and commerce, although even in these areas the European companies dominated the heights, leaving much of the rest of the activity to the Chinese. As far as the indigenous Indonesian labour force was concerned, 63 per cent were employed in small-scale agriculture (including livestock, fisheries and forestry) while the rest were scattered through a range of occupations, the most important of which were manufacturing, trade and plantations. The distribution of income between Indonesians revealed far less glaring disparities than between ethnic groups; government employees and large farmers were, on average, earning several times the average Indonesian income, while small farmers and labourers were earning rather less.

The distribution of income in the late colonial economy in Indonesia was very different from that found in other parts of Asia. If we compare the Indonesian situation with Maddison's estimates for India, for example, it is striking how much smaller the 'village' (here interpreted as the smallholder agricultural) economy was in Indonesia (Booth 1986: 29). The expatriate share of the non-village economy was, by contrast, much larger, partly because the Dutch economic presence was so much larger than that of the British in India, and partly because of the importance of the Chinese, who had no equivalent in South Asia. The indigenous capitalist, merchant and professional class accounted for a larger share of income in India and, although the small traders, clerical workers and artisans accounted for about the same proportion of national income in both countries, they were a much larger part of the labour force in Indonesia. Small farmers, tenants, and landless labourers fared about the same in both countries.

THE STANDARD OF LIVING AND THE DISTRIBUTION OF INCOME IN AN ERA OF TRANSITION: 1950–65

There can be little doubt that during the decade of the 1940s the great majority of Indonesians experienced falling living standards. Even allowing for inaccuracies and understatement in the official food production data for Java, it is clear that per capita food availability declined very sharply after 1941. Sato (1994: 154–61) argues that in addition to the forced deliveries of rice, forced labour demands in Java grew rapidly, and by late 1944 over 2.6 million Javanese were working for the Japanese armed forces and the military administration. Outside Java, the policies of self-reliance imposed by the Japanese meant that those regions dependent on food imports from Java and other parts of Asia suddenly had to produce enough to feed not just the local populations but also the Japanese armed forces and conscript labourers who had been brought from Java. In some areas the result was a rapid descent into near-famine conditions.

Everywhere in the archipelago non-food basic needs such as cloth, which had either been imported or produced locally, vanished from the marketplace. By 1945, starving people dressed in rags were a common sight in Java and elsewhere (Reid 1980: 21).

Matters improved only slightly after the defeat of the Japanese. Although in the Dutch-controlled areas food and other imports resumed, per capita availability of basic foods in Java recovered slowly, and indeed had not returned to pre-war levels by the latter part of the 1950s. Per capita availability of cotton cloth was also slightly lower in 1960 than in 1940 (Table 3.3). After 1950, the private consumption component of GDP, computed from the official GDP series reported by the World Bank (1976: 122), registered a considerable increase until 1962 in per capita terms (Table 3.4). There was some decline between 1962 and 1963, but thereafter per capita consumption expenditure in Indonesia was fairly stable. This suggests that the main impact of the GDP decline in the early and mid-1960s was on investment expenditures rather than consumption. However, the series of poor monsoons from 1961 to 1967, coupled with the declining ability

Table 3.4 Real per capita consumption expenditure and rice availability, Indonesia, 1950–67

Year	Real per capita consumption expenditure (rupiahs, 1960 prices)	Rice availability (kg per year)
1950	2,615	n.a.
1955	3,126	87
1960	3,263	109
1961	3,461	101
1962	3,617	106
1963	3,409	92
1964	3,371	96
1965	3,387	92
1966	3,274	94
1967	3,497	91

Sources: World Bank, *World Tables* (1976: 122); Mears (1984: 126).

to import, led to a sharp decline in the per capita availability of rice, although, as in the pre-independence era, this was partly compensated by increased production of other staples such as corn (Mears 1984: 125). The series on cloth production and imports compiled by Palmer (1972: Table 39) showed that domestic cloth production in 1963 had fallen back to the level attained in 1955, while imports after 1961 fell below the figures for the 1950s. The declining per capita availability of rice and cloth in the decade from 1955 to 1965 is strong evidence of a general deterioration in living standards, and indeed much of the contemporary literature asserted that such a decline was taking place. It was also asserted that, in spite of declining incomes for the majority, a minority were growing steadily richer (Castles 1965: 38; Mackie 1967: 63). Certainly, worsening income distribution would be one explanation for the coexistence of constant average per capita consumption figures with declining rice consumption, and other evidence of falling consumption standards for the mass of the population.

In what ways did the distribution of income and wealth in Indonesia in the years from 1950 to 1965 change? This question has several facets, some easier to quantify than others. The explicit distinction between different ethnic groups which characterised the colonial statistics made it easy for researchers to quantify differences in income both between and within races. After independence this distinction was dropped, and since then information on the inter-racial distribution of income and wealth has been extremely difficult to obtain. Scholars have to rely on rough guesstimates. Anspach (1969: 182–3) cited figures from East Java in the early 1950s which indicate that 'alien' (mainly Chinese) interests dominated industries such as rice milling, printing, ice plants, machine-made cigarettes, and mechanical weaving. Chinese also owned the great majority of the bus and trucking companies. In addition, more often than not it was Chinese who acquired the enterprises of the departing Dutch throughout the 1950s, enabling them to move into sectors from which they had been excluded in the colonial period.

Anspach (1969: 182) asserted that 'Chinese enterprise, backed by experience, financial capacity, and associative spirit, proved highly resistant to the pressures of indigenism in the 1950–7 period'. He claimed that it was the growing feeling among indigenous Indonesian businessmen that they could never compete with the Chinese which led to the massive socialisation of assets after the final expulsion of the Dutch in 1957–58. But, at the same time, there appears to be little doubt that it suited many indigenous 'businessmen', who had obtained their import licences and bank loans on favourable terms largely because of their political connections, to become fronts for Chinese entrepreneurs. This led to the widespread incidence of 'Ali-Baba' firms, where the well-connected Indonesian secured the necessary licences, and the Chinese partner supplied the managerial and marketing expertise (Feith 1962: 375). Such practices became more and more widespread during the first cabinet of Ali Sastroamidjojo, when the use of the licensing system as a way of rewarding political supporters became more blatant. These practices not only increased the role of Chinese entrepreneurs in the Ali-Baba companies themselves, but made it even more difficult for Indonesians with entrepreneurial skills, but without the political connections, to establish viable enterprises (Soedarpo 1994: 50–1). Almost certainly, they must have led to a redistribution of wealth in favour of the Chinese minority.

The second important distributional issue, which by the late 1950s had become even more politically sensitive than the inter-ethnic issue, concerned the regional distribution of income, and especially income from foreign trade. The share of the Outer Islands, and particularly Sumatra, in total export production, grew steadily throughout the last five decades of the colonial era; in 1938, the last year of normal foreign trade before the outbreak of war in Europe, Sumatra accounted for 48 per cent of commodity export earnings and Java for only 32 per cent. By 1957, according to the official figures, exports from Sumatra accounted for 66 per cent of the total, and by 1967, 75 per cent (Table 3.5). At the same time Sumatra's share of total imports was steadily declining, so that by 1967, imports into Sumatra amounted to only 23 per cent of the rupiah value of exports. In interpreting these figures it has to be borne in mind that the export data are undervalued relative to the import data, because of the way the increasingly complex system of multiple exchange rates discriminated against exporters, and because of under-invoicing and smuggling. These last two problems mean that the US$ values of exports, as reported in international publications, are also unreliable. Rosendale (1978: 150) calculated revised estimates of commodity exports which suggest that official data in US$ terms were understated by almost 30 per cent in 1964 and 1965. Moreover, it is probable that the smuggling was more widespread in Sumatra than elsewhere, because the close proximity of ports such as Singapore and Penang reduced both the costs and the risks. Thus, the true share of Sumatra in Indonesia's total exports by the early 1960s was almost certainly understated in the official data. This implies that the Sumatran export surplus would also have been understated, although it is probable that some imports into Java ultimately found their way to Sumatra.

Table 3.5 Regional distribution of exports and export surpluses, 1938–68

Year	Regional distribution of exports (% of total)			Export surplus (exports as a % of imports)		
	Java	Sumatra	Other islands	Java	Sumatra	Indonesia
1938	32	48	20	71	276	144
1939	36	48	16	89	325	164
1940	33	52	15	104	470	217
1954	20	62	18	38	432	138
1955	18	67	15	37	485	150
1956	16	68	16	25	341	107
1957	14	66	20	26	308	119
1958	13	71	16	30	351	145
1959	12	69	19	40	433	193
1960	14	71	15	29	472	146
1961	12	71	17	15	401	99
1962	10	73	17	14	389	105
1963	13	73	14	25	439	134
1964	15	72	13	20	487	105
1965	12	76	12	15	567	99
1966	17	69	14	26	689	129
1967	13	75	12	17	443	102
1968	12	74	14	16	349	102

Source: *Statistical Pocketbook of Indonesia*, various issues.

But even allowing for problems in interpreting the data, it is clear from Table 3.5 why many outside Java, and especially in Sumatra, felt that they were subsidising Java in the late 1950s and early 1960s. To an increasing extent the export-producing provinces felt that Java was draining their wealth away in the form of unrequired export surpluses, much as the nationalists had accused the Netherlands of draining wealth from the colonial economy. The widespread smuggling of the 1960s was only the most obvious manifestation of what Mackie (1967: 65) termed the tendency towards 'de facto federalism', which in turn was hastened by the 'atrophy of the central government's machinery'. Pitt (1981: 202–3) argued that the smuggling was so widespread that, in fact, it led to a considerable increase in the domestic price of rubber beyond the 'legal trade price', thereby modifying the impact on producer incomes of the overvalued exchange rate. But, in spite of the smuggling, the effective tax imposed on producers in Sumatra, and in the other export-producing regions, through the under-pricing of exports must have been considerable, although in the absence of a 'true' equilibrium exchange rate its magnitude can only be guessed at. Such a tax could be considered a replacement for more orthodox taxation methods which the central government was patently unable to implement. But it was hardly equitable, especially as those bureaucrats and businessmen in Java reaping large rents from their privileged access to foreign exchange and other scarce resources were almost certainly paying trivial amounts of income tax. These glaring disparities added to the sense of frustration and anger outside Java.

The extent of the disparities in consumption expenditures between provinces in the mid-1960s is most clearly shown in the data from the second round of the National Socioeconomic Survey (*Susenas*). Ranking provinces by average per capita monthly expenditure produces the not unexpected result that the main exporting regions in Sumatra, Kalimantan and Northern Sulawesi had the highest nominal expenditures, and the densely populated provinces of Central and East Java and Bali the lowest (Booth 1988: Table 4.19). But nominal figures are unsatisfactory as indicators of relative living standards when regional price disparities were clearly substantial. It is striking, for example, that per capita cereal consumption correlates very poorly with per capita money expenditures on food. We can, in fact, estimate the price of cereals (rice and corn) from the data contained in the *Susenas*, and use that to compute a poverty line in the manner suggested by Sajogyo (1975). Such an exercise confirms that the provinces with the highest proportion of poor people were in Java, Central Sumatra and Nusa Tenggara, while those with the lowest were in Northern and Southern Sumatra and in Kalimantan (Booth 1988: Table 4.19). Thus the transfers to Java from the export regions were not sufficient to equalise real incomes or alleviate the problems of mass poverty in Indonesia's densely settled inner core.

This supports the views of those who argued that the profits which were made from importing in the early and mid-1960s accrued largely to a small number of well-connected people in Jakarta and other urban areas who 'enjoy luxuries which seem incredible to an outsider' and 'control funds of an order which would have been out of the question ten or fifteen years ago' (Mackie 1967: 62). Mackie went on to argue that the government schemes such as the *sandang pangan* programme which were intended to provide basic goods at subsidised prices foundered because of the high budgetary costs, and the inevitable black marketing to which they gave rise. Even the allocations of rice and cloth at cheap prices to civil servants were insufficient for their needs, forcing them to buy on the open markets at prices which were increasing far more rapidly than their wages. Certainly, all the evidence which we have on trends in real wages in sectors such as estates and manufacturing over these years indicates that there was a sustained decline from the mid-1950s onwards, reaching the nadir in the mid-1960s (Papanek 1980: Tables 4.3, 4.5). Although these series may not fully take into account the fact that most formal sector employees were receiving a considerable part of their wages in kind, there can be little doubt that the purchasing power of wages and salaries dropped precipitously in these years, and even those with permanent employment found themselves reduced to near-penury.

Those in self-employment, particularly in agriculture, on the whole fared rather better, and this was probably the main reason for the fact that in most provinces, average per capita expenditures were only about 37 per cent higher in urban than in rural areas in 1964–65 (Table 3.6). This urban–rural disparity was, in fact, quite moderate in comparison with other Asian countries (Sundrum 1973a: Table 6). But, at the same time, the proportion in poverty was higher in rural

Table 3.6   Urban–rural disparities in Indonesia, 1964–65 to 1993

Year	All urban areas*	Jakarta*
1964–65	137	
1969	145	
1970	143	
1976	173	
1978	195	
1980	169	207
1981	179	234
1984	189	250
1987	185	271
1990	181	275
1993	192	305

*Average per capital consumption expenditures in urban areas (only Jakarta) as a percentage ratio of rural expenditures.
Source: *Survei Sosial Ekonomi Nasional, Pengeluaran untuk Konsumsi Penduduk*, Jakarta: Central Bureau of Statistics, various rounds.

than urban areas in most regions. This indicates that the gap between rich and poor in rural areas was widening as well; while those families with land could insulate themselves against the impact of inflation on food prices, those reliant on wage labour were probably worse off than urban workers because they had less security of tenure. Inequalities in per capita expenditure in Java in 1964–65, as measured by the Gini coefficient, were lower in urban than in rural areas (King and Weldon 1977: 702). The lower urban inequality suggests that the incidence of inflation was particularly severe on the urban middle classes in salaried employment, who in turn were more numerous in Java than elsewhere. To the extent that their consumption standards were depressed to levels nearer those of the urban poor, overall inequalities would have been reduced. This trend might have been offset by the gains which accrued to the very rich, although these are unlikely to be fully reflected in a household consumption survey.

In spite of the increasingly strident socialist rhetoric which characterised the Guided Democracy era, little serious attempt was made to redistribute productive assets from rich to poor. Even the nationalisation of Dutch companies and their conversion into state enterprises could hardly be considered a measure designed to redistribute assets towards the poor, especially as it became obvious that many senior managers in the state enterprises were running them for their own private profit (Castles 1965: 23–4). The one important sector where legislation was enacted which was at least redistributive in intent was agriculture. The purpose of the 1960 Basic Agrarian Law (BAL) was to unify the two very different land tenure systems which had developed in the colonial period, the one based on Western legal concepts and the other on customary *adat* law. In addition, in response to increasing population pressures and land scarcity in Java and Bali, the legislation introduced both maximum and minimum holding sizes. The minimum size (two hectares, at a time when the average holding size in Java was already well below one hectare) was obviously unrealistic, as were many of the conditions imposed on leasing contracts. Although eye witnesses of the implementation of the laws in the early 1960s claimed that 'fairly large sections of the country have no land to redistribute at all; and where such land is available, it is available in small amounts', the legislation did give many former tenants or squatters on land belonging to estates some security of tenure (Ladejinsky 1977: 342–3). Utrecht (1969) estimated that by 1968 about one million hectares of land had been distributed to one million people, although some of this was subsequently reoccupied by former owners.

The 1963 Agricultural Census revealed that the average holding size in Indonesian agriculture (excluding the large estate sector on the one hand, and holdings under 0.1 hectares on the other) was slightly over one hectare; in Java it was 0.71 hectares. The top 5 per cent of farmers for the country as a whole controlled 32.9 per cent of the land, while the bottom 40 per cent controlled only 10 per cent (Booth and Sundrum 1976: 96). While such a distribution of land was not highly skewed by Asian standards, let alone in comparison with Latin America, it was hardly as egalitarian as many urban Indonesians liked to imagine. Furthermore, many rural families owned little or no land at all. The 1964–65 *Susenas* showed that of the 16 million workers giving agriculture as their main source of income, fewer than half were 'independent farmers'; most of the rest were either wage workers or unpaid family workers. Only 58 per cent of male workers were independent farmers (Huizer 1980: 106). The violent confrontations organised by the Communist-controlled peasant organisations in East Java in the early 1960s showed clearly how deep the divisions had become in rural Java between those who controlled land and those who were denied access to it (Mortimer 1974: Chapter 7). Although the distribution of assets in rural Java might have appeared quite egalitarian to outsiders familiar with South Asia or Latin America, there can be little doubt that, to those living there, rural Java, and indeed rural Indonesia as a whole, in the mid-1960s had become a divided, even polarised, society.

DISTRIBUTIONAL CONSEQUENCES OF ACCELERATED ECONOMIC GROWTH AFTER 1970

There seems to be little doubt that the 1960s was a time of declining consumption standards for the great majority of Indonesians. However, because those on fixed incomes suffered the most drastic declines in real purchasing power during the years of high inflation, and because they comprised a higher proportion of the labour force in urban areas, the degree of urban-rural disparity in consumer expenditures was quite modest in Indonesia in 1964–65, and one of the most striking developments of the 1970s was an increase in this disparity, especially for non-food items (Booth 1992: Table 10.1). The explanation for this increase is not hard to find. The oil revenues accrued in the first instance to government, and much of the first-round impact of the increased government expenditures occurred in urban areas. Not only did civil servants enjoy a rapid increase in their real rates of remuneration, but there was also a substantial growth in expenditures on infrastructure which benefited the urban-based construction sector, and indirectly most other parts of the urban economy.

The increase in urban–rural expenditure disparities was greater for Java than for the Outer Islands (Sundrum and Booth 1980: Table 4). It could be argued that the increase in these ratios was mainly due to faster inflation in urban areas, which in turn could be attributed to the higher weight given to non-traded goods, such as housing, in the urban cost of living indexes. But, in fact, the Jakarta cost of living index rose at almost exactly the same rate in the 1970s as the rural Java index of nine basic commodities, although the difference between urban and rural inflation was rather greater outside Java. If the increase in per capita consumption expenditures are adjusted by appropriate price deflators for urban and rural areas in Java and elsewhere, it is clear that in the first part of the 1970s, real expenditure growth in urban Java was much higher than anywhere else (Booth 1992: Table 10.2). In the latter part of the 1970s, real expenditure growth in rural Java caught up with that in urban areas, implying that disparities stayed constant in real terms. Consumption expenditures in both urban and rural areas of Java grew faster than in other parts of the country.

The urban–rural differential showed little decline after 1981, in spite of the cutbacks in government expenditure as a result of falling oil prices. Indeed, the differentials were much the same in 1990 as they had been in the mid-1970s (Table 3.6). As the available price indexes suggest that rural inflation, in both Java and the Outer Islands, was rather faster than inflation in Jakarta over the decade 1976–86, and faster than the growth in the household expenditure component of the GDP deflator, it is probable that in real terms the urban–rural, and especially the Jakarta–rural, differential could have widened in the decade from the mid-1970s to the mid-1980s. This is confirmed by the figures on real expenditure growth by province between 1980 and 1987 (Booth 1992: Table 10.3). These show that Jakarta consumption expenditures grew more rapidly than in other urban areas in Java, and in urban Indonesia as a whole. While these results could be influenced by declining understatement in urban expenditures through the 1980s, it still seems probable that consumption standards in the national capital, already higher than elsewhere in 1980, have been increasing more rapidly since then. Particularly striking has been the widening gap between Jakarta expenditures and the average for rural areas since 1980 (Table 3.6).

The evidence that real per capita expenditure growth was faster in Java than elsewhere in the 1970s again raises the issue of regional disparities. These have usually been studied in Indonesia since the late 1960s using the provincial gross domestic product data prepared by the Central Bureau of Statistics. But if we are interested primarily in estimating disparities in living standards, rather than in gross regional domestic product, it is more instructive to look at provincial disparities in household per capita consumption expenditures which are collected in the *Susenas* surveys. If we convert the provincial *Susenas* data on per capita consumption expenditure to Jakarta prices and calculate population-weighted coefficients of variation, there appears to have been an increase in regional disparities in the 1980s in urban areas, although in rural areas the coefficient fell (Booth 1992: Table 10.5). These data indicate that different forces are influencing growth in consumption in urban and rural areas of Indonesia in the last two decades of the twentieth century, with the result that disparities are widening within urban areas, and between the capital, Jakarta, and the rest of the country.

Another important set of questions relates to trends in inequality between socioeconomic classes in Indonesia since the late 1960s. What has happened to incomes of professionals, managers and government workers compared to the average? What has happened to incomes of highly educated workers relative to those of the less well educated? We know that in Indonesia, as in most other societies, educational attainment is an important determinant of earnings, because access to highly paying jobs in both the public and the private sectors is determined mainly by qualifications. In the late 1960s, the monthly earnings of a worker with a university qualification in Jakarta was over five times that of a worker with incomplete primary education (Booth and Sundrum 1981: 199). Although comparable data are not available from later surveys, it is widely believed that during the 1970s the incomes of highly qualified workers rose relative to the national average because demand exceeded supply. Many of these workers were employed in the public sector, and data collected from the urban cost of living surveys carried out in the late 1960s and late 1970s allow us to estimate the disparity between incomes of households where the household head was in government service relative to the average. This disparity widened in the 1970s in almost all cities.

But in the latter part of the 1970s and the early 1980s it seems that differentials in remuneration between well educated professional and technical workers and others began to narrow. Between 1976 and 1982, the evidence from the Labour Force and *Susenas* Surveys suggests that the household income of managerial, professional and administrative households declined relative to the average, and relative to that of farmers, the poorest category. The degree of income disparity within each of these classes, as measured by the Gini coefficient, also declined over these years. There was also evidence of a decline in earnings differentials by educational attainment (Keyfitz 1989: Table 9). By 1986, the Labour Force Survey showed that an employee with a tertiary qualification earned about four times more than one with incomplete primary schooling, compared with over seven times more a decade earlier (Booth 1992: Table 10.12). The rapid decline in differentials by educational status was no doubt due to the growth in supply of educated workers, and the decline in demand due to slower growth after 1981. Between 1986 and 1990, differentials between those with completed primary education, and those with secondary education declined further, although the earnings gap between those with primary and those with tertiary qualifications was constant (Booth 1994: Table 16).

While few observers of Indonesian economic and social change over the last two decades would be surprised by the evidence of large and growing urban-rural income differentials, especially in Java, the apparent decline in inequalities within rural areas since the late 1960s is more controversial. Asra (1989) has argued that once allowance is made for differential rates of inflation in different expenditure groups, the decline in the Gini coefficient in rural areas in the 1970s could well have been lower than shown in the unadjusted data, although he still finds evidence of a decline. But many scholars have argued that, in rural Java in particular, disparities in income and wealth have widened since the late 1960s, even if in absolute terms most people have experienced some improvement in living standards. Much of the evidence for these arguments comes from village studies, rather than from analysis of data collected by the Central Bureau of Statistics (CBS), but it is frequently argued that data collected by the CBS are unreliable in that they underestimate income and expenditure on the part of the richest people in rural areas. Therefore, inequality indicators calculated from them are unreliable, and possibly misleading. Such criticisms may well be valid, although they are very difficult to test.

Are there any firm conclusions on trends in inequality in Indonesia since the 1960s which can be drawn from the welter of available data, some of it apparently conflicting and much of it of dubious quality? There does seem to be considerable statistical support for the argument that consumption expenditures in urban areas, especially in Jakarta, have been growing faster than in rural areas. While urban income inequalities may not have increased greatly since the 1970s, there is evidence that, by the late 1980s, they were quite high, especially in Java. The urban cost of living surveys carried out in 1989 showed that the Gini coefficient of household income inequality in the main cities of Java was over 0.4, indicating a fairly skewed distribution by international standards (Central Bureau of Statistics 1990: 25). Such a finding would not surprise most observers of urban Java in the late 1980s and early 1990s. In rural areas, the data are more contradictory, but it does seem clear that off-farm income now accounts for a considerable part of the total incomes of rural households, especially in Java. The sample survey of farm household incomes that was carried out as part of the 1983 Agricultural Census found that the average agricultural household in Indonesia earned only 55 per cent of its total income from its own agricultural holding, and that the rest of the household income was derived from a variety of sources including wage labour and from activities such as trade and transport (Central Bureau of Statistics 1987: 18). Thus, the determinants of off-farm employment, and especially its relationship to ownership of land and other assets, have become crucial issues in the study of income distribution, and of poverty, in rural Indonesia.

TRENDS IN INDICATORS OF POVERTY: 1969–90

Since the early 1970s, there has been much discussion in Indonesia about trends in poverty. As in many other countries, attempts have been made to compute poverty lines, and to estimate the proportion of the population who fall below that line, and how it has changed over time, for the country as a whole, and for different regions. Individual scholars, the Central Bureau of Statistics and the World Bank have all published estimates of trends in poverty, each using rather different poverty line concepts, and thus reaching rather different results. In recent years, however, the poverty line estimates put forward by the Central Bureau of Statistics have gained prominence as the 'official' figure, and it is these data which are referred to by the President and cabinet ministers. They show that there has been a steady decline in the percentage of the population living below the poverty line in both urban and rural areas of Indonesia since 1976. The decline has been particularly marked in rural areas; whereas 40.4 per cent of the rural population were below the poverty line in 1976, by 1990 this percentage had fallen to 14.3. The decline in urban areas was less dramatic, although the percentage was almost halved over the fourteen-year period. However, the urban population had been growing more rapidly than the rural population over these years, so the decline in the absolute numbers in poverty had been much slower in urban areas, and the urban poor accounted for almost one-third of the total poor by 1987 (Central Bureau of Statistics 1992: 19).

The Central Bureau of Statistics poverty estimates have several controversial aspects, which have been discussed in detail elsewhere (Booth 1993). However, other poverty lines widely used in Indonesia over the New Order period show a decline over time in the numbers in poverty, in both urban and rural areas (Booth 1992: Table 10.14). This is particularly true of the poverty line put forward by Professor Sajogyo, which is set in terms of the rice price. The Sajogyo poverty line is vulnerable to the obvious criticism that rice prices have not risen as rapidly as prices of other basic needs since the late 1960s, and thus a poverty line based exclusively on the rice price will exaggerate the fall in the incidence of poverty. In contrast to the Sajogyo approach, the poverty line put forward by Hendra Esmara (1986: 320 ff) is set in terms of actual expenditures on a basket of 'essential' goods and services as revealed in successive rounds of the Susenas surveys. Because it captures both the effects of inflation and the impact of higher real incomes on the quantity and quality of essential goods consumed, this poverty line increases more rapidly than the others. But it also shows a steady decline in the incidence of poverty in Indonesia since the mid-1960s (Booth 1992: 343).

Growing household incomes in Indonesia over the New Order period have led to improved per capita consumption of both food and non-food items. The food balance sheets which have been published since the late 1960s give estimates of per capita calorie availability from different types of foods for the whole country. Total calorie availability has increased by 36 per cent between 1968 and 1990, while protein availability has increased by over 40 per cent (Table 3.7). Furthermore, this increase in per capita calorie intake has come from increased consumption of superior foods, especially rice, sugar, meat, fish and eggs, while consumption of starchy root-crops has fallen. It is true that these are average figures, and do not by themselves indicate anything about improvement in food consumption for the lower expenditure groups. But the Susenas data indicate that food consumption expenditures are much less skewed than non-food expenditures, and, indeed, cereal expenditures vary very little as total expenditure increases (Booth 1988: 191). Thus, the improvement in average consumption of foods such as rice would be reflected in improvements for all income groups.

Table 3.7   Changes in per capita availability of calories and proteins, 1968–90

Foodstuffs	Calories		Proteins (grams)	
	1968	1990	1968	1990
Cereals	1,346	1,817	28.2	36.6
Tubers	284	165	2.4	1.5
Sugar	109	150	n.a.	0.1
Fruits*	133	325	6.6	15.2
Vegetables	19	25	1.1	1.2
Meat	20	28	1.1	1.9
Eggs	1	10	0.1	0.8
Milk	2	6	0.1	0.3
Fish	22	24	3.4	4.2
Oils	97	231	n.a.	0.1
Total	2,035	2,781	43.0	61.8

* Including oilseeds.
Sources: *Neraca Bahan Makanan di Indonesia di Indonesia 1968–74*, Jakarta: Central Bureau of Statistics, April 1977; *Neraca Bahan Makanan di Indonesia di Indonesia, 1990–91*, Jakarta: Central Bureau of Statistics, October 1992.

Has the decline in poverty which has undoubtedly occurred in Indonesia since the late 1960s been uniform across all parts of the country? Since the Dutch colonial authorities began to be concerned with the problem of 'declining native welfare' in Java at the turn of the century, the problem of rural, and indeed urban, poverty in Indonesia has tended to be regarded as primarily a Javanese problem. Certainly the regional distribution of poverty as shown by the *Susenas* survey for 1964–65 supported this view (Booth 1988: Table 4.19). In 1969–70 almost 60 per cent of the poor population of Indonesia were located in rural Java, compared with 53 per cent of the total population (Booth 1992: Table 10.17). But by 1990, the regional distribution of both the total population and the poor population had altered quite dramatically. According to the Central Bureau of Statistics figures, less than half the rural poor were located in Java, compared with almost 56 per cent of the rural population. Although a high proportion of the urban poor were located in Java (72 per cent of the total) this was only slightly higher than the proportion of the total urban population located in Java (Booth 1993: Table 10).

What led to this change in the regional distribution of poverty in Indonesia in the space of only two decades? Regional variations in poverty in Indonesia are closely correlated with per capita consumption expenditures, which in turn are correlated with per capita non-oil GDP (Booth 1992: Table 10.19). Thus the shift in the locus of poverty away from Java since the mid-1970s reflects the fact that household consumption expenditures have been increasing more rapidly there in per capita terms than in the Outer Islands. This, in turn, is partly due to the fact that agriculture still accounts for a higher share of regional GDP in most of the provinces outside Java than in Java, and the pace of technical change in agriculture outside Java, in both foodcrops and cashcrops, has been quite slow since the late 1960s (Tabor 1992: 191 ff). Another factor impeding the economic growth and diversification of provinces outside Java has been the neglect of infrastructural development. This, in turn, is related to the extreme centralisation of budgetary expenditures in both the colonial and the post-colonial era, which has led to a drain of resources from the resource-rich provinces to the centre. These issues are examined further in subsequent chapters.

A remarkable feature of the decline in the incidence of poverty in Indonesia since the 1960s is that it appears to have continued almost regardless of changes in macroeconomic conditions. Certainly, there is little support for the argument that the poverty decline was entirely due to the oil boom, because it began in the latter part of the 1960s, and has continued after 1981, in spite of slower GDP growth, budgetary cutbacks and economic restructuring. During the period of budgetary austerity, the government cut back on expenditures which did not directly affect the poor; as budgetary subsidies on staple foods and non-food items such as fuel were relatively modest, their reduction did not lead to sudden, large increases in the cost of living for the poorer groups in society, as happened with structural adjustment programmes in other parts of the world. The rapid industrial growth of the latter part of the 1980s, based in part on labour-intensive sectors such as textiles, garments and footwear, also led to a considerable increase in manufacturing employment in Java, and has led to diversification of household income even in rural areas.

LONG-TERM TRENDS IN LIVING STANDARDS

To what extent has the income growth and poverty decline of the last two decades led to an improvement in living standards beyond what was attained in the final part of the colonial era? This question can only be addressed in the context of Java, as the income and expenditure surveys carried out in the inter-war years refer only to Java. Apart from the so-called 'coolie-budget' studies, which have already been mentioned, a number of other family budget surveys were carried out. Most of them were too limited in their sample coverage to permit comparisons with more recent surveys, such as the household expenditure surveys (HES) carried out by the Central Bureau of Statistics since the 1960s. Bijlmer (1986: 153) attempted a comparison of average family incomes in Java and Madura between 1886 and 1976, drawing on a variety of colonial studies, and the 1976 HES. Some of his estimates refer to recommended dietary allowances and some to estimates of actual household incomes or expenditures. He points out that the average family income for the sample of households in Java surveyed by Meijer Ranneft and Huender (1926), converted into rice equivalents, was rather lower than the monthly 'hygenic ration' estimated in 1921 by Muhlenfeld on the basis of prison rations. In fact, the Muhlenfeld hygenic ration was still higher than average family expenditures in rural Java in 1976 in rice equivalents. Bijlmer (1986: 153–4) draws the following conclusions from his results:

> We see a striking similarity of the outcomes of 1924 and the average rural income of 1976, which are very close to the minima advised by the Labour Commission. This suggests that the average income of the rural population largely stagnated in these fifty years, whilst the growth is almost exclusively generated in urban areas.

Several criticisms can be made of Bijlmer's results; he does not adjust his estimates of family income to allow for changes in household size, and the use of rice equivalents, while widespread in both the colonial and the post-colonial literature, is obviously unsatisfactory if increases in the price of rice have not been commensurate with increases in the price of other basic foods, or with non-food necessities such as clothing and housing. Furthermore, none of the colonial surveys used as large a sample as the 1976 HES; for example the Meyer Ranneft and Huender sample consisted of only 1425 households, while the 1976 HES sample would have been at least ten times that size. In addition, the sampling procedures in most of the colonial surveys were far from random; in some cases the households were specially chosen from particular groups which the colonial authorities considered vulnerable, while in other cases, such as the urban household survey carried out in 1925–26, European households accounted for a disproportionate share of the total (Weinreb and Ibrahim 1957: 743 ff).

There are, in fact, good grounds for arguing that, given the differences in sample coverage, comparisons cannot be made between the colonial and post-colonial household surveys. Certainly, the rather sweeping claims made by Bijlmer need to be treated with caution. But if we do attempt a comparison using those colonial surveys which appear to be most similar in sample coverage to the post-independence HES, Bijlmer's stagnation hypothesis is not confirmed. The survey of plantation labourers and farmers carried out in the late 1930s, and reported in van Niel (1956: 77ff) was based on a sample of some 2,000 households, and the results disaggregated according to the job status of the household head. If we compare the reported food and total expenditures with those from the 1964–65, 1969–70 and 1980 HES for rural Java, only the relatively privileged category of field labourers on the plantations had expenditures which were higher in real terms than the 1969–70 and 1980 averages for rural Java. Even in 1964–65 food expenditures were higher than those for the control group of farmers in the 1939–40 sample (Table 3.8). By 1980, food expenditures were almost 50 per cent higher than in the 1939–40 sample.

Table 3.8   Comparison of real per capita consumption expenditures, 1939–40 to 1980 (1913 cents per day*)

	Food	Total	Food as a percentage of the Total
1939–40			
Field labourers	2.61	3.56	73.2
Factory labourers	1.27	1.69	75.0
Farmers	1.34	1.89	71.2
1964–65			
Rural Java (all households)	1.46	1.82	80.7
1969–70			
Rural Java (all households)	1.94	2.48	78.2
1980			
Rural Java (all households)	1.99	2.75	72.3

(Cont'd)

(Cont'd)

* The deflator used was the rural Java 12-food index, using the 1913 weights reported in Central Bureau of Statistics (1938), and prices reported in *Statistik Konjunctur* and *Indikator Ekonomi*, various issues. 1964 data were adjusted to December 1964–January 1965 prices using the Jakarta cost of living index, as price data were not available for these months.

Sources: Van Niel (1956:77); Central Bureau of Statistics, *Survey Sosial Ekonomi Nasional*, 1964–65, 1969–70, 1980. Java rural 12 commodity food index for 1969–70 estimated using 1913 weights as given in Central Bureau of Statistics (1938: 25–6).

This, indeed, is what would be expected, given the improvement in per capita food availability which occurred in the 1970s and was sustained into the 1980s. This evidence can be combined with that of falling infant and child mortality, greatly expanded access to basic education and other amenities such as electricity and running water to present a convincing case that there has been a broadly based improvement in living standards in Indonesia since the 1960s. By the early 1990s, Indonesia was ranked by the United Nations among the 'medium' human development countries, according to a composite indicator which included per capita GDP (corrected for differences in purchasing power), educational attainment and life expectancy. While still below neighbouring countries such as Malaysia and Thailand, Indonesia ranks well above the countries of the Indian subcontinent, much of the Middle East and Africa (UNDP 1995: 155–9).

4 Government and the Economy in Indonesia in the Nineteenth and Twentieth Centuries

THE ECONOMIC ROLE OF GOVERNMENT IN INDONESIA

What have been the main engines of growth in Indonesia since the early nineteenth century, and what has determined the distributional outcomes of that growth? These are complex questions which do not admit of any simple answer. Many students of Indonesian economic development both in colonial times and more recently have emphasised the crucial importance of external factors in determining the performance of the domestic economy. Certainly, the whole issue of the vulnerability of primary-exporting countries to fluctuations in their terms of trade, and the consequences of this vulnerability for their longer-term growth has generated an enormous international literature, which we will be looking at in more detail in the Indonesian context in the next chapter. But, for a deeper understanding of Indonesian economic performance since the early nineteenth century, we must also develop a better understanding of the domestic factors promoting, and inhibiting, economic growth. In this chapter, it is argued that the actions of successive governments, in both the colonial and post-colonial periods, are crucial to such an understanding.

This is true, not just because government policy has often placed obstacles in the path of economic change, but also because successive governments have assumed responsibility for altering its direction and accelerating its pace. This was certainly the case during the last four decades of the colonial period, when the ethical policy led to considerable growth in government expenditure as a proportion of national income, and in the numbers of government enterprises. It also led to increasing government intervention in, and regulation of, both domestic and foreign trade. In the immediate aftermath of independence, in spite of much use of socialist rhetoric, government attempts to plan the economy and regulate economic activity were unsuccessful, so that by the early 1960s the economic role of government was considerably diminished compared with the late colonial period. However, the twenty-five years of New Order economic policy-making from 1965 to 1990 have seen a considerable resurgence of government power, and several commentators have drawn attention to the apparent similarities between the last decades of Dutch rule and the policies pursued under Suharto (Willner 1981; McVey 1982; Anderson 1983).

The validity of these arguments are examined in this chapter, together with an assessment of the extent to which the government in Indonesia has facilitated, or retarded, the growth process. Indeed, Indonesia over the last 150 years offers a fascinating laboratory in which to study the impact of government on the process of economic development, first under Dutch colonial rule and then under successive independent governments. It can be argued that, for most of this time, Indonesian governments have exhibited traces of the traditional 'predatory' state as descibed by Lal (1988: 294), the planned state (Little 1982: 132) and the developmental state, as the term has been used by Johnson (1982: 17–34). The main objective of the predatory state, according to Lal (1988: 294), is to extract 'the maximum continuing flow of resources . . . for the members of Government and its associates'. The ruling class in the predatory state have some interest in the growth of the economy, through, for example, the provision of public goods such as law and order, transport infrastructure etc., in so far as 'this raises the potential flow of their own income'. However, they have little interest in any initiative which may eventually lead to the erosion of their own position of dominance. Historically, the power of predatory rulers has been eroded only where the citizens have been able to enforce constitutional limits to the powers of kings, aristocrats etc., and institute some form of representative government, with exclusive powers to tax and control public expenditure vested in an elected assembly or parliament.

Economists continue to argue over what 'rational economic planning' should involve, but even the more conservative would probably agree with Little (1982: 132) who argues for government programmes 'in the non-traded goods sectors of the economy – in health, education, roads, ports, power supply etc.' Many may go further and concede the case for government regulation of sectors producing traded goods in some circumstances (for example to stabilise prices of food staples in times of international shortages). The stronger argument, that the government has a responsibility to help late-developing economies catch up with the leaders goes back a considerable way in the literature of economic development. Recently, it has been used with considerable persuasiveness by scholars seeking to explain the high growth rates achieved by the East Asian economies such as Japan, Korea and Taiwan (Johnson 1982; Amsden 1989; Wade 1990). The argument is not that these economies have had a 'large government sector' (in fact, they have tended to have smaller ratios of public expenditure to GDP than other, slower growing economies in both the developed and the developing world). Rather, it is that they have developed sophisticated economic bureaucracies which have become extremely astute in assisting those industries with export potential to grow rapidly through penetration of foreign markets. An important message of this literature is that the economic bureaucracies have managed to insulate themselves from pressures exerted by special interest groups and have thus been able to withdraw support from those industries which have not met performance targets.

In this chapter, six phases between 1830 and the late 1990s are distinguished in the role of government in the Indonesian economy:

1 Government-led exploitation, 1830–70
2 *Laissez-faire* liberalism, 1870–1900
3 The rise of 'welfare interventionism', 1900–42
4 Gradual attenuation of government control, 1942–65
5 Stabilisation and boom under the New Order, 1965–81
6 The new liberalism and its enemies, 1982–present

In Indonesia, these phases have not involved a sequential progression from exploitation under a colonial predatory state to either a 'rationally planned' state, or an East Asian 'developmental' state. Rather, over the past 150 years or so, there have been attempts at such a transition by successive governments in Indonesia, both colonial and post-colonial. But they have been frustrated by an array of vested interests, some of them well entrenched within the government apparatus. Thus, in the late twentieth century, vestiges of the predatory state are still apparent in many areas of government policy.

GOVERNMENT-LED EXPLOITATION: 1830–70

In a survey of the Dutch colonial fiscal system written at the turn of the century, Day (1900) divided the nineteenth century into three periods. The first of these, from 1800 to around 1830 was 'a period of experimentation', but most of the experiments, most notably the

British attempt to establish a uniform system of land taxation based on individual assessment, failed (Bastin 1954). After the termination of the British interregnum, the colony went through a period of badly organised financial administration, and by 1829 the accumulated government deficits came to 38 million guilders, rather more than twice the level of imports in that year (CEI Vol 2: 17). Various proposals were put forward for reforming the colony's finances in the 1820s; Muntinghe suggested that cash crops could be grown on plantations outside Jakarta, making use of free labour, and that a company should be established to transport and market these crops (van Baardewijk: CEI, Vol 14: 11–12). Partly as a result of these proposals the *Nederlandsche Handel-Maatschappij* (NHM) was established in 1824. But after 1830, another system was implemented to reform the colonial budget.

Van Baardewijk (CEI, Vol 14: 13) has stressed that the original intention of van den Bosch was not just to increase revenues from the colony but also to improve indigenous living standards through the provision of paid labour. But during the 1830s, idealistic experimentation gave way to systematic exploitation, the main aim of which was to secure as large a surplus as possible for remittance to the Netherlands. Indigenous cultivators were forced to grow specified products which were then collected by government agents, shipped to Europe by the NHM and sold there. The NHM's monopoly in the transport and sale of Indonesian products in the Netherlands enabled it to rapidly become an extremely profitable company, and as van Zanden (1993: 144–6) has argued, the company's activities in the Netherlands had a considerable impact on industry and trade in Amsterdam and the surrounding regions. In the 1830s, the textile industry in Twente was given a considerable boost by Dutch protectionism which limited access of English cotton goods to the Java market, and opened it to Dutch products. Javanese consumers of cotton goods thus paid higher prices in order to subsidise the development of the textile industry in the Netherlands.

While the cultivators, and domestic middlemen in Java did receive payments for their deliveries, these were well below the amount derived by the government from the sale of crops. In addition, other imposts were levied, including land and trade taxes, and considerable revenues accrued to the government from monopolies. On the other hand, as Day (1900: 77) pointed out, expenditures 'especially on items like education and the administration of justice, were reduced to a point that menaced the permanent welfare of the people'. In fact, it is unclear to what extent expenditures, particularly on items such as education, were reduced beyond the very low levels that prevailed prior to 1830, but it is obvious that the colonial government kept all expenditures within the colony to an absolute minimum. The net outcome was a budget that was almost continually in surplus from 1835 to 1875. The surplus, in turn, financed the payments made to the exchequer in the Netherlands, although the size of the unrequited government transfers shown in the balance of payments data exceeded the fiscal surplus for the 1830s and the 1840s (Table 4.1). This disparity suggests that not all transfers made on government account to the Netherlands were recorded in the budget figures.

Table 4.1 The fiscal balance and unrequited transfers on government account, 1821–30 to 1931–40 (million guilders: decade averages)

Decade	Total fiscal balance	Unrequited government transfers	Net revenues from sale of products
1821–30	−4.1	2.3	n.a.
1831–40	4.9	10.1	n.a.
1841–50	10.8	20.0	6.1
1851–60	29.5	27.7	32.1
1861–70	26.3	22.8	40.4
1871–80	6.6	11.7*	6.6
1881–90	−1.0	0	20.4
1891–1900	−7.8	0	15.5[†]
1901–10	−5.7	0	0
1911–20	−78.6	0	0
1921–30	−39.4	0	0
1931–40	−102.4	0	0

* To 1877.
[†] To 1899.
Sources: Total fiscal balance: CEI, Vol 2, Table 2, line 11 and Table 3, line 17. Net revenue from sale of products: CEI, Vol 2, Table 2, lines 15 and 16 less line 17; Table 3, lines 21 and 22 less line 23. Unrequited government transfers: CEI, Vol 7, Table 1, Lines 17 and 18.

The data assembled by Creutzberg (CEI, Vol 2) also indicate that not all the net revenue accruing to the government from the sale of products was remitted back to Holland; from the 1850s onwards, net revenue from sale of products exceeded the fiscal balance, and government transfers abroad by a widening margin (Table 4.1). The balance was spent in the colony, mainly on general administration and defence. In the two decades from 1846 to 1865, defence expenditure was just under 20 per cent of total revenues from all sources, and about 13 per cent of total expenditure (Booth 1990: Table 10.1). For the entire period from the mid-1830s to the mid-1870s, when large overall budget surpluses were recorded, total expenditures in the colony exceeded revenues raised locally from taxes, sale of products in the colony, and other sources including revenue farming (Diehl 1993: 198–9). The colonial authorities were always under pressure from the Netherlands to curtail expenditures and increase revenues in the colony, although at the same time public opinion in the Netherlands was increasingly hostile to deriving more revenue from sources such as opium farming (Diehl 1993: 200). It was inevitable that, over time, at least part of the revenues from sales of products would be used domestically rather than remitted to the Netherlands.

Throughout the period of the Culture System (CS), gross revenue from sale of products accounted for between 50 and 60 per cent of total revenues; the balance came from monopolies farmed out mainly to Chinese, of which opium was the most important, the land tax and taxes on exports and imports. The land tax (*landrente*) was the most important single tax, although it only accounted for about 12 per cent of total revenues, on average, in the decades between 1846 and 1875 (Van den Berg 1895: Appendix D). At the height of the CS, total expenditures amounted to only 70 per cent of gross budgetary receipts, although in the decade 1866–75 this figure jumped to 85 per cent, at least partly because of increased military expenditures. It is striking that, even as late as 1871, the cost of collecting and selling sugar and coffee in both the colony and the Netherlands amounted to over half the budgetary revenues earned from those two crops (Van den Berg 1895: Appendix D). Certainly, the CS had become an inefficient method of earning government revenues, compared with conventional taxes such as customs duties and excises, whose collection costs were a small fraction of total revenues. This was no doubt a further reason for the erosion of political support for the CS in the Netherlands, apart from those discussed by Fasseur (1991).

The fiscal 'drain' under the CS ensured that the domestic economy of Java captured few of the potential benefits of the export growth which took place in the fifty years from 1820 to 1870. Had government revenues from sale of crops and from other taxes been spent in Java on productive infrastructure, and on education, the subsequent economic development of the colony might have been very different. Instead, a considerable part of the gains from Javanese trade went on providing the citizens of metropolitan Holland with the infrastructure and education which were denied the colonial population, and with exemption from income taxes. While it may be true that the liberal critics of the system exaggerated its deleterious impact on native living standards, there can be no denying that if government expenditure policies had been directed more towards providing infrastructure and services in Java, indigenous living standards could have been considerably higher by the end of the nineteenth century than, in fact, turned out to be the case.

LAISSEZ-FAIRE LIBERALISM: 1870–1900

Day regarded the outbreak of the Aceh War in 1873 as the major factor in bringing to an end the long era of colonial fiscal surpluses, a view which has been confirmed by more recent scholars (Fasseur 1991: 43). However, the size of the budget surplus was already diminishing perceptibly in the late 1860s; this was due in part at least to the growth in non-military expenditures, particularly on the so-called 'utilities', which expanded in number to include railways, mining industries, and government estates (CEI, Vol 2: 52). In the last three decades of the nineteenth century, expenditures on what we would think of today as 'development' activities, in particular infrastructure and education, showed some increase as a percentage of the total, as did expenditures on pensions, most of which were paid in the Netherlands (Table 4.2). There was a steep decline in the proportion of expenditures devoted to the cultivation and selling of export crops, in turn reflecting the decline in the proportion of revenues derived from this source. By 1895, revenues from taxation amounted to over 40 per cent of total revenues, although the proportion of government expenditure devoted to tax collection appears to have fallen slightly (Booth 1990: Table 10.3). Certainly, taxes were a much 'cheaper' source of government revenue in terms of collection costs, than revenues from sale of produce. Between 1876 and 1899, the budget was in surplus in only six years; in order to finance the deficits, loans were contracted by the Department of Colonies from the Netherlands Department of Finance. As the century drew to a close, these loans increased considerably; in 1898, a law was passed in the Netherlands authorising a loan of 57.8 million guilders, a sum equal to almost 40 per cent of budgetary expenditures in that year. Interest and debt repayment charges in 1900 amounted to 4.3 million guilders, about 3 per cent of budgetary expenditures (Day 1900: 97–8).

Table 4.2 Percentage breakdown of budgetary expenditures, 1871–1921

	1871	1895	1905	1913	1921*
Justice	4.2	4.9	4.5	3.2	2.3
Finance	7.8	11.7	17.5	19.6	17.0
(Pensions)	(3.6)	(7.6)	(8.3)	(5.6)	(4.7)
Interior	45.3	22.9	20.1	12.2	9.8
(Adminstration)	(7.3)	(9.2)	(7.9)	(3.8)	(1.8)
(Crops)	(30.1)	(6.0)	(4.0)	—	—
Education	1.7	3.4	3.7	4.1	3.5
(European)	(0.7)	(1.7)	(2.0)	(1.7)	(n.a.)
(Native)	(0.3)	(1.0)	(1.1)	(1.9)	(n.a.)
Medical	0.8	1.6	1.7	1.9	1.7
Mines/Industry	4.6	6.1	7.5	3.4	2.5
Public Works[†]	8.5	20.4	18.5	37.7	39.2
(Railways)	(0.7)	(8.1)	(8.9)	(11.3)	(16.4)
War Department	19.2	21.5	21.7	12.3	11.5
Navy Department	7.9	6.0	5.6	5.6	4.4
Other	—	1.4	—	—	8.1
Total	100.0	100.0	100.0	100.0	100.0

* Provisional figures
† Includes expenditures on roads, bridges, public buildings, irrigation works, and government enterprises including railways and post and telegraphs.
Sources: 1871, 1895: van den Berg (1895), Appendix D; *Jaarcijfers*, various issues.

Day (1904: 388) has claimed that the changes in colonial fiscal policy which occurred between 1870 and 1900 amounted to 'nothing less than a revolution'. While this might seem something of an exaggeration, there can be no doubt that public expenditures in the colonial economy did show some real growth in the period 1870–1900, although this growth decelerated after 1885 (Table 2.1). But there was only a marginal increase in the share of total national income accounted for by the public sector (Figure 4.1), and by international standards, public expenditures in late nineteenth century Indonesia were not high. In per capita terms they were lower than in British India up to 1885, and lower than in other British dependent colonies until 1912 (Table 4.3). On the other hand, total government revenues per capita (in sterling) were higher than in British India for the entire period from 1860 to 1912. This indicates that for most of the nineteenth century the fiscal surplus in Indonesia was larger than in the British Empire; total revenues were higher relative to expenditures, and even when deficits were incurred they were much smaller in per

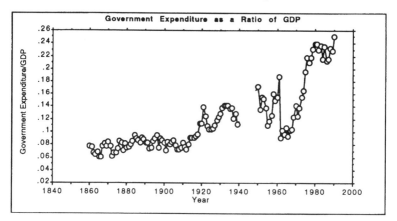

Figure 4.1 *Sources*: Government expenditure: CEI, Vol. 3, Tables 3 and 4; nominal GDP data from Pierre van der Eng. See Fig. 4.2 for sources post–1950.

Table 4.3   Government revenues and expenditures per capita in Indonesia and in India and other British dependent colonies, 1860–1912 (sterling pounds per capita)

Year	Indonesia		India		Other British colonies	
	R	E	R	E	R	E
1860–64	.39	.28	.31	.38	.66	.64
1865–69	.36	.29	.31	.44	.65	.68
1870–74	.37	.31	.29	.46	.62	.65
1875–79	.37	.38	.31	.49	.61	.65
1880–84	.34	.36	.33	.51	.67	.78
1885–89	.30	.29	.23	.33	.76	.89
1890–94	.28	.29	.18	.25	.72	.99
1895–99	.27	.29	.20	.29	.57	.81
1900–04	.28	.29	.23	.33	.42	.61
1905–09	.31	.31	.23	.36	.38	.55
1910–12	.40	.41	.22	.34	.39	.64

R = Total government revenues
E = Total government expenditures
Sources: Davis and Huttenback (1986:123, 222). Indian data exclude the princely states and refer to the national government only. Dependent colonies include all British colonies in Asia, the Pacific, Africa, the Caribbean and Latin America, excluding those which were self-governing. Indonesian data from CEI, Vol 2, Tables 2 and 3; exchange rates from CEI, Vol 6, Table 8.

capita terms than in either India or in the other dependent British colonies. After the turn of the century, the cessation of hostilities in Aceh permitted the government to reduce military spending. It might have been expected that this in turn would have led to a considerable reduction in taxation, and a smaller budget. But this was not the option taken by the colonial officials charged with the implementation of the new Ethical Policies after 1901.

GROWTH OF GOVERNMENT REVENUES AND EXPENDITURES AFTER 1900

The immediate impact of the ethical policy on the public finances was not dramatic, but over the first two decades of the twentieth century public expenditures did grow, both in real terms and relative to a growing GDP. By 1920, public expenditures had reached 14 per cent of GDP as estimated by van der Eng (Figure 4.1). There was also a considerable redirection of expenditure away from military and defence and towards salaries and perquisites of the civilian bureaucracy, public works, and to a lesser extent health and education (Table 4.2). By 1921, public works accounted for almost 40 per cent of the total budget. In 1903, an Act of the Dutch Parliament clearly separated the metropolitan finances from those of the colony, thus making it possible for the colonial government to raise loans to finance expenditures. The Minister of the Colonies, Idenburg, was convinced that loan authorisation powers were essential if the kinds of projects envisaged by the ethical policy were to be implemented (Creutzberg 1972: xxvi). In 1905, the Dutch government relieved the colonial government of 40 million guilders of floating debt, although the improvement in colonial revenues after 1905 meant that further loans were not negotiated until 1915.

To begin with, as Creutzberg (1972; xxxiii) points out, the departments of the colonial government had some difficulty framing development projects. Not surprisingly, it was the Department of Public Works which was first to submit 'concrete proposals for complete projects' in sectors such as railways, roads and irrigation. In 1904, the Department of Agriculture was established, and extension services and research establishments placed under its jurisdiction. In 1908, both the Public Works and the Education Departments were reorganised, and their functions expanded. The composition of revenues also changed; by 1909 taxes accounted for over 40 per cent of all government revenues and government enterprises a further 33 per cent (Paulus 1909: 122–3). The practice of revenue farming had been terminated in Java by 1910, and was gradually being phased out elsewhere; opium farms were replaced by a state opium monopoly, but revenues were expected to decline as the use of opium was restricted to 'medicinal purposes' (Paulus 1909: 125). In fact, by 1925, the opium monopoly still accounted for about 6 per cent of government revenues (Diehl 1993: 208).

But government revenues from all sources did not keep up with growing government outlays, and the budget deficit in the second decade of the century averaged more than 78 million guilders per annum (Table 4.1). By 1920, it had reached 3.4 per cent of GDP as calculated by van der Eng (1992). These deficits were met after 1915 by increased government borrowing, and by 1923 the accumulated stock of public debt amounted to over 21 per cent of national income and debt service payments to around 6 per cent of commodity exports (Table 4.4). Although these ratios were low compared with what they were to become later in the century, the Dutch Central Bank objected to the 'increasingly larger advances given to the Indies government by the Netherlands treasury', which in turn had to be covered with short-dated Dutch treasury bills (Creutzberg 1975: xxix). It became more difficult for the colonial government to borrow in the Netherlands, and, in 1922 and 1923, loans were secured from the USA and Britain. But the Dutch monetary authorities were increasingly unhappy with the colonial budgetary situation, and the colonial government was put under intense pressure to curb expenditures. Although government expenditures continued to grow in real terms in the 1920s, the rate of growth fell sharply (Table 2.1). Government expenditures fell as a proportion of GDP, from the peak of 14 per cent in 1921 to around 10 per cent by the mid-1920s (Figure 4.1). The budget deficit was reined in, and the debt stock fell somewhat compared with the early part of the decade.

There can be little doubt that the squeeze on public expenditure implemented in the 1920s affected capital works programmes far more than current expenditures on salaries and other perquisites of the civil service. The severe depression of the early 1930s led to even more draconian cuts in capital works, and by the mid-1930s, extraordinary (mainly capital) expenses had declined to virtually zero. General administrative expenses amounted to almost 80 per cent of total budgetary outlays. But even in spite of the cutback on capital works, revenues still fell more rapidly than expenditures in the early 1930s,

Table 4.4 Trends in public debt and debt service payments in Indonesia, 1911–90

Year	Public debt as a percentage of:		Debt service as a percentage of:	
	GDP	Exports	Exports	Total public expenditure
1911	2.9	17.5	0.8	1.8
1914	4.8	25.0	0.8	1.7
1919	8.8	24.8	1.1	3.6
1923	21.3	93.9	5.7	11.9
1928	15.8	63.2	6.2	13.1
1933	43.0	290.0	20.0	20.8
1938	34.2	199.7	11.0	14.6
1952	*	63.5	n.a.	n.a.
1958	*	77.8	n.a.	n.a.
1965	*	333.2	n.a.	n.a.
1970[†]	25.3	206.3	13.9	5.6
1980**	20.8	67.6	12.7	6.7
1985**	32.0	132.6	25.1	14.6
1990**	44.6	150.5	28.4	27.1

* The overvalued exchange rates makes comparisons with GDP difficult, especially in 1958 and 1965.
[†] 1970 data refer to long-term public debt only. GNP used rather than GDP.
** Data refer to long-term public debt only. GNP used rather than GDP. Debt service payments include private as well as public debt payments.
Sources: 1911–38: CEI Volumes 2 and 12a, GDP data from van der Eng (1992); 1952 and 1958: Bank Indonesia *Annual Reports*; 1965: Panglaykim and Arndt (1966:5); 1970–90: World Bank, *World Debt Tables*, and *Indikator Ekonomi*, various issues.

and government borrowing again increased. By 1933, the budget deficit amounted to over 4 per cent of national income and debt servicing accounted for 21 per cent of total budgetary expenditure (Table 4.4). Although a decline in the size of the budget deficit, combined with accelerated economic growth after 1935, permitted some reduction in the size of the accumulated public debt relative to national income by the late 1930s, debt servicing still accounted for 11 per cent of export receipts in 1939.

Given the sophistication of the late colonial administrative apparatus, it is perhaps surprising that more effort was not made to reduce the public sector borrowing requirement by increasing government revenues, and particularly tax revenues, in the interwar years. In fact, these two decades did see a considerable change in the relative importance of tax and non-tax revenues, compared to the pre-1913 situation. Although the ratio of total revenues to national income did not alter much, the share of total revenues accounted for by taxes grew fairly steadily, and by 1939 accounted for 67 per cent of all revenues (Booth 1990: Table 10.9). This was mainly due to the growing importance of taxes on incomes (both personal and corporate), taxes on foreign trade and specific excises. This increase occurred in spite of the fact that prominent civil servants argued strongly in the early 1920s that, in Java at least, the people were already being taxed 'to the utmost limit', and that further increases in the burden of taxation would adversely affect indigenous welfare (Huender, as quoted in Penders 1977: 96).

There was an attempt to increase government revenues from taxes which would fall on upper income groups, rather than from the land tax or from other sources such as the government monopolies whose incidence was probably more regressive. But, in spite of the diversification in revenue sources which occurred after 1920, the tax burden on the indigenous population increased over these two decades, while at the same time powerful business interests objected to the growing burden of personal and corporate income tax, which they claimed adversely affected the international competitiveness of export industries, especially the agricultural estates. By the 1930s, it was considered out of the question to attempt to increase tax revenues by raising the rate of income tax, although with the improvement in the business climate after 1934 revenues rose with growing personal and corporate incomes.

The Indonesian tax structure exhibited the same broad changes in the first four decades of the twentieth century as those which occurred in other parts of Asia. The proportion of total government revenues accruing from land taxes fell, and the proportion accruing from taxes on foreign trade, on both personal and corporate incomes, and from specific excises, rose. Like most other countries in the region, Indonesia derived a large share of total revenues from non-tax sources, such as government monopolies and charges for publicly provided services, including utilities and education. Although their share of total government revenues fell over the last four decades of Dutch colonial rule, they still accounted for almost 37 per cent of the total in 1939 (Booth 1990: Table 10.9). Foreign trade taxes increased their share from under 10 per cent in 1913 to 25 per cent in 1936 (Table 4.5), although this proportion fell back again after the special export tax on exports of native rubber was abolished.

Table 4.5   Foreign trade taxes as a percentage of total government revenues and as a percentage of commodity exports and imports, 1900–90

Year	Foreign trade taxes as a percentage of:	
	Total government revenues*	Commodity export and import receipts[†]
1900	8.1	2.7
1910	8.5	2.3
1913	8.5	2.3
1920	9.4	1.9
1925	12.5	3.3
1929	14.1	4.2
1933	14.5	5.8
1936	25.1	11.7
1939	16.8	6.2
1951	57.8	82.3
1954	23.1	15.9
1958	36.4	55.6
1961	16.2	14.1
1965	5.6	81.9
1969–70	38.6 (28.3)	24.3 (20.0)**
1973–74	50.5 (29.9)	21.2 (13.1)
1980–81	68.0 (20.2)	33.9 (9.3)
1986–87	33.7 (6.7)	19.8 (4.4)
1990–91	40.9 (8.0)	21.2 (3.9)

* Figures in brackets show foreign trade taxes excluding the oil company tax as a percentage of total government revenues excluding the oil company tax.
[†] Figures in brackets show foreign trade taxes excluding the oil company tax as a percentage of non-oil exports and imports, converted at the prevailing exchange rates.
** Export and import data refer to calendar year 1969.
Sources: 1900–39: *Jaarcijfers* and *Indisch Verslag*, various issues; 1951–65: Bank Indonesia, *Annual Reports*, various issues; 1969/70–1990/91: Bank Indonesia, *Indonesian Financial Statistics*, various issues.

INFRASTRUCTURE DEVELOPMENT AND THE GROWTH OF STATE ENTERPRISES

Even before the Ethical Policy was announced in 1901, the colonial authorities had placed considerable emphasis on the development of infrastructure, and certainly considered its development too important to be left entirely to the private sector. Nowhere was this more obvious than in railway development. By 1940, there was over 5,400 kilometres of rail and tram track in Java, which meant that the island had an integrated rail network whose density compared favourably with many parts of Europe (Naval Intelligence Division 1944: 414). The construction of this network began in the 1860s when a concession was granted to a private company to construct a railway from Semarang to the sultanates of Yogyakarta and Surakarta to the south. During the latter part of the 1840s, the notion of a state-owned rail system in Java had vigorous advocates, but the Minister of Colonies was reluctant, and in the rather different climate of the 1860s, private enterprise was favoured. But although the line was considered to be immediately profitable, the government guaranteed a return of 4.5 per cent on the capital invested for thirty-three years, and, in fact, after twenty-five years the government had an option to buy the entire railway at an agreed price (Wellenstein 1909: 189; CEI Vol 9: 28). Even with this assistance, the private company granted the concession still had difficulty raising sufficient capital, and the line was only completed in 1872, by which time the government had been forced to offer further financial assistance in the form of interest-free loans.

At this time, few railways had been constructed in equatorial regions and the technical problems were more formidable than either the company or the government had at first realised. The private company involved in the first line also constructed a line from Jakarta to Bogor, but the reluctance of private capital to enter the field unassisted, combined with considerable pressure from planter interests to construct more lines in Java forced the government to assume complete responsibility for the construction of a line from Surabaya to Pasuruan. The line was, in fact, more profitable than the government had expected, and both government and private companies continued to invest in rail and steamtram development in Java, and to embark on projects in Aceh and North Sumatra. In 1889, government operations accounted for 65 per cent of all track in Java (including town tramways), and 38 per cent in Sumatra; these percentages were to fall only slightly in Java and to rise sharply in the Outer Islands in the early years of the twentieth century (CEI Vol 9, Table 13).

The great heyday of railway construction in Indonesia was the two decades up to 1914. In 1894 there were 1,600 kilometres of track in Java and 320 kilometres in Sumatra. By 1914, length of track in Java had almost trebled to 4,526 kilometres, while in Sumatra there were

980 kilometres of track (CEI Vol 9: 30). During the 1920s, another thousand kilometres of track were laid in Java and a further three hundred outside Java, including 47 kilometres in South Sulawesi. During the 1930s, there was a decline in length of track in Java as uneconomic lines were closed, but some expansion continued in Sumatra. But the ambitious plans outlined in the early 1920s to extend the rail network in Kalimantan, Sulawesi, and to Bali and Lombok were never realised (Fowler 1923: 51–2). Outside Java the motivations for railway development were mixed; the first railway in Sumatra was built in Aceh for use by the military during the Achinese War, and was only transferred to the government rail system in 1916. Government played a larger role in rail development outside Java than in Java, and by 1929 controlled 75 per cent of all track (CEI Vol 9, Table 13).

The state rail system was one of the largest enterprises to be placed under the control of the Department of State Enterprises which was established in 1908 to manage the railways, the post and telegraph system, and assorted salt mines, coal mines, tin mines and an opium factory (Houben 1994: 192–4). Although railways were viewed by the colonial government at least partly as a public good, they were expected to make a profit, and indeed, between 1908 and 1921, made larger profits than any other government enterprise except the Bangka Tin Mine. The Post and Telegraph Enterprise, by contrast, consistently made a loss (Houben 1994: 196). Other government-owned assets such as the ports, whose capacity was continuously expanded between 1890 and 1930, were not placed under the Department of State Enterprises but were managed by separate authorities. The larger ports of Jakarta and Surabaya had both floating and dry docks, some of which were run by the government and some by the private sector.

As with the railways, the development of electric power generation also depended heavily on government initiative. Until the second decade of the twentieth century, power for industry had been provided mainly by steam boilers. As the technology of hydro-electric power generation became more widely used, a special section of the Department of Public Works was established in 1917 to plan the development of power generation both in Java and in other parts of the country. The problem was that in Java, where the demand for electric power was highest, water resources were quite limited, whereas outside Java they were more abundant, but demand was quite restricted. The government responded with a characteristic blend of direct action and incentives to private enterprise within a tight regulatory framework. The broad policy was to 'reserve as much power as is necessary for general lighting, railways and other public services, and to place the surplus at the disposal of private enterprise...the larger sources for the generation of electric energy are mostly retained by the government, while the distribution is entrusted either to joint companies, in which the government works jointly with private capital, or to private companies or local authorities' (Naval Intelligence Division 1944: 281).

While the colonial government played a crucial role in the development of railways, ports and electric power generation, these enterprises were expected to generate income through user charges. By contrast, roads and irrigation were a direct charge on the government budget. Modern road development in Java began with the construction of the *Grote Postweg* (Great Post Road) in 1808. Although the main reason for the construction of a road from west to east across the island was military, economic considerations were also in the minds of both Daendals who initiated the project and Raffles who completed it. However, a road across the north coast of Java was 'of negligible economic significance' during the period of the *cultuurstelsel*, when the main need was for transport links into the interior (CEI Vol 9: 26). By the 1840s, the need for railways was being mooted, although as we have already seen, nothing was done until the 1860s, and then only with government assistance. Roads continued to be the principal means of transporting produce in Java until the last decade of the nineteenth century, by which time a network of over 20,000 kilometres had been constructed. Much of this was gravelled which meant that it was usable throughout the year. Regional roads were constructed and maintained under the supervision of the indigenous administration, usually with corvee labour, although the main highways were the responsibility of the central government. A third type of road was wholly maintained by private sector interests, mainly estates (Thieme 1909: 204–6).

The road network in Java did not, in fact, expand very rapidly between 1892 and the late 1930s, although the quality of the surfaces improved, and by 1938 there was more than 8,000 kilometres of asphalt road. Outside Java the growth over these decades was much faster, and by 1938 there were 42,000 kilometres of sealed road, compared with under 12,000 in 1892. But as with the rail network, road development outside Java was regionally fragmented, and, with the exception of Sumatra, integrated island-wide networks were never completed. Instead, the practice was to link roads to river transport, which was adequate for the purposes of transporting agricultural output to the coast but seldom overcame the natural barriers that divided districts and regions. Even in Sumatra, where by 1940 a continuous metal road did extend from Teluk Betung in the south to Banda Aceh in the north, a subsidiary network of feeder roads was never completed and many regions relied entirely on river transport or on rough tracks through the jungle for their links to the outside world.

The development of a modern road network with sealed surfaces in the early twentieth century inevitably led to the growth in numbers of motor vehicles, although up until 1940 the vehicle fleet was dominated by passenger cars and motorcycles. There can be little doubt that trucks transported only a small part of all freight traffic in those parts of the archipelago where there was a rail network, while in the more remote areas the lack of roads was a barrier to the use of motor transport for moving goods. Buses were of negligible significance compared with trains and trams as a means of moving people. An important reason for the very slow development of motorised freight and passenger transport during the inter-war years was a regulatory regime designed to protect the railways (Gotz 1939: 279–81). The financial situation of the state railways deteriorated sharply with the onset of the depression, and pressure to protect them from 'chaotic competition' culminated in a road traffic ordinance which stipulated that public motorbuses could only run with a government licence. Both routes and fares were carefully monitored to protect the railways. Although road freight traffic was not subject to general licensing restrictions, the Governor General was empowered to restrict road traffic on certain routes where its growth was causing the railways 'serious economic difficulties' (Gotz 1939: 281). This interventionist regime was to change only slowly in the post-independence era.

The development of both land and sea transport in colonial Indonesia was obviously determined in large part by the demands of the export economy, with defence against external interference an important secondary consideration. The motivations behind the considerable government investment in irrigation which occurred in the last five decades of Dutch colonial rule were rather different and more complex. The indigenous populations in many parts of Indonesia, especially in Java and Bali, had long practised irrigation as a means of providing assured water supplies to dry-season rice crops, and in some areas very sophisticated community organisations evolved for the operation and maintenance of village irrigation facilities. By the middle years of the nineteenth century, over half of all *sawah* in Java was 'irrigated' (according to the definitions of the day); in some residencies the irrigation ratio was, well over 65 per cent (Booth 1988: 74). The extent of irrigation was, in turn, a significant determinant of yields of *sawah* in different parts of the island.

Until the middle decades of the nineteenth century, there is little evidence that the colonial government felt under any obligation to concern itself with the provision or administration of irrigation infrastructure, and almost all the infrastructure in Java and Bali as well as in other parts of the archipelago were constructed and operated by the local communities. But after the establishment of the Department of Public Works in 1854, and the recruitment of some qualified engineers to staff it, more attention was given to the development of irrigation. Given the long history of water control and management in their homeland, it was hardly surprising that the Dutch authorities emphasised the role of 'scientific irrigation' in increasing both the area under rice (through double cropping) and yields per planted hectare. In 1885, an Irrigation Brigade was established within the Corps of Engineers, and work commenced on the systematic application of modern engineering techniques to the control and supply of water in Java.

By 1914, almost 600,000 hectares were under 'permanent irrigation' in Java, and by 1930 this had increased to over one million hectares. By 1937, it was estimated that, of the 3.4 million hectares of *sawah* in Java, 1.25 million were 'technically' irrigated and a further 0.9 million 'semi-technically' irrigated (Metzelaar 1946: 204). But although these increases looked impressive, in fact only about 2.3 per cent of total government expenditures was devoted to irrigation construction and maintenance in 1913, and the proportion fell thereafter (van der Eng 1993: Table A8.2; CEI, Vol 2, Table 4). Irrigation development never managed to capture as large a share of budgetary resources as rail development, in spite of the great emphasis which it received in Ethical Policy pronouncements. An important reason for the larger share of resources going to rail development was that railways were seen as profit-making concerns, while irrigation development generated no revenue, because of official reluctance to impose a water charge (van der Eng 1993: 60–1). Outside Java far less government money was spent on irrigation development than on Java (van der Meulen 1940: 149). By far the most important government project in Sumatra was in the Way Sekampung transmigration site in Central Lampung where almost 43,000 hectares were under permanent irrigation works by 1940. The largest project in Sulawesi was on the Sadang river north of Pare Pare where 64,000 hectares were irrigated. Elsewhere little was done by government to develop irrigation, although there were almost certainly many successful systems in operation which were constructed and maintained by local people. Very little information is available on the extent of these systems at the end of the colonial period, and apart from the *subak* in Bali, little is known about their operations.

The substantial government investment which took place in Indonesia in the nineteenth and early twentieth centuries in railways, roads, irrigation and electric power generation facilities meant that the government was heavily involved not just in initial construction, but also in operation and maintenance. Even outside Java, where infrastructure development was more the result of a series of piecemeal responses to the requirements of the export economy, rather than any 'ethical' considerations about improving popular welfare, much of the response came from the public sector, rather than from private initiative. In this, Indonesia was probably not very different from many other tropical colonies. But the heavy government involvement in infrastructure development in the colonial era in Indonesia had an important consequence. If the power of the government, and especially the central government, were to become weaker, much of the infrastructure would inevitably fall into disrepair. This indeed is what happened after 1942.

THE RISE OF 'WELFARE INTERVENTIONISM': 1900–42

Several students of the late colonial history of Indonesia have used the Dutch term *beamtenstaat*, or administrative state, to describe the system of government which evolved in Indonesia over the last decades of colonial rule. The essence of this system was its emphasis on law and order, and political demobilisation (McVey, 1982; Anderson, 1983). It was hardly a system unique to Dutch colonial territories. Benda (1966: 238) argued that

> colonial governments are almost without exception *Beamtenstaaten,* apolitical, administrative polities par excellence. The maintenance of peace and order being the *summum bonum* of what . . . could be called a nightwatchman state, colonial policy is above all an instrument for the implementation, not of competing social demands but of 'sound administration' per se.

And yet colonial Indonesia, at least in the twentieth century, was far more than just a nightwatchman state, concerned purely with law and order and the collection of taxes. Benda (1966: 238–9) has argued that the last four decades of Dutch rule were 'seemingly dominated by the constant theme of reform', and speaks of the 'enthusiastic emphasis on rapid modernisation of colonial, but especially indigenous, society' which characterised the ethical policy. That this policy led to considerable growth in the size of the administrative apparatus, and a rapid proliferation in its functions has been widely noted. Vandenbosch (1941: 171–2) points out that the total size of the government establishment increased from 154,000 to 212,000 between 1917 and 1928; almost all this increase was accounted for by indigenous Indonesians. Sartono (1984: 122–3) has stressed the importance of civil service employment for Indonesian graduates of the Dutch-language school system after 1920, and the frustration felt by those who were not able to find public sector employment.

The growing emphasis on development policies was reflected in the growth of specialist services charged with implementing road and rail development, irrigation expansion, agricultural extension, rural credit, indigenous education, public health and land settlement outside Java (Boomgaard 1986). In both size and prestige, these services began to eclipse the traditional administrative service and assume the role of a 'developmental technocracy', similar in functions to those which have proliferated at both national and regional levels since the second world war. Van Doorn (1994: 118–19) estimates that, from 1878 to 1928, the number of engineers working in the Indies grew from under 100 to 1300. Around 30 per cent of all engineers trained in Delft, the leading technical university in the Netherlands, found employment in the colony. Compared with the Netherlands, a much higher proportion of those working in the Indies were in government service; in 1930 almost half of all electrical engineers, 71 per cent of agricultural engineers and 75 per cent of civil engineers were employed by government agencies (van Doorn 1994: 164).

But the changing role of government in the colonial economy in the four decades up to 1942 was manifested not just in the growth of government expenditure on a range of development activities. There was also increasing intervention on the part of the government in the economy to attain objectives which would not have been achieved had product and factor markets been left to the vagaries of national and international trends. In this aspect of their behaviour, the last generation of colonial civil servants foreshadowed many of the policies which would be enthusiastically adopted by newly industrialising countries in many parts of the world after 1945. A major preoccupation was the stabilisation of markets for basic commodities, especially in times of international shortages. From 1911 onwards, the government was concerned about ensuring stable rice supplies and, in April 1918, the government took over the entire rice import trade (Creutzberg 1974: xxxii). The immediate concern was the shortage induced by poor harvests in many parts of Asia and severely disrupted shipping services as a result of the hostilities in Europe. As a consequence, the government became heavily involved in domestic food procurement and storage, and indeed in regulating international shipping.

After 1921, many of the emergency measures were withdrawn, but the onset of the depression threw up a new and even greater set of problems. Boeke (1953: Chapter 23) discusses in detail the regulation of rice exports necessitated by shrinking world markets, and the growth of government intervention in markets for basic foodstuffs, especially rice. Government intervention was not just confined to basic foods; in the 1930s the colonial government joined in a number of international commodity stabilisation programmes and attempted, with varying degress of success, to regulate output of rubber, tea and tin (van Gelderen 1939). The motivations for these interventions were mixed, although there is little evidence that it was due to any concern on the part of the colonial bureaucracy to 'protect peasants from capitalism' (Alexander and Alexander 1991). Rather, the intention of the regulation of domestic markets was to protect farm incomes from fluctuations in prices of food and cash crops on world markets. Inevitably, this meant that goals of domestic self-sufficiency became prominent.

If the extent of intervention in agricultural markets signified a considerable departure from previous colonial policy, the trend was even more marked in the case of industrial production. The industrial branch of the Department of Economic Affairs was established in the early 1930s with an explicit mandate for promoting those industries which would use labour-intensive techniques to supply basic needs to the population. It was, according to Boeke (1953: 285), 'especially responsible for the introduction of relatively simple improvements in technique, for better organisation of the procurement of raw materials, for arranging the connection of such enterprises with central establishments that are better equipped to handle the technically more difficult processes and are in a better position to standardise and finish off the product, and for the regulation of sale'. Government intervention yielded variable results. Boeke (1953) and Palmer (1972: Chapter 2) give considerable detail on attempts to improve technology and efficiency in the textile sector where the main aim of government policy was to encourage the adoption of the improved hand-loom. Attempts to regulate production were frustrated by the sheer number of establishments, although the government persisted in its attempts right up to 1942. The government's concern about 'cut-throat' competition extended to the cigarette industry where it was on the one hand concerned with the battle for market share between the modern white cigarette industry and the traditional hand-made industry, and on the other hand determined to regulate ouput within the traditional sector. In fact, in 1937 a general Regulation Board was established which was concerned with the planning and regulation of industrial activity across the entire range of industrial activity.

Placed in a broader historical perspective, the growth of government regulation in the 1930s can be seen as one phase in the continuing cycle of deregulation and intervention, *dirigisme* and *laissez faire*, which has characterised Indonesia over the last two centuries. A North American economist, writing some thirty years after the events of the 1930s, argued that an important effect of the 1930s depression was 'a shift from a relatively free to a highly regulated economy' (Higgins 1968: 693). But the 'relatively free' economy was itself very much a creation of the Dutch colonial system after the gradual retreat from the *dirigisme* of the years from 1830 to 1870. As Fasseur (1991: 49–50) argued, the 'aversion to a system of government intervention in economic activities' in Dutch government circles was an important reason for the gradual demise of the Cultivation System after 1870. Similarly, the publicity given to the growing gap in living standards between an increasingly prosperous bourgeois society in the Netherlands and a poor agrarian society in Indonesia led to the inauguration of the ethical policy after 1900, and with it the growth of 'welfare interventionism'. But to some observers these interventions smacked of 'administrative tyranny' (Bousquet 1940: 51). This perceptive French observer pointed out that:

In India officialdom concerns itself with as little as possible with the personal affairs of the natives; in the Indies it meddles in everything. The French administration in North Africa stands between these two, but it definitely has more in common with the liberal spirit of the British ... The Dutch administration considers the native to be a child and meddles with the pettiest trifles in native life.

THE COLONIAL FISCAL SYSTEM IN INTERNATIONAL PERSPECTIVE

An influential argument in the literature of colonial economic development is that government expenditures were primarily determined by revenues which in turn, in an underdeveloped open economy, were largely a function of export earnings. According to this view, to the extent that colonial governments were interested in providing infrastructure at all, such provision was directed entirely to the export sector. Thus models have been developed (e.g. Birnberg and Resnick 1975) where export earnings are seen as a function of government expenditure and, in turn, generate revenues, mainly through trade taxes. These revenues, in turn, generate further government expenditures leading to further exports and so on. A major implication of this model is that revenue and expenditures will be closely correlated with exports, although the 'best fit' may involve some lags.

When a partial adjustment model of the type used by Leff (1982: 119–21) on Brazilian data is applied to the Indonesian data for 1840 to 1913, the short and long-run elasticities of both revenue and expenditure growth with respect to exports are found to be rather lower than in the case of Brazil in the nineteenth century (Table 4.6). This suggests that factors other than export fluctuations were important in determining trends in both government revenues and expenditures. It would appear that both were considerably influenced by the deliberate actions of government, taken in response to changing national priorities. One such change occurred after 1870, when the Cultivation System was gradually abandoned in favour of more liberal economic policies, and it was no longer necessary to devote such a substantial proportion of government expenditure to the extraction and sale of products. A further reorientation of priorities occurred at the same time because of the outbreak of the war in Aceh, which led to more spending on the military. And with the inauguration of the ethical policy at the beginning of the twentieth century, the government embarked on an ambitious programme of public investment. While the increases in public expenditure which occurred in the first decade of this century were no doubt facilitated by buoyant export earnings, they were not determined solely by them. But, as we have seen, a much more conservative approach to fiscal policy was adopted in the 1920s, and expenditures were cut back with falling export receipts. Thus, for the five decades from 1890 to 1940, the long-run elasticities of both revenue and expenditure with respect to exports were close to unity, and indeed remarkably similar to those for other colonies during the same years.

Table 4.6   Elasticities of government revenues and expenditures with respect to export earnings: Indonesia and selected comparisons

Country	Years	Revenue elasticities*			Expenditure elasticities*		
		SR	LR	Lag†	SR	LR	Lag†
Brazil	1823–1913	0.32	1.08	2.41	0.37	1.04	1.82
Indonesia	1840–1913	0.27	0.52	0.92	0.14	0.64	3.46
Ceylon	1895–1938	0.16	0.97	5.09	0.13	1.07	7.21
Egypt	1889–1937	0.18	1.13	5.19	0.36	1.12	2.09
India	1888–1936	0.08	0.76	8.13	0.06	1.15	12.64
Indonesia	1890–1939	0.26	0.89	2.45	0.18	0.93	4.20
Jamaica	1884–1938	0.35	1.13	2.20	0.23	1.18	4.21
Philippines	1902–38	0.29	0.85	1.92	0.25	0.90	2.56
Thailand	1892–1938	0.14	0.82	4.75	0.15	0.90	5.04

*Following Leff (1982: 119–21), a partial adjustment model was fitted to the data. In cases where autocorrelation was detected, an appropriate autoregressive model was fitted using an iterative least squares procedure. *SR* = short run; *LR* = long run.
† Mean adjustment lag in years.
Sources: Indonesia: CEI, Vol 2, Tables 1 and 2: CEI, Vol 12a; Brazil: Leff (1982: 120–1). Other countries: Birnberg and Resnick (1975), Appendices.

International comparisons also indicate that, at the end of the colonial era, a rather low proportion of total government revenues in Indonesia were derived from taxes on foreign trade, and the rather high proportion derived from taxes on personal and corporate incomes. By the end of the 1930s, the proportion of total government revenues derived from foreign trade taxes was lower than in India, although Indonesia was much the more open economy. It was also much lower than in Burma, Thailand or Egypt. On the other hand, Indonesia was deriving a higher proportion of its total revenue from income taxes than most other Asian countries, higher even than Japan in the first decade of the century (Booth 1990, Table 10.9).

It was pointed out above that per capita government expenditures in Indonesia were lower for much of the nineteenth century than in India, and much lower than in other dependent British colonies (Table 4.3). In 1895, per capita public expenditures were higher in Indonesia than in Thailand, but slightly lower than in India or in Japan (Table 4.7). In the first decade of the twentieth century, per capita expenditure in Indonesia remained low relative to India, to Thailand, and to Japan. But after 1910, per capita expenditure grew more rapidly than in India and Thailand, so that by 1920 it was considerably higher than in either of these countries, although still lower than in Japan. It remained higher than in Thailand up to 1940 but, during the 1930s, per capita public expenditures in Indonesia fell more sharply than in British India, and by 1940 were considerably below them. Fiscal policy is generally considered to have been conservative in both British India and Thailand. The Thai government was advised by British financial advisers who advocated balanced budgets and fiscal prudence, while British India never attempted the kinds of 'welfare policies' which gained official support in Indonesia after 1900. But the rhetoric of the ethical policy was slow to be translated into fiscal practice, and when public expenditures did grow rapidly after 1910, and outstripped growth in revenues, the colonial authorities were soon induced to apply the fiscal brakes. These brakes stayed on for much of the period from 1920 to 1940.

Table 4.7   Average per capita government expenditures (US$)

Year*	Indonesia	India	Thailand	Japan
1895	3.54	4.75	2.01	4.00
1900	3.49	4.66	3.05	6.47
1905	3.62	5.34	5.29	12.93
1910	4.53	5.49	7.81	11.45
1915	6.62	5.97	7.81	11.45
1920	14.98	10.43	10.16	28.03
1925	11.56	9.10	10.65	37.59
1930	11.85	9.27	8.65	44.60
1935	7.23	10.05	5.14	126.31
1975†	43.90	19.14	66.45	691.89

*Five-year moving averages centred on the year shown, except for India in 1975, where the data refer to 1974–6.
† Data refer to total expenditure, excluding lending less repayments (line CII in the source document).
Sources: 1895–1935: Indonesia: CEI, Volume 2, Table 4, line 13; Table 3, line 9; India: Reddy (1972: 186–9); Thailand: Ingram (1971; 328–30); Japan: Ohkawa and Shinohara (1979: 370 ff). 1975: International Monetary Fund, *Government Finance Statistics Yearbook* Volume IV, 1980; International Monetary Fund, *International Financial Statistics Yearbook*, 1979.

A further comparative issue which has attracted the attention of several scholars concerns the relative size of the colonial administrative establishment in different colonies. Maddison (1989: Table 11) has shown that metropolitan nationals and other 'Europeans' (a term the Dutch used to include non-Dutch nationals from Europe and Japan, although not from China, South Asia and the Middle East), amounted to about 0.4 per cent of the population in 1930. This was a considerably larger percentage than that found in British India, French Indochina or the American Philippines, although smaller than in Malaya (including Singapore) and much smaller than the Japanese presence in Korea and Taiwan. About 25 per cent of those Europeans who were economically active in 1930 were in government service, including the armed forces, while the rest were in various professional, business and commercial occupations. Polak (CEI Vol 5: Table 10.1) shows that in 1932 about 9.2 per cent of the civil service (some 19,000 officers out of almost 210,000) were European. This was certainly a much higher proportion than, for example, in British India, where Indian officers rose to even the most senior echelons of the civil service and the judiciary in the inter-war period. Vandenbosch (1944: 173) claimed that by the 1930s 'in relation to the population served the Netherlands at present imports four times as many persons for the East Indian service as the United States does in the Philippines'. As was noted above, this larger bureaucratic presence led to the perception that there was a greater degree of government regulation in the Indonesian economy than was considered either feasible or necessary in other Asian colonies.

It is important to remember that this impression was not the result of the ethical policy *per se*, but of more than a century of intensive government involvement in the colonial economy, especially in Java. The policy objectives of government involvement altered over time, with emphasis shifting between the raising of revenues, the maintenance of law and order, the regulation of production and trade, and investment in both infrastructure and directly productive activities. As we have seen, this involvement was not reflected in much higher levels of public expenditures per capita compared to other parts of Asia. Rather, it led to a greater degree of government 'presence' in the form of official intrusion into people's workplaces and homes. This was to be an important legacy of the Dutch colonial period to the independent economy.

REVENUE AND EXPENDITURE POLICY: 1950–65

When we turn to examine the role of the government in the economy in the years from 1950 to 1965, we are immediately confronted with a paradox. On the one hand, as was the case in most of the newly independent Asian countries in the 1950s, the leaders of the Indonesian independence movement were greatly influenced by European socialist thought, including its Marxist-Leninist derivatives, in formulating policies for economic development. Reviewing developments in the last phase of the Guided Economy era, Castles (1965: 13) argued that 'rejection of capitalism and espousal of socialism as the preferred pattern of economic organisation has been an almost universal element in Indonesian political thinking since independence'. But, in spite of this pronounced ideological inclination to the left, the entire period from 1950 to 1965 can be viewed as one of gradual attenuation of government control of the economy. We have seen that the interwar years witnessed a considerable growth in the role of government in the colonial economy. This was most obvious in the rising ratio of government expenditures to national income; in addition, bureaucratic regulation of production became widespread. The government of the newly independent nation was not committed to any diminution of the economic role of the state. On the contrary, it had a long list of sectoral plans which it wanted to carry forward as rapidly as possible, in agriculture, transport, irrigation, health and education (de Meel 1950). By the mid-1950s, it embarked on a more ambitious five year plan. But all these plans were only partially implemented, usually through lack of funds. In fact, the 1950s and early 1960s witnessed a gradual decline in the ratios of government revenue and expenditure to GDP. By the early 1960s, the ratio of government expenditures to GDP was almost certainly lower than that attained in the last decade of the colonial era (Figure 4.1).

Why was a newly independent nation, apparently committed to planned economic development, if not on the Russian model at least along Indian lines, incapable of increasing the share of government expenditure in national income? (In India, by contrast, the share of government expenditures in national income more than doubled in the first fifteen years of independence). Yet another paradox arises when we look at the data on the government deficit. Almost all students of the Indonesian economy in the years between 1950 and 1965 claim that it was persistent government deficits which fuelled the almost continual inflation which by the mid-1960s had reached the point where consumer prices were more than doubling annually (Sundrum 1973: 77). But, in fact, these deficits never exceeded 7 per cent of GDP, which meant that they were not much larger, relative to national income, than in the early 1930s (Figure 4.2). And yet the 1930s were characterised by deflation rather than inflation. Why was the effect of budget deficits on monetary stability so dramatically different in the immediate post-independence period from the inter-war years?

In order to answer these questions, we must begin with an investigation of revenue policy, as it was the failure of revenue policy which was ultimately responsible for the failure of fiscal policy over these years. By the end of the colonial period, tax revenues accounted for about 60 per cent of total government revenues, the rest comprising revenues from government monopolies and utilities. About one third of all tax revenues accrued from personal and corporate income taxes, and a further one third from import and export taxes, the remainder comprising land and property taxes and excises (Booth 1980, Tables 1 and 2). In short, it was a fairly diversified revenue system, with total government revenues amounting to about 12 per cent of national income. In the immediate post-independence era, it appeared that the aim of government was to build on the colonial foundation, by further strengthening and diversifying the revenue system. A general sales tax was introduced in 1950, and officials of the Ministry of Finance were sent abroad for training in tax administration (Cnossen 1971: Chapter 1).

As it turned out, in the early 1950s the ratio of revenue to GDP was rather higher than in the late 1930s, but this was mainly because of the surge in foreign trade taxes, due to the Korean War boom. The structure of revenues had changed considerably, with foreign trade taxes assuming a dominant role (Table 4.5). Foreign trade taxes were, in turn, a mixture of 'orthodox' export and import taxes, and revenues from the so-called 'inducement certificates', and import surcharges which in the early 1950s actually exceeded revenues from trade taxes. Corden and Mackie (1962: 39 ff) have described the working of these certificates and surcharges in detail; in effect, they amounted to a subsidy to exporters (in the sense that they allowed exporters to convert their export earnings into rupiah at a more favourable rate than the official one) while at the same time imposing an even greater tax on importers. The difference between the payment to exporters and the tax on importers accrued to the government budget.

With the collapse of the Korean War boom and the subsequent slump in export prices, revenues from trade taxes and other levies on trade fell, both as a percentage of total revenues, and also as a percentage of total export and import earnings (Table 4.5). In 1952–53, much of the fall in revenues from trade was made up through higher earnings from non-trade taxes, and other income including mining concessions, and revenues from government enterprises. But with the advent of the first Ali Sastroamidjojo cabinet in 1953, fiscal discipline deteriorated. Both trade and non-trade revenues fell as a proportion of GDP, so that total revenues were less than 10 per cent of GDP by 1955. Expenditures fell also but not as rapidly, so that by 1954 the deficit was twice as high relative to GDP as in 1951 (Figure 4.2). Inflation gathered pace, the balance of payments deteriorated and quantitative restrictions on imports proliferated. When Sumitro returned as Finance Minister in the Harahap cabinet, a number of measures were adopted to increase the supply of imports and to curb the growth in the money supply, including the complete dismantling of the 'regulatory gadgets' of the previous government, and a steep rise in import surcharges (Corden and Mackie 1962: 48; Pitt 1991: 49–52). This led to an increase in the ratio of revenues from trade to import and export earnings (Table 4.5), although the impact on the ratio of total revenues to GDP was muted by a decline in non-trade revenues. But this liberalisation episode was brought to an abrupt end by the relatively poor showing in the 1955 election of the parties that made up the Harahap coalition cabinet. The new cabinet, headed again by Ali Sastroamidjojo, had little commitment to ongoing economic reform until forced into action by the deteriorating foreign exchange position.

Further changes to the already complex system of trade taxes and inducement certificates in 1957 led to a considerable jump in the ratio of trade revenues to import and export receipts, although the ratio of total government revenues to GDP remained fairly constant until 1960. The sharp jump in the ratio of revenues to GDP in 1960 and 1961 was not due to intensification of taxes and other levies on foreign trade; in fact, these revenues declined relative to GDP (and also as a percentage of import and export earnings). Rather, the improved revenue performance was due to higher receipts from domestic taxes on the one hand (income and sales taxes and excises) and higher revenues from sources such as the 'excess profits' levy on the petroleum companies on the other. As a result of these efforts, the ratio of total revenues to GDP was by 1960 back to the level attained in 1953.

But the improved revenue performance of 1960–61 was not maintained, and 1962 witnessed a dramatic collapse in revenues, from 13.2 to 5.5 per cent of GDP. Most commentators have attributed this collapse to the steep decline in the value of recorded exports which occurred 'partly because of an adverse trend in world prices of rubber and other Indonesian export products and partly because of declining exportable surpluses and diversion of exports into unrecorded trade' (Sundrum 1973: 75). But, in fact, even the exports and imports which were recorded in the trade figures, and were thus presumably available to the government to tax were, in fact, being less intensively taxed in 1961–62 than at any time since 1954 (Table 4.5). There were two main reasons for this; on the one hand the rate of export tax was reduced in 1960 as part of a package of measures designed to improve producer incentives, and appease the rebellious Outer Islands, while on the other hand most recorded imports were in the 'necessity' category which attracted low or zero duties. It seems more likely that the reason for the decline in revenues in 1962 was the marked jump in inflation in that year. Prices tripled between 1961 and 1962, and given the lags in revenue collection, this ensured that the real value of revenues would decline (Hicks 1966: 215).

It is noteworthy that expenditures also declined as a proportion of GDP in 1962, and, in fact, the deficit as a percentage of GDP fell to less than 4 per cent of GDP (Figure 4.2). Indeed, following the argument put forward by Sundrum (1973), it is clear that given the ratio of government revenue to GDP, it was impossible for the ratio of expenditure to GDP to have been more than about 5 percentage points above this ratio. This is because there is a limit to the amount of real resources which a government can procure through the 'inflationary tax'.

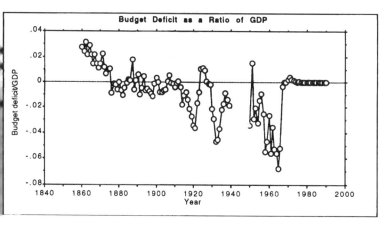

Figure 4.2 *Sources*: Government deficit up to 1939: CEI, Vol. 3, Table 3 and 4: after 1950: Bank Indonesia *Annual Reports*, various issues. Nominal GDP data up to 1939 from Pierre van der Eng; after 1950 from United Nations (1960); Nugroho (1967: 537–42); Central Bureau of Statistics (1970) and *Statistical Yearbook of Indonesia*, various issues.

In order to secure a given volume of goods and services, the increase in money supply had to cover, not merely their value at the previously prevailing prices, but also the increase in prices resulting from the expansion in money supply. (In effect, the resources which the government was no longer able to obtain from the public through taxation, it now tried to bid away from them by offering higher prices.) Moreover, as prices rose, confidence in the stability of the currency declined; rising price expectations raised the velocity of circulation, so that prices began to rise faster than money supply. Thus to secure a given percentage increase in its share of GDP through budget deficit finance, government needed to increase the money supply by a substantially larger percentage (Sundrum 1973: 75).

As Sundrum demonstrates, for an elasticity of income velocity with respect to prices of about 0.35, the limit to the amount of GDP which governments can procure through inflation is about 5 per cent, which suggests that in the years from 1961 to 1966 the inflation tax instrument in Indonesia was being used to its limit. However, the continued reliance on this means of raising revenue entailed ever-increasing inflation, which in turn meant that the performance of conventional taxes continued to deteriorate, not just because of assessment lags, but also because civil service incomes failed to keep up with prices which in turn meant that taxation officials were demoralised and easily corrupted. By 1962, the government was caught in a vicious spiral of inflation leading to poor revenue performance leading to deficits leading to further inflation from which it seemed impossible to break free.

Given that expenditures were effectively constrained to about 10 per cent of GDP from 1962 onwards, and given that GDP was itself growing very slowly, real government expenditures actually declined over these years. Their composition reflected the extremely high priority accorded defence; given that expenditures on more 'developmental' activities such as agricultural extension and public works were a residual after allowing for expenditures on defence and general administration, it is not surprising that they accounted for more than 20 per cent of total expenditures in only one year, 1963 (Bank Indonesia 1968: 30–5). Defence expenditures fell in this year because the Irian campaign had been concluded and the Malaysian campaign had only just begun; by 1965, they again comprised more than 40 per cent of the total. Indeed, in the entire period from 1950 to 1965, defence expenditures never dropped below 20 per cent of total govern-ment expenditures, and were frequently much more. Expenditures on public works, education and health, by contrast, never reached 20 per cent of the total at any time in the 1950s. This situation can be contrasted with the second decade of the twentieth century when over 40 per cent of total government expenditures were devoted to public works, health and education (Table 4.2).

Almost all commentators on the Indonesian economy in the 1950s and early 1960s stressed the failure of successive governments to allocate funds to investment projects. In the late 1950s, Indonesia ranked lowest among major Asian countries in terms of the ratio of government investment to GNP, and in terms of the percentage share of government in total investment (Table 4.8). Although other coun-tries, such as Burma, Pakistan and Thailand were devoting an even higher proportion of total government expenditures to defence than Indonesia, they also managed to spend more on economic services and infrastructure, both as a proportion of GDP and as a proportion of the total budget (Anspach 1960: 41). In the early 1950s, Sumitro (1953: 7–8) pointed out that a minimum programme of capital works was so important that, if necessary, it should be financed by deficit spending, although he admitted that because of prior commitments to

Table 4.8 ECAFE countries: government investment* in the late 1950s

Country	Government investment as % of GNP, 1957	Share of government in total investment, 1957–59
China	13.6	(100)
Japan	10.2	38
Burma	9.5	47
Taiwan	9.5	71
South Korea	8.9	69
Ceylon	7.3	62
India	7.1	69
Pakistan	5.2	58
Thailand	4.7	24
Malaya	3.3	49
Philippines	2.6	28
Indonesia[†]	2.6	24

*See sources for full details of data used and adjustments made.
[†]Indonesian data adjusted using data from United Nations (1964: 211).
Sources: *Economic Survey of Asia and the Far East* (1960: 71); *Economic Survey of Asia and the Far East* (1961: 36).

routine expenditure, it might prove difficult in the 1953 fiscal year to allocate adequate funds to priority capital works. 'One may hope for a 1954 capital budget that will consist entirely of priority items within a balanced development-plan'. This goal was to elude both Sumitro and subsequent policymakers right up to 1965. We examine the reasons for this failure in Indonesia in the 1950s and early 1960s in later parts of this chapter. But first we look at the stabilisation policies implemented between 1950 and 1965, and the reasons for their failure.

THE FAILURE OF STABILISATION POLICIES: 1950–65

When one studies the voluminous literature on fiscal, monetary and trade policy in Indonesia in the 1950s from the perspective of the 1990s, one must wonder why a succession of governments, some of them quite sophisticated in terms of their economic expertise, continued to rely on a highly complex system of multiple exchange rates which was patently impossible to administer honestly and efficiently, and which, in effect, discriminated against exporters. Why did the government not move swiftly to devalue and unify the exchange rate in the wake of the Korean War boom in the early 1950s? In fact, there were two formal devaluations, in 1952 and again in 1959, but neither was successful in solving the country's fundamental imbalance in its foreign payments. The official and black market rates of the rupiah continued to diverge, and smuggling became endemic. One approach is to explain the persistence of successive governments with an apparently unworkable system in terms of models of rent-collecting; although the economy as a whole suffered from the policies pursued, powerful vested interests gained in terms of their access to licences, bank loans and so on, and it was obviously in their interests to maintain a system which conferred on them considerable private wealth.

But given the continual changes in governments and the constantly shifting power alignments in Indonesia, at least up to 1958, this explanation appears less plausible than, for example, in a country such as India where the Congress Party was perpetually in power, producing a stable and well-entrenched set of interests to which the ruling party became increasingly beholden. Indeed, several Indonesian cabinets did try to reform the situation; we have already referred to Sumitro's attempts during his two spells as Minister of Finance to restore order to the public finances, and remove the controls over imports which were leading to blatant abuse. Even after the demise of parliamentary democracy, repeated attempts were made to tackle the twin problems of the budget deficit and inflation; there was the devaluation and monetary purge of 1959, the rationalisation of export and import taxes and surcharges in 1960, and the so-called Economic Declaration (*Dekon*) and subsequent measures of early 1963. Why were all these attempts by government to put the economy on a stable growth path ultimately unsuccessful?

Let us begin by addressing the issue of the multiple exchange rate. In the early 1950s, multiple exchange rate regimes in one form or another were widespread in many parts of the world, and indeed even IMF officials conceded that there were conditions where they could be advantageous, particularly if import demand and export supply were inelastic, and if poor standards of public administration ruled out more sophisticated tax instruments (Bernstein 1953). In the Indonesian context, informed opinion in the early 1950s was clearly on the side of multiple rates. Higgins (1953) argued that the conditions set out by Bernstein did, in fact, apply in Indonesia, which could benefit considerably from a multiple exchange rate regime, and especially one implemented through a system of import surcharges. Higgins argued against the alternative of devaluation on several grounds: a devaluation sufficient to restore equilibrium to the balance of payments would lead to a considerable increase in the price of basic necessities, and while at the same time it would bring large windfall profits to exporters, and such profits would not induce much extra output, at least in the short run. Further, Higgins argued, the effects of a devaluation would probably be rapidly eroded, particularly as trade unions would immediately demand wage increases. Higgins was mindful of the fact that the devaluation of 1952 had not suppressed the black market for the rupiah, and a further devaluation after little more than a year would probably be no more successful. He concluded his paper with the assertion that

the present system of import surcharges is advantageous for Indonesia. The system contributes to improvement of both the budget balance and the balance of payments. It does not appear to be very harmful to other countries. Devaluation, or a free exchange market, on the other hand, might lead to runaway inflation and collapse of the rupiah; at best it would probably bring a deterioration of the terms of trade (Higgins 1953: 235–6).

Subsequent studies published in the latter part of the 1950s did not dissent from this judgement. Corden and Mackie (1962: 59) ended their review of the Indonesian exchange rate regime with the following objection to the 'chase after the equilibrium rate of exchange':

> free trade (with or without freedom of capital movements and profit remittances) is in no sense an optimum in the conditions of Indonesia, especially when there is little likelihood that there are serious fiscal alternatives to taxes on trade.

Of course these authors were mindful of the objections which could be raised against the system operating in Indonesia, but in the prevailing conditions in both the domestic and the international economy they could see little alternative. They stressed the futility of considering exchange rate reform in isolation from the other problems besetting the economy, of which the budget deficit and inflation were obviously the most serious. From the early 1950s onwards, it was obvious to informed observers that it was not the budget deficit *per se* which caused inflation but the way in which it was financed. In his 1953 discussion of fiscal and monetary policy, Sumitro had stressed that, while in the short run the deficit could be financed in a non-inflationary manner by drawing down foreign exchange reserves (which were still substantial as a result of the Korean War boom), and soaking up the increase in domestic purchasing power through increased imports, in the longer run both budgetary and balance of payments deficits would have to be eliminated, or at least brought into line with the economy's ability to borrow abroad and service the resulting debt. Of course the domestic money supply could be allowed to expand, but such expansion would only be consistent with stable prices in an environment of rapid economic growth leading to growing demand for cash balances on the part of private individuals and corporate bodies. Such rapid growth, in turn, required accelerated investment by both the public and private sectors. Thus, Sumitro insisted that deficit finance be used only for purposes of investment in projects which would, in turn, lead to a prompt increase in the supply of consumer goods, especially food (Sumitro 1953: 18).

In the early 1950s, and again in 1956, the foreign sector did play a significant role in reducing the growth in the money supply by offsetting the expansionary impact of the government sector. But after 1960 its deflationary impact was insignificant in comparison to that of government (Nugroho 1967: 477). In addition, the inflationary impact of the growth in the money supply was offset to some extent in the

1950s by declining velocity of circulation (Thomas and Drysdale 1964: 546–7; Sundrum 1973: 78). Whether this decline was due to a 'widespread and increasing tendency to hoard cash, induced primarily by increasing political uncertainty' as Thomas and Drysdale claim, or by structural change and growing monetisation, as Sundrum suggests, there can be little doubt that it did counteract the inflationary impact of continued budget deficits. But after 1960 income velocity increased rapidly as a result of increasing expectations on the part of the public that inflation would continue.

In the face of the growth in money supply due to the public sector on the one hand, and falling demand for money on the other, there was little that conventional monetary policy could achieve. In his discussion of the 'monetary purge' of 1959, which involved the devaluation of all 500 and 1,000 rupiah notes to 10 per cent of their value and the freezing of bank deposits above Rp 25,000, Anspach (1960: 15) argued that

> conventional tight money measures (higher interest rates, increase of bank reserves), are not effective in Indonesia because of the lack of a well-organised money market. Direct restrictions to bank credit apply to too small a part of the stock of money – and in any case enforcement is difficult because of lack of trained personnel. Once-over tight money policies used by previous cabinets have for various reasons been foreclosed to this government. For example importers prepayments were already 100% .... Flooding the market with imported goods paid for out of foreign exchange reserves was out of the question because of the deterioration of the exchange reserves and because no dramatic improvement in the terms of trade appeared as deus ex machina – as was true with rubber prices in the case of the Harahap cabinet.

Other commentators have also stressed the gradual reduction in policy tools available to the government, so that, by the end of the 1950s, 'sledgehammer blows have become increasingly necessary' in place of the fine tuning of economic regulators which was possible in the earlier part of the decade (Mackie 1964: 55). The 1959 measures, blunt though they were, did slow down money supply growth in that year, while the serious attempt to prune expenditures and increase taxes over the following few months actually resulted in the government sector having a contractionary impact on money supply in 1960 (Nugroho 1967: 477). But the acceleration in military expenditures in 1961–62 which was associated with the West Irian campaign led to a blowout in the deficit in 1961, and a trebling in the price level between 1961 and 1962. The black market price of dollars and gold soared and hoarding of basic commodities became widespread.

The final serious attempt at stabilisation occurred in May 1963, with a package of reforms, usually referred to by the acronym *Dekon*, which were aimed at stimulating exports by what amounted to a *de facto* devaluation, increasing domestic production by lifting price controls and facilitating imports of raw materials, and reducing the budget deficit through removal of subsidies and increased revenues from import levies and other taxes (Pitt 1991: 64–6). The measures did lead to a jump in the ratio of levies on trade to imports and exports (Table 4.5) but their political support was tenuous. As Weinstein (1976: 315) argued, 'the stabilisation plan's foreign sponsorship and the belief that the stringent anti-inflationary regulations had been forced on Indonesia by the IMF and the United States as preconditions for aid left its backers exceedingly vulnerable to criticism'. The stabilisation programme basically relied for its success on substantial foreign loans from the USA and other Western countries, and as the Malaysia campaign gathered strength in the latter part of 1963, this support was withdrawn. It is arguable how much impact the *Dekon* measures would have had anyway; Pitt (1991: 65) argues that they were nowhere near as dramatic a liberalisation attempt as the Sumitro reforms of the mid-1950s. But the failure of the government to implement the reforms led to a loss of foreign funding, and this, combined with accelerating defence expenditures, led to increases in the deficit as a proportion of GDP in 1963, 1964 and 1965 and thus to accelerating inflation. But the political polarisation which had by then occurred made any consensus on remedial action impossible, and the economic situation drifted until September 1965.

THE GROWTH OF THE PUBLIC ENTERPRISE SECTOR AFTER 1950

Although the period from 1950 to 1965 can be seen as characterised by a continual decline in the size of government expenditures relative to GDP, and a progressive failure of government stabilisation policies, it was also a period during which the size of the state-owned enterprise (SOE) sector grew. Indeed, it can be argued that the growth of the SOE sector was the main exception to the trend towards the attenuation of government control over the economy in the years from 1950 to 1965. But, in fact, the SOE sector as it developed under the Old Order embraced a very diverse and heterogeneous range of enterprises, many of them only very loosely under the control of the central government. After independence, the Indonesian government shared the opinion then prevalent in many parts of the world, that the government should own and control the 'commanding heights' of industry, trade and commerce. In developed countries, especially in West Europe, this opinion was based on politically influential theories of socialism. In the newly independent countries, socialist ideology was buttressed by a profound suspicion of foreign control. Not only did governments want to control what was then seen as the 'natural monopoly' industries such as telecommunications, railways, and electricity generation, which had been government enterprises in the colonial era, but also banking, and wholesale trade. A particularly strong argument was that both small producers and consumers were being exploited by a trading system which was riddled by market imperfections and that government intervention was essential if the supply of basic needs at 'reasonable' prices was to be achieved.

For most of the period of parliamentary democracy, successive governments were frustrated in their attempts to impose control over key sectors of the economy because of the continuing domination of foreign, and especially Dutch-controlled, interests. The wholesale nationalisation of Dutch interests which occurred in late 1957 meant that, virtually overnight, the size of the state-owned sector increased dramatically. Not only agricultural estates and large manufacturing enterprises, but also the main Dutch trading houses were suddenly placed under government control. The prevailing political situation made payment of compensation impossible. Equally impossible was the sale of the Dutch enterprises to domestic interests, or indeed to other foreigners. The domestic entrepreneurial class was too small, and too dominated by Chinese, to make such sales feasible from either a financial or a political point of view. Besides, the government benefited from the patronage that the dramatically enlarged SOE sector brought in terms of appointments.

It was also expected that the nationalised sector of the economy would play an important role in funding the ambitious eight-year development plan which was scheduled to run from 1961 to 1968. This plan, in spite of its overtly ideological framework and populist rhetoric emphasising 'Indonesian socialism', did attempt to accelerate the pace of government investment in a number of key sectors of the economy including food production, basic industries such as steel, cement and fertiliser, education and scientific research, transport, defence and social welfare. Although foreign observers such as Paauw (1963: 223) pointed out that considerable care had obviously gone into the choice and planning of individual projects, the circumstances of the early 1960s were hardly conducive to speedy implementation. Pond (1964: 98) calculated that only about 17 per cent of targeted expenditures were realised in the first two years; the main problem was finance. Given the poor performance of public enterprises, planners were depending on revenues from the petroleum sector (still largely in foreign hands) to finance plan expenditures; in fact, one minister claimed that as much as 75 per cent of all resources for plan expenditures would come from the petroleum industry (Paauw 1963: 229). But government revenues fell markedly as a proportion of GDP after 1961, and although the end of the Irian campaign allowed a higher proportion of budgetary expenditures to be devoted to plan projects in 1963, defence expenditures were again accorded priority in 1964 and 1965 (Bank Indonesia 1968: 30–5). Even those plan projects which were commenced in 1963 were distinguished more by their high public visibility than by their economic benefits.

By the early 1960s, the Indonesian economy was, in effect, divided into three distinct sectors. First, there was small-scale, or peasant agriculture, including livestock, fisheries and smallholder cashcrops as well as foodcrops, which accounted for about 50 per cent of GDP in 1960. This sector remained the preserve of 'uncollectivised peasants' (Castles 1965: 23), and production decisions were taken by millions of small producers, influenced only indirectly by government policies. The second part of the economy consisted of nationalised enterprises, many of which had been formerly owned by Dutch interests. It is difficult to estimate what proportion of GDP this sector comprised, but it is unlikely to have been much more than 20 per cent. The residual share of GDP (of around 30 per cent) was produced in the privately owned non-agricultural sector, and included about 70 per cent of the large and medium-scale manufacturing sector, all the small-scale manufacturing sector, as well as a substantial share of construction, road transport and domestic trade (Table 4.9). In many of these activities it could be assumed that the role of Chinese businessmen was very important, if not dominant. Anspach (1969: 182) argued that many Dutch businesses were taken over by Chinese when the Dutch left in the 1950s, and that their Chinese owners 'proved highly resistant to the pressures of indigenism in the 1950–57 period'. This indeed was, according to Anspach, the 'real frustration' of the policies of indigenism, that they reduced the power of the Dutch in the economy only to increase that of the Chinese. This ongoing dilemma is examined in greater detail in Chapter 7.

Table 4.9 Breakdown of GDP, 1960, according to sector and ownership of enterprise (Rp billions)

| Sector | Ownership | | | Total |
	Smallholder agriculturists	*Private**	*Government*	
Foodcrops	134.0			134.0
Cashcrops	28.1			28.1
Livestock[†]	26.3			26.3
Estates		5.1	7.6	12.7
Forestry	2.6	6.0	0.7	9.3
Mining		10.8	3.6	14.4
Manufacturing:				
Large/Medium		14.6	6.3	20.9
Small		11.7		11.7
Construction		3.2	4.7	7.9
Utilities			1.1	1.1
Transport:				
Rail/Air			1.7	1.7
Other		9.0	3.8	12.8
Trade:				
Export-Import		10.9	16.5	27.4
Other		22.7	5.7	28.4
Banking		1.1	2.8	3.9
Dwellings		6.9	0.8	7.7
Public Sector**			17.6	17.6
Services:				
Personal		15.7		15.7
Community		1.6	7.0	8.6
Total GDP	191.0 (49.0)	119.3 (30.6)	79.9 (20.5)	390.2 (100)

* Includes foreign enterprises.
[†] Includes fisheries.
** Includes defence.
Source: BPS, *Pendapatan Nasional Indonesia 1960–8*, Table 1. Weights assigned on the basis of evidence contained in the source document and Nugroho (1967).

LESSONS FROM OLD ORDER PUBLIC POLICY

Not surprisingly, given the state of the Indonesian economy in 1965, the lessons which have been drawn subsequently from the conduct of fiscal and monetary policy in the first fifteen years of independence have been very negative. In particular, the idea has become deeply rooted in the minds of most Indonesian economists that the inflation was caused by budget deficits, and that a 'balanced budget' was therefore essential to attain stable economic growth. In fact, as we have already stressed, it was not the deficit *per se* which was inflationary but the way in which it was financed. Had successive Indonesian governments been prepared to rely on foreign borrowing to fund the budget deficit, as did the colonial government in the 1930s, higher levels of budgetary expenditure could have been sustained with little pressure on prices. Although there was some concern at the size of Indonesia's foreign debt in the early 1950s, it was in fact much smaller relative to exports than had been the case in the 1930s. The overvalued exchange rate makes it difficult to compare ratios of debt to GDP in the 1950s with those from the 1930s, but the ratios of debt to exports, and debt service payments to exports in 1952 were much below those of 1933 (Table 4.4). This suggests that there was scope for borrowing abroad to cushion the budgetary and balance of payments effects of the fall in export prices in 1951–53. Of course, as Sumitro (1953: 18) emphasised, such borrowing should be used only for funding public capital formation, and not for routine expenditures. Had successive governments through the 1950s been prepared to rely more on foreign loans for development finance, much more could have been done to increase public investment in badly needed infrastructure projects.

To what extent could foreign borrowing have cushioned the impact of the very steep decline in the terms of trade which occurred after 1960? Given the severity of the decline, which was even steeper than that which occurred in the 1930s, some effect on real GDP growth would probably have been inevitable. But given that in December 1958 total foreign debt was well below the level of the early 1950s (as a result of the cancellation of the remaining colonial debt), there was obviously scope for a judicious increase in foreign borrowing in the early 1960s to enable government to accelerate the pace of capital formation without undue pressure on prices. In fact, there was a rapid increase in foreign borrowing in the Guided Democracy period, so that by the end of 1965 the total foreign debt was estimated to be $2.4 billion (Panglaykim and Arndt 1966: 5). Given that recorded exports had fallen to little more than $700 million in 1965, this meant that the ratio of outstanding foreign debt to officially recorded exports was higher than it had been in 1933 (Table 4.4). But much of this borrowing was extra-budgetary;

more than half was, in fact, borrowed from Communist bloc countries and used largely for defence purchases. Thus, the government had little choice but to fund the budget deficit by printing money, with the inevitable inflationary consequences.

The main lesson to be learned from the conduct of fiscal and monetary policy in the 1950s and 1960s is not that budget deficits are always inflationary, but rather that government expenditures should be permitted to exceed domestic revenues only if the expenditures are devoted to capital works projects which can be justified according to the standard criteria of economic efficiency, and if the required foreign or domestic borrowing does not impose too heavy a burden on the budget and the balance of payments. Indeed, foreign borrowing to maintain recurrent government expenditures (on salaries and wages and other items necessary to maintain existing provision of government services) could be justified to protect the domestic economy from an adverse trend in the terms of trade, if such a trend were of short duration. The substantial foreign borrowing undertaken by the colonial government in the 1930s was mainly used to finance recurrent expenditures; such borrowing was not inflationary and nor did it precipitate a debt crisis. Without it, the effect of the depression on the Indonesian population would have been even more severe than in fact it was. Had similar policies been pursued in the 1960s the effects of the fall in the terms of trade on the domestic economy would have been mitigated, if not entirely offset.

The other important lesson to be learned from the Old Order was that if economic policy-making was to be effective there must be continuity at least of policies, and preferably of policy-makers. Although there was a shortage of skilled personnel in the early 1950s, especially in the senior levels of the civil service, this was not the main reason for the problems faced by those, such as Sumitro and Sjafruddin, who were struggling to implement policies which they considered were in the interests of long-term economic development. Rather, it was a political system which was inherently unstable, and which meant that most ministers, however competent, had only a few months in which to frame and implement policy before surrendering office, often to someone of quite different political persuasion with quite different policy goals. Although the demise of parliamentary democracy could have led to greater continuity of policy-making, in fact the growing political polarisation which ensued aggravated rather than ameliorated the problem of implementation. Several sensible reform packages were drawn up between 1959 and 1963 which tried to tackle the country's economic problems, and some attempt was made to implement them. But each attempt failed because the political will necessary for a sustained reform process was lacking. This lesson was not lost on the military officers and the civilian technocrats who assumed power in 1966.

STABILISATION POLICIES AND THE RETURN TO GROWTH: 1966–73

The stabilisation programme embarked on by the Indonesian government with the advice and support of the International Monetary Fund (IMF) in 1966 has come to be regarded as one of the most successful such programmes undertaken anywhere in the world since 1950 (Sutton 1984: 68). Not only was the government able to reduce the rate of inflation to virtually zero within the space of three years, but this success was not accompanied by the declining production, rising unemployment and deteriorating living standards which have characterised IMF stabilisation programmes in many other countries. Indeed, as we have seen in Chapters 2 and 3, the economy embarked on a sustained process of economic growth after 1967 which faltered only with the decline in the world oil price in the early 1980s. Furthermore, there was a considerable fall in the proportion of the population in both urban and rural areas living under the 'very poor' poverty line in the latter part of the 1960s; this decline is particularly marked if we use a rice-based poverty line (Booth 1988: 193). This remarkable experience of stabilisation with equity deserves close examination.

The triumvirate which assumed effective power in early 1966 immediately set about tackling the nation's economic problems, with the assistance of a number of economists from the University of Indonesia, and from international agencies such as the International Monetary Fund and the World Bank. The stabilisation package drawn up in August and September 1966 in conjunction with a team from the International Monetary Fund stressed the paramount importance of balancing the budget as a means of reducing inflation. Other policy measures emphasised were a systematic move towards 'decontrol' of the economy, reform of the banking sector and credit policy and the establishment of an appropriate link between the domestic and the international economy through the realistic pricing of foreign exchange (Arndt 1966: 4). A balanced budget was to be achieved through more intensive collection of taxes and 'severe austerity' on the expenditure side.

In the event, the budget deficit for the calendar year 1967 was drastically reduced to only 0.3 per cent of GDP. This was achieved not by severe cutbacks in expenditures (which, in fact, grew slightly relative to GDP compared with 1966), but by a remarkable doubling in revenues as a proportion of GDP. There were two main reasons for this improved revenue performance. First, the government intensified collection of import and export taxes and the tax on oil company profits; together these taxes accounted for over 40 per cent of total revenues in 1967 (Tandjung and Nazar 1973: 156). Second, the consortium of major Western countries and multilateral lending organisations which had first met in Tokyo in 1966 decided, in February 1967, to commence a long-term programme of assistance to Indonesia under the auspices of a specially constituted Inter-Governmental Group on Indonesia (IGGI). In 1967, this aid amounted to Rp 24.7 billion, or almost 30 per cent of budgetary revenues. As development expenditures only amounted to Rp 17.5 billion, a considerable part of the aid was, in fact, used to finance recurrent expenditures including debt repayments. Donor compliance with this use of aid was encouraged by the drastic reduction in military expenditures following the termination of confrontation with Malaysia.

Although most of the donor countries had a strong preference for project aid, the Indonesian government and the IMF managed to persuade them that such aid was not feasible given the state of the Indonesian economy. The government was simply not in a position to prepare a list of development projects for foreign financing, let alone implement such projects if funding became available. Rather, the government proposed that all available aid should be integrated into the foreign exchange market. In 1966, import licensing had been abolished and replaced with certificates issued by the Central Bank at a fluctuating rate. These certificates could be freely traded, and gave importers the right to import any goods from the BE list. What was proposed was that special BE certificates would be created against aid funds for use in importing goods from the donor country. These could then be sold on the open market and used to import goods on the BE list from the donor country. Although the system was not without its operational problems, it did permit far more speedy and efficient utilisation of foreign aid revenues than would have been the case if the 'decrepid bureaucracy were left to do the job'

(Glassburner 1971: 413–17). Additional programme aid was also provided in the form of foodgrains, mainly from the USA (Posthumus 1972: 59–61).

The growing availability of foreign aid also assisted the government in bringing order to the foreign exchange market. In 1966 the government returned to a multiple exchange rate system not dissimilar to the one which operated in the 1950s (Glassburner 1971: 397), although in the 1950s experiments with a freely functioning market for export certificates were always shortlived. Glassburner (1971: 398) argued that 'all earlier attempts at a free market for certificates ran afoul of political or economic instability or both, while the present system, being accompanied by serious efforts to establish monetary and fiscal equilibrium, appears to have some chance of long life and continued expansion'. In fact, the government had by 1970 managed to achieve the goal of a unified exchange rate, with the merging of the markets for BE (essential) and DP (luxury) foreign exchange. While the unified rate was nominally floating, Bank Indonesia intervened in the market to support it. In August 1971, there was a further devaluation of the rupiah, which 'marked the end of a liberalisation phase that had transformed Indonesia's trade regime from one of the more restrictive among LDCs to one in which there was full exchange convertibility and a complete absence of foreign exchange licensing' (Pitt 1981: 199).

Paradoxically this was not such a boon to exporters as might have been predicted. Pitt's analysis of trends in the real effective exchange rate for rubber producers indicated that for much of the period from 1958 to 1965 'smuggling . . . counterbalanced a significant amount of the price distorting effects of government trade policy' (Pitt 1981: 203). Thus, the realised rupiah return for a dollar's worth of rubber export was in real terms rather greater during the years of greater distortion than it was at the end of the period of stabilisation in 1971. This was due to the sharp deterioration in the world price for rubber which occurred throughout the 1960s; by 1972 the real price was less than half what it had been a decade earlier (World Bank 1982: 97). The unification of the exchange rate and the rationalisation of the foreign trade regime was not in itself sufficient to offset the impact of this decline on producer prices.

An important goal of the post-1966 stabilisation policy was reform of the banking sector and credit policy. After 1957, political priorities became dominant in decisions regarding the quantity and allocation of bank credit and both Bank Indonesia and the state trading banks lost whatever autonomy they had had *vis-à-vis* government

departments and powerful individuals. Data are scarce on the allocation of credit in the years from 1958 to 1965 but Arndt has argued
that:

> Much the largest volume of credit...went directly from the Bank
> Indonesia to the government for budgetary and extra-budgetary
> expenditures. For budgetary expenditures, the departments of the
> central government drew directly on the central bank under author-
> isations by the Department of the Budget, although in the last
> phase these became little more than a formality with little pretence
> at budgetary control. All other central bank credit appears to have
> been channelled through the general banking department. It con-
> sisted of two parts. One was credit extended to other banks, par-
> tly...in the form of advances – mainly to the government foreign
> exchange banks and the state development bank – for approved
> specific projects and priority sectors, and partly in the form of
> informal overdrafts. The other was credit granted by the Bank
> Indonesia for the president's 'special projects', and other 'vital'
> purposes (Arndt 1971: 380).

The upshot of this was that by the early 1960s the central bank had
degenerated into a vehicle for the discretionary use of funds by the
governor for his own and the president's purposes. It was obvious that
a 'balanced budget' would have little impact on macroeconomic stabilisation if the government continued to resort to extra-budgetary
finance through the banking system to fund expenditures. The reim-
position of discipline within the banking sector had to assume equal
priority with attempts to impose fiscal discipline. The new government
wasted little time in implementing monetary reforms. A combination
of severe restrictions on bank credits – none for imports, no long-term
loans, no overdrafts, no preference for state enterprises, no credit to
finance debts of government enterprises – and higher interest rates
were imposed in 1966 (Arndt 1971: 384–5). In 1967, this very tight
monetary policy was relaxed in the interests of 'stimulating production'. Credit restrictions were eased and interest rates lowered. This,
together with a new law on foreign investment and a larger budget
allocation for development expenditures, especially roads, led to an
improvement in the investment climate and greater optimism that
accelerated growth was possible.

One result of the years of hyperinflation was a severe contraction in
the money supply in real terms, as the growth in nominal money
supply failed to keep pace with accelerating inflation after 1958. As

public confidence in the currency declined there was a sharp decline in the demand for money and increasing use of goods both as a means of exchange and as a store of value. The success of the stabilisation programme meant that demand for money both for transactions purposes and to build up money balances grew rapidly. As Arndt (1971: 386) pointed out, there was a very real danger that the increased demand for money combined with a shift in price expectations would lead to uncontrolled price deflation. Faced with this problem, the government began to channel large increases in central bank credit to government agencies, such as the rice procurement agency, and indirectly to the private sector through the state banks. By mid-1969, real money supply was more than three times what it had been in 1965, although it had still not returned to the 1960 level (Arndt 1971: 388).

In its reform of both the foreign exchange market and the banking system the government demonstrated considerable determination to move away from a highly regulated and controlled economy to one where the market could play a greater role in determining the allocation of scarce resources in the economy. But as the stabilisation programme progressed it became clear that the government was unwilling to expose the economy to the full rigours of the market, especially as far as basic needs were concerned. In the latter part of 1967 rice prices began to increase as a result of a prolonged dry season and an overly rapid decline in government imports. The ensuing popular unrest reinforced the conviction of many in both the military and the civilian bureaucracies that the supply of basic (or 'strategic') goods was too important to leave to the vagaries of market forces, and more credit was channelled to the government logistics agency to build up and distribute stocks. Another old problem that returned to prominence as the government began to permit the private sector a greater role concerned the ethnic Chinese community. The Guided Economy had done nothing to foster an indigenous entrepreneurial class; indeed, as Panglaykim (1968: 58) argued, it was the Chinese who filled the void left by the expulsion of Dutch capital in the late 1950s. It soon became obvious that it was the Chinese business community, already well-entrenched in both manufacturing and trade, who would be the major beneficiaries of economic liberalisation and a more open market economy. Ugly anti-Chinese riots in many cities in 1967 served to warn the government that this was a problem that was not amenable to easy, short-term solutions.

By 1969 the success of the stabilisation programme was clear. The consumer price index was stable, production of food and other basic necessities was increasing, and annual per capita rice availability was more than 10 kilos higher than two years previously. GDP was growing at a faster rate than at any time since the early 1950s. There were probably three main reasons for this dramatic success. First, Indonesia remained a predominantly agricultural economy, and the improvement in agricultural output in 1968 and 1969, due partly to good weather and partly to government policy, had an immediate impact on both GDP growth and popular welfare. Second, the successful absorption of both financial and commodity aid led to a considerable increase in the availability of basic needs (foodgrains, textiles etc). Third, both the increased supply of foreign aid and improved domestic revenue performance meant that the budget could be balanced without draconian expenditure cuts. The small size of the government sector at the height of the Guided Economy period, together with the fact that little expenditure was directed to such 'welfare' purposes as food subsidies meant that the vast majority of the population had little to lose from a period of fiscal austerity. Indeed, budget expenditures as a percentage of GDP stayed quite constant in 1967 and 1968, and the redirection of expenditures away from defence and towards salaries and wages and a modest programme of development expenditures probably helped rather than harmed most people, especially in urban areas.

THE RETURN TO DEVELOPMENT PLANNING UNDER THE NEW ORDER

With improved domestic revenue performance and foreign aid receipts running at more than 3 per cent of GDP, the government felt sufficiently confident by 1969 to shift the focus of economic policy from stabilisation to the promotion of long run economic development and structural change. While balanced budgets and monetary discipline were an essential pre-requisite for sustained economic growth, the government was clearly of the opinion that some medium-term direction of the economy through an indicative plan was essential to reassure foreign investors, aid donors and domestic public opinion that economic development was now to be accorded top priority. No doubt partly because of the conspicuous lack of success in implementing the two Old Order development plans, the first five year plan (*Repelita 1*) of the New Order was quite modest in aims and content. The plan document commented that 'the Indonesian people have been disappointed for too long by all kinds of development plans and slogans. Too often plans are started with much fanfare only to be completely forgotten afterwards' (Department of Information 1969: 23). The tone of the new plan was pragmatic rather than ideological, and technically quite unsophisticated; there was no reliance on planning models of the Indian variety. In the words of one observer,

> The Plan has been variously described as 'a strategy for action' and, more modestly, as 'a Government five year capital budget'. Indonesia's weak administrative apparatus precluded strong overall planning with enforced and rigid targets even if this had been the desire of the economic policy-makers. The government even now has at its disposal very few 'levers' with which it can effect the direction of the economy and enforce priorities. Even conventional monetary and fiscal controls are fettered by the small budget ... and the continuing need to exercise credit restraint.
> The Plan is unusual in that it is not couched in the customary macro framework, with a target increase in National Income stipulated as the starting point, and investment and savings requirements determined by relating this target growth-rate to the capital–output ratios. Instead, the Plan is a series of targets and estimates of some of the more predictable of the 'macro' magnitudes and a statement of general policy objectives, linked together in a loose overall framework (Anon 1969: 69).

The plan projected a 150 per cent increase in real investment between 1969–70 and 1973–74 with 75 per cent of the investment coming from the central government development budget. It was expected that budgetary savings (the difference between all domestic revenues and routine expenditures) would fund only a relatively small share of the development budget; 19.5 per cent in 1969–70 rising to 24 per cent in 1973–74. The balance would come from the rupiah counter-value of programme aid, and from project aid. By 1973–74 it was expected that project aid would be funding almost half of all development expenditures. In the event, budgetary savings grew far more rapidly over the plan period than was initially predicted, and by 1973–74 covered 56 per cent of development expenditures, with a corresponding decline in the proportion financed by foreign aid. The reason for this was the faster than expected growth of domestic revenues, and especially oil revenues which by 1973–74 accounted for almost 30 per cent of total government revenues (Booth and McCawley 1981: Tables 5.1 and

5.6). The increase was mainly due to increased volume as the OPEC-induced increase in prices occurred too late in the plan period to have much impact. By the end of 1973, the index of petroleum production stood at 289 compared with 100 in 1966 and 130 in 1968.

Among the major economic sectors, agriculture was accorded priority in the allocation of investment funds, and within agriculture rice production, which was projected to grow by almost 50 per cent. According to the plan, the focus on agriculture was due to the fact that 'the greater part of the Indonesian people lives in this sector, working either as farmer producers or as farm labourers... the development of agricultural sector is expected to open up growth possibilities in other sectors so that an opportunity will be created to combat the backwardness of the Indonesian economy on many fronts' (Department of Information 1969: 13). Thirty per cent of the government development budget was devoted to agriculture and irrigation, and a further 20 per cent to the rehabilitation and upgrading of the road system which would facilitate farmers' access to agricultural inputs (especially fertiliser) and marketing of output. Although rice production did not grow as fast as the plan document predicted, the actual increase achieved, almost three million tons between 1968 and 1973, represented an annual growth of 4.6 per cent, which was a considerable improvement over the performance of the 1960s.

The *Repelita 1* document also set out a number of goals for the industrial sector, although the criteria for industrial promotion were so general that most parts of the industrial sector appeared to qualify (McCawley 1979: 35–7). McCawley noted that the broad government strategy for industrial promotion was 'unmistakably protectionist' and the general emphasis on favouring 'weaker' (i.e. non-Chinese) entrepreneurs was a carry-over from the immediate post-independence era. He also pointed out that there was virtually no attention paid 'to the need for Indonesian industry to operate more efficiently, to specialise in areas where Indonesia might have a comparative advantage, or to move toward a situation where less protection was needed'. These aspects of industrial policy only began to achieve rigorous government attention in the mid-1980s.

By the final fiscal year of *Repelita 1* (1973–74) the Indonesian government could look back with some satisfaction on the achievements of the previous five years. Although inflation returned to double digit figures in 1973 as a result of the rise in rice prices of 1972–73 and the accompanying monetary expansion (Grenville 1979), there could be little doubt that substantial progress had been made towards the restoration of fiscal and monetary discipline. Government revenues had risen relative to GDP because of improved domestic revenue performance, and reliance on foreign aid and borrowing to finance the development budget had declined. Government expenditures had been redirected away from routine expenditures and defence and towards development expenditures on much needed infrastructure rehabilitation and extension. The low ICOR achieved during these years testifies to the care with which projects were selected for their potential to generate economic benefits quickly. Of particular note in this respect was the expansion of the so-called INPRES programmes. These were grants from the central government budget to the *kabupaten* and village governments which were strictly earmarked for the rehabilitation of infrastructure (de Wit 1973). Although these expenditures accounted for less than 10 per cent of total government expenditures in 1973–74, they were successful in tapping the substantial capacity for project implementation at the sub-national level and were an obvious target for increased funding under the second plan of the New Order (*Repelita 1*).

One point about fiscal policy in the *Repelita 1* period is worth emphasising as it was to give rise to continuing confusion in subsequent discussion. In spite of the repeated assertions of the government that it was adhering to a 'balanced budget policy', in fact, the government continued to spend more than its domestic revenues plus foreign aid receipts and by 1974 the resulting deficit, as estimated by the International Monetary Fund, amounted to more than 1 per cent of GDP (Asher and Booth 1992, Table 2.8). While this was lower relative to GDP than the deficits of the early 1960s it was still hardly a balanced budget. The resulting borrowing requirement was not shown in the budget documents because of the practice of combining both foreign aid and commercial loans together under 'development revenues'. As government commercial borrowing was always in foreign currency and covered by imports, its domestic inflationary impact was minimal, in contrast to the deficits of the early 1960s which were largely funded by printing money.

MANAGING THE OIL BOOM: 1974–81

It was stressed in Chapter 2 that the dramatic jump in the price of oil which occurred in late 1973 and 1974 did not lead to any perceptible increase in growth of GDP over what had been achieved in the years from 1967 to 1973. The growth in the income terms of trade which had been extremely rapid in the 1967–73 period actually declined somewhat, partly because of the increase in import prices which occurred after 1973, as a result of accelerating world inflation (Table 2.1). The most immediate effect of the oil boom on the Indonesian economy was greatly to expand revenues accruing to government from the royalties paid by the extracting companies, classified in the budget as the 'oil company tax'. Between 1973–74 and 1974–75 budgetary revenues from this source almost trebled, and in the latter part of the 1970s, oil revenues accounted for close to half of all government revenues from both internal and external sources (Booth and McCawley 1981, Table 5.1).

The oil bonanza presented the Indonesian government with a series of difficult policy choices. The first decision concerned how much of the revenues should be absorbed domestically and how much accumulated abroad in the form of foreign exchange reserves. Domestic absorption would greatly aggravate inflationary pressures because, unlike domestic revenues obtained from taxation or borrowing, the oil revenues had no offsetting impact on incomes and expenditures of individuals and companies within the country. The domestic impact of the increased oil revenues could have been completely sterilised if the government had been willing to run a budgetary surplus equal to the balance of payments surplus and hold the reserves abroad, or if it had reduced capital inflow on both private and public account sufficiently to compensate for increased oil revenues (McCawley 1980: 52). If the oil bonanza had been of very short duration the first option might have been sensible; the accumulated reserves could then have been drawn down slowly over time to offset the balance of payments effect of a subsequent decline in the income terms of trade. But the Indonesian government, correctly as it turned out, judged that world oil prices of under two dollars a barrel were a thing of the past, and that the domestic economy must adjust to a regime of high world oil prices. How could this be done without aggravating already serious domestic inflationary prices and placing considerable strain on domestic producers of non-oil tradables, both exports and import substitutes?

In the event, the government reacted to the revenue increase by increasing government expenditures sharply relative to GDP (Figure 4.1). Much of the increase went on salaries of civil servants and school teachers, greatly expanding the INPRES grants to regional governments, and embarking on new programmes in the education and public health sectors, including the construction of thousands of rural schools and health clinics. By the mid-1970s, per capita government expenditures (in US$) were well above India, although below Thailand (Table 4.7). The inflationary impact of these expenditures was offset to some extent by a massive programme of government imports of rice, and fertiliser, which was sold at heavily subsidised prices to encourage domestic food production. In addition, government expenditures on very import-intensive infrastructure projects in the telecommunications sector was increased (McCawley 1980: 53). But, in spite of these initiatives, the rate of inflation increased to an alarming 40 per cent in 1974.

What really contained the inflationary impact of the first oil shock, and indeed sent both the budget and the balance of payments back into deficit in 1975 was the Pertamina crisis. The state oil company had, during the early part of the 1970s, built up a considerable corporate empire centred on oil but branching out in many other directions. Increasingly, Pertamina management sought to avoid government control of long-term borrowing by state instrumentalities by negotiating short-term finance with a range of suppliers and foreign banks. But during 1974, conditions in international money markets tightened, and it became increasingly difficult for Pertamina to continue to roll over its short-term debts. For the better part of a year, it used oil revenues due to the government, amounting to almost one billion dollars, to 'keep its creditors at bay, but in February 1975 government intervention became necessary to save it from default on two overseas loans' (Arndt 1983: 142). The government was forced to assume responsibility for all Pertamina debts, and those that came due in 1975–76 were paid off partly from current oil revenues and partly from a foreign loan negotiated with an international consortium of banks. Pertamina commitments to its non-oil enterprises, notably PT Krakatau Steel and a large tanker-charter deal, were renegotiated, and central bank finance was made available to pay off domestic creditors.

The Pertamina collapse cost the Indonesian government very dearly, and not only financially. The New Order's attempts to build up an international reputation for prudent economic management were severely compromised and Indonesia once again became a by-word in the world media for financial irresponsibility and corruption. But as Arndt (1983: 142) has argued, 'there could hardly have been a more anti-inflationary use of the additional oil earnings than repayment of Pertamina's external debts'. From a peak of 40 per cent in

1974, increases in the Jakarta cost of living index began to trend downwards and in 1977 the annual increase was only 11 per cent. Although the IMF estimate of the budget deficit before borrowing jumped to 3.4 per cent of GDP in 1975–76 and 4.1 per cent the following year, largely because of Pertamina-related expenditures, by 1979 it had fallen back to 2.2 per cent of GDP (Asher and Booth 1992: Table 2.8). Besides moderating domestic inflationary pressures, there were two other benefits. Those members of the military who advocated a 'nationalistic, *zaibatsu* approach to economic management' lost influence with the President, and the role of the economists in the cabinet was enhanced. And at least for the rest of the 1970s, the government was anxious to avoid further short-term borrowing, and pursued a very conservative foreign debt strategy (Woo, Glassburner and Nasution 1994: 124).

But, by 1978, more fundamental structural problems resulting from the oil boom were troubling many observers of the Indonesian economy. These problems were due to the so-called 'Dutch disease' effects of the oil boom on other producers of tradable goods, both exports and import substitutes. Since 1971 the Indonesian rupiah had experienced a substantial real appreciation relative to the currencies of its major trading partners, similar to that which occurred in the 1930s as a result of the Dutch government's determination to stay on the gold standard. The rate of exchange relative to the US dollar had remained unchanged since 1971, while from 1974 onwards Indonesia's rate of inflation had been well above that of its major trading partners. As a result the 'competitiveness index' for Indonesia (obtained as a trade-weighted average of the nominal exchange rate between Indonesia and each of its major trading partners, multiplied by the ratio of consumer prices in the trading partner to consumer prices in Indonesia) fell from 100 in 1971 to only 67 in 1977 (Warr 1984: 67). This decline reflected a rise in costs in Indonesia relative to competitors abroad which made it difficult for producers of traded goods to compete with foreign suppliers in either domestic or international markets.

The government reacted to this problem in a number of ways. On the import side, considerable protection was given to domestic producers through tariffs, quotas and input subsidies. The first two measures were used with increasing frequency in the manufacturing sector where domestic producers of a range of consumer durables were given almost total protection through import restrictions and bans. In the crucially important foodcrop sector, the government controlled rice imports to allow domestic prices to rise slightly above the falling world price, while at the same time giving considerable assistance to domestic producers through subsidies on irrigation and fertiliser. The manufacturing sector boomed under this regime, although much of what it was producing was at higher cost and of lower quality than the foreign competition. Even with substantial government assistance, growth in rice output was slower than in the *Repelita* period. As far as non-oil exports were concerned, production growth was very slow. Paauw (1978: 208) estimated that production volume of the eleven leading non-extractive commodities, all agricultural, stagnated between 1971 and 1976. There was very little growth of any manufactured exports over this period. Such stagnation contrasted sharply with the situation in other parts of Asia where both traditional and new export industries were growing rapidly, exploiting their comparative advantage due to climate, environment and cheap labour.

Opinion was divided over the consequences of these developments for the nation's economic future. Authorities such as Paauw argued that most of the non-oil export staples were produced by smallholders whose incomes and living standards had been severely affected by the oil-boom induced real appreciation of the rupiah. Furthermore, the country was facing an enormous challenge in creating productive employment opportunities for the rapidly growing labour force, and a rapid expansion of labour-intensive non-oil exports was essential for employment purposes. Paauw (1978: 217–8) discussed various policy alternatives and came down strongly on the side of a 'general change in the exchange rate to stimulate exports'. But others argued that Indonesia's medium-term comparative advantage was clearly in resource-based exports, and if these could not provide much employment the solution must lie in absorbing more labour into production of non-tradables such as construction and services. Attempts to boost non-oil exports through a currency devaluation would inevitably accelerate domestic inflation and thus rapidly erode any improvement in competitiveness. To the extent that supply elasticities for many smallholder export crops were quite low in the short run, it was unlikely that a devaluation would lead to accelerated export volume, although it would of course give producers a short-run windfall improvement in income.

If expert opinion was divided over the merits of devaluation as a policy remedy for the Dutch disease, an exchange rate adjustment became more seriously considered during 1978 on the grounds that the oil boom was over and that the balance of payments was likely to deteriorate rapidly (Arndt 1978: 2). But, in spite of widespread discussion of the pros and cons of a devaluation during 1978, the actual decision in November came as a considerable surprise. So did the size of the devaluation. The rupiah–dollar rate rose by 50.6 per cent from 415 to 625 rupiahs to the dollar. It appeared at the time that the devaluation was undertaken 'on structural rather than conventional balance of payments grounds' (Dick 1979: 4) although the IMF was known to have argued the case for a devaluation at least partly for balance of payments reasons at the IGGI meeting in May. However, senior government officials subsequently stated that the devaluation was carried out to improve Indonesia's competitive position (Ismael 1980: 103), and one analyst claimed that the 1978 Indonesian devaluation provides a 'relatively clear example of a devaluation motivated primarily by protectionist considerations' (Warr 1984: 54).

The government was obviously aware of the need to control inflation in the wake of the devaluation in order to prevent the rapid erosion of the impact of the devaluation on the relative prices of tradables and non-tradables in the economy. But the devaluation severely shook public confidence in economic management, and as Dick (1979: 4) pointed out, many businessmen, consumers and indeed government officials 'reverted instinctively to dormant patterns of behaviour typical of earlier periods of economic dislocation'. Irrational rumours of further devaluations spread, and many people withdrew savings and converted them into gold or goods. Many traders increased prices of all goods by the full amount of the devaluation or more, regardless of their import content. Rather than pursue the conventional path of monetary and fiscal constraint, the authorities reacted to this situation by imposing a total price freeze, a move that frustrated the aim of the devaluation which was to raise the price of tradables relative to other goods and services. Even worse, the government moved to protect domestic industries such as plywood, footwear and furniture by preventing domestic prices of logs, leather and rotan rising by the full extent of the devaluation, either through export taxes or, in the case of logs, by outright export bans. In addition, a supplementary export tax was imposed on coffee, palm oil, copra and coconut oil, partly to cream off some of the rupiah increase in exporters' incomes and partly to lower prices to domestic consumers. This move obviously frustrated one of the aims of the devaluation, which was to increase the incomes and living standards of the smallholder producers of export crops.

As 1979 progressed, it became clear that the increase in world oil prices induced by the Iranian revolution would severely test the ability of the government to maintain tight fiscal and monetary control. But in the event, the government was surprisingly successful in containing the rate of growth of the money supply. This was done mainly by running a public sector surplus sufficiently large to sterilise the monetary impact of the balance of payments surplus. Inflation did accelerate in 1979 but declined again in 1980, and by 1981 had dropped back to the 1978 level of under 10 per cent per annum (Arndt and Sundrum 1984: Figure 3 and Table 1). As Arndt and Sundrum argued, the fact that money supply rose less rapidly than prices in 1979 indicates that part of the cost-push effect of the devaluation was accommodated through a rise in velocity of circulation, in turn due to both businesses and households drawing down cash balances in order to maintain real levels of expenditures. Although there can be little doubt that the price of non-traded goods also rose in the wake of the 1978 devaluation, the Indonesian government was quite successful in making the devaluation 'stick' in the sense of maintaining the post-devaluation ratio of tradable to non-tradable goods prices. Warr (1984: 71) argues that 'although the magnitude of the relative price effects of devaluation seems to have been smaller in Indonesia, the effect was more prolonged' compared to devaluations in many other countries.

By 1981, the world price of the OPEC marker crude had reached $33.20, which was close to three times the 1978 price. In 1979 and 1980 a significant part of the increase in foreign reserves due to the oil price rise was, in fact, sterilised; this showed up in the monetary statistics as a decline in central government liabilities with the central bank. One indicator of the impact of this decline is to estimate the financial surplus (which measures changes in the government's net position with the banking system) as a percentage of GDP. In 1980 the surplus was almost 4 per cent of GDP, although that fell to 1 per cent in 1981 (Asher and Booth 1991: Table 2.8). It is not easy to reconcile this surplus with the budgetary data which showed a budget balance, or indeed with the deficit estimated by the International Monetary Fund which is derived by removing government commercial borrowings from the data on budgetary revenues and treating them instead as financing requirements. There can be little doubt that over these years the government, to curb inflation, was understating revenues in the budgetary documents, and possibly overstating expenditures as well (Booth and McCawley 1981: 150). Thus, while appearing to run an expansionary fiscal policy, the net impact on aggregate demand was, in fact, quite contractionary.

But in spite of the fact that they were almost certainly understated in the budgetary documents, oil revenues still accounted for over 60 per cent of all budgetary revenues in 1981–82. In this year, non-oil domestic revenues had sunk to little more than one quarter of budgetary revenues and foreign aid and borrowing made up the balance. The increase in oil revenues also permitted a rapid increase in the percentage of the development budget which was financed from government savings rather than from foreign aid and borrowing (Asher and Booth 1992: Table 2.2). However, development expenditures did not grow markedly relative to GDP during the second oil shock; they already accounted for over 10 per cent of GDP in 1978–79 and increased to almost 12 per cent by 1981–82 (Asher and Booth 1992: 59). There was, however, some change in the sectoral breakdown of development expenditures compared with the period of the first oil shock. The *Repelita III* plan document showed a projected breakdown of development expenditures which emphasised energy, transportation and education; these three sectors accounted for almost 40 per cent of total planned expenditures (Booth 1989: Table 6). The share of development expenditures devoted to agriculture and irrigation fell to only 14 per cent which was less than half the share this sector received under *Repelita 1*. Transmigration by contrast rose to over 5 per cent of planned development expenditures, although the share of regional development excluding transmigration fell.

The extreme and unpredictable fluctuations in oil revenues in the years from 1974 to 1981 made any medium-term planning of government revenues and expenditures very difficult. Both the second and third five year plans of the New Order were overtaken by events in the world oil market almost as soon as they appeared. But there can be little doubt that the two oil shocks together led to a considerable growth in the role of government in the economy. In 1980–81, total government expenditures accounted for almost one quarter of GDP, an historic high (Figure 4.1). At the same time, most commentators agreed that the oil boom years saw a marked retreat from the liberal economic policies of the early New Order period. This was most obvious in the growth of restrictions on foreign investment and international trade, which accelerated after the anti-Japanese 'Malari' riots of early 1974. In their survey of manufacturing protection policy in the New Order, Pangestu and Boediono (1986: 9 ff) argued that after 1972 a range of protective devices were adopted by the government in addition to the tariffs, import restrictions and licences which had been used since the 1950s. They listed twenty-two different policy instruments including government monopolies and procurement policies, preferential credit policies and compulsory use of domestic components by domestic manufacturers which conferred considerable protection on certain industries in addition to the tax and tariff regime.

Pangestu and Boediono were of the opinion that the average rate of effective protection for manufacturing industries fell somewhat between 1975 and 1980, although their estimates did not take into account many of the quantitative restrictions which were in use by 1980. Certainly it was true that in 1979 the government did move to reduce tariffs, although this move had little effect on those industries protected by quantitative import controls or by various types of government subsidy. But even allowing for the tentative steps towards trade liberalisation which occurred in the latter part of the 1970s there can be little doubt that levels of protection in Indonesian manufacturing were high by Asian standards, although there was considerable variation between industries. Not surprisingly, import substituting industries received, on average, much higher levels of protection than export oriented industries, although there was substantial variation within both categories.

POST-OIL BOOM RESTRUCTURING AND PARTIAL LIBERALISATION

In several respects, 1982 was a watershed year for New Order economic policy. Although world oil prices held at 1981 levels for much of the year, Indonesia followed the OPEC-mandated production cuts, and both export earnings and government revenues from the petroleum sector began to fall, both in absolute terms and as a percentage of the total. The balance of payments deficit in 1982–83 increased sharply as a percentage of GDP, and there was growing awareness of a burgeoning resource constraint, particularly for the public sector. The government was faced with a stark choice. Either it could retreat from even the partial liberalisation of commodity trade which had occurred after 1968 and return to the regime of quantitative controls which had prevailed prior to 1965 in the hope of restricting imports, or it could remove the disincentives to export production in the existing trade regime in the hope of encouraging a dramatic acceleration in non-oil exports.

The problem was greatly aggravated by the commitment of the government to supporting the establishment of over 50 new industrial projects, many in the state-owned sector, at an estimated capital cost of over $11 billion (Gray 1982: 36 ff). The World Bank in a major review of the Indonesian manufacturing sector released in 1981 had drawn attention to the dangers of an industrialisation strategy based on the establishment of import-competing industries which were un-likely, given the small size of the Indonesian market, to develop into internationally competitive enterprises which could profitably export at least part of their output. Many of the proposed new 'upstream' industries required imported plant and equipment which would im-pose an added burden on the balance of payments, as would the servicing of new loans undertaken to finance industrial expansion. The danger was that, as oil revenues declined, the balance of pay-ments would deteriorate even further, forcing a drastic reduction in both public and private sector expenditures.

In the years from 1982 to 1985, there was much evidence that the government was resorting to further quantitative controls on imports while at the same time adopting other measures (including the ap-pointment of a Minister for the Promotion of Use of Domestic Products) which appeared to reinforce the emphasis on import sub-stitution rather than export promotion. In November 1982, the gov-ernment introduced the 'approved importers' system which introduced several new import licences in addition to the two then in use, the general import licence and the import licence for producers to import inputs. The net effect of the new arrangements was to restrict the type and amount of goods imported by limiting both the number of importers and the type of goods they could import. In the most restrictive cases, imports of some key raw materials, intermedi-ate goods and agricultural products were limited to a few, or even one importer, frequently a state trading enterprise. Examples included iron and steel products, plastics, cotton, wheat flour, milk and milk products, and some agricultural products such as soyabeans, cloves and sugar. Licences were also granted to producer-importers, which gave domestic producers a monopoly over competing imports. The official reason for the introduction of this restrictive regime was to stabilise the supply and price of 'strategic' commodities and increase bargaining power with overseas suppliers (Pangestu 1987: 28).

On the other hand, 1983 saw several new initiatives in monetary, fiscal and exchange rate policy, as well as the 'rescheduling' of several of the large public sector industrial projects about whose economic viability concern had been expressed in the previous year. The rupiah was devalued in March 1983, and a number of new deregulation initiatives were announced in the financial sector (Arndt 1983a). In December 1983, the Indonesian parliament approved three tax reform laws which were implemented over the following eighteen months. But at the same time as some degree of financial liberalisation was taking place, quantitative restrictions on imports were increasing. By early 1985 a lively debate had emerged within the economics profession and in the media over the causes of the 'high cost economy' and the need for liberalisation of the 'real' economy. Many observers argued that financial deregulation and fiscal reform were not in themselves sufficient to make Indonesia an internationally competitive producer of a range of non-oil export goods and services. A major cause of the high cost economy was excessive protection from both tariff and non-tariff barriers, and these would have to be removed (Dick 1985: 19).

The first intimation that the government was heeding calls for a more export-oriented trade regime came in March and April 1985. In March, the tariff system was rationalised through a reduction in the maximum *ad valorem* rate from 225 per cent to 60 per cent and a reduction in the number of rates. More dramatically, in April the notorious Directorate General of Customs was relieved of all responsibility for the export and import of goods. Customs surveillance was handed over to a Swiss company with long experience in many parts of the developing world, clearance procedures were greatly simplified (the number of signatures required was reported to have declined from around 20 to just one) and the time taken to complete formalities was greatly reduced. Inter-island trade also benefited from the long overdue elimination of customs controls and the introduction of more efficient trans-shipment procedures (Dick 1985: 11).

Such measures certainly served to startle the outside world into acceptance of the seriousness of the Indonesian government's deregulation drive. But they were insufficient in themselves to greatly affect the high cost structure faced by many firms in manufacturing, trade and transport which prevented them from becoming competitive international producers of goods and services. By mid-1986 it was clear that even more drastic measures were needed to improve the balance of payments. Although the 1983 devaluation did give some stimulus to non-oil exports (total export earnings in nominal dollar terms grew between 1983 and 1984, after two years of decline), the real impact of the devaluation had begun to taper off by 1985. The sharp drop in world oil prices in the early months of 1986 led to a decline in total export earnings from oil and gas of almost five billion dollars in 1986 compared with 1985, and of 11.5 billion dollars compared with 1981. In 1982 and 1983, the government had been borrowing abroad to fund the budget deficit rather than cut back on development expenditures, which actually rose as a proportion of GDP in 1983–84 compared with the height of the oil boom (Asher and Booth 1992: 59). By 1986 debt service charges were already 36 per cent of export earnings, and this ratio threatened to increase as the rapidly deteriorating balance of payments situation required further borrowing abroad.

In spite of these problems, it appeared to many that the government was determined to continue with a policy of import restrictions through more systematic and comprehensive licensing, rather than move to a policy of active non-oil export promotion. The turning point came in May 1986 when a wide-ranging package was announced whose aim was to facilitate the purchase of imported inputs at world prices by firms producing in whole or part for export. Exporters were in fact allowed to import their raw materials directly, thus bypassing licensed importers entirely. The scheme was operated not by the Department of Trade but by the Department of Finance which was seen as a major victory for the deregulators in that ministry (Muir 1986: 23). The May package was followed in September by a substantial devaluation of the rupiah which was primarily intended to improve the competitiveness of Indonesian exports, and encourage domestic producers to begin selling in international markets. Its initial impact, however, was on business confidence which was badly shaken. Even the announcement in October 1986 and January 1987 of substantial relaxations of quantitative restrictions on imports did not entirely restore confidence in the credibility of government policy-making (Pangestu 1987). Assessments of the country's economic outlook through 1987 and into 1988 remained rather pessimistic.

But the deregulation drive did not lose momentum. In July 1987, the system of textile and garment quota allocations to exporters was rationalised and in December a package of reforms was announced which were intended to further reduce quantitative import barriers, remove export licences and other barriers to export production, improve incentives for foreign investors, and revive the moribund domestic share market (Booth 1988b). Various incentives were also given to the tourism industry. In October 1988, a long-awaited banking reform package was announced, which was followed by further reforms of the financial system in 1989–91 (Nasution 1993:

290–5; Pangestu 1993: 270–2). In November 1988, further deregulation of inter-island shipping was announced (Dick and Forbes 1992: 277). A start was also made on the complex issue of establishing performance criteria for state enterprises, with the aim of deciding what form ownership and control of such enterprises should ultimately take, although in this area reform has been very slow (Mackie and Sjahrir 1989: 26–30; Pangestu 1993: 274–6).

The latter part of the 1980s also witnessed a substantial change in the compostition of both government revenues and expenditures and in the impact of the budget on aggregate demand. In 1986–87 the proportion of total government revenues derived from oil and gas fell back to 1973–74 levels. Reliance on aid and foreign borrowing returned to the level which prevailed in the late 1960s; indeed, in 1988–89 about 30 per cent of government revenues were obtained from these sources which was a record for the New Order period. At the same time non-oil domestic revenues increased both as a share of total government revenues and relative to GDP. By 1989–90, non-oil domestic revenues were 11 per cent of GDP compared with only 7 per cent in 1984–85. This improvement was due mainly to the better than expected revenue performance of the value added tax, and also to some improvement in income tax collections especially after 1987 (Asher and Booth 1992: 47 ff).

On the expenditure side, total expenditures fell only slightly as a proportion of GDP, but the composition changed markedly. Development expenditures fell from almost 13 per cent of GDP in 1983–84 to only 7.6 per cent in 1987–88. Falling levels of government savings led to a progressively lower share of development expenditures being financed from domestic sources; in 1988–89 aid and foreign borrowing financed more than 80 per cent of development expenditures which was a higher ratio than in 1969–70 (Asher and Booth 1992: 49). Routine expenditures increased from under 11 per cent to 14 per cent of GDP over the same years. The main reason for the increase in routine expenditures was the rapid growth of government debt servicing obligations, aggravated by the devaluation which increased the rupiah burden of government debt servicing obligations by almost 50 per cent. By 1990 the long-term foreign public debt stood at 45 per cent of GDP and 150 per cent of export earnings (Table 4.4). While neither of these ratios exceeded previous peaks, total debt service payments were extremely high at almost 30 per cent of export earnings, and government debt service payments accounted for 27 per cent of total budgetary expenditures, a higher proportion than in the 1930s.

The fall in oil revenues and the rise in government debt servicing obligations together meant that the large domestic deficit (the difference between revenues derived from the domestic economy from non-oil taxes and non-tax sources and rupiah expenditures) which characterised the oil boom era had vanished by the latter part of the 1980s. Indeed, it has been estimated that for 1988–89 and 1989–90 the government actually ran a domestic surplus in order to offset the foreign deficit, which was in turn the result of lower oil revenues and higher debt servicing obligations. The domestic deficit is important mainly as an indicator of the impact of the budget on aggregate purchasing power in the domestic economy; many commentators were of the view that a decline in the size of the deficit would lead to a drastic slowdown in domestic economic activity, slower economic growth and higher unemployment (Glassburner 1986: 22). In the event, the government did draw down its balances with the central bank between 1986 and 1988, thus modestly stimulating the domestic economy and assisting the acceleration in growth which took place in the latter part of the 1980s (Asher and Booth 1991: Table 2.8).

Looking back on the changing role of government in the Indonesian economy from 1983 to 1990, it is obvious that much progress was made towards the goal of making the non-oil traded goods sectors (agriculture, manufacturing, tourism) more internationally competitive and less reliant on exports of oil and gas. The government was extremely successful in controlling domestic inflation after two large devaluations, thus bringing about a large and sustained fall in the real effective exchange rate (Asian Development Bank 1990: 246–7). This, in turn, was a key factor in the growth of non-oil exports. But perhaps the most considerable achievement was in changing the mental attitudes of both government officials and the business community. Although many officials were hostile to the deregulation drive of the latter part of the 1980s, especially when it threatened their jobs, status and monetary remuneration, there could be little doubt that by the early 1990s a sizeable constituency for liberalisation had been built up within the government apparatus. This, in turn, helped the confidence of both the foreign and domestic business community in exploiting the full potential of existing investments and in committing new investment funds.

But at the same time, it would be incorrect to conclude that the role of government in the economy was in any significant way reduced in the 1980s. All the evidence indicates the reverse. After a dip in the early 1980s, the ratio of government expenditure to GDP increased again in the latter part of the 1980s, and was only slightly below the oil boom peak (Figure 4.1). Estimates of ratios of government expenditure to GDP in international prices (i.e. corrected for differences in the purchasing power of currencies) indicate that the Indonesian figure in 1990 was close to the East Asian average, but the ratio has tended to increase faster in Indonesia since 1970 (Table 4.10). An estimate of the government share of GDP, taking into account state-owned enterprises (SOEs), made by Hill (1990: 55) found that the government accounted for 31 per cent of GDP in 1988, a considerable increase over the share for 1960 (Table 4.9).

Table 4.10   Government expenditure as a percentage of GDP, 1960–90
(1985 international prices)

Year[*]	Indonesia	Thailand	Malaysia	Philippines	Taiwan	Korea
1960	13.0[†]	11.7	14.0	14.1	23.2	16.0
1965	11.2	12.2	15.5	13.5	20.3	13.4
1970	10.6	13.4	15.2	15.0	19.0	12.5
1975	12.3	13.8	16.3	18.2	15.4	11.3
1980	15.3	17.0	17.0	16.6	14.9	10.8
1985	14.7	18.1	17.2	15.4	14.4	9.2
1990	14.9	14.4	15.0	15.7	14.0[**]	8.6[††]

[*]Five-year averages centred on the year shown, except where otherwise indicated.
[†]1960–62
[**]1988–90.
[††]1988–91.
Source: Robert Summers and Alan Heston, *Penn World Table*, version 5.6.

Very little attempt has been made to privatise the SOE sector, and indeed total sales of SOEs, as a proportion of GDP, increased over the 1980s, although the rate of return on assets was very low (Hill 1996: 162). An important reason for the low rate of return has been the constraints imposed on pricing; the state electricity corporation, for example, has been forced to supply electricity at well below cost since the late 1960s (Kristov 1995: 100). Regulatory control over parts of the SOE sector remains weak; the so-called 'strategic enterprises' controlled by the influential Minister of Research, Dr Habibie, enjoy access to extra-budgetary sources of finance which are outside the control of the Ministry of Finance, or any other government regulatory agency (McKendrick 1992; Azis 1994: 411–14). This recurrence of the 'Pertamina syndrome' indicates that the problem of controlling the state enterprise sector is far from resolved in New Order Indonesia.

GOVERNMENT AND DEVELOPMENT: A SUMMING UP

It is obvious from Figure 4.1 that the 130 years from 1860 to 1990 have seen a progressive increase in the share of government in GDP. In this sense, the Indonesian experience mirrors that of many other countries, which have experienced similar secular increases in government expenditures relative to GDP. The remarkable feature of Indonesia's post-independence experience is not that public expenditures increased relative to GDP, but that the increase only occurred in the latter part of the 1970s, after the decline of the 1960s. From 1950 to 1965, real growth in public expenditure was, in fact, much lower than in the first three decades of the twentieth century (Table 2.1). Slow expenditure growth was largely the result of slow revenue growth: the failure of revenue policy was in turn due to the desire on the part of the newly independent nation to break with a traditional revenue policy which was seen as colonial and exploitative. The acute lack of administrative capacity made the efficient implementation of new forms of taxation impossible. This failure, together with, in the early 1960s, an aggressive foreign policy, led to increasing defence expenditures, falling foreign aid, mounting budget deficits and hyper-inflation. The problem of poor revenue performance was masked in the 1970s by the growth in government revenues from aid, and from oil. As world oil prices fell in the 1980s, and the importance of oil revenues in the government budget declined, there was no corresponding decline in government expenditures. Rather, the 'ratchet' effect familiar to students of the development of the public sector in other parts of the world came into effect. Instead of pruning back expenditures, the government was forced into diversifying its sources of revenues, increasing government borrowing in the short-term and embarking on a wide-ranging tax reform which increased sources of revenue in the medium term. But the lesson of the 1960s was well learnt, and there was no increase in inflationary borrowing from the banking system.

After 1983, the government embarked on a successful programme of 'deregulation' designed particularly to improve incentives for non-oil exporters, and remove the bureaucratic obstacles confronting them. Indeed, the experience of the 1980s confirms the argument that Indonesia since independence has been prepared to invoke the market principle 'only under economic duress' (Woo, Glassburner and Nasution 1994: 128). The experience of the 1980s can be contrasted with the late colonial era when the Dutch authorities introduced wide-ranging market regulation in response to the problems of the world depression of the early 1930s. But the deregulation which took place between 1985 and the early 1990s was partial in scope. The government sector including state enterprises almost certainly accounted for a larger share of GDP in the late 1980s than in the early 1960s when 'Indonesian socialism' was the official ideology. Large 'para-statal' enterprises, in the public sector but largely immune to budgetary accountability, continued to flourish. Certainly the post-oil boom years in Indonesia saw no dramatic rolling back of government's role in the economy.

Over the New Order era, as in the last four decades of the colonial period, the government has been reasonably successful in maintaining macro-economic stability in the face of massive external shocks. It has also channelled investment into both infrastructure and education, with results which are examined in more detail in Chapter 6. But interventions in markets for traded goods have been more controversial. As in the 1930s, interventions in food markets have been pervasive. It has been claimed that the benefits of rice price stabilisation to the wider economy have been significant, especially in the 1970s (Timmer 1996: 67). On the other hand, there is not much evidence that the Indonesian government has been successful in 'disciplining private firms' through the kinds of performance incentives and sanctions which Amsden (1989: 14) argues have been important in Korea. Selective intervention, especially in the industrial sector, has rather been used to secure favours for certain companies and individuals, and the benefits for the economy as a whole have been negligible (Azis 1994: 411–14; Hill 1996: 168).

5 The Impact of International Trade

THE ROLE OF INTERNATIONAL TRADE IN THE INDONESIAN ECONOMY

There can be no doubt that the last century of Dutch colonial rule in Indonesia witnessed a remarkable transformation of the economies first of Java, and then of many parts of Sumatra, Kalimantan and Sulawesi. Not only did the volume of production of traditional exports increase, but new export staples emerged, sometimes with dramatic speed, in response to growing markets in the industrialising countries of Europe and North America. The emergence of these new export crops in turn transformed the local economies of the producing regions through the provision of infrastructure and the growing demand for inputs and services. And yet, the transformation of Indonesia into an open export-oriented economy in the nineteenth and early twentieth centuries did not lead to rapid structural change, and sustained economic development. Indeed, it was precisely because of this failure that policy-makers after independence adopted less liberal, more inward-looking policy regimes. But they too failed to produce sustained economic growth, and after 1965 there was a partial return to a more open trading system. Even over the three decades from 1965, the commitment to trade liberalisation has been considerably less than whole-hearted, and many in the Indonesian policy-making establishment remain unconvinced of the benefits of closer integration with the global economy.

The purpose of this chapter is three-fold. The first part examines the statistical evidence on the growth and changing composition of exports from Indonesia in the nineteenth and twentieth centuries. The second part discusses the causes and consequences of the changes in the trade regime brought about by successive governments since the 1830s. The final part examines the relationship between export growth and economic growth and suggests reasons why this relationship has varied over time.

GROWTH AND CHANGE IN THE COMPOSITION AND DIRECTION OF EXPORTS

As we saw in Chapter 2, the *culturstelsel* (CS) was extremely successful in increasing the volume of exports from Java in the period from the late 1820s to 1840. Export volume growth was faster than in most other parts of Asia, and indeed faster than in most other parts of the world. According to the estimates of Bairoch and Etemad (1985: 92), Indonesia (which until 1874 meant Java, as far as the official statistics were concerned) accounted for only 6.2 per cent of all exports from Asia in the 1830s, but 13.6 per cent by 1860 (Table 5.1). Over these years, Asia's exports were growing as a proportion of all exports from developing countries, but Indonesia's share of the total still increased. Another increase in Indonesia's share of Asian exports occurred between 1912 and 1928. By 1928, Indonesia accounted for almost 8 per cent of all 'third world' exports as estimated by Bairoch and Etemad. For a country of Indonesia's size, exports were a high percentage of GDP, reaching almost 30 per cent in 1925. This percentage fell with the onset of the depression but rose again to almost 25 per cent in 1937 (Figure 5.1). For the entire period from 1830 to 1938, Indonesian exports in per capita terms were considerably higher than in British India, and comparable to those in smaller Southeast Asian economies such as Thailand and the Philippines (Table 5.2). But after 1930, exports per capita in all these economies were dwarfed by the achievement of Japan.

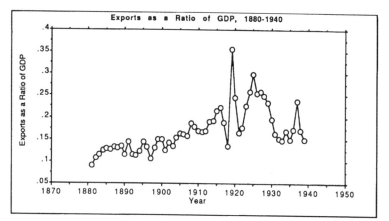

Figure 5.1 *Sources*: Exports: CEI, Vol. 12a, Table 2B; nominal GDP data from Pierre van der Eng.

Although there was some growth in export volume in the early 1950s over the level achieved in the late 1930s, Indonesia participated hardly at all in the dramatic expansion of world trade that occurred in the 1950s and 1960s. Indeed, between 1953 and 1966 Indonesian export volume grew by less than 1 per cent per annum, although there was some acceleration towards the end of the 1960s. Over the same period Hanson (1980: 14) estimates that world trade grew by 7 per cent per annum, which was faster than at any time since 1800. At a time when exports from the developing countries were falling as a percentage of the world total, Indonesia's share of the developing country total was also falling, and had declined to only 2 per cent by 1970 (Table 5.1). From being a major export economy in the late 1920s, Indonesia four decades later was only a minor actor in the unfolding drama of world trade expansion.

It has been argued that the 1950s and 1960s also saw a sharp decline in exports and imports relative to GDP, compared with the ratios which prevailed in the inter-war years (Glassburner 1971:396; Paauw 1981:150–1). But, as was shown in Chapter 2, estimates of these ratios are bedevilled by the problem of the grossly overvalued exchange rate, which undervalued both exportables and importables in the national

Table 5.1   Relative share of Indonesia in Asian export trade and Asian trade in third world total, 1830–1990*

	Indonesia as % of Asia	Asia as % of third world	Third world as % of world
1830	6.1	32.6	27.5
1860	13.6	40.7	22.0
1900	13.9	41.4	19.4
1912	13.5	44.1	24.2
1928	16.5	46.4	25.3
1937	16.4	39.7	26.8
1970	6.3	28.8	20.2
1990	5.6	59.4	23.5

* Asia comprises the South Asian sub-continent, Southeast Asia, Korea, Taiwan, China, and Hong Kong, but excludes Japan. The third world comprises these countries plus Africa (excluding South Africa), the Middle East, and Latin America and the Caribbean. All data refer to three-year averages centred on the years shown.
Sources: Up to 1937: Bairoch and Etemad (1985), Tables 1.2, 3.1, 6.1. 1970: International Monetary Fund, *Direction of Trade Yearbook 1968–72*. 1990: International Monetary Fund, *Direction of Trade Statistics Yearbook 1994*.

Table 5.2   Per capita exports: Indonesia and selected Asian comparisons,
1830–1990 (current dollars)
(three-year averages centred on the years shown)

Year	Indonesia	India	Philippines	Thailand	Japan
1830	0.8	0.2	0.4	0.6	n.a.
1860	1.8	0.6	1.8	0.7	0.1
1880	2.5	1.2	3.2	1.5	0.8
1900	2.8	1.3	2.9	2.3	2.8
1912	5.2	2.4	5.8	4.1	4.9*
1928	10.8	3.7	12.4	9.8	17.6
1938	6.5	1.8	7.4[†]	5.6	16.8
1960	10.0	3.2	18.9	15.5	42.0
1975	58.9	7.7	58.9	60.8	533.9
1990	142.8	20.7	133.3	425.5	2,364.7

* 1910 data.
[†] 1938 only.
Sources: Up to 1938: Bairoch (1991), Tables 9 and 10. Data for 1960, 1975 and 1990 taken from International Monetary Fund, *Direction of Trade Annual, 1958–62*; International Monetary Fund, *Direction of Trade Yearbook 1980*; International Monetary Fund, *Direction of Trade Statistics Yearbook 1994*.

accounts relative to non-traded goods and services. The problem was further complicated by the growth of unrecorded trade. If we compare the export volume index computed by Rosendale (which takes account of unrecorded trade) with the real GDP figures based on the World Bank and other sources, it is clear that both grew at roughly the same rate between 1938 and 1966 (Table 2.12). Of course, it is possible that the GDP data understate the actual growth in volume of output over these years, but at least on the face of it there is little support for the argument that the export sector underwent a 'substantial shrinkage' relative to GDP in the 1950s and 1960s (Paauw 1981:151).

In the latter part of the 1960s and the early 1970s Indonesian export volume grew rapidly as the trade regime was stabilised and liberalised and world prices for key export commodities such as rubber began to improve, which encouraged growers to increase tapping. After 1973 export volume growth slowed, as the OPEC quotas constrained the growth of oil exports and the real appreciation of the rupiah affected the competitiveness of non-oil exports. But for the 1970s as a whole, export volume grew at 8 per cent per annum which was faster than the growth of world trade. Perhaps surprisingly, the decade of the

1980s saw slower export volume growth than the 1970s, in spite of the implementation of successive reform packages intended to deregulate markets and promote non-oil exports. This was largely due to the declining volume of oil exports. At the height of the oil boom in 1980, exports rose to 31 per cent of GDP, although they fell back to around 19 per cent in 1986, and rose to 24 per cent by the end of the decade.

The past two centuries have also witnessed considerable change in the commodity composition of Indonesian trade, although there has been remarkably little change in the commodity concentration of earnings. Through much of the colonial period, Indonesian exports were less concentrated by commodity than in many other tropical colonies. In fact, Hanson (1980: 39–40) has shown that in 1860 the proportion of Indonesia's export earnings accounted for by the largest item was quite low in comparison with most other countries in Asia, Africa and Latin America. By 1900, the Hirschman index of export concentration was lower in Indonesia than in any other country outside Europe and North America except India and China; it was much lower than in Brazil, Egypt, the Philippines, or Argentina. Less than 30 per cent of export earnings were derived from the largest export, sugar (Table 5.3). Thus, unlike many tropical colonies, Indonesia was far from being a monocrop economy, whose fortunes depended crucially on one international price. Not only was the Indonesian export economy more diversified in terms of product mix than most others; it also exhibited considerable diversification in terms of production technologies. To an increasing extent, smallholder producers became involved in the production of many export crops, so that by the late 1930s they dominated production of coffee, copra and spices, and accounted for almost half the production of rubber.

There was an increase in export concentration in the post-independence period, due first of all to the dominance of rubber, and then to oil and gas. In 1981, export earnings from oil and liquified natural gas amounted to 82 per cent of all exports. In this year a higher proportion of export revenues were derived from one group of closely related commodities than had ever been the case in the colonial era. However, the decline in world oil prices which took place through the 1980s, together with the growth in a range of manufactured exports led to a substantial fall in the role of oil and gas in total export earnings, although by 1992 the degree of commodity concentration was still no lower than it had been in 1900. The five largest export groups (petroleum and gas, plywood, textiles and garments, non-ferrous metals and rubber) still accounted for almost 70 per cent of export earnings, compared with over 90 per cent at the beginning of the decade (Table 5.3).

Table 5.3   Concentration of export earnings by commodity, 1825–1990

	Percentage of export earnings accounted for by:	
	largest commodity	five largest commodities
1825*	67.7 (coffee)	84.1
1850*	36.1 (coffee)	89.7
1870*	40.2 (coffee)	88.6
1885	45.4 (sugar)	78.9
1900	28.6 (sugar)	68.1
1925	32.6 (rubber)	75.2
1940	37.7 (rubber)	78.4
1952	46.0 (rubber)	87.4
1970[†]	38.5 (petroleum)	85.1
1981	82.1 (petroleum)	93.2
1990	43.1 (petroleum)	68.5

* Java only up to 1870
[†] After 1970, petroleum includes liquefied natural gas
Sources: 1825–70: *Handelsstatistiek Java 1823–1873, Mededeeling 160*, Batavia: Centraal Kantoor voor de Statistiek; 1885–1925: *Handelsstatistiek Nederlandsch-Indie 1874–1937, Mededeeling 161*, Batavia: Centraal Kantoor voor de Statistiek; 1940: *Statistical Pocketbook of Indonesia 1941*, pp. 78–86; 1952: Bank Indonesia, *Annual Report, 1954–55*, p. 98; 1970–90: *Indikator Ekonomi*, various issues.

CHANGES IN THE DIRECTION OF TRADE

Considerable changes have occurred in the direction of trade over the past two centuries. During the decades of the *cultuurstelsel*, a high proportion of exports from Java were shipped to the Netherlands and sold there; in 1860 almost 90 per cent of exports were disposed of in this way. A lower, although still substantial, proportion of imports came directly from the Netherlands, while most other imports were either sourced directly from Europe or shipped through Singapore (Table 5.4). With the advent of the Liberal reforms of the 1870s, there were significant changes in the direction of trade. On the export side, the share of the Netherlands declined steadily until by 1920 only 16 per cent of exports were sold there. Europe as a whole took only 30 per cent of all exports, compared with 40 per cent to other parts of

Asia, 13 per cent to America and 12 per cent to Africa (mainly Egypt). On the import side, the share of the Netherlands and of Europe fell more gradually; in 1920 Europe was still supplying 47 per cent of all imports, and Asia around 34 per cent. The increase in the American share of Indonesian imports after the First World War reflected in part improved trans-Pacific shipping routes, but also the fact that income growth and industrial development in Indonesia were creating a growing demand for both capital and consumer goods produced by the USA.

By the 1920s another Asian country was emerging as an important market for Indonesian exports and as a source of imports. This was Japan. After 1920, Japan's share of Indonesian exports fell, mainly because of the development of the Taiwanese sugar industry, but Japan's share of Indonesian imports grew steadily, and by 1934 accounted for over 30 per cent of the total (Table 5.4). As the first Asian country to industrialise, Japan was still technologically backward compared with the industrial giants of West Europe and North America. But it could manufacture cheaply a range of consumer goods such as cotton cloth, household utensils, and bicycles which appealed to that part of the indigenous population in Indonesia who were sufficiently affluent to be able to afford a few goods and services beyond what was necessary for bare existence. In fact, Japan's exports to most parts of Asia expanded rapidly in the inter-war years, except in those colonies (principally Indochina) where metropolitan manufacturers were sufficiently powerful to ban or restrict competition for their own exports.

But the growth of Japanese exports to Indonesia in the years from 1928 to 1933 was much more rapid than the growth of Japanese exports to Asia as a whole, so that by 1933 exports to Indonesia comprised 17 per cent of all exports to Asian countries (excluding the colonies of Korea and Formosa) and 8.5 per cent of total Japanese exports. (The corresponding percentages in 1928 had been 8.8 per cent and 3.7 per cent). In absolute terms, the value of exports to Indonesia was higher than to any other Asian country except British India and China by the early 1930s. Furthermore, the official figures almost certainly underestimated the importance of Indonesia as a final destination because a substantial share of Japanese exports to the Straits Settlements found their way to Sumatra and Kalimantan. There were several reasons for the success of Japanese products in Indonesian markets. First, prices were low. This was especially true of textiles and garments, owing to the rationalisation of the Japanese textile industry, which encouraged the adoption of new technologies and thus a reduction in production costs (Sugiyama 1994: 67). Second, the depreciation of the yen and the adherence of the guilder to the gold standard led to a very rapid real devaluation of the yen relative to the guilder (Booth 1994: Table 6.8). Third, Japanese companies built up an extensive marketing network throughout the archipelago, often using Chinese business networks (Post 1993: 157). The colonial government responded to this rapid growth of Japanese commercial influence by imposing quantitative restrictions on a range of manufactured imports in 1934–5. In 1936 the metropolitan and colonial guilders were devalued together. These measures led to a decline in the Japanese share of imports after 1935, although it was to rise again after independence.

The decades since independence have seen a continual decline in the share of Europe in Indonesia's export and import trade, and an increase in the share of both Asia and America (Table 5.4). Asia's dominance is particularly marked on the export side. In 1990 almost 70 per cent of Indonesian exports went to other parts of Asia, of which Japan alone accounted for over 40 per cent. This reflected the importance of Japan as a buyer of Indonesian oil and gas, and also plywood and some metals such as aluminium. Indeed, in 1980 Japan was absorbing a slightly higher proportion of Indonesian exports than had the Netherlands a century earlier. Indonesia's reliance on Asia, and especially Japan as a source of imports reached a peak in 1980 and declined somewhat thereafter, as the share of the USA grew. In 1990 Asia supplied 55 per cent of Indonesia's imports which was the same percentage as in 1934, although the role of both Japan and Singapore had declined while that of Hong Kong, China and Korea had grown.

THE COMMODITY TRADE BALANCE AND THE BALANCE OF PAYMENTS

From the establishment of the *cultuurstelsel* to 1940, Indonesian exports often exceeded imports by a wide margin (Table 5.5). That colonial Indonesia had an unusually large commodity export surplus has been acknowledged by several scholars. Golay (1976, Table 1) has shown that the ratio of imports to exports never rose above 65 per cent before 1870; for most of the nineteenth and early twentieth centuries, the Indonesian ratio was the lowest in Southeast Asia.

Table 5.4   Changes in the direction of trade: 1835–1990 (percentage of exports and imports)

	1835*†	1874†	1910†	1934†	1953	1975	1990
Exports							
Europe	80.9	74.9	38.7	39.6	35.4	6.4	12.8
Netherlands	(77.1)	(61.8)	(26.3)	(20.2)	(22.5)	(2.5)	(2.8)
USA	2.4	8.2	4.5	11.1	20.7	26.3	13.1
Asia	15.7	12.8	45.4	33.1	34.8	58.7	70.4
Singapore**	(5.1)	(11.6)	(20.3)	(19.0)	(21.5)	(8.9)	(7.4)
Japan	(0.9)	(—)	(3.7)	(3.8)	(4.5)	(44.1)	(42.5)
Australasia	0.2	3.5	1.5	4.6	2.9	0.3	1.9
Africa	0.1	0.1	4.8	2.5	1.3	—	—
Other††	0.7	0.5	5.1	9.1	4.9	8.3	1.8
Total	100.0	100.0	100.0	100.0	100.0	100.0	100.0
Imports							
Europe	68.2	63.6	51.5	33.3	34.8	24.3	22.3
Netherlands	(35.4)	(54.7)	(32.3)	(13.0)	(11.7)	(2.8)	(2.5)
USA	2.1	2.4	1.6	6.7	17.9	14.0	11.5
Asia	29.6	33.0	45.1	53.6	43.1	53.9	55.1
Singapore**	(12.6)	(27.6)	(22.6)	(12.6)	(13.1)	(7.2)	(5.8)
Japan	(10.7)	(—)	(1.0)	(31.9)	(16.9)	(31.0)	(24.3)
Australasia	—	1.0	1.7	3.3	2.3	3.6	6.0
Africa	0.1	—	—	0.8	1.1	2.3	0.8
Other††	0.0	0.0	0.1	2.3	0.8	1.9	4.3
Total	100.0	100.0	100.0	100.0	100.0	100.0	100.0

* Data refer to Java's trade with other countries, excluding trade with the Outer Islands.
† Trade in goods only, excluding coin and bullion.
** Includes Peninsular Malaysia until 1953.
†† Includes duty-free ports such as Sabang.
Sources: CEI, Vol 12a; Bank Indonesia, *Report for the Year 1954–5*, pp. 100–1; Central Bureau of Statistics, *Statistical Yearbook of Indonesia, 1979*, pp. 387–409; Central Bureau of Statistics, *Statistical Yearbook of Indonesia, 1994*, pp. 333–56.

Hanson (1980: 124–7) examined the data for thirty-four developing countries in the latter half of the nineteenth century and reached the conclusion that only four 'fit the pattern of experiencing export surpluses amounting to 25 per cent or more of total exports'. These four were Indonesia, Brazil, Thailand and British India. Until 1870, much of the commodity export surplus financed the colonial contribution to the Netherlands. After 1870 private outward remittances on current account began to grow, and these together with inward movements of non-monetary gold and silver accounted for part of the commodity export surplus (Table 5.5). However, in all decades from the 1840s until the 1890s there was on average a substantial surplus on current account, which in turn was used to finance additions to private balances held abroad (Table 5.6).

Table 5.5 Trends in the current account of the balance of payments (Annual averages: millions of guilders)

Period	Balance on commodity trade	Net inward flow of non-monetary gold and silver	Current outward remittances		Current account balance
1831–40	14.7	0.7	15.6	(10.1)	-1.6
1841–50	32.5	0.5	22.8	(23.0)	9.2
1851–60	48.6	-1.1	36.9	(27.7)	12.8
1861–70	51.9	5.1	26.7	(22.8)	20.1
1871–80	70.4	5.8	41.4	(8.2)	23.2
1881–90	61.5	10.1	40.5	(1.6)	10.9
1891–1900	60.3	6.9	57.2	(2.2)	-3.8
1901–10	129.2	4.9	103.0	(3.0)	21.3
1911–20	441.4	13.5	327.8	(10.4)	100.1
1921–30	559.6	11.8	494.5	(59.0)	53.3
1931–39	221.3	-21.3	220.0	(55.9)	22.6

* Figures in brackets refer to outward remittances on government accounts. Up to 1871–80 these were mainly surpluses from the *cultuurstelsel*. From then government remittances were mainly interest payments.
Source: *Changing Economy of Indonesia*, Vol. 7, Table 1.

Table 5.6 Trends in the capital account of the balance of payments, 1831–1940 (Annual averages: millions of guilders)

	Current account surplus/deficit (−)	Net additions to private balances abroad	Private capital imports*	Balancing item[†]
1831–40	−1.6	2.5	−2.5	−1.6
1841–50	9.2	7.0	0	2.2
1851–60	12.8	7.8	−1.0	6.0
1861–70	20.1	23.1	−3.2	0.2
1871–80	23.2	20.1	−3.5	6.6
1881–90	10.9	30.3	−20.1	0.7
1891–1900	−3.8	23.9	−27.6	−0.1
1901–10	21.3	51.3	−42.5	12.5

1911–20	100.1	206.6	−104.3	−2.2
1921–30	53.3	136.0	−56.2	−26.5
1931–40	22.6	39.4	−7.1	−9.7

* Negative sign denotes inward flow of capital.
† Includes imports and exports of monetary gold and silver, changes in official gold and silver reserves, changes in floating debt of the government, issues of government bonds, purchases of securities abroad and remittances of life insurance premiums and pensions funds.
Source: CEI, Vol 7, Table 1.

Although the current account surplus declined in the 1880s, and became a deficit in the 1890s, after 1900 it began to grow again, in spite of the rapid growth in current remittances of interest, dividends and profits. But this growth in the current account surplus was more than offset by net additions to private balances held abroad. This substantial private sector outflow on both current and capital account was in turn offset to some extent by private capital imports, which increased rapidly after 1890. After 1920 private capital imports fell off more drastically than private outflow, and government borrowing was required to bridge the gap between net additions to privately held balances abroad and the current account surplus (Table 5.6).

In the years from 1923 to 1927, the current account surplus averaged 5 per cent of national income, an extraordinarily high percentage for a country at Indonesia's stage of development. On average in the two decades from 1921 to 1939, the current account surplus averaged 2 per cent of GDP (Figure 5.2). The relative scale of Indonesia's

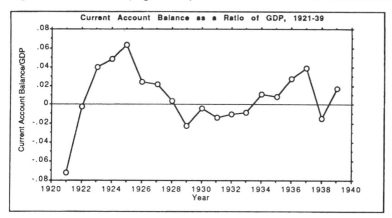

Figure 5.2: *Sources:* Current account balance, CEI, Vol. 7, Table 1; nominal GDP data from Pierre van der Eng.

capital export at this period can be appreciated if we examine the data for the United Kingdom in the late nineteenth and early twentieth centuries, and Japan in the 1980s. The United Kingdom's current account surplus was 5.5 per cent of GDP in the 1880s, and fell somewhat thereafter, while Japan's current account surplus averaged 2.5 per cent of GDP from 1981 to 1988 (Arndt 1990: Table 1). Thus Indonesia in the inter-war years was on average exporting capital at almost the same rate, relative to national income, as the two largest creditor nations in the world economy at the peak periods of their international influence. The consequences of this for Indonesian economic development are examined in the next section.

After independence, it might have been expected that the current account would rapidly swing into deficit, as the policy-makers embarked on an ambitious programme of planned economic development. But this, in fact, was not the case. Rosendale's estimates of the current account balance during the Old Order period indicated a deficit in only six years between 1950 and 1965 (Rosendale 1978: 146). In the early 1950s, the current account surpluses were mainly used to build up foreign exchange reserves. However, in the late 1950s and early 1960s the 'errors and omissions' in the capital account became very large, which Rosendale (1978: 154) argued 'indicated the extent of under-statement of imports of goods, imports of services and capital outflow'. The real break with the tradition of current account surpluses financing large capital outflows which had persisted in Indonesia with few interruptions since the 1830s came with the advent of the New Order government. In the two decades from 1969 to 1989, the current account balance was positive in only three years, 1974, 1979 and 1980. In each of these years there were large and unanticipated increases in export earnings as a result of increases in the world price of oil. In other years, the current account deficits were financed by net inflow of capital on both government and private account. But, perhaps surprisingly, the balance of commodity trade remained in surplus over this entire period, and indeed the commodity trade balance as a proportion of exports was as high in the 1970s and 1980s as in the interwar years. The main reason for the deficits on current account in the New Order period has been a large deficit in 'invisibles', including transport and travel and debt servicing payments.

CHANGES IN THE TRADE REGIME: THE RISE AND DECLINE OF FREE TRADE LIBERALISM IN THE COLONIAL ERA

There can be little doubt that the most dramatic change in the colonial trade regime in the nineteenth century occurred in the 1870s with the advent of the so-called Liberal Policy. Although a desire to protect Dutch commercial interests against British imports and British influence had been one reason for the implementation of the *cultuurstelsel* in the first place, the years from 1830 to 1860 had, as Furnivall (1944: 172) pointed out, witnessed a considerable increase in British influence in the archipelago, most notably in shipping. In the 1830s, Lord Palmerston, then the Foreign Secretary, complained to the Hague about impediments to trade encountered by British exporters in Indonesia. He was told that the duties and preferential arrangements which the British objected to were being revoked as they had served their end which was to prevent the importation of Belgium goods into Dutch colonies during the war between the two countries (Wright 1909: 99). By 1860, British imports into Java accounted for 19 per cent of all imports into Java (excluding those from the Outer Islands), compared with only 13 per cent in 1840 (CEI, Vol 12a, Tables 1A and 3A).

By the end of the 1860s, the climate of Dutch opinion on colonial trade policy began to change. As Fasseur (1978: 157) has argued, a major reason for this change was the growing influence in the Netherlands of political and economic liberalism. A system relying on coercion of cultivators and government intervention in, and regulation of, markets for tropical produce was therefore bound to meet with criticism. In addition, there seemed little point in persevering with a system of colonial economic management that was unsatisfactory for other reasons if it was also unsuccessful in reducing the influence in the Indonesian archipelago of the Netherlands' main commercial rival. The changes influential liberals such as van Bosse and van de Putte brought about in the tariff laws of the Netherlands between 1865 and 1872 led to the abolition of all differential tariff duties in both the Netherlands and the colonies. Although these changes had only limited support in those Chambers of Commerce involved in colonial trade, the case for free trade had powerful support in the press, which emboldened the politicians seeking abolition of all differential tariffs on imports into Indonesia, and weakened those opposing tariff reform (Kuitenbrouwer 1991: 67–72).

From the early 1870s to the early 1930s Indonesia was, at least in appearance, an open and unprotected economy. Not only was there virtually no tariff or non-tariff discrimination against imports from any source, but there was also an open capital account facilitating the inflow of capital and the repatriation of profits. Although both specific and *ad valorem* import taxes were levied, both Dutch and foreign commentators emphasised that tariffs were purely for revenue purposes, and 'the idea of protection is totally foreign' (Paulus 1909: 124; Fowler 1923: 399; Kuitenbrouwer 1991: 67). After 1872, import tariffs were set at 10 per cent for most commodities, and export taxes varied between 3 and 6 per cent. In the early 1920s, the highest *ad valorem* tariff levied was still only 12 per cent, although some luxury goods such as alcoholic drinks were subject to higher specific tariffs. Export duties on products such as rubber and quinine were levied on a sliding scale, so that the *ad valorem* rate increased with rising prices. For rubber, the maximum *ad valorem* rate was 7 per cent (Fowler 1923: 398).

But in spite of the apparently non-discriminatory trade regime, the Netherlands continued to account for a much greater share of Indonesia's imports than its share of total world trade would have justified. Import enforcement ratios certainly fell between 1880 and 1900 although in 1900 the Netherlands' share of Indonesian imports was still almost five times its share of total world exports. By comparison Great Britain accounted for a lower share of Indonesian imports than its share of world exports (Table 5.7). Singapore's ratio was much higher, but this reflects the importance of Singapore as a regional entrepot and transhipment centre, which declined slowly in the years from 1900 to 1930. It is likely that various forms of subtle discrimination against British and other importers persisted after 1870 through the dominance of Dutch trading houses in the export-import sector, and, of course, through a Dutch commercial and legal system which would have advantaged Dutch merchants. In addition, by the early twentieth century, there were complaints that continual changes to the tariff system were making the system less transparent; as Pitt (1991: 18) points out, such criticisms were to become more vociferous as the century progressed. Such lack of transparency again would have disadvantaged non-Dutch merchants who were in many cases unable to read Dutch, and would have been less familiar with the Dutch regulatory system.

In spite of the bias in import trade towards the Netherlands revealed in Table 5.7, Dutch policy-makers were anxious to create a

Table 5.7   Import trade global enforcement ratios,* 1880–1990

	Netherlands	United Kingdom	USA	Japan	Singapore[†]
1880	8.5	0.6	0.4	n.a	29.4
1900	4.8	0.8	0.1	0.2	30.5
1913	5.3	1.2	0.8	0.9	16.3
1931**	6.6	0.9	0.7	5.0	8.8
1953	4.0	0.7	0.8	9.6	1.1
1975	0.6	0.6	1.2	5.0	7.1
1990	0.6	0.3	0.8	4.0	3.5

*Ratios refer to the share of the country in total Indonesian imports divided by the share of the country's exports in total world exports. A ratio of unity implies that the share of the country in Indonesian imports was the same as its share in world imports.
[†]Until 1953 includes Peninsular Malaysia
**Five-year average centred on 1931
Sources: Indonesian import ratios from CEI, Volume 12a, Table 3b(1880–1931); Bank Indonesia, *Report for the Year 1954–5*, p. 101 (1953); Central Bureau of Statistics, *Statistical Yearbook of Indonesia 1979*, *Statistical Yearbook of Indonesia 1994* (1975 and 1990). Export data for the other countries and the global totals taken from Hansen (1980), Table A-3 for 1880 and 1900; Yates (1959: 202–38) for 1913 and 1953; Clark (1936), Table XXIX for 1931; International Monetary Fund, *Direction of Trade Statistics Yearbook*, 1978 and 1994 for 1975 and 1990.

favourable climate in Indonesia for investors, both from the Netherlands and elsewhere. A key element in this strategy was the virtual parity of the colonial with the metropolitan guilder, and the adherence of both currencies to the Gold Standard from the mid-1870s onwards. This move was forced on the metropolitan economy by the German decision to move to the Gold Standard in 1873. There was considerable debate about whether Indonesia should follow suit, or stay with a silver-based system. Powerful voices such as that of van den Berg, the president of the Java Bank, argued that if the colony stayed with a silver-based currency, maintenance of the parity between the two guilders would be impossible (van der Eng 1996: xi). These arguments prevailed. The operation of the so-called guilder exchange standard was largely the responsibility of the Java Bank, which managed the domestic money supply through its monopoly on the issue of bank notes. The colonial government's adoption of this system was not without controversy; in particular, sugar producers blamed the fixed exchange rate for the troubles of the industry in the mid-1880s. The

Dutch government addressed their grievances by reducing sugar export taxes, but there was no change in the exchange rate regime (Kuitenbrouwer 1991: 183–4). In fact, the agricultural estates recovered quite quickly from their problems, through improvements in management and technology and the development of new markets. By the early 1890s, they had come to accept that 'it is a mistake to suppose that the difficulties of 1884–86 were primarily or even largely due to currency legislation' (Kensington 1892: 58; van der Eng 1996: xix).

The guilder exchange standard had the great advantage of eliminating any exchange rate risk for investors from other Gold Standard countries, especially Britain which was by far the largest exporter of capital at the time. The stable exchange rate combined with a low and reasonably transparent tariff regime certainly made Indonesia attractive to foreign investors, compared to many other parts of Asia. It has been estimated that by 1914 almost 60 per cent of all foreign private investment in Southeast Asia (including Indochina) was in Indonesia, and much of this was direct rather than portfolio investment (Svedberg 1978: 770). But as Svedberg (1981: 22) has argued, investors from the mother country enjoyed a number of advantages in Indonesia as in other colonial territories, and the investment enforcement ratios for Indonesia, like the trade enforcement ratios, were well above unity even at the end of the 1930s, when the Dutch share of total foreign investment was lower than it had been earlier in the century (Svedberg 1981: Table 1).

Even if the foreign trade and investment regime in colonial Indonesia was in practice less open and liberal than some Dutch officials claimed, there were those who thought that it should favour Dutch metropolitan interests to a much greater extent. There was a growing debate, especially in the 1920s, about the desirability of creating a customs union between the Netherlands and Indonesia, along the lines of the one between metropolitan France and her colonies. But as Gonggrijp (1931: 158) pointed out, such a union 'must be protectionist if it is to be effective'. In addition, the costs to the colonial budget would have been considerable, as all existing tariffs on Dutch imports would have been abolished. These arguments were forceful enough to carry the day, and nothing came of the various proposals for greater economic integration between the metropolitan and colonial economies.

It was the events of the early 1930s which finally brought about the break with the low tariff regime of the previous six decades. The slump in export prices, the drastic curtailment of traditional markets for key export staples, especially sugar, and the rise in Japanese imports together persuaded the colonial authorities that there was little option but to embark on a strategy of strict regulation of foreign trade. As far as export crops were concerned, the government attempted to regulate domestic production of chincona, kapok, tin, rubber, and sugar, either unilaterally or in the context of international agreements (van Gelderen 1939: 38–62; Furnivall 1944: 435–8). On the import side regulation took the form of import bans, and both general and specific quota restrictions. The most important commodity to be protected through a comprehensive ban was rice; imports of rice into Java were prohibited in 1933, and the major markets outside Java were gradually closed to foreign imports as arrangements were made for their supply from Java and Bali (Furnivall 1944: 439).

A broad range of other imports were restricted through general and specific quotas. The former were not specified by country of origin, and enabled the authorities

> to issue licences for the import of ... goods to all recognised import firms which remained totally free to buy these goods where they liked. Practically this meant that these goods were bought in Japan. However the allotment of licences formed a protection of the existing import apparatus, as the licences were issued to each firm according to its share in total import trade in a basic period (van Gelderen 1939: 24).

The system of specific quotas by contrast was deliberately designed to bring about a redirection of import trade away from cheap Japanese goods and towards goods of Dutch origin, or from other countries 'with which trade arrangements on the basis of some reciprocity would be concluded' (van Gelderen 1939: 25). Typically, specific quotas were used to regulate imports of high quality textiles, wrapping paper, rubber tyres, artificial manures and light bulbs. The Japanese share of all these imports fell over the latter part of the 1930s. Goods not subject to quotas were subject to tariffs which ranged from zero to 20 per cent *ad valorem*; liquor and tobacco products continued to be subject to specific rates (International Customs Tariffs Bureau, 1937).

Official calculations indicated that these restrictions together affected almost 40 per cent of all imports, of which 14 per cent fell under the specific quota system. In addition to imposing tariffs and quantitative controls, the government began to implement an extensive programme of price surveillance which was intended to prevent 'any unfounded increase of prices' (van Gelderen 1939: 26). Particular import firms were often awarded both general and specific licences, and profits made on Japanese imports could thus be offset against losses made on sales of expensive European imports at controlled prices. In effect, the specific quotas should be seen as a tax imposed on both importers and consumers of Japanese products in the colony to finance the partial rehabilitation of the Dutch textile industry. To the extent that consumers of Japanese products were mainly indigenous Indonesians, these policies would have been quite regressive.

Certainly the complex system of import regulations introduced after 1934 was successful in reducing the Japanese import share, a goal which was as much strategic as economic. The growth in Japanese exports was viewed by many in the colonial government as part of a longer-term political strategy to undermine the authority of the European colonial powers in Southeast Asia; even such a balanced observer as van Gelderen (1939: 22) spoke of an urgent need for 'economic defence against monopoly and semi-political penetration'. Other observers pointed to the 'unfair trading practices' of the Japanese, including government support for exporters at a level 'to which the rest of the world was as yet unaccustomed' (de Wilde and Moll 1936: 58). In fact, we have seen that there were obvious economic reasons for the rapid growth of Japanese imports into Indonesia in the late 1920s and early 1930s, and indeed Indonesia remained an important market for Japanese cotton piecegoods after 1934, in spite of the imposition of quotas.

Given that a key reason for the rapid growth of Japanese imports after 1930 was the decision of the Dutch monetary authorities to stay on the gold standard, why did the colonial authorities not unilaterally devalue the NEI guilder? Such a method of countering the Japanese 'threat' would have been more in keeping with previous liberal policies than the imposition of quantitative restrictions. It would also have given much needed assistance to traded goods industries across the board, in both the export and the import competing sectors. In fact the colonial authorities resisted demands to devalue the Indies guilder from members of the *Volksraad* (People's Council) on the grounds that it would sever the close economic ties between the colony and the Netherlands (Prince 1996: 67). The NEI guilder was only devalued in 1936, when the home government decided to abandon the gold parity.

It was stressed in the previous chapter that the main result of the measures taken in the 1930s was an unprecedented level of government involvement in the colonial economy. By 1939 an American observer was writing of 'six years of economic planning in Netherlands India' (Barber 1939). According to Barber, from being a 'stronghold of free trade and free capitalist enterprise', the economic system of colonial Indonesia underwent progressive modification through the 1930s 'in the direction of closer, more detailed and far more studied government control'.

The Dutch have feared the political consequences of Japanese economic penetration and the entire Japanese question in Netherlands India is thus tinged with political considerations. Political considerations weighed heavily in determining the free trade and open door policy of pre-crisis years, since the Netherlands government was well aware that stronger powers, if denied access to the raw materials of the East Indies, might easily be disposed to challenge Dutch control. If free trade, however, enabled the Japanese to achieve economic dominance and political influence in the islands, the traditional policy was useless, or worse. Hence a change was indicated, just as when a century ago the Dutch decided that free trade in that day meant the promotion of British goods and influence at the expense of Dutch interests and would have none of it (Barber 1939: 202).

Thus, the ideology of free trade which had prevailed in colonial Indonesia since the 1870s had been abandoned for a system which involved considerable government intervention in, and regulation of, markets for traded goods. In addition, there was growing support for the use of colonial markets to assist struggling industries in the Netherlands. Indeed, it is probable that measures to effect closer economic integration between the Netherlands and Indonesia, rejected as too protectionist in the 1920s, might have been adopted in the 1940s, were it not for the outbreak of hostilities in Europe and the Pacific. Some members of the Visman Commission, which reported in 1938, strongly advocated further cuts in tariffs for industrial imports from the Netherlands, even if this impeded the pace of colonial industrialisation (Broek 1942: 111). The German invasion of the Netherlands in 1940 meant that all such schemes were shelved, but it also led to the adoption of strict foreign exchange and price controls in Indonesia. These were reimposed when the Dutch returned in 1945.

Several writers have emphasised the importance of these measures for post-independence policy-making in Indonesia. Higgins (1968: 693) pointed out that it was a regulated rather than a free economy which the Dutch bequeathed to the independent republic, and the tendency of subsequent governments, at least until the late 1960s, was 'to add new regulations without removing the old ones'. Pitt (1991: 25) has summarised the Dutch legacy as follows:

> The Dutch established a pervasive system of import and production quotas whose level and distribution were controlled or influenced by associations of affected trading firms and manufacturing enterprises. Price control was widespread. Official discrimination against the 'economically strong group' – meaning Indo-chinese – was first enacted... These same measures characterised the pattern of policy during the first two decades of Indonesia's independence... those forces who proclaimed most loudly the need to destroy the remnants of the Dutch colonial economy were those who adopted its methods of economic control.

THE REGULATED TRADE REGIME SINCE 1950

The truth of these comments was amply demonstrated in the years from 1950 to 1965. During the Korean War Boom of 1950–51, commodity prices surged, and virtually all the pre-war quantitative restraints on exports were lifted. The foreign exchange retention scheme introduced in March 1950 was modified later in the year. The Hatta and Natsir cabinets were keen to liberalise imports, mainly because liberalisation would curtail the power of the large Dutch-owned trading houses which were viewed by many nationalists as trojan horses for Dutch economic interests in the newly independent republic. While technocrats such as Sumitro saw market forces as the best way of ending colonial monopolies, others wanted the system of import controls to continue but indigenous rather than Dutch firms to be the beneficiaries. Such economic nationalists viewed Sumitro with intense suspicion, although Sumitro himself was responsible for the so-called 'Benteng' programme when he was Minister of Trade and Industry in the Natsir cabinet. The Natsir cabinet fell in early 1951, and its successor led by Sukiman was more nationalist in orientation. By early 1952 it had to deal with declining world commodity prices and a sharp decline in official dollar reserves.

The measures adopted to tackle the ensuing balance of payments crisis included a substantial devaluation of the rupiah (from 3.8 to 11.4 rupiahs to the dollar) and more changes to the already complex system of multiple exchange rates. The devaluation in fact made little difference to the exchange rate facing importers, because of the multiple exchange rate system already in place, although it did raise the export rate by 50 per cent (Corden and Mackie 1962: 46; Pitt 1991: 37). From 1952 onwards a range of devices were used to control quantities and prices of both exports and imports, including inducement certificates, import taxes and surcharges, export taxes and subsidies, import prepayments and quantitative licensing of imports. The use of these instruments varied with the government in power. When economic rationalists such as Sumitro were influential, there were attempts to use the price mechanism to control imports, while the cabinets of Ali Sastroamidjojo, in 1953 and 1955, resorted increasingly to arbitrary controls as a means of bringing order to an increasingly chaotic situation. But no government after 1952 was successful in removing the complex regime of multiple exchange rates. As Corden and Mackie (1962: 41) pointed out, post-independence governments had kept almost intact the relatively simple tariff code of the pre-war era, but added to it a complicated system of import surcharges administered as part of the exchange rate system. 'What Indonesia thus lacks in complexity in its tariff system it has to a large extent made up by complexity in its exchange rate system.'

As was argued in the previous chapter, the climate of international opinion had greatly changed in the post-war era and even in the International Monetary Fund there was guarded support for multiple exchange rate systems and even for quantitative import controls. Economic liberalism was a discredited creed as Keynesian ideas of economic management took hold in the industrialised world and planned economic development was almost universally adopted in Asian developing countries. Nobody in Indonesia seriously contemplated a return to the pre-1930s trade regime, which in the eyes of even the most moderate of Indonesian nationalists had enriched the Dutch, other foreigners and the Chinese in that order, at the expense of the indigenous Indonesian cultivator. Those hostile to economic liberalism could reasonably point to the fact that six decades of export expansion under a liberal trade regime from 1870 to 1930 had brought very little improvement in the living conditions of the great majority of the population, and that a more interventionist approach was essential if the benefits of trade were to be retained in the country and used for purposes of long-run economic development. When knowledgeable foreigners such as Corden and Mackie (1962: 59) argued that 'free trade...is in no sense an optimum in the conditions of Indonesia' there were few in Indonesia who would have dissented.

It could plausibly be argued that, had the competent economic managers such as Sumitro and Sjafruddin been able to control economic policy-making over a longer period after 1951, they could have gradually fashioned a trade policy which relied less on quantitative controls and more on the price mechanism to ration scarce resources of foreign exchange among competing uses. Even in the brief period during which Sumitro was Minister of Finance in 1955, in the caretaker cabinet headed by Harahap, quite sweeping reforms were made to the system of import controls and multiple exchange rates (Pitt 1991: 49–52). But with the second cabinet of Ali Sastroamidjojo, rampant corruption and favouritism replaced any pretence of market methods of allocating increasingly scarce and under-priced foreign exchange. An increasing proportion of exports were diverted into smuggling, and the black market value of the rupiah soared. The export-producing provinces outside Java became more and more convinced that the foreign trade regime was designed to exploit them and reward the bureaucrats and politicians, largely Javanese, who ran it. The result was that Indonesian exports stagnated while world trade grew at historically unprecedented rates.

The New Order regime's commitment to exchange rate stabilisation and the restoration of incentives in the export economy was evidenced in the series of measures adopted between 1966 and 1971 which were discussed in the previous chapter. As far as exchange rate management was concerned, the old system was completely abandoned in favour of a unified exchange rate. Indeed, with the unification of the exchange rate in 1971 and a freely convertible rupiah, together with virtually no constraints on capital movement in or out of the country, Indonesia had, in effect, returned to the pre-1930 exchange system. But it can be queried how much actual difference these measures made to the incentives facing individual producers of traded goods. As Pitt (1991: 181) points out, by 1966 'the instruments of economic control were widely evaded by black markets' and a substantial part of the response of producers to the measures of 1966 amounted to a redirection of illegal activities into legal market channels. Producer returns to smallholder rubber exporters, for example, were no greater after the reforms than before, once smuggling was taken into account. The real benefits of the reform measures lay in the much greater climate of certainty created by the return of orderly markets for goods, credit and foreign exchange. Certainly, controls and corruption, favouritism and insider trading remained, but their scale was much reduced.

But the liberalisation of the period 1966–71 was still partial. As far as commodity trade was concerned the restrictions remained considerable. The tariff code had become much more complex, and more overtly protectionist, in the 1960s, and the series of tariff revisions between 1970 and 1973 produced a tariff code whose nature still reflected an uneasy compromise between revenue-raising and protectionist goals. Glassburner (1973: 103) drew attention to the large number of rates, which would have made enforcement difficult for even the most efficient of customs services. Although rates on intermediate goods and capital goods were increased to enhance the revenue productivity of the system, the rate structure as a whole remained sharply cascaded with goods for final consumption attracting a higher rate on average than capital and intermediate goods. Effective protection rates for final consumption goods were thus higher than the nominal rates.

After the 1973 tariff reform it was widely argued that import policies became increasingly protectionist in Indonesia. There was increasing resort to quantitative controls, including outright import bans, or prohibitively expensive import prepayment arrangements which amounted to the same thing (McCawley 1981: 80). In addition, the administrative difficulties involved in importing and exporting became more pronounced as successive attempts to reform the notorious Directorate General of Customs and Excise failed to yield significant results. The upshot was a trade regime that afforded extremely high effective rates of protection to many enterprises manufacturing consumer goods for sale in Indonesia, while exporters enjoyed little government assistance and in some cases, where their inputs were priced well above world levels or where export taxes were levied, they received negative effective protection (Boediono and Pangestu 1986: 41–3). In fact, the gap between the Jakarta wholesale price and the world price for crops such as rubber, coffee and tea was substantially larger after 1968 than it had been in the pre-war period (Booth 1988: 230–2). This reflected the severity of the export tax regime and also, in the case of tea and coffee, the fact that Indonesian exports were of poor quality and their price was frequently discounted relative to the world benchmark prices. In addition, of course smallholder producers of export crops were penalised by high transport costs and various illegal imposts which greatly reduced the price they received at the farm gate compared to wholesale prices in the large cities.

As was noted in the previous chapter, there was considerable evidence in the years from 1981 to 1985 that the government would react to the fall in the income terms of trade consequent upon falling world oil prices by imposing even more restrictions on imports. In the event, the latter part of the 1980s saw a number of notable moves away from a highly regulated trade regime and towards greater simplicity and transparency in the structure of protection, together with a reduction in the disincentives facing exporters. Many quantitative restrictions on imports were removed and there were some moves towards the use of tariffs rather than non-tariff barriers as the principal means of protection. Even so, the trade regime of the late 1980s was still very different from the liberal one which prevailed before the 1930s. The structure of protection afforded the manufacturing sector was still characterised by a very marked dispersion in effective rates, with many industries still enjoying effective rates of protection in excess of 50 per cent, while others faced negative protection (Fane and Phillips 1991: 124–5). Although some exporters received substantial assistance from the duty drawback scheme on imported inputs which had been operated by the Ministry of Finance since 1986, the system remained administratively complex and potentially vulnerable to bureaucratic abuse. The incentive schemes which were introduced in the latter part of the 1980s benefited exporters of manufactures, rather than smallholder producers of agricultural exports, most of whom enjoyed little government assistance. In addition, attempts at across the board trade liberalisation were thwarted by the continuing implementation of policies designed to protect enterprises owned by those associated with senior political figures.

On the other hand, it could be argued that to return to a completely open trade regime, even if it were politically possible, would not be desirable for a country at Indonesia's level of development. The world trading system changed considerably after the boom period of the 1950s and 1960s, and while it was still far more liberal in the 1980s than in the 1930s, protectionism certainly increased. Many of Indonesia's exports including oil, textile products, coffee and tin were still in 1990 subject to various forms of international quota restrictions which, in turn, involved the regulation of domestic production. The challenge for Indonesian policy-makers in the 1990s is to maximise the country's gains from trade in a far from perfectly competitive international trading environment. In the 1980s, as in the 1930s, the Indonesian economy proved remarkably resilient in the face of external instability, which was reflected in both output restrictions and falling prices for key export staples. In both decades there was rapid export diversification and new export products emerged often with surprising speed. In both decades, government policy interventions, including exchange rate adjustments, certainly facilitated the emergence of new exports, but the important point is that domestic producers proved themselves enterprising enough to respond rapidly to the incentives provided. But what impact has this resilience and enterprise had on the growth of the economy as a whole? We turn now to examine this question in more detail.

INTERNATIONAL TRADE AND ECONOMIC GROWTH: THE COLONIAL EXPERIENCE

A major issue confronting an economic historian studying Southeast Asia, or indeed many other parts of the tropical world in the nineteenth and early twentieth centuries, is the impact of increased involvement in international trade on economic development and the standard of living. Although trade was seen as the 'engine of growth' in Europe and in the countries of European settlement in North and South America, Australasia and Southern Africa, the tropical colonies which had been opened up to international trade in the nineteenth century failed to experience the same economic transformation as occurred in Europe and the European dominions overseas. There has been much discussion in the literature of colonial economic development about why this was so, particularly in the light of the many arguments, from the works of Adam Smith onwards, that a liberal international trade regime should facilitate the economic development process. In his survey of export growth in Asia, Africa and Latin America in the nineteenth century, Hanson (1980: 51) listed three conditions which must be fulfilled before 'trade can be expected to contribute significantly to a country's economic development'. These were:

1 a large export sector,
2 rapid export growth in per capita terms,
3 a comparative advantage in products with growth-promoting or at least not growth-retarding production functions.

To this list we should add the presence of a government willing and able to promote the development of market institutions, and to facilitate investment in both physical and human capital, especially by ensuring that a large share of the profits from foreign trade and investment are invested in the domestic economy.

These are a demanding set of conditions and few countries met them before 1900. Indeed, as Hanson points out, few even met the first two. Certainly Indonesia did not. Although there was rapid export growth in Java in the 1830s, it was from a low base, and of course most of the profits were remitted abroad. From 1840 to 1870 per capita export volume growth was less than 1 per cent per annum. It was argued in Chapter 2 that the export regions outside Java were penalised throughout the nineteenth century by their incorporation into the Indonesian economy, a process which involved the rupturing of traditional trading links with regional entrepots and with the wider world. Some regions such as Aceh and Lombok never recovered from this process. Their traditional export sectors contracted and they remained stagnant backwaters until 1940. But even in those regions outside Java such as the East Coast of Sumatra where important export industries such as tobacco began to develop after 1870, the export sectors remained too small to have much impact on the regional economy until 1900. Certainly the income terms of trade improved in Indonesia between 1850 and 1900 (Table 2.1) but the total size of the export sector was too small for this improvement to have a dramatic effect on the domestic economy. As Leff (1982: 91) put it for Brazil in the nineteenth century, the engine was both too small and too slow-moving to have had much impact.

But in the three decades from 1900 to 1930 Indonesia should have been able to utilise the gains from trade to accelerate growth in the national economy. Export volume growth accelerated after 1900, and the income terms of trade showed a continuous upward trend until 1928 (Table 2.1). The export sector accounted for a growing proportion of GDP (Figure 5.1) and Indonesian exports accounted for a growing share of total exports from the third world (Table 5.1). One possible explanation for the failure of this impressive export performance to generate broadly based development within the colonial economy is the third factor mentioned by Hanson. According to this argument, Indonesian export staples lacked 'growth-promoting production functions'. This hypothesis will be addressed in more detail in the next chapter. Here I want to examine another, more controversial explanation much discussed in the colonial development literature, that of the colonial drain.

The Indonesian balance of payments recorded large and sustained surpluses on commodity trade and on the current account over more than a century, which were used to finance capital export on both private and government account (Tables 5.5 and 5.6). These surpluses were almost as high relative to GDP as those achieved by major capital exporters such as Britain in the nineteenth century, or Japan more recently. They were high in absolute terms as well; in the years from 1828 to 1913 the net cumulative surplus on the current account of the balance of payments (i.e. accumulated surpluses less deficits) came to almost £70 million in 1880 prices (Table 5.8). This was more than twice Edelstein's estimate of Britain's entire capital exports in 1880, and 5 per cent of the UK's gross national product in 1880 (Edelstein 1982: 313). Between 1913 and 1940 the accumulated net balance of payments surpluses amounted to $1.44 billion in 1967 prices (Table 5.8).

Table 5.8 Cumulative current account surpluses, 1828–1940

	£ million (1880 prices)	US$ million (1967 prices)
Indonesia		
1828–50	4.593	
1851–90	49.603	
1891–1913	13.915	178.829
1914–30		1,124.005
1931–39		316.670
1969–90		−10,424.570
Japan		
1914–30		513.230
1931–39		−353.518

Note: The deflator used for pounds sterling was the export price index estimated by Imlah. For dollars the US Producer Price Index was used.
Sources: CEI, Vol 7; CEI Vol 6; Imlah (1958: 94–8); *Statistical Abstracts of the USA*; Ohkawa and Shinohara (1979: 332–6).

A persistent idea in the literature of economic growth has been that countries go through stages in the evolution of their balance of payments in the course of their economic development. They begin as 'immature debtor-borrowers' with a deficit in the goods and service accounts of their balance of payments, and a deficit in investment income financed by net capital receipts. They end up as mature creditors, still with a deficit in goods and services, but which is more than covered by investment income so there is a net outflow of capital (Sachs and Larrain 1993: 575). Recent empirical investigations have cast doubt on this progression in that some high-income countries such as Australia and Canada have remained 'mature debtor-borrowers' while the USA has regressed from being a mature creditor-lender in the inter-war years, and in the period from 1945 to 1980, to being a large borrower in the 1980s. But the available evidence does indicate that in the post-1945 period, no low income country has been an exporter of capital (Halevi 1971: Tables 3 and 4). Thus, the experience of Indonesia during the last century or so of Dutch colonial rule is anomalous, to say the least, in the light of the more recent experience of developing countries.

The question thus arises of the causes of these large and sustained commodity trade and balance of payments surpluses in colonial Indonesia. Should they be regarded, as they certainly were by the nationalist movement, as evidence of a deliberate policy of 'exploitation', either in the sense that they were used to finance unrequited transfers to the home government, which were then used for purposes that contributed nothing to the development of Indonesia, or in the sense that they financed outward remittances on private account which were higher than would have been justified by the normal workings of the market? There can be little doubt that the very large unrequited government transfers abroad on government account during the years of the *cultuurstelsel* were the result of deliberate policy and were certainly exploitative in that the domestic economy received virtually nothing back in return. But to what extent did the high level of outward remittances on private account which persisted from the 1880s to the 1930s represent simply a 'fair return' to the foreign factors of production (capital and labour) invested in the Indonesian economy in ever-increasing amounts through the late nineteenth and early twentieth centuries? Certainly some colonial economists thought that this was how they should be regarded. Boeke (1953: 203) argued as follows:

> colonial capital, whether organised as a private enterprise or as a government activity, serves, works, fertilises, produces; and even if the results of its productive achievements are in part intended for export abroad, all that is left over for, or given to, the native community is pure gain for it. Without western leadership, without help and cooperation from western capital, the 'colonial' country would not have developed as it has.

An argument along these lines has been made more recently by van der Eng (1993b). But it begs some important questions. To what extent were the Western enterprises really essential to the growth of the export sector? Were the profits accruing to Western export enterprises in Indonesia, which were remitted abroad, at least in part due to government protection against competition from domestic producers? It can be argued in the case of the rubber estate companies, for example, that smallholder domestic producers were just as efficient as the foreign estates, which only survived in the interwar period because of government assistance through the allocation of export quotas (Bauer 1948: 331–5). In these circumstances, at least part of the funds accruing to the foreign shareholders of the estate companies must be seen as monopoly profits, rather than as a competitive return to 'the enormous risks involved in colonial investment' (Boeke 1953: 203). In addition, as Myint (1971: 110) argued, the large profits made by trading firms in many parts of Asia arose in part from their strategic position which permitted them to exercise 'varying degrees of monopoly power both in the buying of the produce from the peasants and in the selling of the imported goods to them'. It can also be argued that the high salaries earned by European workers reflected an artificial scarcity of skills created by educational policies which in effect prevented all but a few indigenous Indonesians from gaining access to European schools.

But there is a much more important set of issues regarding the persistent colonial balance of payments surplus which have not been addressed in the Indonesian literature, although they have been extensively discussed in the theoretical literature on open economy macroeconomics. It is now widely realised that a country's current account surplus or deficit is the result not just of the difference between domestic savings and domestic investment (on both government and private account), but also of the real effective exchange rate. If an open economy consistently saves more than it invests, either because the private sector has a high savings propensity or because the government is running a large budgetary surplus, then exports will exceed imports, and a current account surplus will result. But in order to bring this about, total domestic spending or absorption must be divided between traded and non-traded goods in such a way that the difference between domestic savings and investment $(S - I)$ equals the current account balance $(X - M)$. The ratio of the prices of traded to non-traded goods (the real exchange rate) must be such as to bring about an allocation of expenditure between them which equalises the two surpluses (Arndt 1991).

The current account surpluses between 1830 and 1870 were the result of both government budgetary surpluses and high rates of domestic savings. The government surpluses were used to finance the remittances to the budget of the Netherlands, while the surplus of private savings over private investment was used to fund private remittances to the Netherlands and elsewhere. While the budgetary surpluses were the result of deliberate government policy, it is important to ask why domestic savings were remitted abroad, rather than invested in the colony. Certainly, the underdeveloped financial system was one reason, but it was also the case that for much of the nineteenth century, with the exception of the 1880s, the Indies guilder underwent a real appreciation, in the sense that the domestic prices of traded goods (imports and exports) declined relative to the domestic consumer price index, as proxied by the rice price index (Figure 5.3). The higher rate of domestic inflation compared with export and import prices was in turn the result of the persistent domestic budgetary deficit through much of the period of the CS. This would have made investment in traded goods industries (both exports and import substitutes) less profitable in Indonesia than in other parts of the world, and encouraged profits earned in the colony to be reinvested abroad. As was noted in Chapter 4, the government did take steps to encourage investment in infrastructure projects such as railways by guaranteeing the rate of return, but given the excess of private savings over investment for much of the nineteenth century, more could have been done to provide attractive investment opportunities in non-traded goods within the colony.

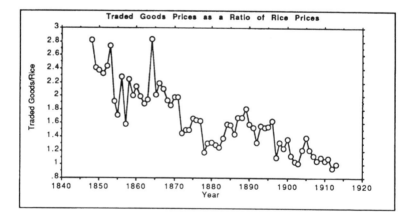

Figure 5.3 *Sources*: The rice price index was taken from CEI, Vol. 4, Table 1; the traded goods index is a weighted average of the export and import price index given in CEI, Vol. 15, Appendix A; weights were 60 per cent for exports and 40 per cent for imports.

We saw in the previous chapter that the size of the budget surplus fell after 1870, and in fact for much of the time from 1880 to 1940 the government budget was in deficit (Table 4.1). As the current account was in surplus for much of this time, private savings greatly exceeded private investment. Certainly, between 1914 and 1930, when the cumulative balance of payments surplus was extremely large, private savings were much in excess of private investment (Figure 5.4). What then accounted for this excess? Certainly, between 1920 and 1933 the price of traded goods fell sharply relative to home goods (Figure 5.5). As in the earlier period, this real appreciation of the guilder could have encouraged firms based in the colony to reinvest profits in other parts of the world. But at the same time the real appreciation should have diverted more domestic consumption towards traded goods, especially imports, and this should have reduced the trade surplus over time. The tighter fiscal policy stance after 1920 was one reason why imports did not grow more rapidly. In addition, the decline in the terms of trade also reduced real domestic incomes, aggravating the effect of the cutback in government expenditure. Taken together, these policies produced the high private savings and reduced incentives to invest in the colony, leading to the high and sustained current account surpluses.

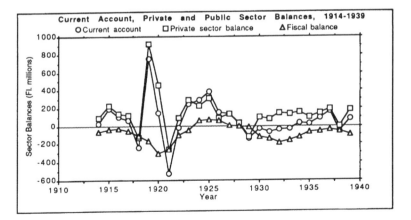

Figure 5.4 *Sources*: Current account balance, CEI, Vol. 7, Table 1; fiscal balance from CEI, Vol. 3, Table 4. Private sector balance derived from $X - M = S - I + T - G$.

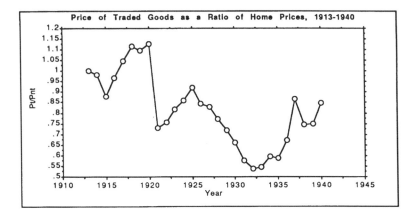

Figure 5.5 *Sources*: The home price index was taken from Central Bureau of Statistics (1938), Table X and *Statistical Pocketbook of Indonesia 1940*, p. 122; the traded goods index is a weighted average of the export and import price index given in van Ark (1986) and CEI, Vol. 15, Appendix A; weights were 60 per cent for exports and 40 per cent for imports

In the inter-war years, some Dutch economists were inclined to advocate direct government action to curb outward remittances on private account. Gonggrijp (1931: 160) stressed the damaging effect of profit remittances by large corporations which operated in the colony but were not resident there,

> and consequently, the profit realized affects the native population little if at all. The authorities should see to it that the part due to the Indian population be as large as possible. It would be expedient to favour governmental exploitation to that end, in all cases where they would be a chance of success (*sic*), without committing the error of excluding private exploitation. Another means of attaining this end would be to levy such high taxes on foreign capital (Dutch, English etc.) that the desire to create new exploitations would just survive, but not be greater than elsewhere.

It is obvious from the last sentence of this passage that Gonggrijp thought that at least part of the profits earned by the large private companies operating in the colony were due to market imperfections in the sense that they were greater than was necessary to attract foreign capital, given the opportunities available elsewhere. Whether this was really the case or not is difficult to establish without detailed examination of individual company records. Such research as is available indicates that only a minority of companies operating in the colony made what could be considered 'excessive' profits, although there can be little doubt that remitted profits from both the tobacco and the petroleum industries were very large (a Campo 1994; Thee 1977: 71–2). If the profits earned by these companies were indeed higher than what was necessary to attract them into Indonesia, then there would have been a case for higher taxation. But, in addition, a larger government deficit could have been run in the 1920s, given the very high propensity to save in the private sector. This would have permitted increased expenditures on both physical and human capital formation, which could have assisted the development of an indigenous entrepreneurial class. We return to these arguments in the next two chapters.

In assessing the consequences of the large balance of payments surpluses in colonial Indonesia, it is important to bear in mind that the surpluses for the export-producing regions were even larger than for the country as a whole. Thee (1977: 69–72) has discussed the debates surrounding the very large trade surpluses from the estate region of East Sumatra between 1913 and 1938. The ratio of exports to imports in this region was much higher than the national average, indicating that this region was benefiting very little in terms of either government or private investment from its rapid export growth. In spite of the fact that, by the 1920s, the majority of exports originated from the Outer Islands, little was done by the government to develop infrastructure outside Java beyond what was essential for the export industries. This was in contrast to Java which, by the 1920s, had probably the most developed infrastructure of any region in Asia, apart from Japan. In addition, the export regions had little opportunity to diversify their economies on the back of the booming export sectors. Huff (1994: 203 ff) has pointed out that it was the port of Singapore that benefited from the linkages which flowed from the huge growth in Indonesian rubber production after 1920, rather than Medan, Palembang or Pontianak. Dutch capital did endeavour to establish rubber milling plants in Sumatra but they could not compete with the traders and millers in Singapore, and a high proportion of all Indonesian rubber was exported in unprocessed form. Rubber milling was labour-intensive, and thousands of jobs were created in Singapore as a result of the Indonesian imports. In addition, it was Singapore that was able to benefit from the the growth of trading and financial services, rather than the towns of Sumatra and Kalimantan.

TRADE AND GROWTH: THE POST-COLONIAL EXPERIENCE

Much of the discussion of Indonesian economic policy-making in the first fifteen years of independence has stressed the 'inward-looking' nature of the policy regime, compared with the more 'outward-looking' stance of other Southeast Asian countries (Paauw 1969: Myint 1971: 271 ff). In a more recent paper, Myint (1984) put forward a typology of outward and inward-looking policies, with the pure inward-looking case being characterised by protectionist and import-substitution policies, 'insulating' domestic economic policies, reliance on domestic savings and resource self-sufficiency, restriction of private foreign investment and restriction on immigration. He argues that, in the Guided Democracy years, the Indonesian economy moved close to this pure case.

According to Myint, international trade was tightly controlled, both for short-run balance-of-payments and for other reasons, compounded of a nationalistic reaction against the 'colonial pattern' of exports and the desire to promote domestic manufacturing industries. The domestic economy was enmeshed in detailed bureaucratic controls, which combined a carry-over from the older Dutch administrative controls with the new desire to use 'planning' as a nationalistic shield against market forces. Private foreign investment was severely discouraged, both by a series of nationalisation measures against existing enterprises and by restrictions on new investment. Oil was the only sector in which foreign investment was permitted to operate on a profit-sharing basis. Immigration was discouraged and discriminatory measures against Chinese living in Indonesia led to a large exodus (Myint 1984: 43).

While this is a reasonable summary of policies at least from 1957 to 1965, two points need to be stressed. First, as Myint acknowledges, at least some of the controls were legacies from the late colonial period, and especially from the period of government-encouraged import substitution which began in the early 1930s. However, in those years, the government encouraged foreign investment, and also permitted the free flow of capital in and out of the country, both policies which the New Order regime of General Suharto adopted after effective power was wrested from President Sukarno in 1966. Second, it is important to realise that the 'inward' policy stance which characterised the Sukarno years did not imply a rapid decline in the ratio of exports to GDP, as has been claimed by several writers. Indeed, as was argued in Chapter 2, this ratio may not have been greatly different in 1965 from 1938, even allowing for the substantial deterioration in the commodity terms of trade which occurred in the 1960s.

On the one hand this reflected the fact that the production and export of commodities such as rubber, copra, coffee, pepper and spices had become a way of life for millions of producers and traders outside Java, most of whom were neither willing nor able to foresake their traditional occupations simply because of discriminatory government policies. To the greatest extent possible they circumvented official marketing channels and sold their output on the most favourable terms they could secure, but there can be little doubt that most received incomes well below those which they would have obtained had the exchange rate been determined by market forces, and had export taxes and other government distortions been removed. The years from 1950 to 1965 saw a marked widening in the disparity between the domestic and international terms of trade for rubber and coffee producers compared with the pre-war period, reflecting the extent to which government policies were discriminating against producers of these crops (Booth 1988: 228–9). The adverse price environment in which the export producers operated in turn discouraged investment in replanting or in the development of new plantations, so that growth in both production and export volume was much lower than in the pre-war years (Booth 1988: Table 6.1). Thus the constant ratio of exports to GDP reflects the slow growth of both in the 1950s and 1960s.

Clearly this need not have been the case. The newly independent government had a unique opportunity to reverse the policies of the colonial period which favoured estate producers at the expense of smallholders, and to develop infrastructure, marketing channels and extension services for smallholder cashcrop producers. By the early 1960s, yield-increasing technologies for crops such as rubber and coconut were already being successfully disseminated to smallholder producers in Malaysia and the Philippines, but very little was achieved in Indonesia. There was not much evidence that such revenues as were raised from exporters through, for example, export taxes and a range of other cesses and levies of varying degrees of legality were ever used in ways which would have benefited the major producing regions. Even when these taxes accrued to provincial and local governments they were almost always dissipated on routine expenditures. The rebellions in several of the major export-producing provinces in the late 1950s and early 1960s did little to

improve the situation, and the regions remained backward, undeveloped and resentful of their treatment at the hands of the central
government.

As was pointed out in Chapter 2, the advent of the New Order
government coincided with a dramatic acceleration in export volume
growth, to over 14 per cent per annum in the years from 1967 to 1973.
This expansion can be seen mainly as a response to the devaluation of
the rupiah and other economic stabilisation policies implemented in
these years. World prices for Indonesia's major export staples, which
had fallen more or less continually through the latter part of the
1960s, began to recover after 1971 (Rosendale 1978: 192). The
combination of improving prices and increasing volume together
meant that the income terms of trade increased at an unprecedented
28 per cent per annum over these years (Table 2.1). Almost all exports
were still produced in the agricultural and mining sectors, and the
export volume growth contributed to growth of output and value
added in both these sectors; between 1967 and 1973 these two sectors
in turn contributed over 40 per cent to total growth of GDP (Table
2.16). There was also some improvement in the commodity terms of
trade after 1969, which meant that domestic income (GDY) grew
more rapidly over these years than GDP (Sundrum 1986: Table 6).
This in turn allowed consumption expenditures on both private and
government account and investment to increase, compared with the
dismal performance of the early 1960s.

During the 1970s, the improvement in export prices, and the net
barter terms of trade was more spectacular than at any period in
Indonesia's modern economic history. Although there had been
previous periods of sustained improvement in export prices, most
notably the years from the late 1840s to the mid-1860s and the decade
up to 1913, the rate of growth was quite modest. By contrast between
1969 and 1981, the index of export prices calculated from the national
income data grew more than twenty-six-fold (Sundrum 1986: Table 3).
Although this growth was in large part due to the dramatic growth in
the world price of oil, it is important to bear in mind that all
Indonesia's main export commodities experienced price increases in
the 1970s including rubber, timber, coffee, vegetable oils and non-
ferrous metals. Even allowing for real appreciation of the exchange
rate which occurred as a result of the oil boom, most export producers
enjoyed some improvement in real incomes over the decade, although
export taxes creamed off around 10 per cent of the increase for
producers of rubber, coffee, timber and tin.

The real volume of export growth fell sharply after 1973, partly because the OPEC quotas effectively placed a ceiling on petroleum production and partly because non-oil export production growth was quite modest. But the growth in prices meant that the income terms of trade continued to improve, albeit at a rather slower rate than between 1967 and 1973. Because a quantum growth in exports is reflected directly in the growth of real GDP, but an improvement in the terms of trade is not, it is necessary to adjust the GDP data for the improvement in the commodity terms of trade in order to examine the impact on the domestic economy. The oil price increases in the OPEC countries were essentially an unrequited transfer payment, or as one writer has put it, 'cash made available to the country in return for nothing in the way of production by the economy in general' (Bruton 1984: 131). In Indonesia, this cash mainly accrued to the government in the form of dollars, and the impact of these dollars on the growth of domestic production of goods and services depended on how they were spent. In this sense, the oil boom of the 1970s had the same effect on the Indonesian economy as the unrequited transfers from the colony to the Dutch budget had on the Dutch economy in the nineteenth century.

One method of disposing of the petroleum rents which was adopted by many of the sparsely populated petroleum economies was to invest it abroad. This option was adopted by the Indonesians to a very limited extent. Sundrum (1986, Table 6) has shown that only about 2.5 per cent of GDY (GDP adjusted for the terms of trade improvement) was used to accumulate reserves abroad in the years from 1973 to 1981. The rest was absorbed domestically. To see how these resources were used, we can look at the three main expenditure components distinguished in the national income accounts: private consumption expenditures, government consumption expenditures and investment. In the years from 1967 to 1973 the rate of growth of investment was very high, partly as a result of the rapid growth in the government development budget, and partly as a result of growth in investment in the private sector, which in turn was influenced by the growth in direct foreign investment (Sundrum 1986: Table 6). But after 1973 the rate of investment growth fell while that of private consumption accelerated. There was also a slight acceleration in the rate of growth of government consumption.

Another way of bringing out the change that occurred after 1973 is to examine the growth in these various categories of expenditure as a proportion of GDY. In 1967–73, private consumption expenditure accounted for just under half of the growth in GDY, while between 1974 and 1981 its share increased to two thirds. This suggests that much of the improvement in the terms of trade after 1973 (indicated by the widening gap between export and import growth) was spent on consumption of both imports and locally produced goods and services, which in turn might have had a high import content. To the extent that investment grew relative to GDP over the 1970s, there is evidence that it was channelled into those parts of the economy where it yielded a low rate of return. The incremental capital – value added ratio increased sharply between 1975 and the early 1980 (Keuning 1991: 103).

It was argued in Chapter 2 that it was the sustained fall in nominal export earnings after 1981, rather than the declining commodity terms of trade, which was the primary cause of the slowdown in economic growth. The high levels of economic growth of the 1970s had been based on extremely rapid rates of growth in the income terms of trade which were obviously not sustainable in the longer term. The challenge facing policy-makers after 1981 was to restructure the economy and the trade regime so that rates of GDP growth in excess of 5 per cent per annum could be sustained on both lower growth of exports and a much slower growth in the income terms of trade. By the early 1990s there was evidence that the successive reform measures adopted since 1983 were achieving some success in meeting this challenge. Between 1987 and 1990, real GDP grew by around 22 per cent; around 30 per cent of the growth in GDP was in manufacturing industry and a further 10 per cent in construction and public utilities. The agricultural sector also accounted for just over 10 per cent, and almost all the rest (45 per cent) occurred in the service sector, including trade and transport.

There can be little doubt that at least part of the growth in both manufacturing and services was due to the resurgence of the export economy after five years of contraction. Between 1981 and 1986, total commodity export earnings declined from $25.2 billion to $14.8 billion; this was entirely due to the fall in oil prices, and non-oil/gas exports actually registered some growth over these years. By 1990, total export earnings had recovered to $25.7 billion, which was slightly above the 1981 peak of $25.2 billion. Again, the improvement was entirely due to non-oil/gas exports which grew from $6.5 billion to $14.6 billion in the four years from 1986 to 1990. In addition, foreign exchange earnings for tourism grew rapidly after 1985. Much of the growth in non-oil commodity exports was due to manufactures, especially plywood, textiles, garments and footwear, and some heavy industrial products, such as fertiliser, cement and fabricated steel.

It is possible to isolate three distinct reasons for this remarkable boom in non-oil exports in such a short space of time. First, the government was successful in containing inflation after the substantial rupiah devaluation of September 1986, so that the real effective exchange rate declined markedly after 1986. Indeed, one set of estimates suggests that the real rate of depreciation of the rupiah was faster in the years from 1985 to 1990 than in any other Asian country (Asian Development Bank 1994: 250). Second, the various liberalisation measures introduced from 1985 onwards, particularly the introduction of the duty drawback scheme for exporters, encouraged both domestic and foreign investors to expand production for export, especially in such labour-intensive industries as garments and footwear. Deregulation measures also benefited the tourist industry, especially the abolition of visa requirements for ASEAN and OECD nationals, and the granting of landing rights in Bali to a number of foreign airlines. Third, the government intervened with a variety of quantitative controls and subsidies to promote particular industries. The best-known example has been the log export ban which was imposed to encourage the domestic plywood industry (Lindsay 1989). The technique of banning or restricting exports of raw materials in order to encourage domestic processing industries was later extended to rotan and palm oil. In addition, a number of heavy industries now exporting part of their output have been assisted with subsidised inputs, particularly fuel, and with cheap liquidity credits.

Unsurprisingly, many economists expressed unease with this third method of export promotion, although there are certainly precedents in the successful export economies of Northeast Asia for such policies. The short-run costs of export restrictions and subsidies are often considerable, and it is not always obvious that they will be recouped in the longer run as export industries expand and their unit costs fall, benefiting domestic as well as foreign consumers. Another adverse effect of policies such as the export ban on rotan is that it operates as a tax on smallholder producers outside Java and a subsidy to the Java-based processing industry. Over time such policies will increase income disparities between urban Java and the rest of the country, and between ethnic groups, and thus promote regional unrest, as indeed happened in the 1950s. Such tensions are likely to be aggravated by the evidence that in the 1980s the balance of payments surplus from the four main resource-exporting provinces outside Java is even larger, relative to GDP, than the colonial balance of payments surpluses (Booth 1992: Table 1.6). A greater decentralisation of the fiscal system than either the colonial or post-colonial governments have been prepared to concede would seem to be essential, if resource-producing regions are to have a greater degree of control over their own export economies.

In conclusion, it needs to be reiterated that the reforms of the past decade have not recreated the type of open trading regime that prevailed in the colonial economy from the 1870s to the 1930s. In spite of a series of tariff reform packages since the late 1980s, tariffs are still higher on average than in the colonial period, and the variation in effective rates of protection remains considerable. Quantitative import controls, while reduced in number, are still significant in certain sectors, especially agriculture. The result is a system of protection which in the late 1980s was still substantially biased against trade (Fane and Phillips 1991: 121). While the use of measures such as duty drawback schemes have been successful in simulating free trade conditions for export producers, their administration is vulnerable to corruption. It is, of course, arguable that the partial deregulation of the trade regime which has occurred in the 1980s has been more successful in promoting economic growth in the domestic economy than the more liberal colonial system, which resulted in large balance of payments surpluses and substantial outflow of capital. But such an argument confuses the impact of the trade regime with the impact of fiscal and monetary policies.

Even after the termination of the remittances to the home budget, fiscal, monetary and exchange rate policies from 1870 to 1930 together produced large balance of payments surpluses which greatly reduced the impact of export growth on the domestic economy, even in periods of rapid export growth. In spite of the evidence of rising consumption and declining efficiency of investment in the latter part of the oil boom, a far greater attempt was made to capture the benefits of improving terms of trade for the domestic economy between 1967 and 1981 than in previous periods of buoyant export prices such as the early phase of the CS, or in the first two decades of the twentieth century. The key mechanism used in the oil boom years was budgetary policy which was able to appropriate the rents accruing from the petroleum price increase and utilise them, at least partially, for productive investment which enhanced the longer term productive capacity of the economy. Certainly, there is plenty of evidence that government investment over the oil boom years was far from optimal. But at least the rents were retained in the domestic economy. Had budgetary policy been used for investment in human and physical capital at earlier periods in Indonesia's economic history, per capita output and living standards could have grown faster than in fact was the case. The actual record of investment in the colonial economy is examined in the next chapter.

6 Investment and Technological Change

SOURCES OF INVESTMENT IN COLONIAL AND POST-COLONIAL INDONESIA

On the basis of the pioneering work of scholars such as Clark, Kuznets and Lewis, it is now widely recognised that economies grow through investment and the adoption of new technologies in all sectors of the economy. But as economists collect more empirical evidence on processes of capital accumulation and technological progress, in various parts of the world since the early nineteenth century, it has become clear that this generalisation must be modified in the light of the experience of different countries and regions. While it is usually true that some acceleration in the ratio of investment to GDP has accompanied the process of economic growth, it is not always clear whether the growth in investment has been a cause or a consequence of the growth process. Some economies have grown much faster than others with broadly similar ratios of investment to GDP; in other words, there have been substantial disparities across countries in the impact a given quantum of investment has had on the growth of GDP. This difference is crudely captured in differences in the ICOR (incremental capital-output ratio) or in more sophisticated estimates of growth in total factor productivity.

Differences in the productivity of investment appear to be linked to the success different economies have had in adopting and adapting new technologies in different parts of the economy. It is often argued that those countries which embarked on the development process in the late nineteenth and twentieth centuries were able to take advantage of the backlog of technology, especially in the industrial sector, and were thus able to catch up and in some cases overtake those countries which initially were in the vanguard of industrial growth. However, it has become obvious in the decades since 1945 that not all countries have been able to share in this catching-up process. It has worked extremely well in cases such as Japan, Korea and Taiwan, and barely at all in sub-Saharan Africa. A country's ability to adopt and adapt the techniques of production evolved in the more advanced economies depends on both its physical infrastructure and on its educational attainment, as well as on the development of market institutions and the size, competence, and freedom of action of its entrepreneurial classes (Abramovitz 1986; Dowrick 1992).

Thus, an examination of investment and technological change in Indonesia must include not just investment in physical capital, but also investment in human capital. For purposes of analysis and quantification, investment in physical capital assets can be divided into the various categories shown in Table 6.1. Government investment can be broken down into that part financed from foreign sources (aid and borrowing) and that part financed from domestic sources (budgetary allocations and domestic borrowing). Private investment also can be divided according to sources of finance. Foreign finance can come either from direct investment from multinational companies into domestic subsidiaries or from portfolio investments. Domestic private investment in corporate enterprises can come either from profits, or from loans or stock market flotations, while investment in unincorporated enterprises comes mainly from private sources and can utilise family labour and land as well as purchased inputs.

Table 6.1 Sources of investment funds

	Private	Government
Foreign	Foreign direct investment Foreign portfolio investment Borrowing from private banks	Foreign aid Foreign borrowing
Domestic	Retained profits Stock market flotations Borrowing from domestic banks Personal savings and labour (household sector)	Budgetary funding Borrowing from central bank Borrowing from banks (SOEs)

In discussing capital formation in Indonesia, it is useful to bear in mind that not all capital formation occurs in enterprises run along capitalist lines. Labour-intensive investment within household production units has been important in the Indonesian economy for centuries, although the last 150 years have been characterised by accelerating investment in capitalist production, where such production is defined not just in terms of scale of operations, but also as entirely based on hiring in labour and selling the output at a profit. This trend is the inevitable consequence of the process of economic growth and structural change; indeed, the 'decline of the importance of the family as a productive unit' has been singled out by economic historians as 'perhaps the most important of all long-run institutional changes that have occurred in advanced economies' (Mathews 1986: 906). To the extent that the Indonesian economy has been characterised by sustained, although slow, economic growth and structural change through the nineteenth and twentieth centuries, we would expect that over time an increasing proportion of productive activity has occurred in large-scale enterprises run along capitalist lines. One question examined in this chapter is just how much investment has gone into capitalist production in Indonesia, and how this investment has been financed. But the chapter begins with an investigation of capital formation in that part of the economy which is often overlooked in discussions of the 'rise of capital', the small-scale, often household-based, enterprise.

PRIVATE INVESTMENT IN SMALL-SCALE ENTERPRISES IN INDONESIA

Until the nineteenth century, in Indonesia as in most other parts of the world, most capital formation was carried out by individuals or small community groups. People engaged in a directly productive activity in an enterprise operated mainly by family labour such as a small farm, a handicraft activity, or a retail outlet, used such surplus labour and materials as they had at their disposal to improve the productivity of their land and labour. Most analysis of capital formation in traditional, family-based activities has centred on the agricultural sector. The most obvious type of traditional agricultural capital is land itself, and the theme that 'the soil of today owes as much to nurture as to nature' (Lakdawala 1946: 127) has been emphasised by many writers. One of the best known, Boserup (1981: 45) has listed a number of investment activities requiring labour and simple tools such as clearing, levelling, terracing, bounding, irrigating and draining. An additional form of agricultural investment which economists began to study only in the 1960s is livestock. In his study of livestock investment in India, Raj (1969: 2) pointed out that cattle can be considered an investment good in that they produce a number of goods and services for the household (milk, manure, traction, young cattle) over an extended period.

Furthermore, farmers in many parts of the world put in considerable labour in preparing seeds, manures, buildings and farm implements.

The above types of investment are necessary in all agricultural production systems, whether purely subsistence, or oriented to local or international markets. But what of the capital requirements of agricultural production for export? It has been argued in the Southeast Asian context that the export expansion which began in the nineteenth century was 'undemanding of capital goods, particularly imported capital equipment' (Drake 1972: 954). Drake argues that the main requirement was capital of a circulating or wage fund nature, 'supplemented by the sort of fixed capital that can be constructed readily from local resources'. The circulating capital often took the form of imported wage goods which were advanced to producers by traders who then took the crop and marketed it. In Indonesia, as in many other parts of the tropical world, the rapid growth of smallholder export production required massive investment in treecrops and other perennials, most of which was carried out using labour and simple tools. In the 1950s, Bauer and Yamey (1957: 30) drew attention to the millions of hectares under crops such as rubber, cocoa, coffee etc. in Asia and Africa which were largely excluded from official estimates of capital formation, but which were 'obvious examples of investments (large-scale in total) made by peasants in the expectation of profitable returns which often occur only several seasons later, or extend over a number of seasons'. Certainly, imported capital goods were necessary for the rapid expansion of major export industries such as sugar and petroleum refining, and, indeed, these imports grew rapidly in the late nineteenth and early twentieth centuries in Indonesia (Table 2.6). But for the smallholder sector, and for part of the estate sector, Drake's argument is valid.

Data from FAO sources indicate that the various types of traditional or labour-intensive agricultural capital are more prominent in the labour abundant developing countries than in other parts of the world. For example, in the late 1970s a much higher proportion of arable land was irrigated in East Asia than in Africa or Latin America, or in any developed economy except Japan. By contrast, those types of agricultural capital which required substantial monetary outlay such as chemical fertilisers, tractors and other types of machinery were more intensively used in the developed countries (Booth and Sundrum 1984, Tables 8.1 and 8.2). Scholars such as Boserup have stressed the role that labour-intensive capital formation has played in permitting a country or region to shift from extensive to more intensive forms of cultivation (the most intensive being multiple cropping) which in turn allow much greater populations to be sustained off a given amount of land. However, the relationship between population densities, and agricultural intensification (defined for example by the cropping ratio) is a complicated one, and several scholars have warned against 'reading an economic relationship into what may in fact be a statistical relationship with the character of an identity' (Booth and Sundrum 1984: 25). There can be little doubt that, as Boserup and others have pointed out, the more densely settled parts of the world tend to be more intensively cropped. But why is this?

If indeed mounting population pressures induce changes in agricultural technology which in turn permit more intensive cropping, what is the nature of the inducement mechanism? Is it simply that in the more densely settled parts of the world the opportunity cost of labour is very low, so that people are willing to invest in those types of land improvement which allow more intensive cropping? How does the land tenure system affect these decisions? Do not the bio-physical conditions prevailing in a particular area, such as rainfall and soil quality affect the extent to which intensification can proceed? And if indeed there is a strong correlation between population densities and intensity of agricultural cultivation, are we justified in arguing that the former causes the latter? Is it not equally plausible to argue that those parts of the world with the greatest potential for agricultural intensification have attracted larger populations through in-migration? Because we have quite detailed statistics on population, arable area and crop production in Indonesia, and especially in Java, stretching back over many decades, the country has been used by numerous scholars as a laboratory for studying the nature of the interactions between population growth and agricultural technology.

In an important study published in the 1960s, Wander (1965: 264) drew attention to the very high positive correlation between population densities and the cultivation ratios in different regions of Java in the late nineteenth century. Booth (1988: 89) has demonstrated that a similarly high correlation obtained for Indonesia as a whole in the 1980s. These findings might appear to support Boserup's argument that, for largely exogenous reasons the population grew more rapidly in some parts of Indonesia than in others, and it was this population growth which in turn encouraged both the increase in arable land and in the cropping ratio. But they might also support an alternative theory, that it was precisely in those regions where the biophysical environment was most favourable that the cultivation ratio could be increased and this in turn attracted in-migrants. Certainly, there is evidence that migration rather than fertility or mortality was the major determinant of inter-regional disparities in population growth in Java in the nineteenth century and more recently for the country as a whole (Booth 1988: 88–90). As the land tenure system became more individualised in the latter part of the nineteenth century, migrants could move out of the densely settled parts of Java and establish new holdings with secure tenure in under-populated regions such as Besuki, or Krawang.

The evidence that migration, and the establishment of new holdings has played such an important role in agricultural expansion in Indonesia, at least since the middle of the nineteenth century, does not support the view that traditional agriculture was static or that the indigenous population were simply passive 'involuters' (Booth 1988: 98). There is considerable evidence that labour was used intensively on the smaller holdings to improve land quality (through manuring and irrigation) and for the raising of cattle (Booth 1988: 116–18). But there were limits to the extent to which household investment in agricultural capital could be used to stave off the impact of the inexorable growth of population on limited supplies of land. This fact became increasingly obvious to the Dutch colonial authorities, and the last five decades of the colonial era were characterised by growing public sector expenditures on smallholder agricultural development, primarily in Java. Public sector irrigation expenditures increased considerably between 1890 and 1930 as did expenditures on agricultural research and extension (van der Eng 1993, Table A8.2).

The magnitude and impact of these public expenditures are examined below. But until the end of the colonial era, they were minor in comparison with household investment not just in land development, but also in both smallholder treecrop cultivation and in livestock agriculture. Over the last four decades of the colonial period, the rate of growth of output of smallholder cashcrops (rubber, copra, coffee, tea, cloves, pepper, tobacco, cotton and sugar) was considerably faster than the rate of growth of output from the large estates (Booth 1988: 196). By the end of the colonial era, smallholders dominated production of coffee, copra, cloves and pepper and were producing almost 50 per cent of rubber exports. Although complete data on land under smallholder treecrop cultivation are not available for the colonial period, it has been estimated that by 1940 about 643,000 hectares of land in Java was planted to farm cashcrops and a further 2.7 million hectares outside Java (van der Eng 1993, Table A7). By 1984, Department of Agriculture data indicated that 7.7 million hectares were planted to smallholder cashcrops, compared with only 4.6 million hectares in 1969 (Booth 1988, Table 2.11).

Clearly, the millions of hectares of smallholder treecrops which have been planted in Indonesia since the late nineteenth century represent a massive investment of labour and a much more modest investment of financial capital by millions of rural producers everywhere in the archipelago, but especially in regions where land was abundant. As numerous commentators have pointed out, these cultivators were responding to perceived market opportunities by utilising the resources available to them in the most efficient way they could. Bauer (1948: 67–8) argued that the paid-out cost of bringing an acre of smallholder rubber to maturity in the Outer Islands was less than 10 per cent of the costs of the large estates, even assuming the smallholder was using hired labour. Both Bauer (1948: 68) and Lindblad (1988: 67) stressed that smallholder rubber stands were often more densely planted than those on estates and to begin with the yields were higher. But in the last years of the colonial era the estates began to invest in higher yielding varieties and inputs such as chemical fertiliser, and their per hectare yields overtook those of smallholders. When comparable data for rubber producers became available after 1950, it was clear that smallholder yields were only about two-thirds of those on the estates. Furthermore, while estate yields showed some improvement, especially in the 1970s, smallholder yields stagnated at about 300 kg per planted hectare. This contrasted sharply with the situation in neighbouring Malaysia, where smallholder rubber yields more than doubled between 1960 and 1980 (Booth 1988, Table 6.8). Most other smallholder treecrop producers in Indonesia have continued to expand production since 1950 by increasing hectarage, rather than by increasing output per hectare.

Indeed, the experience of Indonesian smallholder producers over the twentieth century confirms the point made by Myint (1973: 39) that when peasant producers took to growing cashcrops in many parts of the tropical world, they availed themselves of the market opportunities which international trade offered, but did not take advantage of the technical opportunities which Western science offered to improve their productive capacity. Therefore, productivity per unit of land remained stagnant, and in some cases declined. Output per worker also probably stagnated, although in the absence of reliable data, this is impossible to quantify. Under these circumstances, as Myint pointed out, peasant production was bound to come to a stop sooner or later, as supplies of suitable land ran out. The fact that smallholder output of crops such as rubber, coffee, cloves, pepper and spices continues to grow in Indonesia through extension of planted area testifies to the continuing availability of land, and to the continuing availability of labour with no more lucrative alternative occupation than the planting of cashcrops.

Another important labour-intensive form of household capital formation is livestock. Here the evidence indicates contrary trends for Java and for the Outer Islands over the century from 1890 to 1990. In Java, numbers of large animals (buffalo, cows and horses) stood at 5.5 million in 1890. The buffalo population fell continually in Java from the late 1890s onwards, in spite of the quite rapid growth in the harvested area of paddy land. This decline was partly due to disease, but also probably reflects the fact that the combination of a growing agricultural population and diminishing average farm size rendered uneconomic the use of buffalo for traction. Ploughing could be done more cheaply by other draught animals, or by increasingly abundant human labour, as was the case in other densely settled parts of Asia such as China (Lewis 1978: 207). By 1940 there were fewer than two million buffalo in Java compared with 2.6 million in 1890. Numbers of horses also fell, no doubt reflecting the growing availability of bicycles and motorised transport which made horses an increasingly unprofitable form of investment, even for those farmers who had the land and labour to maintain them. Only numbers of cows rose, from about 2.35 million in 1890 to over four million in the early 1930s (van der Eng, 1993, Table A5). This presumably meant that even in land-scarce Java, demand for meat and milk made the upkeep of cows profitable. However, numbers of small ruminants (sheep and goats) grew much faster than numbers of cows over the five decades from 1890, and by 1942 had reached seven million. To the extent that livestock were being kept mainly for meat and milk rather than for traction, small animals were a much more profitable sideline activity for most farmers.

Numbers of all animals dropped sharply in Java during the 1940s, reflecting both the depredations of the Japanese army and the generally distressed conditions after 1945 which would have forced many farmers to slaughter their animals for food or for cash. After 1950 buffalo numbers began to increase although they never returned to the level reached in 1942 and, by the 1980s, numbers had fallen to one million, which was only 40 per cent of the total recorded in 1890.

During this decade, the use of tractors for land preparation became more common in Java, which made the upkeep of buffalo even less attractive. There was some growth in numbers of cows, especially in the 1980s when the government subsidised the growth of the domestic dairy industry. But the most rapid growth was in the numbers of sheep and goats, which more than doubled between 1950 and 1990. Even in a rural economy where opportunities for non-agricultural employment were growing rapidly, it appears that it was profitable for many households to continue to raise these animals for both milk and meat.

Outside Java, the growth of all forms of livestock has been more rapid than in Java, and by 1992 there were over nine million large ruminants and over thirteen million pigs, sheep and goats (*Statistical Yearbook of Indonesia* 1994: 242). However, in terms of animals per unit of land area, the cattle population was still much more dense in Java than elsewhere. There was less regional variation in the ratio of cattle to the agricultural labour force. This reflects the labour-intensive nature of cattle upkeep in an economy such as Indonesia; small ruminants, in particular, are often kept tethered and fed by hand. Family labour is used to collect food, although increasing use is made of manufactured feedstuffs. Traditionally, livestock rearing has always been a smallholder activity in Indonesia, and the upkeep of small ruminants continues to be mainly a household activity. But some of the rapid growth in cattle numbers outside Java in the 1980s reflects the growth of large-scale ranching enterprises, particularly in Eastern Indonesia.

Taken together, investment in land improvements, in the planting of treecrops and in the raising of livestock has been of enormous importance in Indonesia's rural economy in the nineteenth and twentieth centuries. Although it is impossible to value accurately the assets created through labour-intensive investment of this nature, it is certain to have been a significant proportion of all private investment, both in the colonial economy and more recently. Neither should investments in housing in both urban and rural areas, be overlooked. Most housing units in rural areas and a significant proportion in urban areas continue to be constructed and repaired by their owners, either for occupation or for lease. In many cases private dwellings are also used for business activities, so a clear distinction between residential investment and investment in directly productive activities cannot be made. The estimates of Feinstein (1988: 433–4) for the United Kingdom and Minami (1986: 168) for Japan in 1900 indicate that residential buildings accounted for around 25 per cent of the capital stock in both economies, and it is likely that housing accounted for a similar, or even higher, proportion of total capital stock in Indonesia in the late colonial era, and indeed in the 1960s. Minami's data on the composition of capital stock in Japan in 1900 showed that housing, livestock and perennial plants together accounted for 40 per cent of the total. It is probable that the proportion for late colonial Indonesia would have been even higher. Most of these assets were owned by indigenous Indonesians.

PRIVATE INVESTMENT IN LARGE-SCALE CAPITALIST PRODUCTION

In his introduction to the third volume in the Changing Economy series, Creutzberg (CEI, Vol 3: 11) argued that large private corporations were 'not to be found in Indonesia before the nineteenth century'. The Dutch East India Company 'jealously guarded its chartered status against competition', and was not prepared to allow other companies, either Dutch or foreign, to establish within its area. Under the British interregnum, and immediately after the restoration of Dutch power, several trading houses were established, and a number of plantation companies. The latter were mainly in the Javanese principalities, and little is known about their sources of capital, although short-term credit was probably obtained from the trading houses handling the exports. In the 1820s several corporations were established which were to play a crucial role in colonial development for the next century, including the Netherlands Trading Company and the Java Bank. During the Cultivation System, the processing of cane sugar was transferred to private interests (CEI, Vol 3: 17), and by the mid-1850s corporate investment in sugar refineries was estimated to be in the range of 30 million guilders.

Failure rates among sugar companies were high, and the government made substantial losses on its sugar accounts when private refineries collapsed. One of the aims of the Sugar Law of 1870 was to permit free contracts between sugar refineries and peasant cultivators which, in turn, would enable the government to withdraw completely from sugar cultivation. In the 1870s and early 1880s, private capital took advantage of the new legal framework to increase investment not just in the sugar sector but in other types of estates as well. Creutzberg (CEI, Vol 3:18) estimates that the aggregate value of private corporate investment in Indonesia in 1885 was between 150 and 200 million guilders. Much of this would have been in estates, and in associated transport infrastructure. Some of these companies were incorporated in the colony, while others were based in the Netherlands or in other parts of Europe, and may well have been active in several other countries. It has been estimated that in 1860 there were fifteen colonial corporations, ten of which were established in Java. By 1890, there were 200 corporations based in Java, and about the same number based in the Netherlands (a Campo 1994: 5). In addition to Dutch corporations, two other forms of foreign capitalist enterprise became more prominent in the closing decades of the nineteenth century: those operated by non-Indonesian Asians (usually Chinese but also Arab and Indian) and what Lindblad (1991: 185) has termed the 'truly foreign firms' whose headquarters were in other centres of world capitalism including the UK, the USA and Japan.

Creutzberg (CEI, Vol 3: 27–8) has argued that one of the main characteristics of incorporated enterprises in colonial Indonesia was a 'basic reliance on own (non-borrowed) financial resources'. This point has been emphasised by Drake (1972: 955) who stressed the importance of reinvested profits in colonial capital formation in Malaysia. But loans from the banking system were important for some companies; the agricultural estates, for example, relied on the *cultuurbanken*, as well as loan flotations and retained profits (Soegijanto 1994: 128–9). Some companies resorted to bond issues to raise the additional capital necessary for incorporation, but redeemed these as soon as profits were made, and financed further expansion from retained profits (a Campo 1994: 14). Private capital imports began to accelerate from the 1870s and recovered rapidly from the crisis of the mid-1880s. By 1900, Creutzberg estimated that the aggregate value of corporate investment in the colony had increased to 750 million guilders. Relative to GDP, Creutzberg's data show that both private investment and investment in government services increased considerably in the last fifteen years of the nineteenth century, and then fell again between 1900 and 1913 (Table 6.2). The finding that the total value of corporate capital stock increased more slowly between 1900 and 1913 than in the previous fifteen years, and more slowly than the growth in nominal GDP does not seem very plausible, especially as this period was marked by a steady increase in the value of imports of capital goods, both in absolute terms and relative to total imports (CEI Volume 3, Table G and Table 5).

Table 6.2   Estimates of the aggregate value of corporate capital stock,
1885–1939 (millions of current guilders)

Year	Private	Government	Total*	GDP	Ratio[†]
1885	150–200	90	240–290	1,460	16–20
1900	750	250	1,000	1,729	58
1913	1000	280	1,280	3,619	35
1924	1820	978	2,790	6,034	46
1930	4000	990	4,990	6,078	82
1939	3500	929	4,430	5,081	87

*For a discussion of the way the value of capital stock was estimated see CEI, Vol. 3, Table 4. Government capital stock refers to that in government enterprises only.
[†] Total capital as a percentage of GDP
Sources: GDP: van der Eng (unpublished data made available to the author); CEI, Vol. 3, Table A.

Given that we have so little information on capital stock in non-incorporated enterprises, or indeed in the public sector, it is impossible to use the data in Table 6.2 to estimate aggregate capital–output ratios for the colonial economy, although if we assume that in 1913 corporate capital stock amounted to 50 per cent of the total, then the capital–output ratio for the economy would have been 0.7, which is certainly very low by international standards, but possible for an undeveloped economy at the beginning of the process of economic modernisation. Minami (1986: 190) estimates that the capital–output ratio in Japan was already 1.8 in 1900, and rose thereafter. If we assume that the capital–output ratio in Indonesia was closer to unity in 1913, then it follows that well over 50 per cent of the total capital stock was either in public infrastructure (not included in Table 6.2) or in the small-scale household sector. This indeed is plausible, given what we know about the composition of capital stock in other economies in the early stages of economic modernisation.

There can be no doubt that the years between 1913 and 1930 saw a marked acceleration in the value of corporate investment, so that by 1930, it exceeded 80 per cent of GDP. Lindblad (1991: 190) argues that most firms operating in the inter-war years were quite young, and only 10 per cent had their origins in the nineteenth century. Not only did many new firms emerge after 1913, but the mortality rate among older companies was quite high (a Campo 1994: 4). Creutzberg (CEI, Vol 3:19) is of the opinion that the rapid expansion of investment in the 1920s may not have been justified on economic criteria, given the decline in world prices for Indonesia's export commodities which began in the mid-1920s. But, as Lindblad (1991: 190) points out, many of the new firms were not in traditional activities such as agricultural estates, but in mining and services. An increasing proportion were located outside Java.

Table 6.3 Cumulative expenditure on fixed assets, 1910–39
(US$ millions 1967)

Domestic	2,253.62
Foreign	1,896.06
Total*	4,149.68
Of which	
Plantations	2,026.66
Oil and mining	633.00
Government	561.58
Shipping	153.88
Memo items:	
Private capital inflow[†]	1,142.90
Issue of NI loans**	1,860.02
Increase in floating debt[††]	665.11

*See CEI, Vol 3: 41–3 for a discussion of how the data were derived. Foreign expenditures refer to those made abroad on imports of capital goods
[†] Private capital imports less redemption of private loans
** The amounts refer not to the nominal value of the loans but to the actual drawings.
[††] See CEL Vol 7, 67 for details
Sources: CEI Vol 3, Table 1, CEI Vol 7, Table 1. Deflator used is the US Wholesale Price Index, as reported in the *Statistical Abstract of the United States*, various issues.

For the last three decades of the colonial era, we can use the data on expenditure on fixed assets compiled by Creutzberg (CEI Vol 3, Table 1) to examine both the sectoral breakdown of such expenditures, and the division between domestic and foreign expenditures. Table 6.3 presents the data converted into constant dollars, and accumulated over the years from 1910 to 1939. The total arrived at in this way slightly exceeds four billion dollars (1967 prices). Of this, just under half was invested in the estates sector, and a further 15 per cent in the mining sector. Government expenditure on fixed assets accounted for only 14 per cent of the total. Almost half (46 per cent) consisted of foreign expenditures (i.e. expenditures made abroad on imports of capital goods). As Creutzberg (CEI, Vol 3: 42) points out, the domestic component of expenditure on fixed assets consisted largely of labour and delivery costs, transport and unloading charges. For some categories of expenditure on fixed assets, these domestic expenditures outweighed expenditures on imports; perhaps surprisingly the highest share of domestic to total expenditures on fixed assets was found in the mining sector (CEI Volume 3, Table F). This confirms the point made by Huff (1994: 253) about the impact of the Malaysian tin mining industry on the engineering sector in Singapore. Mining enterprises often demand location-specific plant and equipment, which have to be made or modified on or close to the site, and give rise to a sizeable domestic equipment industry. Expenditures on fixed assets in railways, by contrast, which were built to international specifications, were much more import-intensive in Indonesia, as they were in other parts of the world.

Following earlier authors such as Callis, Creutzberg attempted to estimate the value of corporate investments by nationality (CEI, Vol 3, Table 1). He concluded that in 1922 Dutch investment accounted for over 80 per cent of the total capital value of corporate investment in Indonesia, but this had fallen by 1940 to 72 per cent, mainly because of the growth of British and American investments. But even allowing for this growth, Dutch investment in Indonesia in 1938 was still a much larger proportion of the total than Dutch investment globally or in the Asian region, although the Dutch investment enforcement ratios for Indonesia were lower than those of France and the USA for their Asian colonies (Svedberg 1981: Table 1). As with commodity trade, there can be little doubt that Dutch investors continued to enjoy advantages in Indonesia compared with most foreigners until the end of the colonial era, including familiarity with the language and the legal and regulatory systems.

The tendency, already referred to, to use internally generated funds for corporate capital formation, led to a situation where a substantial proportion of total investment in colonial Indonesia was 'entrepreneurial' rather than 'rentier' (Callis 1941: 36). Van der Eng (1993b: 21) suggests that more than one third of total profits generated in the corporate sector were retained after 1900. But reliance on foreign capital inflows to fund investment was clearly far from negligible. The balance of payments figures assembled by Korthals Altes indicate that net private capital imports (i.e. total private capital imports less the redemption of private loans) amounted to $1.1 billion between 1910 and 1939, or roughly one quarter of the total value of investment in fixed assets over this period (Table 6.3). It seems plausible to argue that, in the case of many corporations, expansion was financed at least partly by equity sales abroad or (to a smaller extent) by foreign borrowing, but these inflows were more than balanced over time by additions to both private corporate and individual balances held abroad.

It is also clear that, given that a considerable part of corporate investment in colonial Indonesia undoubtedly was financed internally, we cannot assume that all investment in foreign-owned firms in Indonesia consisted of inward remittances, whether of equity capital or of loans. Such an assumption appears to have been made by Svedberg (1978) who uses the data compiled by Callis to argue that a high proportion of foreign investment in Southeast Asia, as indeed in other parts of the world in the late nineteenth and early twentieth centuries, consisted of direct capital participation rather than loans. To the extent that much of the direct investment was financed from accumulated surpluses rather than from abroad, these arguments could lead the unwary reader to exaggerate the importance of direct foreign investment in Indonesia's colonial development. Drake's argument that the reinvested profits of foreign-owned companies are conceptually distinct from new capital inflow is very relevant here (Drake 1972: 960).

It would also be wrong to assume that all foreign capital was European or North American in origin. In the inter-war period, investment by overseas Chinese in Indonesia was assuming considerable importance, both in the agricultural sector, and in trade and finance. Many of these overseas Chinese investors were resident in Indonesia, and again it is probable that much of the investment was financed from operating surpluses, rather than from borrowing. Brown (1993: Table 5.6) presents data from a Japanese study which indicates that Chinese investment in Indonesia in 1930 amounted to $620 million, although it is unclear how this figure was calculated. The most interesting point to emerge from this study is that almost 64 per cent of this amount was in trade and finance, and the remainder in manufacturing. To the extent that the Chinese were prominent as entrepreneurs in the colonial economy, it was in trade and commerce rather than in manufacturing industry. As Drake (1972: 958) has argued, it is likely that at least part of their profits was not a return to actual investment, but rather a rent accruing to the scarce resource of marketing know-how, which only they could supply.

The importance of retained profits as a source of investment in colonial Indonesia also reflects the lack of alternative domestic sources of finance. Creutzberg was surely correct in pointing to the rudimentary capital market in Indonesia as a major constraint on firms' ability to finance expansion. This contrasts starkly with the situation in India, where by the inter-war years an active capital market existed, and where local investors could, and not infrequently did, become directors of what had been wholly foreign-owned and managed firms (Kidron 1965: 40). Such a development was virtually impossible in Indonesia where neither Chinese nor indigenous investors had the opportunity to acquire equity in foreign-owned concerns. Had they been able to do so, it is possible that an indigenous entrepreneurial class would have developed sooner and played a far more important role in post-colonial economic development.

During the period of the Japanese occupation, there was virtually no new investment in corporate assets in Indonesia, and existing assets in the estates sector, in the manufacturing sector, and in mining (especially petroleum) were severely damaged. The continuing battle between the independence forces and the returning Dutch colonial administration hardly created a supportive environment for new corporate investment, from either domestic or foreign sources. Creutzberg (CEI, Vol 3: 21) argues that, up to 1957, 'a good deal was sunk into a number of new manufacturing industries, which were greatly encouraged by the authorities', and certainly in the early 1950s, statements by moderate technocrats such as Sjafruddin Prawiranegara supported new foreign investment. But many nationalists viewed foreign investment with suspicion, and the unstable macroeconomic climate did little to encourage it. Joint ventures were encouraged under the government 'Benteng' industrialisation programme, but many of these companies were effectively owned and managed by Chinese, and it is likely that retained profits were the main source of investment funds, although those which had politically prominent indigenous Indonesians as partners were probably able to get access to subsidised bank loans.

The fact that the indigenous entrepreneurial class which had formed during the colonial period was so small, combined with the lack of any domestic capital market, meant that it was virtually impossible for domestic business people to acquire equity in what had been foreign-owned firms in the colonial period, as happened in India in the 1950s. Kidron (1965: 40–5) has described a situation where Indian investors took controlling interests in many British firms after independence, and Indian directors gained representation on the boards of many other companies which remained, at least nominally, in foreign hands. Nothing remotely comparable could have occurred in Indonesia in the 1950s. Schmitt (1962: 272) argues that in the early post-independence years, the government thought that the best strategy to enhance the role of indigenous Indonesians in the capitalist economy was to finance the entry of new, Indonesian-owned, firms in sectors dominated by foreign firms. Thus the emphasis put on nationalisation of the banking system, as this was seen as the only way to channel funds to new firms.

But in spite of government efforts, the indigenous business sector in the 1950s remained weak and riddled with political cronyism. In addition, there was still widespread distrust among many Indonesians of any form of private enterprise, at least outside the small-scale agricultural sector. When, after the loss of the United Nations vote on West New Guinea in 1957, the government acted to expropriate Dutch assets, no attempt was made to sell them to domestic investors. They were turned into state enterprises, and indeed most remain government-controlled to this day. But the expropriation without compensation made Indonesia a pariah state as far as Western investors were concerned, and private foreign investment from Western sources was negligible for the next decade. Rosendale (1978: 81) estimates that cumulative net private inflow over the entire period 1950–65 amounted to only $50 million. The available data on direct foreign investment referred only to the foreign oil companies, and there is little evidence that other sectors of the economy received any significant investment from abroad.

It was not until 1967 that a new foreign investment law was promulgated by the Suharto government. This law attracted much attention at the time, and many observers, both in Indonesia and elsewhere, felt that it would lead to Indonesia once again being dominated by foreign business interests. To deflect such criticism, implementation of the law was from the outset extremely bureaucratic, with approvals taking many months (Hill 1988: 30). After the anti-Japanese riots of January 1974, the government imposed more controls on foreign investors; only joint ventures were permitted and 51 per cent of the equity had to be owned by Indonesian citizens after a stipulated period. In practice a considerable part of the 'local' equity was often in the form of land, and additional local equity participation was often financed by the foreign partner (Panglaykim and Pangestu 1983). A considerable part of total foreign investment in Indonesia in the post-1967 era continued to be in the oil sector and this investment was not subject to the provisions of the 1967 law.

Although complete data are difficult to assemble, Hill (1988: 160) estimates that investment in the petroleum sector accounted for almost 75 per cent of total investment in the years from 1968 to 1984.

Much of the non-oil foreign investment in the years from the late 1960s to the mid-1980s was in import-substituting manufacturing industries. There was a tendency for foreign-owned firms to be more capital-intensive, partly because they tended to locate in more capital-intensive sectors of industry, but partly also because they appear to adopt more capital-intensive technologies than domestic firms in the same sector. Hill (1988: 117) explains this tendency in terms of preferential access to low interest loans, and to more sophisticated production technologies developed in countries where labour is more expensive, and which therefore tend to be more labour-saving. The most important single foreign investor in Indonesian manufacturing up to the mid-1980s was Japan; Japanese investment was particularly prominent in textiles, consumer durables and automobiles (Hill 1992: Table 7.8). Indonesia's large population and rich natural resource base made it attractive for Japanese investors, and for the period from 1951 to 1988, Indonesia accounted for well over half of all Japanese foreign investment in the ASEAN nations. Indeed Indonesia received more Japanese investment than any other Asian country (Yamashita 1990: 8). Through the period of the oil boom; manufacturing industry grew rapidly but much of this growth took place behind high tariff walls and was not internationally competitive. Few of the foreign investors who located in Indonesian manufacturing industry up to the mid-1980s did so with the intention of producing for export. The exchange rate and protection policies of this period encouraged foreign investors to concentrate in relatively capital-intensive industries, and to produce almost entirely for the rapidly expanding domestic market.

In the latter part of the 1980s, partly in response to a decline in foreign investment approvals by the Investment Coordination Board, partly in response to criticism from investing countries (especially Japan) and partly in response to the need to boost non-oil exports, the Indonesian government removed a number of restrictions on the operation of foreign firms, especially those producing for export. This led to a rapid growth in both numbers and value of approved foreign investment, so that by 1990 approvals amounted to almost $8.8 billion dollars (Thee 1991, Table 1). In contrast to the years from 1967 to 1986, when Japanese investment dominated, in the years from 1987 to 1990, the 'Asian NICs' (Korea, Taiwan, Hong Kong and Singapore) were the most important source of funds, accounting for almost 30 per cent of the total in 1990. Thee (1991: 84–5) has argued that this investment has tended to be more labour-intensive and export-orientated than investment from Japan or Europe. Furthermore, Japanese investment after 1985 was also much more directed to export-oriented industry than it had been previously (Thee 1992: 45). The more liberal regulatory climate of the late 1980s and early 1990s attracted foreign investors to invest in export industries in Indonesia for the first time since the early decades of the century. Like other countries in the region, Indonesia was able to benefit from the surge of investment from both Japan and the NICs, induced by rising wages and currency appreciation.

Direct foreign investment in Indonesian corporate enterprises received a considerable amount of scholarly attention after 1970, and many observers argued that the Indonesian economy became very dependent on such inflows. However, in relation to both official capital inflows (aid and government borrowing) and to domestic investment (both government and private) foreign direct investment and portfolio investment flows were quite small, at least until the late 1980s (Table 6.4). As a proportion of total investment, direct private foreign investment flows (as reported by the International Monetary Fund) were only 5 per cent of total investment in 1969–75, and fell thereafter. Direct foreign investment and portfolio investment were under 2 per cent of total investment (as measured in the national income accounts) for the years from 1983 to 1990. The estimates in Table 6.4 have been broadly confirmed by other studies which indicate that foreign direct investment accounted for a much lower proportion of gross domestic capital formation in Indonesia than in other ASEAN countries in the 1980s. One study estimated that in the period from 1986 to 1991 foreign direct investment accounted for only 2.4 per cent of total investment compared with 29.4 per cent in Singapore, 9.7 per cent in Malaysia and 6.3 per cent in Thailand (Yoshida *et al.* 1994: 72; see also Pangestu 1996: 173).

Indeed, all external sources of finance, both government and private, only accounted for around 13 per cent of total investment on average in the years from 1969 to 1990 (Table 6.4). The rest came from internal sources. Government investment is discussed in more detail in the next section; here it is worth noting that private investment from domestic sources has always been a significant part of total investment in Indonesia throughout the New Order era, and in the

1980s appears to have been by far the most important source of total investment. Unfortunately, lack of data make it impossible to estimate the composition of private domestic investment either by sector or by type of industry. While the Investment Coordination Board publishes data on 'domestic investment approvals', it is not possible to determine what proportion of these approvals are actually implemented. Furthermore, domestic private investors are not legally compelled to seek approval from the Investment Board, unless they wish to benefit from certain tax and other incentives, and it is widely believed that a substantial proportion choose not to do so.

Table 6.4 Cumulative value of investment flows, 1969–90
(US$ billion 1982 prices)

	1969–75	*1976–82*	*1983–90*
Foreign Inflows			
Direct foreign investment	1.96	2.17	3.52
Portfolio investment	0	0.64	0.26
Official capital inflows	6.28	15.21	17.64
Other capital inflows	−2.94	−0.96	5.87
Development budget*	17.92	65.43	64.52
Total investment (national accounts)	40.38	126.78	203.92

* Data refer to financial years
Sources: *International Financial Statistics Yearbook*, 1992: 410–11, lines 77ba, 77bb, 77ga, 77gc; *Indonesian Financial Statistics*, various issues

How do inflows of direct foreign investment since 1967 compare with those from the colonial era? Given data problems such comparisons are hazardous, but a comparison can be made of the data on private capital inflows compiled by Korthals Altes (CEI, Vol 7, Table 1) with more recent Bank Indonesia data on realised inflows of direct foreign investment (Figure 6.1). Converted into dollars (1967 prices), and expressed in per capita terms, the post-1969 figures have never been as high as the peak in the colonial era. Given that real per capita GDP has been higher since 1970 than in the pre-1940 period, foreign capital inflow has been lower, in relation to GDP, in the New Order era than in the boom years of the 1910s and 1920s. Certainly there are no grounds for arguing that Indonesia in the New Order era became substantially more dependant on private capital inflows from abroad than in the colonial era. Indeed, some scholars argue that Indonesia's heavy-handed regulatory policies towards foreign investors have deterred many potential investors who have found a more congenial investment environment in countries such as Malaysia and Thailand, and more recently China and Vietnam. This, in turn, has seriously affected the rate of growth of the manufacturing sector in particular (Hill 1992: 234).

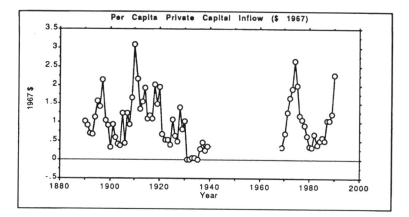

Figure 6.1 *Sources*: Private capital inflow, CEI, Vol. 7, Table 1 (line 19b) up to 1940; after 1967 data taken from Bank Indonesia *Annual Reports*, various issues. Population data from CEI, Vol. 11 and *Statistical Yearbook of Indonesia*, various issues.

The data in Figure 6.1 for the post-1969 period exclude private capital inflows for purposes other than direct investment. For much of the New Order era, these flows have been highly unstable, and largely speculative in character. But since the late 1980s, many large private firms have been negotiating long-term foreign loans, and private (non-guaranteed) loans grew rapidly in absolute terms and as a proportion of the total stock of foreign debt (World Bank 1995: 222). According to Bank Indonesia data, in 1990–91 and 1991–92, private long-term capital inflows other than direct investment were larger than inflows of equity capital (Bank Indonesia 1994: 129). Although the government has attempted to control these loans as part of an overall policy of containing foreign debt, it seems probable that loans, as distinct from equity, will become an increasingly important source of corporate finance in Indonesia.

THE ROLE OF GOVERNMENT IN INVESTMENT

Estimating the precise role of the government in the creation of capital assets in the colonial economy is not easy. Chapter 4 outlined the growing role of government in the construction of roads, railways, irrigation and ports in the latter part of the nineteenth century and the early twentieth century. The methods used, such as budgetary subsidies and government guarantees of minimum returns to private investors were also widely used in the British Empire, both in colonies such as India, and in the self-governing dominions (Headrick 1981: 183–7; Eichengreen 1995). In the Indonesian case, a number of enterprises were built and operated directly by the colonial government. The data assembled by Creutzberg indicate that in 1900, government commercial enterprises accounted for around 25 per cent of the aggregate value of corporate investment, and this ratio increased to 35 per cent by 1924 (Table 6.2). The railways and harbours must have accounted for a high proportion of this total, although after 1900 the government began to invest in mining enterprises and by 1930 there were five state-owned mines, and the government held substantial equity in a number of other enterprises including oil and tin mines (Callis 1941: 38). After the early 1920s there was a considerable decline in the government share of total corporate assets, as private sector investment accelerated (Table 6.2).

In addition, of course, the government invested in public goods which did not yield it an immediate financial return such as roads and irrigation works. The colonial government did not levy a water charge on government-provided irrigation, mainly because the land tax (*landrente*) was assessed at a higher rate on irrigated land, and colonial officialdom considered that an additional water levy would be too burdensome. Government expenditures on new irrigation works as estimated by van der Eng (1993, Table A8.2) accounted for over 6 per cent of total government expenditure on fixed assets in 1912, although this proportion fell sharply in the 1920s, and rose again in the 1930s. But government projects of all kinds accounted for only a small part of total investment expenditures in the final three decades of the Dutch colonial era. From 1910 to 1939, the government on average only accounted for 13.5 per cent of total expenditures on all fixed assets (Table 6.3). This reflected the cutbacks in government expenditures which occurred in the 1920s and the growth in private investment financed from both foreign and domestic sources.

Most writers on foreign investment in the colonial economy emphasise the importance of government borrowing; as Callis (1941: 35) argued 'no one can appreciate the extent to which the Indies had recourse to foreign capital without taking into account the large sums poured into the country by way of government loans'. Certainly between 1910 and 1939, the cumulative total of new Netherlands Indies loans and increases in the floating debt together amounted to well over twice private capital inflow (Table 6.3). But it is indisputable that a substantial proportion of this government borrowing was used to finance current government expenditures rather than capital formation. Callis (1941: 37) argued that in relatively prosperous years government loans raised abroad were used to finance capital works but in relatively depressed years they were used for current expenditures.

A considerable part of the capital stock extant in 1942, both infrastructure and plant and equipment in productive enterprises, was either destroyed during the Japanese occupation and the subsequent struggle for independence, or fell into disrepair. The newly independent government had ambitious plans to rehabilitate and extend investment in infrastructure, but there was a substantial gap between plan and achievement. Paauw (1960: 88–9) estimated that net investment in a 'typical' pre-plan year was Rp 5.65 billion in 1952 prices, or roughly 6 per cent of GDP on average in the years from 1950 to 1955. Of this, around 45 per cent was in the public sector, and a further 37 per cent in the capital-intensive private sector. A significant aspect of Paauw's estimates was that regional and local governments accounted for almost half of total public sector capital formation. The first five year plan was drawn up in the mid-1950s, and scheduled to run from 1956 to 1960. Its main aim was to accelerate the pace of government investment, especially in agriculture, transmigration, irrigation, energy, transport and education. Up to 1958, when it was largely abandoned, implementation was reasonably successful (Pond 1964: 96). The same could not be said for the next attempt at development planning, the eight-year plan drawn up after the return to the 1945 constitution in 1959 which was intended to direct the allocation of government investment from 1960 to 1968. Although most observers agreed that the choice of projects was sensible (many were carry-overs from the 1956–60 plan), the political and economic circumstances were hardly propitious for project implementation, and little was achieved after 1961 (Paauw 1963: 222–31).

The national income data for the 1950s suggest that aggregate investment expenditures in nominal terms did not increase much through the 1950s, and declined sharply in real terms, and relative to GDP (United Nations 1960: 114). The revised national income estimates for the 1960s published in 1970 show that gross domestic capital formation in real terms fluctuated between 7.4 and 10.7 per cent of GDP. In the early 1960s, construction projects accounted for over half of total fixed capital formation. It is probable that many of these were prestige projects undertaken by the government in the larger cities, with little impact on the productive capacity of the economy. Only in 1968 did investment in plant and equipment account for more than half of total investment (Central Bureau of Statistics 1970: 48–53). From the late 1960s onwards, the national accounts figures show that domestic investment rose steadily relative to GDP. The Sixth Five Year Plan document showed that investment comprised 23 per cent of GDP in 1983–84 and 30.5 per cent of GDP in 1993–94 (Booth 1994: Table 4). But these ratios of investment to GDP are inflated by the relatively high cost of capital goods in Indonesia, and for the purposes of international comparison, investment/GDP ratios should be shown adjusted for differences in purchasing power parities (Table 6.5). The adjusted data show that by 1988–92 the investment/GDP ratio was 26 per cent, which was lower than the official figures, but still high in comparison with most other countries in the region.

Table 6.5   Investment as a percentage of GDP*, 1960–90
(1985 international prices)

Year	Indonesia	Thailand	South Korea	Taiwan	Philippines	Malaysia
1960	7.3[†]	11.5	7.9	12.6	11.5	14.0
1965	6.5	16.5	14.1	16.3	13.0	17.1
1970	11.0	18.3	22.0	21.6	13.8	19.2
1975	16.9	17.7	24.3	26.8	17.3	24.1
1980	22.1	17.8	29.4	27.3	19.8	27.9
1985	26.0	16.8	28.9	21.6	14.7	27.8
1990	25.9	25.5	35.5**	23.8[†]	15.7	29.6
Annual average per capita GDP growth rate: 1960–90[§]						
	4.9	4.0	6.9	6.3	1.4	4.4

*Five-year averages centring on the year shown.
[†]1960–2.
**1988–91.
[†]1988–90.
[§]Growth of real per capita GDP, in 1985 international prices, adjusted for changes in the terms of trade.
Source: *Penn World Tables*, version 5.6.

Different sources give rather different estimates of the share of the public and private sectors in total investment in Indonesia since the early 1980s. The Sixth Plan showed that private sources accounted for 73 per cent of total investment and government sources 27 per cent in 1993–94, compared with 52 per cent and 48 per cent a decade earlier (Booth 1994: Table 4). Chant and Pangestu (1994: 264) quote a series which shows the private sector share of total investment rising from 56 per cent in 1981 to 59 per cent in 1989. In contrast, a set of comparative data on investment trends in developing countries showed that private sector investment in Indonesia accounted for around 43 per cent of total investment in 1992, and this ratio had changed little since 1981 (Miller and Sumlinski 1994: Table 1).

One reason for the differing estimates is that data on public sector investment over the New Order period are difficult to assemble and interpret. A distinction should be made between government investment funded through the development budget, some of which takes the form of equity participation in state enterprises, and investment in state enterprises funded through loans. While budgetary data on equity participation are published, it is extremely difficult to obtain information on other investment in the state enterprise sector, although it is known to be considerable. Recent estimates of the total value of assets of state enterprises (BUMN) indicate that in 1992–93 they amounted to Rp 230.3 trillion, or 90 per cent of GDP in 1992 (Department of Information 1993: XXII/73). Direct government equity participation in state enterprises has fallen sharply as a proportion of total development expenditures since the 1970s; by 1993–94 it accounted for less than 1 per cent of total development expenditures. The sectoral allocation of government development expenditures has changed over successive plans from a focus on agriculture to growing emphasis on transport infrastructure, energy, and education (Booth 1994: 12). But not all government development expenditure can be considered 'investment' in the national accounting sense. A considerable, although unknown, part is devoted to salary supplements.

INVESTMENT IN HUMAN CAPITAL THROUGH EDUCATION

As in other parts of colonial Asia, the Dutch authorities in Indonesia assumed responsibility for education only slowly, in response to a number of different, and often conflicting, pressures from liberal opinion in the metropolitan power and from various domestic interest groups. The first real acknowledgement that the colonial government had a responsibility for the education of the indigenous people came in 1854 when the constitutional regulations of that year devoted an entire chapter to education, which in many respects resembled the article on education in the constitution of the Netherlands promulgated in 1848 (van der Wal 1961:5). These provisions reflected prevailing European liberal and humanitarian ideals on the role of education in improving both the material and the spiritual condition of the population, and on the responsibility of government in providing free access to secular education for all children. In 1861 a separate government department was established to oversee educational development and a decade later the first regulations for native education were enacted by royal decree (Hutasoit 1954: 22).

But, in spite of the earnest rhetoric of liberal reformers in both the Netherlands and the colony, little had been achieved by the end of the nineteenth century. Furnivall (1943: 45) commented that in most parts of Asia at this time 'humanitarian sentiment created a new atmosphere and gave a new colour to policy, but had little practical effect until economic circumstances were propitious'. Particularly striking in Indonesia as in most other Asian societies was the failure to develop any mass system of primary vernacular instruction. While European-language instruction was making some headway, especially among the official classes, who viewed it as the main avenue for their offspring's social advancement, many parents saw no point in sending children to schools which only offered a few years of secular education in a vernacular language. In addition, in the Indonesian context, the government favoured the principle of making posts in the native administration hereditary, and traditional rulers were reluctant to send their sons to school if they were guaranteed jobs anyway (Schrieke 1938: 15). Some urban dwellers may have wished to send their children to the Dutch schools where they could have acquired a qualification leading to a clerical job in a government office, or with a foreign company, but such schools were few in number, located only in large towns and cities and prohibitively expensive. In 1900 only 2,440 Indonesian children were enrolled in Dutch primary schools and just thirteen in Dutch secondary schools (van der Veur 1969: 11). A further 98,200 were enrolled in the so-called 'second class schools' which offered primary education in vernacular languages.

The ethical policy reinforced the earlier liberal emphasis on educational development but the government was now prepared to increase expenditure. During the last three decades of the nineteenth century, government expenditures on 'native education' rose from 0.3 per cent to 1 per cent of all budgetary expenditures (Table 4.2). Real government expenditure growth more than doubled after 1900, and the share devoted to native education increased to amost 2 per cent of the total by 1913 (Tables 1.1 and 4.2). Much of the increased budget went on expanding the network of vernacular language schools in both urban and rural areas. In 1907 the *volksschool* were introduced, whose aim was to enrol children in three-year courses teaching the elements of literacy and numeracy. Enrolments at both the *volksschool* and the second-class schools increased quite rapidly between 1900 and 1920, although only 780,000 children were enrolled in 1920, and a further 43,400 had gained access to the Dutch-medium primary schools (van der Veur 1969: 7–11). The 1920 population census revealed that only 5.1 per cent of indigenous males aged over fifteen in Java were literate in Roman script, and 0.2 per cent could read Dutch; the corresponding figures for the Outer Islands were 7.9 per cent and 0.2 per cent. The higher literacy figure outside Java reflected in part the greater presence of missionary activity, although the 1920 census certainly under-counted populations in the more remote regions outside Java and the literacy figures could be inflated for this reason. Female literacy figures were well below those of males everywhere in the country (SJO 1925: 94).

The 1920 census made it painfully obvious just how unlettered the Indonesian population was, especially in the language of the colonial power. There was considerable further growth in indigenous enrolments in both the vernacular and Dutch-medium schools in the 1920s, and the 1930 Census found that almost 11 per cent of indigenous males were literate and 2 per cent of females (Furnivall 1943: 76). But Dutch fears grew about the consequences of rapid expansion of access to education, especially in the Dutch language schools. Such education was seldom sought for its own sake but rather as a passport to a clerical job in the government or in a private company, and the willingness of even the top layer of the indigenous population to pay for a Dutch education was thus much influenced by their expectations of monetary return. Sartono (1984: 123) estimated that almost half the total output of graduates from Dutch-language schools between 1900 and 1928 were absorbed into government jobs, but it was already clear by the 1920s that the supply of graduates was outstripping the number of suitable job openings. Many indigenous Indonesians who did get government jobs occupied lower grades than their paper qualifications equipped them for. While access to Dutch education was a means of rapid social mobility for a few Indonesians, especially in the early phase of the ethical policy, by the 1920s it was producing a generation who were forced to look to other occupations in order to exploit their newly acquired skills.

On the Dutch side, as van der Veur (1969: 9) argued, it was always official policy to regard Dutch education for non-Europeans as the exception and to avoid at all costs the emergence of an 'intellectual proletariat' with European attitudes and expectations but unable to acquire a European income. Such people, it was argued, would only cause social and political unrest (Kahin 1952: 55). Many children whose families were able to pay the fees were, in fact, rejected from the Dutch-medium primary schools because the colonial government feared the consequences of rapid growth of indigenous enrolments (van der Veur 1969:35). In the early years of the depression, as the number of job openings in the modern sector of the economy contracted, there was a marked slowdown in the growth of indigenous enrolments in the Dutch medium schools. Even after 1935, enrolment growth was still below that achieved in the 1920s, although it was faster than the growth of the primary school age cohort as a whole.

Enrolments in the vernacular schools also slowed after 1930, although they accelerated again after 1935. Dutch officials wished to promote vernacular education, both general and vocational, as a means of raising the skill level of the population in their traditional agricultural occupations and in 'new' occupations in the manufacturing and tertiary sectors as these became available (Furnivall 1943: 78). The education offered in the vernacular schools was designed to provide basic literacy and numeracy while at the same time not raising expectations regarding the nature of the employment which education would lead to. By 1940, it was estimated that 44.5 per cent of all children aged between six and nine were enrolled in vernacular schools, compared with 34.7 per cent in 1930 (van der Wal 1961: 7). Although this may appear a creditable achievement, especially for a colonial government which was frequently accused of neglecting education, several caveats need to be borne in mind. As Furnivall (1943: 111) showed, the ratio of primary enrolments to total population was still rather low in Indonesia in the 1930s, in comparison with other Southeast Asian countries. Although this partly reflected differing population age structures, it seems clear that in countries such as Formosa (Taiwan), the Philippines and Thailand a much higher proportion of school-age children were actually enrolled in school than was the case in Indonesia. Furthermore, as van der Veur (1969: 6) has pointed out, most of the enrolments in vernacular schools were in the *volksschool*, where the education offered was of low quality and short duration. There was also a considerable disparity between numbers enrolled and numbers graduating; in the 1920s it was estimated that only about one-third of those who entered the first class actually went to complete the three-year course. Of these, a tiny proportion went on to any kind of further education.

Indeed, it was at the secondary and higher levels that Indonesia fell markedly behind other Southeast Asian countries in the inter-war years. Furnivall (1943: 111) argued that secondary enrolments were not much higher in Indonesia in the late 1930s than in Burma, Formosa or Malaya despite the fact that the Indonesian population was much larger. Total secondary enrolments in 1938 were estimated to be just over 20,000, which was only about one-quarter of the Philippine figure. Secondary enrolments were also a much lower proportion of primary enrolments in Indonesia than in other parts of the region with the exception of Indochina, indicating lower continuation rates. However, Indonesia did stand out in having very high enrolments in technical vocational schools compared with neighbouring countries. Indonesia and Indochina were the only two countries where vocational enrolments exceeded those in general secondary schools. The nature of the vocational training varied greatly. Much of it was in the vernacular and involved little more than practical extension of the courses offered in the *volksschool*. But, at the other extreme, vocational training included the training of 'native doctors' in the medical schools in Jakarta and Surabaya. Although these doctors underwent training for eight years and were legally entitled to practice in Indonesia, their courses were not considered to be of university standard (van der Wal 1961: 11).

That the colonial education system was highly segregated, with educational opportunities differing enormously by ethnic group, was never denied by the colonial authorities. In 1940 about 14,300 students graduated from Dutch-language primary schools; of these slightly more than half were Indonesian. When it is recalled that Indonesians comprised over 97 per cent of the total population it is obvious how restricted access was to the Dutch-language school system for indigenous Indonesians even at the end of the Dutch era. And it was only the Dutch system which offered prospects for upward mobility. At the lower secondary level, slightly under half the graduates were Indonesian, but at the higher levels of education the proportion of Indonesian graduates dropped off. Only 220 of the 859 students graduating from the senior high schools were Indonesian in 1940, and only thirty-seven of the seventy-nine graduating from tertiary institutions. Indonesians accounted for 51 per cent of the 3,800 graduates from vocational, technical and commercial schools; these schools included the medical, dental, veterinary, forestry and law schools as well as a range of other institutions (van der Veur 1969: 14–14a). Some Indonesian students found their way to universities and other institutions of higher learning in the Netherlands, but their numbers were tiny. Van der Wal (1961:13) estimates that 344 Indonesians matriculated in the Netherlands between 1924 and 1940, compared with 360 Chinese students.

There was a marked inverse relationship between the quality of the school, as reflected in the annual cost per student, and the proportion of Indonesians attending. Van der Wal (1963:666) has shown that the annual pupil cost in the *volksschool* (village school) was about 5 guilders per year, compared with between 45 and 90 guilders in the Dutch-language primary schools. At the secondary level, annual costs per pupil ranged from 65 guilders a year in the schools catering largely for indigenous children (MULO) to over 200 guilders per year in the Dutch academic high schools. A good part of these costs were recouped in fees, especially in the Dutch-language streams. Van der Veur has argued that although the fee structure in the Dutch primary schools was based on parental incomes, all parents with incomes below 1,300 guilders per year had to pay 36 guilders per child. As more than 90 per cent of Indonesian parents would have been in this income group,

> what constituted a minimum and reasonable fee for paying-European parents... was in effect a uniform and heavily regressive one for the overwhelming majority of Indonesian parents. Under these circumstances, it is not surprising that the slightest change in a parent's income could spell the end of a child's school career (van der Veur 1969: 16).

The fee structure was undoubtedly an important reason both for the failure of many children to enter the school system in the first place and for the high dropout rate. Even those vocational schools designed exclusively for indigenous Indonesians charged fees that were high in relation to average incomes and, in addition, students usually had to live away from home and pay for room and board. Van der Wal (1963: 378) quotes an official memorandum of 1924 pointing out that the total monthly cost for a student attending the school for training village-school teachers was 6.50 guilders, a substantial sum in comparison with Polak's estimate of total income accruing to indigenous Indonesians of 5.33 guilders per capita per month in 1924.

The educational legacy bequeathed to independent Indonesia was thus an extremely meagre one. Because the expansion of access to the village schools had only occurred quite late in the colonial period, the majority of the population at independence had had no experience of formal schooling. A leading Indonesian authority estimated that 63 per cent of the population were illiterate in 1947 (van der Wal 1961: 7). Of those who had entered the formal educational system, the great majority had had at most three years' instruction in a rural school. Another consequence of the colonial educational system was the marked difference in educational attainment between indigenous Indonesians and the ethnic Chinese. Although the absolute numbers of Indonesians in all the Dutch language schools except the three-and five-year high schools and the very prestigious 'lyceum' exceeded the numbers of Chinese, a much higher percentage of the Chinese population had access to Western education, often in the Dutch-language schools which were established for the Chinese community in the early years of the twentieth century (Suryadinata 1972: 54–6). In the academic high schools and the universities, both in the colony and in the Netherlands, absolute numbers of Chinese enrolments were about the same as, or only slightly lower than, indigenous Indonesian enrolments. Some Indonesian Chinese students were also educated at secondary and tertiary institutions in China. Thus, at independence the average educational level of the Chinese population in Indonesia was much greater than that of the indigenous Indonesian population. This was to have a considerable influence on the subsequent role of the Chinese in the independent state.

The coming of political independence brought with it an enormous demand for education, both for its own sake and as a means of accelerating social mobility. Many people who had had their own hopes of personal advancement frustrated in the colonial period sought education for their children so that the new generation could benefit from the wider range of opportunities which political independence was expected to bring. Enrolments of indigenous Indonesians in all types of schools were estimated at 2.3 million in 1940; by 1953–54 they had more than doubled to 5.8 million. Over the next decade enrolments continued to grow at over 8 per cent per annum, so that

by the mid-1960s over fourteen million young Indonesians were enrolled in some sort of formal educational institution. In 1960–61,
primary school enrolments amounted to almost 63 per cent of children
in the 7–12 age group, compared with only 22 per cent in 1940 (Table
6.6). As Daroesman (1971: 61) pointed out, this growth was remarkable 'not only in relation to the low starting point, but also in relation
to the magnitude and variety of the other problems faced: the creation
of a new system, the adoption of a national language, emergency
training of teachers, and provision of buildings and equipment, all
under the most stringent financial difficulties'. For much of the period
between 1950 and 1965, growth of primary and secondary enrolments
in Indonesia were well above the Asian average.

Table 6.6   Trends in enrolment ratios,* 1940–93/4

Year	Primary		Lower Secondary	Upper Secondary	Tertiary
	C	R			
1940	22.2	n.a.	n.a.	n.a.	n.a.
1960–61	62.8	n.a.	n.a.	n.a.	n.a.
1968	68.7	41.4	16.9	8.6	1.6
1973–74	78.8	66.6	17.4	9.3	1.9
1983–84	122.3	97.2	44.4	26.1	5.3
1993–94	110.4	93.5	43.4	30.3	9.5

* Primary enrolment rates are given in both crude and refined forms. Crude
rates refer to total primary enrolments as a percentage of total population
aged 7–12. Refined rates refer to children aged 7–12 enrolled in school as a
proportion of the total population aged 7–12. Lower secondary rates refer to
all enrolments as a percentage of the population aged 13–15. Upper secondary
rates refer to all enrolments as a percentage of the population aged 16–18.
Tertiary rates refer to all enrolments as a percentage of the population aged
19–24.
Sources: 1940; van der Veur (1969: 7–11); population aged 7–12 in 1940
assumed to be the same proportion of the total population as in 1961.
1960–61: *Statistical Pocketbook of Indonesia 1963*, pp. 15, 31. 1968, 1973–74
and 1983–84: *Lampiran Pidato Pertanggungjawaban 1993*, Tables XVI–1
to XVI–4. 1993–94: *Lampiran Pidato Kenegaraan 1994*, Tables XVI–1 to
XVI–4.

There can be little doubt that this expansion took place at the
expense of qualitative improvement, and that the standard of
Indonesian education was low in comparison with other parts of the
region, where education had progressed more in the colonial era.
Class sizes were high, many teachers were inadequately trained, and

shortages of buildings resulted in overcrowding and reduced teaching hours. Basic equipment, textbooks and teaching aids for staff and pupils were grossly inadequate and often had to be provided by the teacher or pupil at their own expense. Although the great majority of schools were supposedly run and financed by the government, in almost all cases funds had to be supplemented by contributions from parents, and indeed it was explicit government policy to encourage the community to take responsibility for not only the non-salary recurrent costs of government schools, but also for supplements to teachers' salaries (Daroesman 1972: 65; Beeby 1979: 43–4). Inevitably 'community responsibility' involved parental liability for fees both at the time of enrolment and on a monthly basis while the child was attending school. These fees, in turn, acted as a barrier to entry, and encouraged high drop-out rates.

Thus, in spite of the rapid growth in school enrolments which occurred in the years from 1950 to 1965, the problems which faced educational planners at the beginning of the New Order period were formidable. Children aged 7–12 who were actually enrolled in primary school comprised only 41 per cent of the 7–12 age group in 1968 (Table 6.6). Enrolments at the secondary level in 1968 were estimated to be around 1.63 million, or 17 per cent of children in the 13–15 age group; less than half of those children who managed to finish primary school continued on to the secondary level. Although the first *Repelita* document contained a frank discussion of the deficiencies of the educational system and suggested a number of policies for improving both its quantitative and its qualitative performance, the *Repelita 1* implementation report showed that enrolments in both private and government primary schools had increased by only 1.5 per cent per annum between 1969 and 1973 (Republic of Indonesia 1974, Table IX–1). In 1973 only 57 per cent of children aged 7–12 were actually enrolled in government or private schools, although a considerable number were attending the Islamic schools which offered a secular component in the curriculum, so the total participation rate was around 67 per cent.

It was the greatly expanded budgetary revenues from the first oil price increase which allowed the government to increase dramatically funds for educational expansion. In 1972–73, capital expenditures on education accounted for only about 6 per cent of the central government's development budget, and 0.3 per cent of GDP. By the end of the second *Repelita* (1978–79) education accounted for almost 10 per cent of government expenditure and government expenditures on education comprised almost 3 per cent of GDP (International Monetary Fund 1980). The main channel through which the increased capital budget for education was disbursed was the so-called *Inpres* SD programme. This programme disbursed funds to provincial and *kabupaten* authorities for the construction of new school buildings in locations where previously there had been no primary education facility. The programme was designed for the express purpose of absorbing children who had not previously been enrolled, and the emphasis was on new infrastructure rather than the rehabilitation and upgrading of existing schools. In allocating funds for construction of the new schools, particular attention was paid to regions where primary enrolments were low (Heneveld 1978: 67).

By 1983–84, the results of the accelerated school-building programme, together with accelerated recruitment of teachers were obvious in the enrolment figures. Total enrolments in primary schools had jumped to 122 per cent of the 7–12 age group, and 97 per cent of children aged 7–12 were in school compared with only 41 per cent in 1968 (Table 6.6). At the secondary level progress was slower; total lower secondary enrolments comprised only 44 per cent, and senior secondary enrolments comprised only 26 per cent of children in the relevant age groups. As primary enrolments approached 100 per cent in the early 1980s, it might have been expected that more funds would be devoted to expanding access to secondary enrolments. However, government educational expenditures as a proportion of GDP actually fell in the latter part of the 1980s, and although private sector facilities expanded, lower secondary enrolments as a proportion of the 13–15 age cohort were lower in 1993–94 than a decade earlier (Table 6.6). This decline reflected both the increasing direct costs of post-primary school attendance, and the greater opportunity costs in terms of forgone earnings, as job opportunities for young people increased. On the other hand, there was a modest expansion in upper secondary enrolments, and considerable growth in tertiary enrolments as a proportion of the relevant age cohorts. The impact of the post-1970 expansion of access to educational facilities on the educational attainment of the population can be seen most clearly from a comparison of the results of the 1961 and 1990 population censuses (Table 6.7). In 1961, 59 per cent of males and 84 per cent of females over twenty years had had no formal schooling at all. By 1990, these percentages had fallen to 15 and 30 per cent. Although the great majority of both men and women in 1990 had still had no education beyond the primary level, an improvement in average attainment was obvious, especially in the younger age groups.

Table 6.7   Working age population by educational attainment: Indonesia and Japan

Indonesia	Male		Female	
	1961	*1990*	*1961*	*1990*
No schooling	59.4	14.6	83.9	29.7
Incomplete primary	22.3	26.6	9.7	26.8
Complete primary	13.9	29.6	5.0	25.2
Junior high school	3.1	10.2	1.1	7.0
Senior high school	1.1	16.0	0.3	9.8
Tertiary	0.2	2.9	0.1	1.4
Total	100.0	100.0	100.0	100.0
Japan				
	1900	*1940*	*1900*	*1940*
Incomplete primary	78.3	9.8	92.8	22.3
Complete primary	21.5	64.1	7.1	61.8
Above primary	0.2	26.1	0.1	15.9
Total	100.0	100.0	100.0	100.0

Sources: Indonesia: *Population Census* 1961, Series SP1, Table 7; *Population Census* 1990, Series S2, Tables 11.7 and 11.8. Data refer to the population aged over twenty. Japan: Ohkawa and Kohama (1989), Table 6.3.

Impressive though the progress has been since 1961, Indonesia still lagged behind many other Asian countries in terms of educational attainment in the early 1990s. The percentage of the population with completed primary education or more was still lower in 1990 than in Japan in 1940 (Table 6.7). In 1993–94, only 37 per cent of youngsters between 13 and 18 were in secondary school, which was a lower ratio than in Taiwan in the 1960s (Chou 1995: 109). Although the enrolment ratio for all levels of education in 1990 was slightly above Thailand, and the same as Malaysia, it was still well below countries such as Sri Lanka and the Philippines (UNDP 1995: 162–3). And public expenditures on education were only 1.8 per cent of GDP in Indonesia in 1992, compared with over 5 per cent in Malaysia, 3.3 per cent in Thailand and 3 per cent in the Philippines (International Monetary Fund 1995: 6–25). Low levels of government expenditure on education in Indonesia meant that parental contributions still accounted for a considerable part of school budgets, with the inevitable result that children from families unable to make such contributions were excluded from education, especially at the post-primary level.

In addition, many of the quality problems which plagued the system in the immediate post-independence era have not been resolved. In opting for quantitative expansion of enrolments rather than for improvement in existing facilities since 1970, there can be little doubt that educational quality, already low in the 1960s, has not greatly improved, and indeed in some respects could have deteriorated even further. The problem is made worse by the rapid growth of private education, often in response to perceived market demand, and often of dubious quality. It is certainly aggravated in both the state and private sectors by continuing poor salaries for teachers and lecturers, and inadequate budgets for the maintenance and extension of existing facilities and for the purchase of new equipment and teaching aids. These continuing problems of educational quality, in turn, affect the impact of educational expansion on the quality of the labour force, and thus on economic growth. This point is pursued in the next section.

EFFICIENCY OF INVESTMENT

Students of the process of long-term economic growth have devoted considerable attention to physical capital accumulation, as this is seen as the key to sustained growth of output. But international evidence also shows that countries with similar ratios of investment to GDP have achieved very different growth rates. Thus, attention has centred on the efficiency of investment, or its impact on generating further growth of GDP. One crude measure of investment efficiency is simply to look at the capital-output ratio. There can be little doubt that this has been rising in Indonesia over the course of the twentieth century. It was suggested above that the capital–output ratio was probably around unity in 1913; by 1980 it had increased to around 2.1, according to the estimates of the total value of capital stock in 1980 produced by Keuning (1991, Table 2). This is broadly similar to the Japanese figure in 1920 (Table 6.8). A comparison of sectoral capital–output ratios for Indonesia in 1980 and Japan in 1920 indicates that the ratio for the agricultural sector was lower in Indonesia, the ratios for the manufacturing sector were broadly similar, and the ratio for the service sector was much higher in Indonesia. This last disparity is largely due to the impact of the real estate sector, which according to Keuning (1991, Table 2) accounted for about 20 per cent of total capital stock in Indonesia in 1980. Keuning's figures indicate that the real appreciation induced by the oil boom skewed capital investment towards real estate in Indonesia through the 1970s. There is not much support from the comparison with Japan for the argument that the oil boom led to the adoption of extremely capital-intensive production techniques in other sectors of the economy such as manufacturing, construction or public utilities.

Table 6.8 Capital–output (K/Y) ratios: Japan 1920 and Indonesia 1980

	Japan 1920	*Indonesia 1980*
Agriculture	2.46	1.35
Mining	n.a.	1.53
Manufacturing etc.*	3.25	3.24
Services	0.78	2.37
Total	2.16	2.09

* Includes utilities, transport and construction, and mining for Japan.
Sources: Japan: Minami (1986), Tables 6.11 and 6.12. Indonesia: Keuning (1991), Tables 1 and 2.

A more sophisticated estimate of the productivity of investment involves an attempt to estimate the contributions of capital, labour, and total factor productivity growth to growth of output using a production function approach. Several such estimates have been made for Indonesia for the 1970s and 1980s. Woo, Glassburner and Nasution (1994, Table 10.2) decomposed the growth in non-oil GDP in 1973–81 (the oil boom era) and 1982–88 (the period of post-oil boom restructuring). They found that growth in capital stock and labour supply accounted for around 90 per cent of GDP growth in 1973–81, the residual being attributed to growth in total factor productivity (TFP), or growth in output per unit of factor inputs. In 1982–88 by contrast, the combined effect of growth in capital stock and labour supply more than accounted for the observed growth in non-oil GDP. The contribution of TFP growth was in fact negative. The Sixth Plan document presented estimates of sources of total GDP growth for the years from 1989 to 1993. According to these calculations, growth in capital stock and labour supply accounted for 83 per cent of GDP growth while the balance was accounted for by TFP growth (Booth 1994, Table 6).

Both these estimates indicate that the contribution of TFP growth to total growth of GDP in Indonesia in the years from 1973 to 1993 has been low or negative. A recent analysis by the World Bank of growth in East Asia classified Indonesia (with Singapore and Malaysia) as an 'investment-driven' economy in contrast to Japan, Korea, Hong Kong, Taiwan and Thailand where more growth over the last two decades has been attributed to growth in productivity (World Bank 1993:57). This finding is probably less serious for Indonesia than for Malaysia and Singapore, as most international comparisons of sources of growth have reached the conclusion that low income countries such as Indonesia are less likely to experience rapid TFP growth than middle income countries. But the Indonesian findings do pose some worrying questions. Woo, Glassburner and Nasution (1994: 121) argue that it was 'dirigiste microeconomic policies' which accounted for the low growth of TFP in Indonesia. But the low levels of education among the labour force, inadequate infrastructure and the weak legal and institutional support for the market economy which still prevails in many sectors must also have contributed to the low TFP growth. In addition, as the comparison with Japan in Table 6.8 indicates, the real appreciation which occurred during the oil boom encouraged investment in low-yielding sectors such as real estate, which in turn reduced the residual allocated to total factor productivity growth.

PROCESSES OF TECHNOLOGY TRANSFER IN INDONESIA

Both investment (the process of adding to the capital stock) and growth in factor productivity (an increase in output per unit of input of labour and capital) involve the adoption of new technologies. In many sectors of the economy, such as manufacturing industry, construction and the modern service sector, new technologies are embodied in new plant and equipment and their adoption involves additions to the national capital stock. But in addition, the acquisition of new technologies involves the learning of new skills and new approaches to production. Indeed, it is possible for some new technologies to lead to a considerable growth in output with only a modest amount of investment. Thus, the process of technology transfer in an economy tells us much not just about the pace of investment but also about the capacity of the population to learn new skills.

Dutch scholars in the 'dualism' tradition tended to emphasise the great gap between the sophisticated capital-intensive production technologies characteristic of high capitalism and the much simpler, even primitive technologies which were used by indigenous Indonesians to produce their daily necessities. But progressively throughout the nineteenth and twentieth centuries, Indonesians were borrowing and adapting Western production methods both in agriculture and in other sectors of the economy. Sometimes this happened as a result of deliberate government policy, and sometimes in spite of the efforts of government or private interests to prevent technology transfer. Lindblad (1991: 196–7) has pointed out that in the colonial economy 'the very nature of production of raw materials implied a low level of technology geared towards labour-intensive techniques and little mechanisation in estate agriculture and most mining enterprises'. In the case of rubber, local farmers took jobs as coolies on foreign estates in Kalimantan and elsewhere 'only as long as needed to master the techniques required to set up production on their own'. But rapid though the adoption of the new crops was, there was a limit to what small cultivators could achieve on their own with little capital and few opportunities to learn better cultivation practices or adopt higher yielding varieties. Yields stagnated and additional output could only be achieved by replicating the existing technologies over more land.

In the foodcrop sector, the ethical policy ushered in a range of policies in agricultural extension and dissemination of improved cultivation practices, although the numbers employed in the extension service remained below 100 until 1918, and never exceeded 250 (van der Eng 1993: Table 3.10). Extension officers were expected to both carry out research into existing agricultural practices with a view to their improvement and convince farmers to accept their innovations. The best of the colonial agricultural extension officers saw the need for what in the latter part of the twentieth century has become known as integrated rural development. But their numbers were too small to make a significant contribution even in Java, let alone elsewhere, and the research backup was inadequate. Government researchers in foodcrop agriculture were concentrated in the General Agricultural Research Station in Bogor, and their activities were spread over a range of crops and cultivation problems. Foreign visitors to Java in the inter-war years praised the 'wonderful knowledge of scientific methods' displayed by many Javanese farmers (Gore 1928: 125), but how much of this was due to the activities of government extension officers, and how much to their own efforts is unclear. As the network of village schools expanded in the 1920s, and more young people became literate, popular magazines in both Indonesian and Javanese were also used to disseminate knowledge about improved farming practices (van der Eng 1993: 114).

The most dramatic breakthrough in the dissemination of new technologies in smallholder agriculture in Indonesia came in the 1970s and 1980s, with the advent of the new seed-fertiliser technologies in rice agriculture. Building on the experience of small-scale programmes initiated in the early 1960s, the government launched an ambitious programme of mass dissemination of the new seed-fertiliser technologies developed at the International Rice Research Institute in Manila. The new rice varieties spread rapidly through Java, Bali, and the better irrigated parts of Sumatra and Sulawesi, and yields accelerated rapidly (Booth 1988: 146–58). The reasons for this success have been much debated in the literature, but three salient features stand out.

1 Supporting infrastructure was already in place, especially an irrigation system dating from the colonial era, which was rehabilitated and extended in the late 1960s and 1970s.
2 The government played a key role in subsidising fertiliser, providing extension services and credit, and supporting domestic procurement prices through purchases and sales from the national rice stock administered by the National Logistics Board (BULOG). This board controlled all rice imports.
3 Within this controlled environment individual producers had the freedom to purchase inputs as required, although government extension agents often controlled planting and harvesting, especially when pest outbreaks were threatening. Fertiliser distribution and rice marketing were largely in private hands and quite competitive, although BULOG often intervened in rice markets to influence prices.

The Green Revolution in the Indonesian foodcrop sector was a remarkable example of government-sponsored technology transfer to millions of smallholder farmers who proved extremely responsive to new cultivation technologies, even where they involved the purchase of inputs. Contrary to the rather bleak predictions of early observers of the original BIMAS programme, the introduction of the new rice technologies in Indonesia does not appear to have led to a sharp polarization in income distribution in rural areas, or to widespread displacement of labour. The increase in output more than compensated for the decline in labour use per unit of output which the introduction of new planting and harvesting technologies brought about (Booth 1988: 176ff). But the successful strategy of technology transfer in the foodcrop sector proved extremely difficult to replicate in other sectors of the agricultural economy, and especially in the small-scale treecrop sector, where the yields achieved by many small-holders for crops such as rubber, coffee and coconuts continue to be little higher than in the pre-independence period. Tabor (1992: 193ff) has pointed out that the Indonesian government has, in fact, put substantial resources into smallholder treecrop development projects, so the lack of success in disseminating new technologies cannot be attributed to lack of finance. Perhaps the real reason should be sought in what Tabor calls the 'administrative difficulty of sustaining man-agement and technical support for a multi-year investment venture, and in sharp comparison to the Javanese rice case, the inability to use non-market forces to command technological change'.

The non-agricultural sectors of the Indonesian economy also pro-vide many contrasts in production technology, and a variety of tech-nologies are frequently in use in the same industry. As in the agricultural sector, the late colonial period saw the development of an industrial extension service designed to introduce new technologies into a range of small scale manufacturing industries. By the late 1930s, there was an extensive network of over 700 government industrial and vocational schools, and several research institutes (Sitsen: c. 1943: 36). The Bandung Textile Institute developed the non-power weaving loom which could produce five times the output of the traditional loom in 1922. At first its dissemination was slow, mainly because of the rapid growth in cheap cloth imports from Japan. But after the imposition of quotas on Japanese imports in 1934, the number of Bandung looms in use grew rapidly, from only 1,300 in 1933 to 44,000 in 1940 (Boeke 1953: 287; Palmer 1972: 31–47). In addition, imports of fully mechanised looms increased rapidly. As Palmer (1972: 47) has pointed out, there is little evidence that the rapid growth in use of both the Bandung looms and the imported power looms destroyed the traditional weaving sector. In fact, the data on yarn imports in the latter part of the 1930s suggests that all three technologies coexisted side by side, although output from traditional looms did not grow as rapidly.

The introduction of new technologies in the pre-war weaving in-dustry supports Hill's argument (1980: 335) that in many industries the traditional 'dualistic' notion of two sharply contrasting technolo-gies, one labour-intensive and one capital-intensive, was frequently not valid. Rather, a range of efficient techniques exists, and the one chosen usually depends on the prices for labour and capital. Hill (1983) and Timmer (1973) have presented empirical evidence for this in the case of the weaving and rice-milling industries in the 1970s. They argued that distorted capital markets, and especially the access which some borrowers had to subsidised credit in the 1970s and 1980s frequently led to the adoption of very capital-intensive techniques in some factories while small-scale producers who faced much higher interest rates, but who hire labour cheaply (in the case of family labour often at zero cost) adopt intermediate technologies which use more labour, and less capital, per unit of output.

Studies of technology transfer in Indonesian manufacturing industry are still very limited in number, but Braadbaart's work on engineering industries in the Bandung region has highlighted the importance of a few key industries, established in the colonial period, in disseminating engineering skills which have then been utilised elsewhere. Of particular importance was the Army Ordnance works which moved to Bandung in the 1920s. By the late 1930s these works had a sophisticated metallurgical laboratory and employed a large indigenous staff. Of forty-six engineering shops surveyed in Bandung in the early 1990s, over 25 per cent were founded by people who had had experience in the colonial works (Braadbaart 1995: Table 2). After independence, the Ordnance works were transferred to the Indonesian government, but low pay and bad management induced many workers to leave for the private sector, taking their engineering skills with them. Although many of the engineering workshops established by the former Ordnance workers did not survive the inflation of the 1960s and subsequent import liberalisation of the 1970s, which was especially damaging for the relatively unprotected engineering industries, those that did managed to pass on skills to a new generation of workers.

Braadbaart's study highlighted the importance of the private sector in technology dissemination. Other studies have suggested that government attempts in the New Order era to disseminate improved technology to small scale manufacturing plants have met with at best limited success (Sandee 1995: 163–4). In other sectors of the economy, government attitudes to small scale producers using labour intensive technologies have been hostile rather than supportive. Officialdom has often intervened to ban such technologies which are viewed as old-fashioned, unhealthy or dangerous. Probably the most controversial of such policies has been in the urban public transport sector, where the bicycle rickshaw has been banned from the centres of most large cities, to allow freer flow of motorised transport. In addition, street hawkers are frequently driven away from the precincts of modern shopping centres and forced to restrict their trade to less affluent parts of the large cities. Such heavy-handed regulatory policies which discriminate against efficient labour-intensive technologies are obviously labour-displacing, but attractive to city planners who want to establish a modern image in urban areas, and to urban middle classes who wish to simulate a Western lifestyle for themselves and their families.

Many economists now argue that processes of technology transfer are most likely to occur efficiently in Indonesia through market mechanisms, and government interventions almost always introduce distortions, where they are not completely futile. While there is plenty of evidence to support such arguments, the experience of rice agriculture does indicate that the government has a role to play in disseminating new technologies quickly to large numbers of producers. Another, quite different, area where remarkable success has been achieved with government assistance is family planning. The Indonesian programme, initiated in 1969, has disseminated knowledge about modern family planning practices to millions of families, with relatively little of the coercion which has disfigured similar programmes in China (Hull and Hull 1992: 412ff). The provision of modern contraceptives has been heavily subsidised by the government, and as with the green revolution technologies, there can be little doubt that these subsidies greatly speeded up the rate of adoption of new technologies. There is indeed now some alarm in the public health services that with the increased privatization of health provision, and the greater use of private pharmacies to distribute contraceptives, use may decline.

On the basis of the experience in foodcrop agriculture and family planning on the one hand, and manufacturing industry and services on the other, it could be argued that government assistance is essential if new, standardised, technologies are to be disseminated to millions of households very rapidly. But such assistance in the industrial sector, where technology is far more specific to particular firms, is much more likely to introduce distortions and encourage inefficiencies. Almost always it is preferable to allow the process of technology transfer to proceed using well-tested market methods such as direct foreign investment, and licensing agreements, buttressed by specialised skills purchased from external consultants as needed (Hill 1995: 112–14). Certainly there has been, and continues to be, much useful technology transfer to the Indonesian private sector by precisely these means. But in Indonesia, as elsewhere in Asia, there is considerable doubt that such market-induced technology transfer is really making a substantial contribution to the development of indigenous technological capability, at least beyond a very basic level. Studies of Japanese investment in Indonesia, for example, indicate a considerable reluctance to transfer 'managerial know-how' as distinct from basic production skills (Thee 1992: 55–6). An increasingly powerful group of 'technology nationalists' argue that, given this reluctance, leaving the process of technology transfer to the market will mean that the gap between Indonesia and the technology leaders in North Asia, North America and West Europe will widen over time, leaving Indonesia further behind.

The most prominent of the technology nationalists in recent times has been Dr B. J. Habibie, the State Minister of Research. His preferred strategy for technological catch-up is based on heavy government subsidies to especially designated high technology industries, most notably the aerospace industry. In addition, he urges the development of national research capacity by providing scholarships for talented young people to study science and engineering abroad. This combination of technological leap-frogging through state-supported industries and heavy investment in technical education is argued to be the key to the impressive success of economies such as South Korea in catching up with world leaders in a range of medium or high technology sectors such as automobiles, computers, and consumer electronics. Critics of the Habibie strategy point to the high cost of his enterprises, although given the absence of full accounts it is impossible to estimate just how much the aeroplane factory does cost (McKendrick 1992). While few would question the need for Indonesia to invest more in education, especially in the sciences, such training can be provided most efficiently in universities and government-assisted research institutes, rather than in unprofitble state enterprises, however 'high-tech' their image might be.

INDONESIA AND THE 'LUCAS PARADOX'

For much of the period from 1870 to 1990, successive Indonesian governments have encouraged private foreign capital inflow into the domestic economy. But the evidence indicates that in both the colonial period and since 1967, private foreign capital inflow has accounted for only a small share of total capital formation. Why has Indonesia not been able to attract more capital inflow? In posing the wider question, 'why doesn't capital flow from rich to poor countries?' Lucas (1990: 92–6) pointed to a fundamental paradox in international economic relations. If indeed the marginal product of capital is higher in poor, capital-scarce countries, which is what the law of diminishing returns would predict, then 'if world capital markets were anywhere close to being free and complete', investment goods should flow rapidly from the rich countries to poorer ones. This has happened only to a very limited extent in the world economy over the past century. Why has there been so little investment by rich countries in poor ones?

One obvious explanation is that governments in poor countries have regarded foreign investment as a threat to their sovereignty and used a range of regulatory devices to prevent its entry. This was obviously true in Indonesia in the decade from 1957 to 1967. In addition, the macroeconomic instability and chronic over-valuation of the exchange rate which characterised those years deterred most investors, even in the petroleum sector. Although foreign direct investment in Indonesia was made much easier with the passage of the 1967 Investment Law, regulatory barriers were by no means abolished, and, indeed, from 1974 to the mid-1980s many controls were tightened. It was only after 1985 that the official policy became more supportive, especially if the foreign investment was in export-oriented sectors of manufacturing, or in tourism.

Lucas suggested that an important part of the answer to his question lay in the very different education and skill mix of the labour force in poor countries compared with rich ones. Using data produced by Krueger (1968: 653) he pointed out that even if Indonesia (or India or Ghana) had the same stock of physical capital per worker as the USA, their much lower endowment of human capital would effectively constrain their per capita incomes to around 38 per cent of the USA level. This obviously reduces the gap in income per effective worker between the USA and Indonesia. If it is further assumed that a worker's productivity depends not just on his or her own skill level, but also on the skill levels of those around them, then it is possible entirely to eliminate the difference in effective incomes per capita between rich and poor countries and thus explain the lack of capital flow. He also suggested that some governments in both the colonial and the post-colonial eras may have been interested in restricting capital inflows in order to suppress wage rates, thus maximising incomes less wages and interest payments. This is not a very plausible story in the late colonial era in Indonesia, if only because the Dutch were not able to exert a monopoly over capital inflows, but were forced to share the colony's investment opportunities with investors from other countries.

It has already been argued that, in spite of the educational improvements which have taken place since the 1950s, the gap in educational attainment and skill levels between Indonesia and other fast-growing Asian economies remains very large. This gap is partly the result of the very low investment in education in the colonial era, but also reflects low levels of government funding in more recent decades. This, in turn, means that income per effective worker in Indonesia continues to be constrained at levels well below other parts of Asia, let alone West Europe and North America. Thus, an improvement in the educational attainment of the labour force will be essential to make Indonesia more attractive to foreign investors, especially those looking to relocate intermediate manufacturing technologies.

7 Markets and Entrepreneurs

COLONIAL PERCEPTIONS OF INDIGENOUS ENTREPRENEURSHIP

'The development of native enterprise must be a chief object of policy in any dependency which is valued as a market for the products of the colonial power' wrote Furnivall (1948: 293) in his comparative study of Indonesia and Burma. But as Furnivall went on to point out, while the European colonial powers in many parts of Asia and Africa wanted to bring indigenous populations into the cash economy in order to expand the market for their own manufactures, at the same time many colonial officials were ambivalent about the consequences of rapid commercialisation on the welfare of the populations under their control. Nowhere was this ambivalence more obvious than in colonial Indonesia. Dutch officials debated endlessly the extent to which Indonesians were being incorporated into the 'Western sphere' of economic influence, the factors which promoted or inhibited such incorporation, and its effects on the economic and social welfare of the population. In the early nineteenth century, the cultivation system was imposed at least partly because the Dutch authorities felt that government coercion was the only reliable way to secure a large exportable surplus of crops from Java's peasant producers. Market forces could not be relied on to achieve this goal. But, by the early twentieth century, the debate had become far more complex.

Certainly many of the colonial researchers and policy-makers working in Indonesia after 1900 would have concurred with van Gelderen (1927: 144), that 'the inhabitant of the tropics is further removed from the classical *homo oeconomicus* than the Westerner'. But the reasons for the apparent lack of 'rational economic behaviour' on the part of the indigenous population in Indonesia were much disputed. Some colonial officials were content to ascribe this perceived lack to culture, religion and the climate, but others thought differently. In 1941, van der Kolff published a remarkable paper which argued that, to the extent that Indonesians adopted short time horizons and were unwilling to invest in risky operations which would yield results only in the longer term, this was because they were ignorant, poor and insecure. It was, according to van der Kolff (1941: 246–50), poverty and insecurity which led to practices such as *ijon* (selling the crop while still immature), and such behaviour was perfectly rational given the constraints within which the average Indonesian had to make decisions on consumption, saving and investment. Such views were held by others who, like van der Kolff, studied at the Wageningen Agricultural University and worked in the agricultural extension service in Indonesia in the inter-war years. Some, such as de Vries, argued that essentially the economic motivations of Indonesians were little different from those prevailing in other parts of the world (van der Eng 1991: 42–3). Given these views, it is not surprising that van der Kolff argued that such interventions in factor markets as the forced renting of rice land to the sugar estates in Java was 'a chief obstacle to the development of a strong middle class of land-owning farmers' (van der Kolff 1956: 194). The real problem was not that indigenous Indonesians were prevented by an inherent lack of commercial ability from participating in the market economy. Rather, it was that large and powerful conglomerates were allowed to subvert market forces to the detriment of smaller producers.

Another revealing strand in colonial thinking about the role of the market can be found in van Gelderen's assertion that the indigenous cultivator was likely to be exploited in his or her dealings with the market economy because of the 'great difference in bargaining power between the buyer on the one hand and the seller on the other' (van Gelderen 1927: 147).

> The buyer usually has both superior knowledge of the market situation and greater possibilities to reach and make use of more than one local market. This preponderance is even greater if the buyer is the only one, or one of a very small group of competitors, as against a larger number of persons offering the commodity for sale. In such a case it is very easy for a monopoly or semi-monopoly situation to develop, so that the local price of a commodity is forced downwards. Another factor producing the same effect is the vast difference in the value of the same unit of money for the two parties to the transaction....In many cases, in fact, the normal situation is one in which the necessity to sell is so urgent that what takes place is actually a forced sale (van Gelderen 1927: 147).

The underlying implication was, of course, that the monopsonistic middlemen were almost always Chinese, and it was their superior knowledge and bargaining power that led to the exploitation of the indigenous producer. Regardless of the truth or otherwise of these assertions, it is indisputable that they were held by almost all colonial administrators, some of whom, as early as the 1890s, were calling for much tighter controls on migration from China (Fernando and Bulbeck 1992: 74–5). In addition, as the new century arrived, many indigenous Indonesians were unwilling to tolerate what they perceived as Chinese commercial domination. The rapid growth of the *Sarekat Dagang Islam* in the second decade of the twentieth century into a political-nationalist movement was in large part due to 'sharp Chinese trading practices' on the part of 'aggressively competitive Chinese entrepreneurs' whose commercial presence outside the large cities had increased as a result of the lifting of travel restrictions between 1904 and 1911 (Kahin 1952: 67). The SDI attracted many members, at least partly by offering them 'mutual help and support in the economic concerns of life' (Dobbin 1980: 258–9). Cooperatives were established to compete with Chinese retailers, and in some parts of Java the movement took on an adult education function, providing lectures to Moslem traders on economic and commercial topics, as well as religious ones.

Both to colonial administrators and to the nascent nationalist movement the issues of indigenous participation in the modern cash economy and the role of the Chinese were, by the early twentieth century, closely linked. It would, however, be wrong to assume that the attitude of the colonial establishment was one of purely paternalistic concern that the commercially incompetent indigenous population should be protected from the rapacity of the clever Chinese. After 1900, there was a growing awareness in the expanding colonial civil service that living standards of the indigenous population in Indonesia would only improve to the extent that they could participate more fully in the modern, non-agricultural economy. Two facts were widely acknowledged by most scholars and administrators who had studied the empirical evidence: the proportion of agricultural output, including foodstuffs which was sold on the market was increasing in most parts of the country, and most rural households were diversifying their sources of income away from purely agricultural pursuits to manufacturing, transport, trade and wage labour (van Laanen 1990: 265; Boomgaard 1991: 34–6). Burger (1939: 329) in discussing the government's 'native economic policy' in a thesis defended in 1939 was able to quote numerous officials including van Gelderen, Meijer Ranneft and Boeke to support his argument that the indigenous economy was becoming ever more monetised and commercialised, and, as a result, a native business class was slowly emerging.

It was the slow speed at which this business class developed that was a source of frustration to many Dutch administrators, as well as to Indonesians themselves. Burger (1939: 329) was no doubt correct when he argued that 'if a vigorous group of native entrepreneurs had arisen, the authorities would almost certainly not have gone so far with their welfare policies as they have done'. Boeke (1927), in a lecture delivered in the late 1920s, in fact called for a different type of government policy which put less emphasis on improving the general level of welfare and more on encouraging the emergence of outstanding individuals with genuine entrepreneurial ability, a policy later characterised by Wertheim (1964: 264–5) as 'betting on the strong'. Only the emergence of such individuals could, according to Boeke, pose an effective challenge to European and Chinese domination of the economy. But the 1930s were hardly a propitious time for such a new breed of entrepreneurs to emerge and consolidate their position within the colonial economy. By the late 1940s when Boeke's best-known works were published 'the gradualistic approach to rural society, via well-to-do advanced farmers' no longer occupied a central place in his thinking (Wertheim 1964: 266).

THE DEVELOPMENT OF LABOUR AND LAND MARKETS IN THE COLONIAL ERA

While the debate was continuing within the colonial establishment about the entrepreneurial capacities of the indigenous population, it could hardly be denied that their involvement with market institutions was steadily increasing. In the recent literature on the development of the labour market in Java, several authors have stressed that 'free wage labour' was, in fact, far from unknown in the early part of the nineteenth century. Boomgaard argues that in such medium and large-scale industry as existed at that time 'free wage labour and corvee labour were employed side by side, frequently in one establishment, and often at the same wages' (Boomgaard 1989: 123). He also points out that, although there were disparities in wages between the three large cities of the northern littoral, and between the cities and the countryside, there is evidence of some movement of young unattached male workers (*bujang*) in search of wage employment. However, most of these 'coolies' were not interested in permanent employment and were looking for cash either to pay off debts or to finance one of the many life-cycle ceremonies in which they were obliged to participate.

During the years from 1830–50, the labour demands imposed on the population by the cultivation system 'led to a virtual disappearance of free wage labour in the industrial sector' (Boomgaard 1989: 124). However, by the 1860s the situation was changing again as the growth of the population and the labour force, together with growing scarcity of land for subsistence agriculture, had 'created a situation in which a clear surplus of labour was becoming apparent in the villages' (Knight 1988: 265). While there can be little doubt that a part of the labour supplied to the sugar factories as well as to public works projects was corvee, contributed under duress, other workers were supplying their labour voluntarily because they had few alternatives open to them for securing a livelihood. Knight is properly cautious about using the term 'proletariat' but his argument that by the mid-nineteenth century capitalist modes of production, based on the hiring in of workers, were becoming established in Java seems to be well supported by the evidence.

Certainly, as the nineteenth century progressed, the proportion of the population in Java which was either landless or dependent on non-agricultural activities for a substantial part of their income had increased, while at the same time many employed in agriculture diversified their sources of income into various types of 'by-employment'. Boomgaard (1991: 34) suggests that the proportion of the economically active population which were agricultural landholders in Java declined from 71 per cent in 1815 to 40 per cent by 1905. Surveys of 'average peasant households' carried out at the turn of the century in Semarang suggest that only about 10 per cent of total income came from wage labour, although 68 per cent of all households surveyed engaged in some wage labour (Boomgaard 1991: 36). The 1905 data on the distribution of the indigenous labour force by occupation shows that about 40 per cent of the agricultural labour force and one third of the non-agricultural labour force in Java (excluding the native states) were 'employees', while the rest were self-employed either in agriculture or in trading, transport, industries and crafts (White 1991: 44–6). White argues that this indicates that the level of 'proletarianisation' was already quite high in the early twentieth century. However, the 1905 data did not distinguish between those working for wages and those who in modern population censuses would be classified as 'unpaid family workers'. It is probable that quite a high proportion of those enumerated as employees in the 1905 survey were either family workers or family retainers of the traditional kind, receiving lodgings in return for labour services (Booth 1988: 49).

Unfortunately, neither the 1920 nor the 1930 population censuses collected labour force data disaggregated by work status (employer, employee, family worker etc.), although the 1930 census did contain very disaggregated tables on the labour force by occupation. It is thus impossible to judge to what extent the 'proletarianisation' of the Javanese labour force continued after 1905. The breakdown of the rural population in Java by economic status presented by Meijer Ranneft and Huender (1926: 10) indicated that 12.4 per cent were agricultural labourers possessing no land, and a further 19.6 per cent were 'coolies'. Again, it is difficult to know how many of these were family workers and how many wage labourers, although by the late 1920s van Gelderen (1929: 94) argued that 'an ever increasing group of the population, who own no land, provide the permanent farm labourers and the casual labourers'. In the large cities of Java, Meijer Ranneft and Huender reported that about 31 per cent of the working population were described as 'coolies', while 22 per cent worked in factories owned by Europeans and Chinese, and a further 22 per cent were artisans or small traders operating their own enterprises. In the smaller cities, a rather larger proportion were coolies (40 per cent) and 16 per cent were artisans and small traders.

Outside Java, the 1905 data indicated that the proportion of the agricultural labour force working as employees was considerably lower than in Java, especially in Kalimantan and Sulawesi (Booth 1988: 48). This indicates that the processes of commercialisation had progressed less rapidly there than in Java and that a larger proportion of the rural population were owner cultivators, renters or sharecroppers. However, there was a rapid growth in wage employment in the areas where the foreign-owned estates companies established themselves in the latter part of the nineteenth century, most notably on the east coast of Sumatra. The rapid growth of the plantation labour force in East Sumatra from the 1870s to 1930, and the means used by the planters to secure their labour force attracted considerable criticism in colonial times, and several scholars have examined the controversies more recently (Pelzer 1978; Stoler 1985; Breman 1989). In the last decades of the nineteenth century, the planters found it impossible to obtain sufficient wage workers locally to work on the tobacco, nutmeg and other plantations which had developed after 1870. At first the planters recruited labour from southern China, often by paying them a cash sum before departure which then had to be worked off when they arrived in Sumatra (Breman 1989: 28–9). Coolie brokers sprang up who specialised in recruiting labour and, in 1880, a Coolie ordinance was promulgated which held both parties to a written contract specifying the nature of the work and the type of payment to be made. The labourer was obliged to work as specified on the plantation for a maximum of three years, and was entitled to accommodation, food and health facilities. At the end of the contract the worker should be returned to the place of recruitment (Breman 1989: 39–40).

It was the widespread abuse of these provisions which began to attract unfavourable attention in the late nineteenth and early twentieth centuries. By the end of the nineteenth century, the planters had begun to switch their source of recruiting from China to Java, where workers were considered less disobedient and troublesome than the Chinese, and were, of course, closer and thus cheaper to transport (Breman 1989: 59–62). By 1900, it was estimated that some 59,000 Chinese labourers had been imported from outside into the East Coast plantation sector, and a further 35,000 Javanese (Breman 1989: 60). To begin with, many of the Javanese workers were not covered by the Coolie Ordinance, although that changed after 1900. By the early twentieth century, Java's abundant labour supply was being eyed not just by planters in North Sumatra, but also in Malaya, Indochina, Australia, New Caledonia and Surinam. The Javanese responded to this growth in demand for labour by moving in ever greater numbers. But because of the relative closeness of North Sumatra, and because demand for labour there was continuing to grow with the introduction of new estate crops, especially rubber, it remained by far the most important destination for estate labourers. By 1928, it was estimated that 446,000 coolies were employed on estates outside Java, of which 251,000 were indentured workers on the East Coast of Sumatra (SJO 1928: 195). A further 115,000 indentured workers were employed in other provinces including Aceh, West Sumatra, Bengkulu, West and East Kalimantan. The great majority of workers, both indentured and free, were Javanese, predominantly from Central and East Java (Hugo 1980: 106–10).

The abolition of the Coolie Ordinance in 1931 led to a rapid decline in the numbers of contract coolie estate workers from more than 350,000 in the late 1920s to only 6,200 by 1940. Over the same time, the numbers of 'free workers' rose from fewer than 100,000 to 325,000. It is probable that most of the indentured labourers stayed on as free labourers in the 1930s after the expiry of their contracts, as employment opportunities would have been even bleaker at home than in Sumatra or Borneo, and most of them would probably not have been able to pay the return fare. In 1931 a tax on the import of alien labour from China was imposed which brought to an end the importation of Chinese labour, but by then ethnic Chinese accounted for only about 12 per cent of the total estate labour force in the Outer Islands (*Statistical Pocketbook* 1940: 65).

The increased willingness of poor Javanese to migrate to take advantage of employment opportunities in other parts of the country, even if in so doing they had to commit themselves to contracts which deprived them of many of their economic and civil rights, clearly contradicted the stereotype of the indolent native who did not respond to economic incentives. By the end of the colonial era these Javanese migrants formed a large wage labour force in many parts of the Outer Islands, especially in regions where estates, mines or other Western enterprises dominated the regional economy. Pelzer (1945: 260) tabulated the results of the 1930 census on the population of various Outer Island residencies by birthplace; on the east coast of Sumatra 31.4 per cent of the population were born in Java. It seems certain that many more Javanese were employed on estates outside Java than on the sugar estates in Java. In 1930 almost 400,000 male and female coolies were working on estates outside Java, while only around 130,000 were working on sugar estates in Java.

The availability of wage labour on estates was not the only incentive to migrate in the last decades of the colonial period. The government also began to implement a programme of sponsored land settlement in the Outer Islands, known as the transmigration programme. The most important region for pre-independence land settlement or 'colonisation' by Javanese migrants was the southernmost region of Sumatra, Lampung, and by 1941 it was estimated that some 141,000 Javanese settlers were established there (Hardjono 1977:18). The Dutch authorities favoured *sawah*-based settlements on the grounds that this was the type of farming with which the Javanese were familiar. This involved considerable investment in irrigation, and once these facilities were in place each migrant household was allocated one hectare of land. This was substantially larger than the average holding size in Java by 1940, so it is hardly surprising that there were large numbers of migrants willing to take up the government offer. In total some 222,586 people migrated to Sumatra and Sulawesi between 1933 and 1941 under the official programme and considerable numbers also moved voluntarily to work as labourers and open up their own holdings (Pelzer 1945: 230).

Just as labour was becoming a marketed commodity by the inter-war era, so was land, both agricultural and urban. There has been much discussion in the literature on nineteenth century Javanese economic development about the evolution of property rights. Although a consensus does appear to have been reached that in the early years of the century 'hereditary private ownership of arable fields was the predominant form of tenure', communal tenure systems were also in place in the northern coastal areas of Central Java, probably because they facilitated the extraction of taxes in both labour and kind (Boomgaard 1989: 56–7). But the growing demands for both labour and land to grow export crops in Java led to pressures to communalise more land in both Central and East Java, especially in the years from 1830 to 1850 which Boomgaard (1989: 58) regards as the 'heyday of communal tenure', even though large areas in West Java and the eastern part of East Java remained under freehold tenures. Both Boomgaard and Kano (1977: 15–21) have argued that there is little evidence that the trend towards communal tenures in the middle years of the nineteenth century led to a dramatic increase in the proportion of the rural population who controlled land. Access to land depended, above all, on the ability to furnish enough labour to grow export crops and those who could not supply labour did not receive land.

By the latter part of the nineteenth century, the increasing scarcity of land relative to both labour and capital led to pressures for change from the liberal establishment in the Netherlands, who needed to know more about land tenure in Java 'in order to justify the liberal policies' (Goh 1986: 256). What came to be known as the *Eindresume* survey was carried out in 1868–69, and the Agrarian Law was enacted in 1870, although it is unclear to what extent the data from the detailed village surveys influenced the legislation. The 1870 law, and subsequent legislation, was intended to facilitate the use of market contracts, especially medium- and long-term leases for land. While the legislation prevented the alienation of land under 'native tenure', through sale it did make possible the large-scale acquisition of land both in Java and in other parts of the country for use by foreign enterprises for long periods. At the same time, it was possible for the indigenous population to sell or rent land which they possessed under freehold tenures to other indigenous citizens.

The impact of these changes became apparent over the next fifty years. The large estates acquired land both in Java and the Outer Islands (mainly North Sumatra) on a range of leases. In Java the so-called 'private lands' which had been contracted to Chinese and European planters at the time of the British occupation remained in existence, although the hectarage shrank after 1900. Most of the land controlled by the estates was either on short-term leases for crops such as sugar, or long-term leases for perennial treecrops. Outside Java, although the amount of land on long leases grew rapidly after 1900, most of the land operated by the estates was on concessions granted by the local sultans. As Pelzer (1978: 87ff) has argued, the local rulers made very large sums of money out of these concessions but increasingly the Dutch colonial authorities felt uneasy about a system which so obviously deprived the local populations of rights to arable land. The problem became worse as the amount of land held in concessions grew (by the 1920s it amounted to almost 500,000 hectares in North Sumatra), and the numbers of migrant workers from Java increased. How were the local populations, whose numbers were also growing rapidly, to secure an adequate livelihood if they were deprived of both land and opportunities for wage labour? By the late 1930s, both lawyers and agricultural specialists were advocating large-scale conversion of land under the control of both the tobacco and the perennial crop estates to more intensive foodcrop agriculture, and by early 1942 the tobacco estates had been compelled to release some 42,000 hectares (about one-sixth of their total land) and the perennial crop estates a similar amount (Pelzer 1978: 120).

There can be little doubt that the acquisition of large tracts of land for use by the large estates (in 1930 the estates controlled some 2.9 million hectares of land, of which around 1.2 million hectares was actually in production) in both Java and the east coast of North Sumatra had a severely disruptive impact on indigenous agriculture, and on indigenous economic development, in both regions. The benefits and costs of the large estates in Indonesia have been discussed in detail elsewhere (Booth 1988: 220–3). What is relevant to our discussion here is their impact on the development of indigenous entrepreneurial activity, and especially indigenous participation in the industries which the large estates dominated. As we have seen, Indonesians did become increasingly involved in the production of export crops in the late nineteenth and early twentieth centuries, and to some extent the demonstration effect of the large estates did assist in the growth of smallholder cashcrop production. But, at the same time, the presence of the large estates also retarded such growth, most obviously by monopolising so much of the available land, but also because many planters were reluctant to allow smallholders to engage in cashcrop cultivation (Pelzer 1978: 50; Mackie 1985). Indeed, it is striking that the areas where smallholder cashcrop cultivation expanded most rapidly in the latter part of the colonial era, such as South Sumatra and West Kalimantan, were well away from the main concentrations of estate activity in Java and North Sumatra.

Within what writers such as Boeke referred to as 'the native sphere of influence' there was certainly a considerable growth in the land market in the late colonial period. With the establishment of a network of land revenue offices in Java and Bali in the 1920s, all land transactions were carefully recorded, and these records show in the 1920s some 400,000 sale transactions (Boeke 1953: 131). Rather surprisingly, Boeke concluded that this amount of sales did not necessarily indicate the existence of a land market, although the explanations which he put forward to justify this claim hardly appear convincing to a modern reader. He argued that the high incidence of land donations showed that 'land is not regarded as an article of commerce', although the practice of parents giving land to adult children is obviously widespread in Western countries. Boeke also argued that sharecropping, and annual rental contracts could not be regarded as 'market transactions' either, although once again the reasons which he put forward were far from convincing.

The evidence on, and debate over, the development of land and labour markets in colonial Indonesia can be summarised as follows. For much of the period from the early nineteenth century until 1940, European entrepreneurs wished to secure enough land and labour to grow crops for export; they did this by paying indigenous rulers to obtain land concessions and labour, and by making sure that the colonial authorities sanctioned these arrangements through the legal system. Only when labour became abundant relative to land, and workers were willing to work for wages on a full-time basis and migrate where necessary to do so, were expatriate employers willing to trust the labour market to supply them with the workers which they required. But even so, systems of indentured labour lasted far longer in Indonesia than in other parts of Southeast Asia. Land, of course, became an increasingly scarce factor not just in Java but in other parts of the country, and increasingly the estate companies had to rely on state power to back up contracts which the indigenous population saw as inequitable. Thus, in the eyes of many indigenous Indonesians, whether they were full-time wage labourers on estates or peasant cultivators forced into renting rice land to estates, government coercion and the market economy were inextricably linked. But at the same time, the indigenous population had little option but to become more and more enmeshed in markets for both labour and land; by the early twentieth century, 'subsistence' production was simply not an option for most people in Java, and for increasing numbers in other parts of the country.

THE DEVELOPMENT OF COLONIAL CREDIT FACILITIES

By the latter part of the nineteenth century, segmentation in the financial sector was probably more marked than in any other market in the colonial economy. A banking system run along Western lines had emerged to service the European economy, centred around the Java Bank, which was the bank of note issue, the Netherlands-Indian Trading Corporation (usually known by its Dutch initials NHM), the Netherlands-Indian Commercial Bank (NIHB) and the Netherlands-Indian Escompto Company (NIEM). In addition, the so-called agricultural banks concentrated on lending to the large estates (van Laanen 1990: 248). In the aftermath of the banking crisis of 1884, precipitated by the sharp fall in world sugar prices, a sharper distinction was made between normal banking business and loans to the large agricultural estates; the latter business being taken over by what became, in effect, agricultural holding companies (van Laanen 1990: 256). Because most of the large companies in all sectors of the economy were owned by Dutch or other foreign nationals, who chose for the most part to keep their cash surpluses in foreign financial centres, there was little opportunity to develop a money and capital market within the colony. Most banks and financial institutions saw their role in terms of providing short-term working capital to European enterprises, and even the largest Chinese enterprises found it difficult to obtain credit from the European banks except indirectly through European wholesalers (Williams 1952: 42; Panglaykim and Palmer 1969: 5). Chinese traders with links to Singapore and beyond could utilise credit from what Ray (1995) termed the Asian bazaar economy, but for the great majority only the informal credit market was available.

By the turn of the century, narrow money (coins, notes and bank money balances) amounted to slightly under 9 per cent of GDP

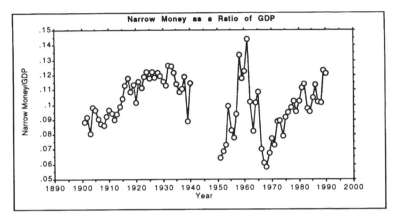

Figure 7.1 *Sources*: Money supply data from CEI, Vol. 6, Table 2; 1950: Bank Indonesia *Annual Reports*, various issues. Nominal GDP data up to 1939 from Pierre van der Eng; after 1950 from United Nations (1960) and *Statistical Yearbook of Indonesia*, various issues.

(Figure 7.1). This was a low ratio in comparison with Western Europe and some parts of Asia. In Japan in 1888 the ratio of narrow money to GNP was already over 30 per cent (Minami 1986: Table 10.9). The high ratio in Japan might have been partly due to greater involvement by the population in market activities, but a more important reason was the far greater diffusion of banking facilities. It has been estimated that there were almost 2000 commercial banks in Japan in 1900 (Arndt 1983b: 93). With the growth of concern over rural poverty in Java at the end of the nineteenth century, there was considerable pressure for extending the reach of the formal credit system. The credit needs of the indigenous population were, for the most part, provided by traders who bought up standing crops at a discount (the *ijon* system). By the early twentieth century these traders were often of Chinese origin and also operated small shops. In addition, the *mindering Chinees* (instalment Chinese) grew in numbers after 1900; they were usually new arrivals from China who went around the rural markets lending small sums to traders and farmers. They obtained their capital from better-off Chinese merchants from the same clan or dialect group, and often boarded with them (Fruin 1938: 113; Dobbin 1980: 255–6). Unsurprisingly, given the small sums and the high risks of default involved in this kind of lending, interest rates were extremely high. Often twice the amount of the original loan would have to be paid back after six months.

Dutch officialdom considered these practices exploitative and, from 1900 onwards, considerable effort went into developing an indigenous 'people's credit system'. The aim of these endeavours was to encourage greater productive activity among the indigenous population by providing them with reliable sources of credit at interest rates which, although higher than those charged by the European banks, would be much less than those prevailing in the unorganised credit market.

By the 1920s, the people's credit system had evolved into a substantial banking system centred around three separate, although linked, institutions. At the regency level, the people's banks (*volksbanken*) extended loans to officials and merchants, and the wealthier farmers, in both urban and rural areas. At the village level, the village banks (*desa banken*) lent money in small amounts for short periods; around 40 per cent of their loans were to women, mainly small traders. The rice banks (*desa lumbung*) made loans in the form of *padi*, usually to tide farmers over the pre-harvest months when food was in short supply and prices high (van Laanen 1990: 258–64; Furnivall 1934a). Furnivall pointed out that the rice banks were found mainly in the relatively poor, densely settled rice growing areas of Java, while the village banks tended to be most successful in the more commercialised regions. He credited the rice banks with some success in levelling out the seasonal fluctuations in the price of rice in rural areas, because they could supply the farmer with paddy at the time when supplies were scarce and, at the same time, sell some of their surplus to depress prices (Furnivall 1934a: 22). Certainly, by the end of the 1920s, the coefficient of variation of monthly rice prices in rural Java markets was little more than 2 per cent, indicating a remarkably low level of seasonal fluctuation (Table 7.1).

However, the single most successful credit institution established after 1900 was the network of state-owned pawnshops. Under Raffles, rights to operate pawnshops had been auctioned to Chinese, who ran them with little regard for government regulations. In spite of spasmodic attempts to assert greater government control, this arrangement continued essentially unchanged until 1901, when a government-operated pawnshop was opened in Sukabumi, in West Java. The objective of the government system was twofold; on the one hand to free the people from the clutches of Chinese money-lenders, and on the other hand to provide better service for those who relied on pawnshops as a convenient source of cash for investment, or to assist

Table 7.1 Coefficient of variation of monthly rice prices in rural Java
markets, 1928–81

Year	Coefficient of variation	Year	Coefficient of variation
1928	2.88	1970	9.91
1929	2.19	1971	7.31
1939	3.15	1972	28.35
1940	2.23	1973	10.22
1955	16.65	1978	4.53
1956	15.01	1979	10.91
1961	54.89	1980	5.83
1962	15.73	1981	3.82

Sources: *Indisch Verslag*, 1930, 1941, Table 254; *Statistik Konjunktur*, 1958, 1963; *Lampiran Pidato Kenegaraan*, 1974, Table V-2; *Indikator Ekonomi*, February 1979, February 1980, February 1981, February 1982, Table 1.18.

them over difficult times. The second objective was to be achieved through more honest and efficient valuations, better storage of pawned goods, prompt redemption of pledges, and full compensation to the owner when unredeemed pledges were sold for more than the amount of the pledge plus interest. The amount of lending through the system grew rapidly, and by 1930 total credit amounted to almost 200 million guilders (van Laanen 1990: 260). For most of the inter-war period, lending via the pawnshop system amounted to almost 60 per cent of total lending of the people's credit system (Table 7.2). Lending from all parts of the system, including the pawnshops, amounted to 48 per cent of lending by the 'big four' commercial banks in 1920, and 86 per cent in 1930, although it dropped back in relation to lending by the commercial banks in the 1930s.

The credit system as a whole was far more developed than any similar scheme elsewhere in Southeast Asia, and attracted attention and admiration from both English and French colonial officials. Apart from Furnivall's studies, the French colonial agricultural expert Yves Henry wrote an extensive appraisal (Henry 1926). Another French observer pointed out that by the mid-1920s 'the Netherlands Indies was infinitely more advanced than Indochina' in the provision of small-scale credit (Angoulvant 1926: 283). The literature in Dutch has been discussed by van Laanen (1990), Alexander and Alexander (1991) and van der Eng (1996: 127–33). Although most writers acknowledged that the Dutch colonial authorities had done far more in extending credit than other governments in South and Southeast

Table 7.2 Real value of credit extended by the people's credit system, 1920–40 (million guilders)

	Total value*	Food price index	Deflated value	Percentage from pawnshops
1920	216.07 (29)	270	80.03	63.2
1923	233.42 (48)	158	147.73	64.5
1925	272.00 (58)	165	164.85	61.1
1928	315.24 (55)	148	213.00	57.6
1930	331.17 (86)	152	217.88	58.6
1933	121.38 (49)	62	195.77	64.4
1935	107.96 (52)	64	168.67	62.5
1938	141.85 (53)	70	202.64	60.1
1940	149.58	68	219.97	59.0

* Figures in brackets refer to total lending by the popular credit system as a proportion of total lending by the 'big four' banks (Java Bank, NHM, NIEM and NIHB), as reported in CEI, Vol 6, Table 5.
Sources: Van Laanen (1990), Table 11.4; Java food price index taken from *Statistical Pocketbook of Indonesia* (1941: Table 186).

Asia, there was criticism about the 'excessively high' interest rates, and also about the pronounced tendency for interest rates to be higher on smaller loans made through the rice banks and the village banks than on the larger loans from the district banks. The pawnshop interest rates fell sharply according to the value of the pledge; loans made against goods valued at under 25 guilders were charged an annual rate of interest of 72 per cent, while those made against goods valued at more than 75 guilders were charged only half this amount (van Lannen 1990: 262). These differential interest rates were justified on the basis of the high fixed costs of lending small sums, together with the greater risk of default, but the high average rates of interest (most loans were of small sums, especially through the pawnshop service) were the main reason for what Furnivall termed the 'substantial profit' made by the pawnshops (Furnivall 1934b: 7).

Furnivall (1934a: 26) was at pains to emphasise that, even in the depths of the depression, the entire credit system was solvent, and required no state subsidies. He argued strongly against the assertion that the government-operated institutions simply displaced private ones, especially those run by the Chinese. Certainly there appears to be little doubt that the government pawnshop service was operated more efficiently than the nineteenth century Chinese pawnshops, and while the relaxation of the laws on Chinese residence might have led to greater Chinese activity in rural areas in the twentieth century, it cannot be argued that taxpayers' money was used to subsidise financial institutions which the private sector would have provided more efficiently. The private system did continue to expand alongside the state one, although in the absence of data, it is impossible to tell how important privately supplied credit was compared with state provision.

Given that the people's credit system did develop so rapidly in the inter-war years, what was its impact on the indigenous economy? Scholars seem divided in their opinions. Alexander and Alexander (1991: 386–7) argue that there is little evidence that the various rural credit institutions served to stimulate economic diversification and the main effect of the government-sponsored initiatives was to institutionalise the two-tier credit market in the rural economy. The relatively wealthy could get access to credit at lower rates of interest which they could then lend on at higher rates to the relatively poor, making large profits in the process. While no doubt correct, this argument ignores the basic economic point that credit markets always reflect a degree of segmentation in the sense that some people will always be seen as more 'credit-worthy' than others. Given that the government initiatives did greatly increase the supply of loanable funds to rural areas, were these funds used for productive investment or for consumption purposes? Alexander and Alexander (1991) and Cribb (1993: 237) suggest that most went on consumption, ceremonial expenditures, and for tiding people over emergencies such as ill-health, unusually long dry seasons and so on.

Other authors argue that the credit available from both the pawnshops and the other credit institutions was at least partly used for productive purposes. Furnivall (1934b:11) pointed out that 'a man may pawn his wife's bangles and use the proceeds as the first instalment towards buying a motor bus on the hire purchase system'. Both Furnivall and van Laanen observed that the pawnshops were not the last resort of the desperate (as they tended to be in Europe), but rather a convenient source of credit to many people who were far from destitute, but who kept their savings in commodities rather than in cash or bank deposits. Van der Eng (1996: 131) suggests that the village banks were probably not well geared to the needs of agricultural producers because their loans were small on average and of short duration. Given that many of their clients were women, it is likely that these loans were used mainly to finance trade. The larger district banks were used by the more commercial farmers, but smaller cultivators probably relied on the informal sector for whatever loans they needed. The fact that the real value of credit advanced through the government institutions dropped so sharply after 1930 indicates that borrowings were related to investment opportunities rather than to financial pressures, and when the investment climate deteriorated as a result of the depression, the demand for loans fell.

The growth of the people's credit system was one explanation for the increase in the ratio of money supply (coins, notes and demand deposits) to GDP in the years from 1900 to 1930 (Figure 7.1). By 1930 money supply had risen to almost 13 per cent of GDP, but the ratio dropped sharply thereafter. The credit system, and indeed the entire formal financial system was largely Java-based, and in 1940 lending within Java accounted for 86 per cent of total lending by the district and village banks and the pawnshops. This bias in the regional availability of credit facilities was to survive long into the post-independence era.

INDIGENOUS ENTREPRENEURSHIP AND THE ROLE OF THE CHINESE IN THE COLONIAL ECONOMY

In 1860 official figures put the number of Chinese in Indonesia at 221,000 of whom 149,000 lived in Java. By 1900 the Chinese population had more than doubled to 537,000, of whom 277,000 were in Java (*Statistical Pocketbook*, 1941: 5). Much of this rapid growth in population was due to in-migration, both to the estate regions outside Java (particularly the East Coast of Sumatra) and to the cities of Java and Eastern Indonesia, with their long-established Chinese communities. According to Rush (1991: 17–18):

Every city or town of consequence had its own Chinese quarter... and the Chinese were generally required to reside there... From top to bottom, commerce marked the Chinese. They were shippers, warehousemen, and labor contractors; builders and repairmen; and suppliers of all things to town and country. They were tinsmiths, leather tanners and furniture makers. They bought and sold real estate, worked timber concessions, and speculated in the plantation economy. They organised the manufacture of batik and tobacco products. The Chinese brought the products of village farmers to market... aside from their own wares, they supplied indigenous vendors with goods like gambir, salt, trasi, and cooking oil for the village trade...Chinese merchants, shopkeepers, and petty traders were also often the first source for loans and credit, and certainly the last.

Much of this diversified activity grew out of the traditional Chinese role as holders of monopoly leases, granted first by the VOC and then by the colonial government, to run a variety of establishments including markets and bazaars, slaughterhouses, gambling dens and pawnshops, and to sell tobacco, alcoholic liquors and opium. As Cator (1936: 98) pointed out, these leases in fact permitted the Chinese to transact a broad range of business well beyond the confines of their urban ghettos, and as these various leases were gradually abolished in the second half of the nineteenth century, the Chinese continued to operate as traders, merchants and money lenders. The development of the port of Singapore in the middle decades of the nineteenth century as 'the centre of a dense web of Chinese finance and trade' stretching through the Indonesian archipelago and as far north as Bangkok meant that Indonesian Chinese traders could exploit the growing opportunities for trade on many regional routes of little interest to the Dutch, or to other Europeans (Ray 1995: 502–14). Often working closely with indigenous traders such as the Buginese, the Chinese built up a vast trading network throughout the archipelago which was very largely independent of European control. Over time the Chinese became dominant in many trading and marketing networks, effectively sidelining their indigenous competitors, as happened in the South Sumatran rubber industry in the 1920s, and the Javanese batik trade (Thomas and Panglaykim 1976: 141; Dobbin 1980: 258–9).

But, in spite of this growth, the economic role of the Chinese in nineteenth century Indonesia should not be exaggerated. As late as 1890, Chinese and other 'foreign Asians' (mainly Arabs and Indians) accounted for only about 11 per cent of the total population of towns in Java with more than 20,000 inhabitants. They were a larger minority in urban areas outside Java, but still were greatly outnumbered by indigenous Indonesians everywhere except in Medan and Pontianak (CEI, Vol 11, Tables 15.2b and 22b). Rush (1991: 19) has argued that revenue farming made a few Chinese in nineteenth century Indonesia very rich indeed, but the gains to the great majority were far more modest, and many Chinese merchants suffered losses in the economic downturn of the 1880s. The data on assessed incomes from the commerce tax (*bedrifsbelasting*) which began to be published in the *Koloniale Verslag* from 1875 onwards, indicate that in Java there were fewer Chinese in the highest income brackets than indigenous Indonesians. Even as late as 1900, there were a roughly similar number of Indonesians and 'foreign Asians' (mainly Chinese) in the upper income groups (Table 7.3). The distribution of income was far more skewed for Chinese than Indonesian taxpayers, indicating that the gulf between rich and poor within the Chinese community was considerable (Booth 1988a: Table 4).

Table 7.3   Numbers of Indonesian and Chinese taxpayers,* 1891–1900

	Numbers of taxpayers with assessed annual incomes:					
	under 2500 Guilders			*over 2500 Guilders*		
	I	*C*	*OA*	*I*	*C*	*OA*
1891	774,683	55,341	4,363	702	531	29
1895	912,019	62,742	5,195	707	582	36
1900	1,005,694	65,398	5,192	688	651	33

I = Indonesian
C = Chinese
OA = Other Asian
* *Bedrijfsbelasting* (Commerce Tax)
Source: *Jaarcijfers*, 1900 pp.32–2

After the turn of the century, the division between the newly arrived Chinese and the established families became more pronounced. Many children from the latter group began to assimilate; they ceased speaking Chinese dialects, learned Dutch and wherever possible gravitated towards salaried jobs. As educational opportunities increased they were, as Rush (1991: 24) and Mackie (1991: 89) have pointed out, attracted to the 'genteel professions' rather than to the hurly-burly of commerce. As they moved upwards into professional occupations, it was inevitable that educated Chinese became more oriented to Dutch, rather than to Indonesian society (Skinner 1960: 90). By contrast, the new arrivals from China, mainly single men, became coolie labourers, itinerant pedlars, and artisans. Mackie (1991: 84) suggests that it was only in the 1920s that 'large numbers of Chinese began to move away from other occupations, mostly less desirable ones . . . into what today are commonly regarded as their characteristic roles as small-scale traders, *warung* operators, commodity dealers, and money lenders.' Total numbers of Chinese immigrants continued to grow until 1930, when the census of that year enumerated 1.23 million Chinese in the colony, and more Chinese rose to positions of considerable material affluence after 1920, as the income tax data make clear (Booth 1988a). But increasingly they did so as doctors, lawyers, or salaried managers, rather than as dynamic entrepreneurs.

The lack of interest in commercial careers on the part of the assimilated (*peranakan*) Chinese in late colonial Indonesia led Williams (1952: 34) to argue that 'the Chinese in Indonesia did not achieve entrepreneurship'. His thorough survey of the evidence from the inter-war years led him to the conclusion that the Indonesian Chinese were unable, or at least unwilling, to extend their commercial and industrial enterprises beyond the 'limits imposed largely by tradition' (Williams 1952: 55). Certainly there were exceptions, the most famous of whom was the 'sugar king' Oei Tiong Ham, whose family wealth originally came from opium farms. Unlike most revenue farmers, Oei managed to diversify, and built up a large conglomerate based mainly on plantations in the early part of the twentieth century (Panglaykim and Palmer 1989; Yoshihara 1989; Dick 1993a). Apart from a few very prominent magnates there were a larger number of medium-scale enterprises, although trade was more common than manufacturing. According to a government survey, there were by the early 1920s almost 1,700 Chinese-owned industrial firms employing more than five people, compared with 2,800 European firms and 870 owned by indigenous Indonesians (Fernando and Bulbeck 1992: 254–9). But these numbers pale into insignificance when compared with developments in other parts of Asia (especially Japan) at the same time, or with industrial development in Indonesia in more recent times. Prominent though the Chinese might have appeared in the commercial life of the colony in the 1920s and 1930s, they were hardly laying the foundations for an industrial take-off. That was to wait until much later in the century, and then the main players would be the offspring of unassimilated migrants (*totok*) rather than from assimilated *peranakan* families.

Given that many assimilated Chinese abandoned commerce for more secure and prestigious occupations in the colonial economy, why were there so few indigenous Indonesians able to take their place in the world of business and commerce? Why did so few of the many businesses started by Moslem (*santri*) Javanese in the early years of the century manage to grow and compete with the Chinese in industries such as *batik* and *kretek* cigarettes? Outside Java, why were ethnic groups such as the Buginese, who had traded throughout the archipelago since pre-colonial times, unable to exploit the growth in inter-regional trade in the nineteenth and early twentieth centuries? Dobbin

(1994: 97) has argued that in the Javanese *batik* trade, a group of Javanese traders from Yogyakarta and Solo 'with diaspora characteristics similar to the Chinese' were successful in displacing other Moslem traders in the production centres of East Java. But these traders were not themselves capable of building durable businesses, and after independence, *batik* manufacture and trade was increasingly dominated by Chinese companies. As with the Moslem *kretek* manufacturers in Kudus studied by Castles (1967), and the Kudus traders in East Java described by Geertz (1965: 94–5), their 'excessive individualism' led to commercial jealously and in-fighting, rather than the kind of networking and mutual support so typical of the immigrant Chinese.

In addition, Ray (1995: 552–2) has suggested that the main reason for the failure of the Buginese and other trading groups to establish large transport and trading concerns was that they could not come to terms with the 'bazaar economy' which developed throughout the Indian Ocean and East and Southeast Asia in the nineteenth century. This economy, while distinct from that of the European imperial powers, was also far removed from the fragmented indigenous market economy based on peddling and small-scale credit. The bazaar economy described by Ray was based on paper credit, which enabled traders to finance long-distance trade with the same facility as Europeans. Interest rates were not always higher than those prevailing in European financial institutions, and trade credit was available through negotiable instruments, as in European financial markets. But participation in this economy demanded literacy, numeracy and commercial skills which few Javanese, Buginese, Minang or other indigenous Indonesians possessed. As the nineteenth century progressed, Javanese, Arab, and Buginese traders all fell behind their Indian and Chinese competitors, and remained behind until the end of the colonial era.

SOCIALISM, PLANNING AND THE PRIVATE SECTOR: 1950–65

The newly independent government which assumed control in 1949 faced the task of building a national economy with the same ambivalent views as many colonial officials had possessed towards the role of the private sector and market forces. On the one hand there was a profound distrust of capitalism as a system of economic organisation.

Many Indonesians who would not have considered themselves 'socialist' in the Western sense of the term inevitably equated capitalism with colonialism, and felt that capitalist economic development under the Dutch led only to foreign exploitation and economic inequality. On the other hand, in spite of the attraction of the Soviet economic model of planned economic development, dominant figures in the new government recognised that the wholesale rejection of the capitalist model might be too disruptive, and a better alternative could be to encourage the participation of many more Indonesians in that part of the economy which was run along capitalist lines. In the early 1950s this included the large-scale agricultural estates, much manufacturing industry and the modern service sector. It also included smaller-scale enterprises in both agriculture and other sectors which made use of hired labour and sold their output on the market.

In his 1953 review of fiscal and monetary policy, Sumitro stressed the importance of allocating a substantial part of government budgetary expenditures to capital works, preferably within the framework of a coherent medium-term development plan. However, he realised that in order to increase the participation of the indigenous population in the nation's economic development, the government would have to do more than simply allocate budgetary funds to infrastructure development, badly needed though such development certainly was. It was also necessary to encourage an indigenous entrepreneurial class to emerge which could compete with, and ultimately replace, both the Chinese and the expatriate firms who continued to dominate much of the non-agricultural economy, including manufacturing, transport, financial services and wholesale and retail trade. Such policies seemed even more necessary because in the aftermath of the Japanese occupation and the struggle for independence, the narrow money supply had fallen sharply relative to GDP compared with the pre-independence period (Figure 7.1). The real value of lending through the people's credit institutions established in the colonial period, including the government pawnshops, was also much lower in 1951 than in 1940 (Table 7.4).

In his first cabinet position, as Minister of Trade and Industry in the Natsir cabinet, Sumitro was responsible for drawing up, and implementing the so-called Economic Urgency Plan or 'Benteng' programme, which was based on the 1934 Regulation of Enterprises Ordinance (Anspach 1969: 164). The plan was described by Glassburner (1971: 85) as a:

highly nationalistic attempt to diminish the nation's dependence on
foreign economic interests in several ways: by developing small,
nasional (i.e. indigenous) industry to produce import substitutes in
the hope of reducing dependence on foreign trade; by means of
capital assistance to indigenous enterprise; and by restricting certain
markets to indigenous sellers.

Sumitro himself was under few illusions about the risks inherent in
such a strategy of 'hothouse' development of entrepreneurial talent.
More than thirty years later, he claimed that the main point of the
policy 'was to try and set up a counter-force to Dutch interests... I
thought that if you give assistance to ten people, seven might turn out
to be parasites but you might still get three entrepreneurs' (Sumitro
1986: 35). The main aim of the policy was to encourage the small
producers of export commodities to move into processing and marketing, areas which had been dominated in colonial times by the Chinese
entrepreneurs and the large Dutch trading houses. This was to be
done primarily through the provision of credit, and several new banks
were established by government specifically to assist indigenous producers. Wibisonso, who was the Finance Minister at the time when
the Urgency Plan was implemented viewed such preferential credit
systems as 'a kind of government scholarship in the school of business
experience' (Anspach 1969: 124).

That there was an urgent political need for policies of this kind in
the early years of the Republic can hardly be disputed. All contemporary observers have stressed that, while Indonesia was reluctantly
granted political independence by the Dutch in 1949, economic domination by foreign interests continued until the late 1950s. This domination was manifest both in the continued role of the large Dutch
trading houses in trade and transport, and also in the considerable
numbers of Dutch 'experts' in the higher echelons of the civil service.
In addition, during the Japanese occupation and the independence
struggle, the role of the Chinese in many parts of the economy underwent important changes. While businesses run by assimilated, Dutch-
speaking Chinese often did not prosper under the Japanese or subsequently, the occupation and the ensuing period of struggle saw the
growth of new Chinese businesses run by younger Hokchia and
Hokkien males who were better able to profit from the economic
turmoil of the times (Twang 1987: Chapter 2). The attitudes of leading
nationalist politicians towards both Dutch and Chinese capital varied.
Hatta and Sjahrir recognised that the new republic would continue to

The Indonesian Economy

need capital and expertise from the West, and were probably more favourably disposed to the returning Dutch than to the Chinese, but others were deeply suspicious of all 'foreign' capital, and indeed the institution of capitalism itself.

Such differences among the nationalist leaders did little to boost the confidence of the indigenous majority in their own entrepreneurial talents. As one of the few successful indigenous entrepreneurs to emerge in the 1950s pointed out, virtually all Indonesians believed at the time of independence that there was no native middle class in Indonesia, and certainly no indigenous bourgeoisie to take over the running of the private sector from the Dutch and the Chinese (Soedarpo 1994: 50). Thus, one had to be created. But, although some genuine indigenous businesses did emerge in the early 1950s, albeit with assistance from their political allies, many of the beneficiaries of government aid were still unable to compete against the far bigger and better organised foreign and Chinese enterprises. Panglaykim (1968: 47) argued that:

> Rather than carry on the unequal struggle, most of the former in practice simply 'accommodated' their business to the situation. This commonly took the form of selling the license obtained from the Government, leaving its use entirely to the foreign and alien firms. The national importer might receive a lump sum for the license or compensation on a profit-sharing basis. Basically 'accommodation' in one form or another led to a situation where the foreign and alien enterprise controlled the majority of the licenses granted to the national private firms.

As in the late colonial era, the government in the 1950s saw easier access to bank credit as one means of encouraging indigenous entrepreneurs, and after 1952 the real volume of lending through the People's Bank (*Bank Rakyat*) grew rapidly. Indeed, by 1960, when it had become the Bank for Cooperatives, Farmers and Fishermen, new loans were larger in real terms than the total achieved in 1940 by the *Algemene Volkscrediet Bank* (Table 7.4). But the proportion going to rural borrowers dropped sharply, to less than 10 per cent by 1960. It seems probable that the bulk of the lending went to politically well-connected urban dwellers, including many civil servants, who used the loans to finance house purchases and business ventures, often with Chinese partners. Most of the staff of the government banks 'had very little experience in the business of banking' and came from backgrounds far removed from commerce (Weckstein 1959: 200).

Inevitably, considerations of commercial viability played little role in lending policy. The real volume of lending through the village banks and the pawnshops never regained pre-war levels.

Table 7.4   Loans from rural banks and pawnshops, 1938–62 (million guilders/rupiah 1953 prices*)

Year	People's bank†	Village banks	Pawnshops	Paddy banks ('000 tons)
1938	1013 (39)	641	2844	108.8
1939	1174 (49)	745	3068	110.7
1940	1050 (51)	746	3026	110.0
1951	353 (38)	32	587	n.a.
1954	858 (19)	154	1087	61.4
1957	1014 (8)	145	1276	47.8
1960	1996 (8)	95	2573	45.6
1962	758 (37)	37	1434	38.8

* Deflator used was the rural Java 12 commodity price index, as reported in *Statistical Pocketbook of Indonesia 1963*, p. 265.
† *Algemene Volkscrediet Bank*, 1938–40; *Bank Rakyat Indonesia*, 1952–59; *Bank Koperasi Tani dan Nelajan*, 1960–62. Figures in brackets show rural loans as a percentage of the total.
Source: *Statistical Pocketbook of Indonesia 1959*, pp. 200–7; *Statistical Pocketbook of Indonesia 1963*, pp. 232–9.

If government attempts to develop a countervailing power in the private sector to both foreign and Chinese dominance met with only very partial success in the early post-independence years, the same was true of government efforts to accelerate the pace of public capital formation through medium-term economic planning. The five-year development plan, begun in 1956, emphasised agricultural investment (including transmigration and irrigation) and investment in energy, transport, and education, but the political circumstances were not propitious for speedy and effective implementation, and after 1958 any serious attempt at implementation ceased. That year also saw the abandonment of official attempts to build up a class of indigenous entrepreneurs. Instead, the government decided to solve the problem of continuing Dutch domination of the economy through outright nationalisation of all Dutch-owned enterprises. While most of the productive enterprises continued to operate without major changes to their company structure, the commercial houses were subject to quite sweeping changes (Panglaykim 1968: 50; Panglaykim and Palmer 1969: 7–35). In 1959, six of the former Dutch 'Big Ten' trading companies were converted into wholly government-owned companies and, together with two government trading companies already in existence, they were given exclusive entitlement to foreign exchange to import the nine most essential commodities. But, as Panglaykim pointed out, the old Dutch trading companies had extensive linkages backwards to a number of estates, manufacturing and other productive enterprises, and forwards to insurance and freight enterprises. These linkages were broken, with a resulting parcelling out of the production and distribution functions of the old trading houses to several newly created state enterprises and government departments. This, in turn, meant that, for example, a rubber estate or textile company that had hitherto existed as part of an integrated production and trading company, was forced to look for new sources of credit, and also to create new marketing channels. In addition, the new enterprises were often not permitted to retain old staff but were forced to make new appointments of people picked largely on grounds of political patronage.

It could be argued that, given the failure of the 'Benteng' approach to the development of a class of indigenous private entrepreneurs on the one hand, and given the pressing political need for a dramatic end to the continuing foreign domination of the economy on the other, there was little alternative to the nationalisation measures adopted between 1957 and 1960. Certainly, the Dutch trading houses could have been forced to break up their highly integrated enterprises and divest themselves of at least some of their subsidiaries. Such a move could well have enhanced economic efficiency through greater competition, while at the same time reducing if not eliminating Dutch control of the economy. But who would have bought those enterprises which the Dutch companies would have been forced to sell? It seems probable that most would have been purchased by politically well-connected people who could get access to bank 'loans', and who would then have run them in conjunction with their former Dutch managers, or with Chinese partners. Such arrangements might have led to greater operating efficiency, although this is far from clear, but they would not have solved the political problem of foreign domination.

As Castles (1965) pointed out, the rapid emergence of a large number of state enterprises in the late 1950s and early 1960s, many run by people who obviously lacked technical competence, and were interested mainly in using the enterprises as a means of self-enrichment, in turn gave rise to new types of political friction. There was increasing denunciation of 'bureaucratic capitalists', especially by those groups, such as the educated young, who saw little prospect of themselves getting access to the kinds of salaries and perquisites which were so obviously at the disposal of the new class of state managers. In addition, many new graduates found it impossible to earn an income by 'legitimate' entrepreneurial activities in a stagnant economy which offered few openings to those who had only their ability to sell. Frustration and bitterness were the inevitable result, and it was not surprising that educated urban youth were among the most vociferous supporters of General Suharto and his New Economic Order, established in the wake of the abortive coup of September, 1965.

It was pointed out in Chapter 4 that the eight-year plan, intended to run from 1960 to 1968 and to create a more 'socialist' and egalitarian economy in Indonesia through expanding the size of the public sector and drastically curtailing the role of both foreign and domestic capital in the private sector, in fact ended up reducing public expenditures relative to national income. The plan document stated that 'the right of private entrepreneurs to operate is not derived from natural law but is given by the government, and therefore the government has the right to guide the process of economic development' (Pauker 1961: 118). But government 'guidance', in effect, meant increasing official hostility to all forms of private capitalism, and even indigenous business people faced enormous problems (Soedarpo 1994: 51–2). Most private entrepreneurs devoted their time and energies to avoiding government restrictions and disincentives, especially in the foreign trade sector where smuggling became widespread. While a few well-placed individuals were in a position to earn large rents from their access to government licences, the vast majority of indigenous producers, especially those in the agricultural sector, were exposed to the full rigour of market forces, with little protection from any government agency. In spite of the official rhetoric in favour of socialism and the 'collectivist economy', no attempt was made in the Guided Democracy period to collectivise agriculture, or even to make rural cooperatives more effective, in spite of the many government statements emphasising their virtues. Discussing the question, what do Indonesians mean by the term 'socialism'?, Mackie (1964: 44–5) distinguished two elements:

First, for some it has meant little more than 'Indonesianisation' – breaking the grip of foreign capital, mostly Dutch and Chinese, over the trading and industrial sectors and plantation agriculture.

Whether this was to be done by state nationalisation or by the creation of an Indonesian business class was, for a long time, an unresolved argument... In the second place, great stress has been put on 'collectivist' organisation of the economy, on the 'family principle', or the *gotong royong* (mutual assistance) method of performing certain agricultural tasks in the villages (and hence on the rejection of individualism, private self-interest, and the profit-motive). Co-operatives were regarded as an excellent expression of Indonesian social ideals, which devalue the bourgeois virtue of thrift and provision for the future. On the other hand, it is noteworthy that collective farming has almost no advocates, even among the communists. One even hears frequent complaints that the peasants are not 'cooperatively minded'. In fact the peasant economy is intensely individualist and mercenary; after all, village *pasar* (markets) reveal the forces of supply and demand in their most naked form with intense bargaining for almost every transaction.

As inflation gathered pace in the 1960s, the contradiction between the official rhetoric stressing socialism and cooperation and the harsh economic realities facing the vast majority of the nation's producers and consumers became more glaring. By 1964–65 more than half the rural population were below a very modest poverty line in Central and East Java, and more than 40 per cent in several other provinces (Booth 1988: 126). Paddy loans through the paddy banks which had helped to smooth out fluctuations in rural rice prices in the 1920s and 1930s had dwindled to only about 40 per cent of the pre-war total by 1962 (Table 7.4). Partly as a result of this, rural markets in Java in the early 1960s were characterised by enormous fluctuations in prices (Table 7.1). Those who had to depend on markets for their food were forced to consume cheaper non-rice staples for much of the year. Real lending through the rural banks and the pawnshops, which had recovered to pre-war levels by 1960, fell rapidly thereafter (Table 7.4). *Socialisme à la Indonesie* had certainly reduced the role of foreign enterprises in the domestic economy, but it had not led to any improvement in living standards for the great majority of the people.

THE MARKET, THE STATE AND ENTREPRENEURSHIP IN THE NEW ORDER

The New Order government led by President Soeharto has seen two distinct phases of 'liberalisation' of the economy. The first of these occurred between 1967 and 1973. During these years inflation was reduced, the exchange rate unified and controls on capital flows into and out of the country were removed (Cole and Slade 1996: 42–5). A new law on foreign investment was passed which encouraged joint ventures between foreign and domestic partners, and performance criteria were established for state enterprises. But, at the same time, the government took responsibility for the dissemination of new agricultural technologies, especially in the smallholder foodcrop sector, and for improving access to education and public health. Although most of the overtly socialist rhetoric of the Guided Democracy era was dropped, many of the old attitudes remained. Most senior government officials who occupied key decision-making positions in the New Order era had spent their formative years under Sukarno, and the old doubts about the suitability of capitalism in the Indonesian context remained. At the same time, many officials and their families were not slow to grasp the opportunities for making money that faster economic growth brought. Many foreign business people enticed back to Indonesia by the 1967 legislation rapidly realised that the regulatory system was still being used for personal enrichment, and that the payment of bribes and kickbacks was part of the costs of doing business in Indonesia. No attempt was made to privatise the large state enterprise sector built up under Sukarno, and indeed the power of the state oil company, *Pertamina*, grew rapidly to the point where it was considered to operate as a 'state within a state'.

A government commission established in 1970 to investigate corruption and bureaucratic mismanagement was especially critical of *Pertamina*, and its continued immunity from any form of external audit (Robison 1986: 235–7). But, in spite of a number of recommendations concerning improved accountability, little was achieved until *Pertamina* collapsed under the weight of its debts in 1975. With the dramatic growth in foreign exchange earnings from oil after 1974, much of the momentum towards economic liberalisation was lost. The riots which followed the visit to Jakarta of the then Japanese prime minister, Mr Tanaka, in 1974 served notice on the government that the issue of foreign domination of the economy was still a very sensitive one. In the latter part of the 1970s and the early 1980s, there was much talk of '*Pancasila* Economics', which emphasised the role of state enterprises and cooperatives in the economy, the importance of egalitarian social and religious values in tempering the selfish and individualistic aspects of market capitalism, and the need for economic nationalism, and consequently of limiting the role of foreign and Chinese businesses in the economy (McCawley 1982).

By the early 1980s, Indonesia was a highly regulated and controlled economy, and the role of government was undoubtedly stronger than at any time since the 1930s. Indeed, most of the regulatory devices introduced to control agricultural markets, and license firms in the manufacturing, transport, trade and financial services sectors in the 1930s were still in force. In addition, capital markets remained undeveloped, and the country was severely 'under-banked', with one of the lowest ratios of broad money to GDP in Asia (Arndt 1983b: 92). But the progressive liberalisation of both the financial sector and the real economy which took place the 1980s and early 1990s, and the improved growth performance that it engendered did not win universal acclaim. Indeed, the concerns expressed by many commentators, both Dutch and nationalist, in the inter-war years have again been expressed about the growth which has occurred since the late 1960s, and especially about the impact of the economic liberalisation measures of the decade from 1985 to 1995. To what extent have these policies benefited foreign and domestic Chinese interests compared with indigenous Indonesians? Is a robust domestic entrepreneurial class emerging which will assume increasing control of the nation's economic development in the twenty-first century? If not, what should be done to promote such a class? Given the fact that many indigenous Indonesians have been involved with the modern market economy for the better part of a century, it is perhaps surprising that it is still necessary to be concerned about the issue of indigenous entrepreneurship at all. Surely, given that Indonesia has been an independent nation for over fifty years, given the overwhelming numerical superiority of indigenous Indonesians over the Chinese minority, and given the greatly improved access to education and to credit facilities since the 1950s, ethnic Indonesians should be in a position to dominate and control their own economy?

By the end of the 1980s, there was considerable evidence to indicate that they were not. In 1989, a Jakarta business magazine published a list of the forty largest private business groups in Indonesia, together with an estimate of their annual sales and assets (Widyahartono 1993: 70–1). Total annual sales of these forty groups in 1988 were estimated to be Rp 37 trillion (just under 15 per cent of GDP). The top ten groups, which accounted for almost 57 per cent of all sales, were all owned by Indonesian families of Chinese descent. The three largest *pribumi* businesses were controlled, in order of sales, by Julius Tahija, an Ambonese who was formerly general manager of Caltex Pacific, Bambang Trihatmodjo, the second son of President Suharto, and Soedarpo Sastrosatomo, who had established himself in general trading and shipping in the 1950s and had subsequently diversified into banking and pharmaceuticals. In total, twelve of the forty groups listed were controlled by *pribumi* interests, four of whom were closely connected with the family of President Suharto. Other prominent indigenous businessmen included Aburizal Bakrie, the son of Achmad Bakrie, a Sumatran who founded a commodity trading enterprise in the 1930s, Ibnu Sutowo, the former head of *Pertamina*, and Sumitro Djojohadikusomo, a former cabinet minister and university professor with close connections to the Suharto family.

The list served to highlight the degree to which the Indonesian economy in the late 1980s was still dominated by a relatively small number of business groups, most of which were owned by ethnic Chinese. Indonesia is, of course, hardly unique among developing countries in possessing a highly concentrated industrial structure. Writers such as Leff (1979) and Amsden and Hikino (1994: 138–9) have argued that there are good reasons, stemming from highly imperfect markets for products, finance and information, why conglomerates emerge in many parts of the developing world. Indeed, vertically integrated conglomerates can, under some conditions, confer real gains on consumers. Some Indonesian policymakers, probably influenced by what they perceive as the 'Japanese' or 'Korean' model of late industrialisation, seem convinced that large conglomerates, whether owned by the state or by private interests, are essential if Indonesia is to catch up with modern technology and compete internationally. This equation of size with efficiency persists in spite of the fact that there is little evidence that state enterprises, or indeed many of the large private conglomerates, are especially efficient or even profitable. There is, however, considerable evidence that they owe their size at least in part to political patronage.

Robison (1986: 329) has suggested that the major indigenous business groups in New Order Indonesia could be divided into three categories: the survivors from the 1950s, the 'politico-bureaucrats' of the New Order who have established business groups based largely on preferential access to government contracts and licences, and the 'new capitalists' who have emerged over the 1970s and 1980s on the basis of their entrepreneurial abilities, albeit with some government patronage. What was most striking about the 1989 list was that the third group was so little in evidence. In addition to the conglomerates controlled by members of the Suharto family, many of the large Chinese-owned conglomerates of recent provenance were known to have strong links to, and backing from, high government officials and their immediate families. Indeed, a Japanese observer has argued that the 'close ties between business activities and political power are everyday realities in Indonesian society, indicating perhaps that there has been no real fundamental change in the country's business environment since the days of the Benteng Programme in the 1950s' (Kano 1989: 165). While the new breed of corporate tycoon which emerged under the New Order, whether Chinese or indigenous, employs staff well versed in modern management techniques, they still rely on family ties to secure contracts and enter lucrative new lines of business.

Although the rise of conglomerates certainly pre-dated the deregulation and liberalisation of the economy over the 1980s, there was by the early 1990s a widespread perception that the one has been caused by the other, and that economic liberalisation had favoured both the Chinese and politically well-connected *pribumi*, and indeed enhanced their control over key sectors of the economy. This perception is clearly false; in fact, the rapid growth of large conglomerates who were able to exploit political connections was rather a symptom of the limitations of the deregulation process. But the argument that economic liberalisation favoured the Chinese was increasingly exploited by the influential organisation of Islamic intellectuals (ICMI) in the early 1990s (Ramage 1995: 101–2). ICMI activists have argued, with some justification, that the rise of conglomerates has been at the expense of the development of a more broadly based entrepreneurial class, which in turn would be more representative of the country's diverse ethnic groups. Critics also point to the inadequacy of government programmes to foster small-scale indigenous enterprise. There is certainly evidence for this; for example, the successful rural credit programme, *Kupedes*, which grew rapidly through the 1980s was still not lending as much in real per capita terms in the early 1990s as the colonial credit programmes fifty years earlier (Table 7.5).

Table 7.5 Real volume of lending by people's credit institutions and
KUPEDES (millions guilders/rupiah:1913 prices*)

Year	Real volume of lending[†]	Per capita lending** (guilders/rupiah)
Peoples' credit institutions		
1938	202.64	3.04 (1.21)
1940	219.97	3.21 (1.32)
KUPEDES		
1991	221.36	1.21
1993	296.12	1.57

*Deflator used is the rural Java 12-foodstuffs index. As this index was
discontinued after 1982, the index was updated to 1991 and 1993 using the
rural Java 9-commodity index, as reported in *Indikator Ekonomi*, October
1994, Table 1.5.
[†]Data for 1938 and 1940 refer to disbursed loans; data for 1991 and 1993 refer
to loans approved over the year.
**Figures in brackets refer to lending per capita, excluding the pawnshops.
Sources: 1938–40; van Laanen (1990: Table 11.4); 1991–93; Soeksmono (1994:
Table 16.4).

The parallels between the 1990s and the colonial and immediate
post-colonial eras are clear. It was argued by economic nationalists
during the independence struggle that 'free-fight liberalism' only benefited the Western capitalists and the Chinese. This conviction ushered
in the largely misconceived programmes of the 1950s which were
intended to enhance '*pribumi* entrepreneurship', nationalise foreign
companies and encourage state enterprises. The recent debate could
trigger one of two reactions. It could lead to a backlash against the
evils of liberal capitalism, similar to that which occurred in the years
from 1950 to 1965. Or it could provoke stronger demands from the
'new capitalists' who are not part of the large conglomerates for a
level playing field, a more transparent regulatory regime, and stricter
control over the business activities of the families of high government
officials. Such demands, in fact, have been increasingly heard during
the 1990s, reflecting the growing strength and confidence of the
indigenous middle class, working in the private sector as white-collar
employees, as employers or as independent, own-account workers. In
addition, the growing numbers of unskilled and semi-skilled wage
workers in the non-agricultural sectors of the economy were demanding more autonomous worker organisations which could press for
better wages and working conditions.

An analysis of the changes in the structure of the Indonesian labour force between 1971 and 1990 indicates the growing importance of non-agricultural employment in both industry and services (Table 7.6). Particularly striking is the increase in the proportion of the labour force comprising employees in both industry and services; in 1990 they accounted for 27.3 per cent of the labour force compared with 17.6 per cent in 1971. Numbers of wage workers in agriculture declined to 5.4 million in 1990, only 7.5 per cent of the labour force. While part of the growth in non-agricultural wage employment can be attributed to growth in public sector employment, most is due to expansion of private sector enterprises. In addition, there has been a considerable growth in the numbers of employers and own account workers in industry and services. By 1990 they numbered 13.3 million, and accounted for 18.8 per cent of the labour force. Only a small minority of these people would have been Chinese.

Table 7.6 Percentage distribution of employed workers by sector and employment status, 1971 and 1990

Year	Agriculture	Industry	Services	Total	% growth 1971–90
Employers/own account workers					
1971	28.4	2.3	9.7	40.4	
1990	26.2	3.3	15.5	45.0	107.2
Employees					
1971	15.1	5.4	12.2	32.6	
1990	7.5	12.0	15.3	34.9	98.8
Family workers					
1971	21.3	1.0	4.7	27.0	
1990	16.2	1.4	2.5	20.1	38.9
All workers					
1971	64.8	8.7	26.5	100.0	
1990	49.9	16.7	33.3	100.0	86.1
% growth 1971–90					
	43.4	259.4	133.9	86.1	

Sources: Central Bureau of Statistics, *Population Census 1971*, Series E, Tables 47, 47A; Central Bureau of Statistics, *Population Census 1990*, Series S2, Table 44.9

The trends indicated in Table 7.6 need to be borne in mind in assessing the increasingly strident debate over conglomerates in the 1990s. Behind the emergence of a small number of very large business groups dominated by a few prominent Chinese businessmen, and the families of high officials, a much more profound change is taking place in the structure of the Indonesian economy, and in the way in which many millions of Indonesians are earning their living. By the early 1990s, only about half the employed labour force was working in agriculture and, of those, many were earning a considerable part of their income from other activities. The proportion of the employed labour force working within the household as family workers has fallen since 1971, and this trend is certain to continue. Of those employed as 'own account workers' whether in agriculture, industry or services, almost all would be involved with the market economy, selling output, and in many cases hiring in labour. Over one third of all employed Indonesians are employed as wage workers and this proportion will increase with continuing economic growth and structural change.

For much of the twentieth century, Indonesia has had, and indeed still possesses, a huge pool of surplus labour, employed often as unpaid family labour in small enterprises. Accelerated economic growth in the early years of the century, and again from the late 1960s, has pulled labour from what Lewis (1972) termed the traditional economy into wage employment in modern enterprises run along capitalist lines. The Lewis analysis would predict that, as long as the pool of surplus labour lasts, there will be little upward pressure on wages, and indeed the available evidence does suggest that real wages have not changed much in Indonesia over the twentieth century. The series on daily wages for male factory workers in the sugar industry shows considerable fluctuations, but no clear upward trend between 1921 and 1981 (Table 7.7). An analysis of wage trends over the 1970s and 1980s reached the conclusion that for most categories of unskilled workers, in agriculture and in industry, there was little evidence of any sustained increase in real wages, and that the evidence pointed to a 'continuing overall surplus of unskilled labour in major sectors and regions of the country' (Manning 1994: 108).

As economic growth in Indonesia continues, it is probable that the correlation between ethnicity and economic status will become weaker, and economic disparities along more conventional occupational and educational lines will override racial differences. To the extent that the industrial and commercial dominance of the Chinese is due to what Braadbaart (1995a: 193) has termed the 'headstart factor' rather than to greater innate business acumen or managerial expertise, this advantage will erode over time as more *pribumi* businesses emerge and prosper. This process is in turn part of broader societal changes as

Table 7.7   Daily wages of male factory coolies in the sugar industry in
Java, *1921–81*
(cents/rupiahs per day, 1913 prices)

1921	26	1971	35
1924	28	1973	32
1929	29	1976	27
1933	50	1979	26
1936	38	1981	43
1940	41		

Note: Deflated by the rural Java 12 commodity price index.
Sources: *Indisch Verslag, 1931, 1941*, Table 160; Central Bureau of Statistics, *Rata-Rata Upah Buruh Perkebunan 1970–73*; Central Bureau of Statistics: *Rata-Rata Upah Perkerja Perkebunan, 1976–81*.

a large urbanised middle class develops, based on the growing numbers of professional, managerial and clerical workers, whose living standards and consumption norms are very much influenced by international trends. At the same time, the numbers of unskilled workers in the non-agricultural economy are growing rapidly. Given that the wages of the latter group are unlikely to rise rapidly as long as there is a large pool of surplus labour, while those possessing technical and professional skills in short supply can expect to earn considerable rents, it is probable that pronounced income inequalities in urban areas will continue. Thus in the twenty-first century, social differentiation along class lines will increasingly replace the ethnic cleavage which has been such a marked characteristic of Indonesian society in the twentieth century.

8 Conclusions

In several crucial respects, the study of the economic history of Indonesia since 1800 is a study of missed opportunities. A country colonised by one of the most prosperous and enlightened states in Europe should surely have developed, in step with the metropolitan power, through the nineteenth and twentieth centuries, into a modern industrial nation, and into a stable constitutional democracy. In the nineteenth century, many visitors to Java, the seat of Dutch power and the most intensively governed part of the archipelago, were convinced that such as transition was underway. In the 1860s the English naturalist, Alfred Russel Wallace enthused:

> Good roads run through the country from end to end; European and native rulers work harmoniously together; and life and property are as well secured as in the best governed states of Europe. I believe, therefore that Java may fairly claim to be the finest tropical island in the world, and equally interesting to the tourist seeking after new and beautiful scenes; to the naturalist who desires to examine the variety and beauty of tropical nature; or to the moralist and the politician who want to solve the problem of how man may best be governed under new and varied conditions (Wallace 1869: 76).

Almost a century after Wallace wrote this, in the early 1960s, western visitors to Java, and to other parts of the country, were appalled at the deterioration of infrastructure, the weak authority of the central government, and the poverty of the great majority of the population. Even after thirty years of accelerated economic development under President Suharto's 'New Order', Indonesia remains a relatively poor country, with marked regional variations in the level of development, and doubts remain about its longer-term economic and political future. In seeking reasons for Indonesia's frustrated economic development, it is tempting to blame the colonial power and this study has indicated a number of reasons for the economy's sluggish economic progress from 1800 to 1942. The reforms initiated by Daendels and Raffles were not continued after the Dutch returned to Java in 1815, and during the four decades from 1830 to 1870, fiscal, monetary and exchange rate policies were subordinated to the need to remit a large annual contribution to the Dutch budget. Even after the termination of these remittances, there was little attempt on the part of the government to increase expenditures on infrastructure or on education until the end of the nineteenth century. Although more enmeshed in the market economy as the century progressed, the great majority of the population lived in rural areas, and indeed in Java the urbanisation ratio declined between 1815 and 1890 (Boomgaard 1989: 111).

There was a change in both official rhetoric and in policies after 1900, and a more assertive fiscal policy combined with an improvement in the terms of trade did lead to accelerated economic growth. Indeed, if the growth momentum achieved in the years from 1900 to 1920 could have been sustained over the next fifty years, Indonesia in 1970 would have been unrecognisable. Indonesia, like most other primary exporters, suffered a decline in the net barter terms of trade in the inter-war years, but this alone cannot account for the disappointing inter-war performance. An overvalued exchange rate inhibited export growth, and almost certainly deterred foreign capital inflow into export and import-competing industries. Exchange rate policy together with tight monetary and fiscal policies again produced substantial balance of payments surpluses. The confident belief of the early years of the ethical policy that education, agricultural development and population movements from Java to other parts of the country could together lead to improved living standards was replaced by an official distrust of lavish 'welfare' expenditure which had simply led to popular unrest and challenges to the authority of the colonial regime.

The failure to accelerate access to education was probably the greatest of the sins of omission of Dutch colonialism. The fact that so few managed to get beyond a few years in a vernacular school meant that fluency in the language of the colonial power was confined to a tiny privileged minority. Senior posts in the civil service, the judiciary, the armed forces and the police were the almost exclusive prerogative of the Dutch until 1942. Thus, in 1949, when full sovereignty was transferred, there was a very small pool of competent people to staff a civil service which was required, not just to run the routine administration of a vast archipelago, but also to implement an ambitious set of development programmes in sectors as diverse as power generation, education and agricultural extension. In spite of the efforts made after independence to increase access to education, the very meagre colonial legacy meant that, in the 1950s and 1960s, the great majority of the working age population had had no schooling at all, or at most a few years in a rural primary school.

Related to the failure to provide access to education, and even more damaging, was the failure of the colonial regime to facilitate the emergence of a robust class of indigenous entrepreneurs, able and willing to challenge the role of the Chinese in the urban, commercial economy. Although the much admired people's credit programmes did assist in developing indigenous businesses in manufacturing, trade and transport, most such businesses were small-scale and in many cases could not withstand the vicissitudes of the years from 1930 to 1950. Perceptive outside observers such as Furnivall (1944: 455-6) noted many signs of the development of an entrepreneurial culture among the native population in the 1930s, but he also pointed out that

> throughout the whole period of Dutch rule, the Chinese have been strengthening their position by building up a barrier, growing ever more formidable, to shut the Native off from industrial development and from stimulating economic contact with the West.

Could different policies have produced different results? Many nationalists in Indonesia, as in other parts of Asia, were only too happy to blame the country's poverty and economic backwardness on the pernicious consequences of European colonialism, and some anti-colonial Western scholars encouraged this conviction. They pointed to Japan as an example of an Asian nation which had not fallen under Western domination, and which had managed to industrialise rapidly after the Meiji restoration, implying that if Indonesia had been left alone, it too could have followed this route. Such an argument ignores the rather obvious point that modern Indonesia is itself an artifact of Western colonialism, and would not have been brought into existence at all in the absence of external forces. It also ignores the point, made by many Japanese historians, that Japan at the end of the Tokugawa era had a number of social, economic and demographic characteristics which set it apart from the rest of Asia, including a highly developed urban culture, quite high literacy rates and a well-developed financial system (Rosovsky 1972: 232-3; Waswo 1996: 9-17). Kiernan (1995: 65) is surely correct when he points out that assertions that Java could have done just as well as Japan ignore the cultural and mental gulf between the two societies in the mid-nineteenth century, and 'Java's far more rudimentary nationhood'.

But even if none of the pieces of what eventually became Indonesia could have emulated Japan's economic achievements since the latter part of the nineteenth century, had they been free of colonial control, it is still useful to ask if a different type of colonialism could have produced better economic results. Those who wish to defend the Dutch record argue that however poor Indonesia's economic performance was in the nineteenth and early twentieth centuries, it was certainly better than that of British India, and probably better than most other parts of Southeast Asia, including the quasi-independent nation of Thailand. Given the geo-political realities of the nineteenth century, it was inevitable that the Indonesian archipelago would fall under the control of one or other of the European powers, and there is little persuasive evidence that economic development would have been faster under another regime. While this may well be true, it is hardly an adequate defence of Dutch stewardship. The Dutch administration failed to produce the sustained improvements in living standards which were the goal of the ethical policy, and unlike the British in India, they bequeathed no durable constitutional framework to independent Indonesia. The federal constitution which was imposed on the new state in 1949 had, as Legge (1961: 7) pointed out, no historical antecedents, and was distrusted by the nationalist leaders. It was speedily dropped although its replacement lasted less than a decade, to be replaced in its turn by the constitution drawn up in 1945, which was based on the concept of a unitary state. But, as one eminent Indonesian lawyer has pointed out, the 1945 constitution must still be regarded as a provisional constitution, and debates about its improvement are certain to continue (Nasution 1992: 432).

The weakness of the indigenous business class in the late colonial era together with the very small numbers of indigenous Indonesians in the upper echelons of the administrative service, or in the professions, meant that these groups had far less influence on the leaders of the independence struggle than in, for example, British India. The group around Sukarno, Hatta and Sjahrir at the time of the proclamation of independence, had little knowledge of, or sympathy for, either private enterprise or public administration. They saw themselves as revolutionaries, and their main aim was to expel the Dutch colonial forces and set up a republic where the state would dominate the economy, control the exploitation of the country's resource wealth, and take responsibility for popular welfare. They argued that in the colonial era, Indonesia's resources were exported and the revenues used mainly to finance foreign remittances. There was enough evidence to make this viewpoint plausible to most Indonesians, who then equated export growth with foreign exploitation. It was not until the 1980s that the Indonesian government began to view broad-based export growth as a means of achieving both faster economic development and improved economic welfare, and this change in view was largely due to the powerful demonstration effect from the successful export economies of Northeast Asia, and from ASEAN neighbours such as Thailand and Malaysia. But even then, there were many who viewed export-led growth as an essentially inegalitarian strategy, which would enrich a few (mainly Chinese) entrepreneurs while trapping most of the labour force in poorly paid, unskilled jobs.

The debates about economic policy in the 1950s, were one part of the wider struggle characterised by Feith (1962: 577ff) in terms of a cleavage between 'administrators' and 'solidarity makers'. The former group was never very strong, and indeed its economic component was very small. After 1953, the influence of the administrator group declined sharply, and the personal antagonisms between its leading members and Sukarno became more bitter. Their complete defeat in 1958–59 led to the incarceration or exile of virtually everyone among the generation of independence fighters who had any interest in, or capacity for, orthodox economic management. The group around. Sukarno claimed to favour socialism, but their notion of a socialist economy was formed very largely in terms of the rejection of liberal capitalism, and disengagement from that part of the international economy controlled by the major Western powers. After 1958, the control of the central government over the major levers of economic policy declined, and the years from 1958 to 1966 witnessed a substantial decline in the role of government in the economy. Not only did government expenditures decline relative to GDP, but many regions outside Java effectively seceded from central control and linked themselves to the economies of neighbouring countries.

In the early 1960s it appeared that the national economy centred on Java, which the Dutch had built up so laboriously over the previous century, was falling apart. The '*de facto* federalism' to which Mackie (1980: 675) drew attention had considerable support outside Java, especially in the export-producing regions, where civilian administrators, military commanders and the producers themselves all benefited from widespread smuggling and the flourishing parallel markets in goods and services, including foreign exchange. The delinking of Java from the outer provinces certainly did not impoverish those provinces, especially in Sumatra, with resilient export sectors and close links to the international economy through regional entrepots such as Singapore. The effects were far more serious in Java, which lost control of a considerable part of the tax revenues accruing from the export-producing regions, and in the poorer provinces of Eastern Indonesia, whose resource wealth was meagre, and who were thus more dependent on revenues from the central government. By the mid-1960s, poverty and malnutrition were widespread in Java, infrastructure was falling into disrepair, and even routine government administration was breaking down as poorly paid civil servants sought alternative employment.

The reintegration of Java and the other islands into a single national economy is certainly one of the most significant achievements of the Suharto era. Less than a decade after the fall of Sukarno, the armed forces were brought under tight central control, regional warlordism had ended, and the 1974 law on regional government had removed any real autonomy from regional parliaments (Mackie 1980: 672). But, by the end of the 1980s, it was clear that the tightly centralised system created after 1970 was causing serious unrest. Not surprisingly, the unrest was most severe in two resource-rich provinces remote from Java, Aceh and Irian Jaya, both of which had been integrated into the Dutch empire quite late, and in the case of Aceh after a long and bitter war. But elsewhere in the country, there was growing unhappiness with a system which appeared to take little account of the aspirations of local populations, whose development needs were subordinated to the requirements of a remote and often rapacious elite based in Jakarta. The evidence that, by the early 1990s, poverty incidence was higher in a number of provinces outside Java than in Java, including a province such as West Kalimantan which had been involved in export production for many decades, reinforced suspicions that the outer provinces were paying a heavy price for their participation in a national economy centred on Java.

The Dutch created a national economy in Indonesia, but they failed to put in place any durable system of centre–regional financial relations, which would prevent, or at least modify, the kinds of abuses which were already in evidence in the early years of this century, and which have not been removed in the half-century since 1945. But the relationship between the constituent parts of the national economy is not the only troubled legacy from the colonial period. Another continuing debate concerns the adoption of capitalism as an appropriate form of economic organisation. One of the most perplexing aspects of contemporary Indonesia to many foreigners is the apparent coexistence of a dynamic, and in some respects rapacious, capitalism with an official rhetoric which is often critical of economic liberalism, and which emphasises the virtues of cooperatives, and the role which government should play in protecting small producers from the vicissitudes of the market economy. Such protection can in turn involve a considerable degree of coercion, especially when it involves the enforced participation in government 'development' programmes, many of which are drawn up with little or no consultation with the intended target group.

It was argued in Chapter 7 that such official suspicion towards the role of markets has a long history in Indonesia. The coercive approach to crop cultivation of the nineteenth century was adopted at least partly because Dutch officialdom doubted that smallholders would respond to international market demand signals. In the early twentieth century, when millions of Indonesians were involved in the voluntary cultivation of export crops, 'ethical' administrators worried about the consequences of the intrusion of the forces of international capitalism into the domestic economy. The Dutch understood both the benefits and the risks inherent in an export economy, as their own nation had developed as a small, open economy surrounded by larger, more powerful neighbours. But they were divided about appropriate policy responses in the Indonesian context. Some wanted to build fences between the indigenous population and the forces of modern capitalism, while others realised that such policies were futile. This second group stressed the need to develop the capacity of the indigenous population to participate more fully and equally in the modern commercial economy, thus diluting the dominant role of foreigners and the Chinese. Such ambivalent attitudes are still found in the contemporary Indonesian bureaucracy. They are accompanied by, and to a considerable extent are a reflection of, even deeper divisions about the economic purpose of the state.

The economic history of Indonesia over the past two centuries, and indeed for much longer, can be seen as a continual struggle between the concepts of the predatory and the developmental state, with the latter gradually becoming the dominant vision but never totally subduing the former. Economic historians seeking to explain the reason why governments in the western world gradually developed an efficient regime of growth-promoting property rights have stressed the role of destabilising influences such as changes in information costs, technology and population, or more generally changes in relative factor prices, which in turn enhance the relative bargaining power of particular groups of constitutents, and force changes in the political system (North 1981). Northern Europe was especially fortunate in that, after the Renaissance, a system of states emerged which were sufficiently large that they were not prone to endemic baronial warfare, but at the same time small enough to be vulnerable to external threats. Thus, the governments did not dare extract the maximum feasible revenues from their citizens for fear of challenges from external rivals. New coalitions could develop as a result of economic and technological change which were ultimately able to change the political order to accommodate their interests.

Pre-colonial Asia was very different; indeed, it has been argued that between 1400 and 1800, virtually the entire territory between Constantinople and Peking 'was an Arthur Laffer nightmare come true: inept and confiscatory government had condemned the population to perpetual poverty by thwarting individual initiative' (Mokyr 1984: 176). In his study of Southeast Asia during the 'Age of Commerce' from 1450 to 1630, Reid (1993: 268) points out that most European observers were in no doubt about the reason why, in spite of the considerable economic progress in the region over this period, most indigenous Southeast Asians remained poor and backward. It was the uncontrolled rapacity of the rulers, against which the population had no protection, save migration to another locality. Visitors to the Netherlands and England from Banten at the end of the seventeenth century were amazed to discover that the property of private citizens in these relatively advanced states of Northern Europe was protected by law against arbitrary confiscation by rulers (Reid 1993: 130). Arbitrary and often brutal exactions were levied on indigenous Indonesians not just by their own rulers, but also by the agents of the VOC. With the establishment of a resident government in the colony in 1800, it was expected by some idealists that such abuses would be curtailed and that indigenous Indonesians would enjoy the same protection from the legal system as Dutch citizens in the Netherlands.

The reality was, of course, rather different. It has been stressed in this study that probably the most pernicious legacy of the cultivation system, both in Java and in the other parts of the archipelago where it was implemented, was to thwart the development of market institutions, especially in the rural economy. Many rural cultivators equated production for the market with coercion and exploitation. At the same time, many colonial officials interpreted reluctance to produce for the market as a lack of economic motivation. The alleged reluctance of the indigenous cultivators to involve themselves in production was in turn used as a justification for further coercion. These attitudes persisted well after the end of the system of forced deliveries in Java, and were in at least some respects reinforced by the ethical policy. Certainly it can be argued that the policy reforms implemented in Indonesia after 1900 laid the foundations for a strong developmental state, and indeed the colonial regime in Indonesia in the early twentieth century was among the first anywhere in the world to accord economic development a top policy priority. But even the most zealous proponents of the ethical policy were to some degree influenced by the old stereotypes about the reluctance of the native population to be involved in the market economy, or to accumulate capital. Furthermore, they were increasingly constrained by conservative fiscal, monetary and exchange rate policies which created large balance of payments surpluses by squeezing domestic expenditures.

It was only after the severe international depression of the early 1930s that the economic reformists in the colonial establishment once again gained the upper hand. In the latter part of the decade there was some progress towards a planned developmental state, with the government taking greater responsibility for accelerated industrialisation, and improved access to education. It is fascinating to speculate on the course of Indonesian economic history had not the Dutch experiment in 'managed' colonial development been brought to an abrupt end by the arrival of the Japanese in 1942. After independence was finally achieved, the new government undoubtedly wished to move further in the direction of a planned development strategy, following the prevailing international ideology of the time which viewed the state as the prime initiator of economic development. But this was frustrated by political instability which made rational economic management impossible. Increasingly, 'economic guidance' became a convenient pretext for xenophobic nationalism which deterred foreign investors and aid donors, while at the same time stifling indigenous, and other, entrepreneurs through controls and regulations. The private sector was viewed with hostility, and the idea that government had any responsibility for developing and supporting a regime of private property rights was totally alien.

While there have been important changes in economic policy-making in the Suharto era, there can be no doubt that many of the legacies from the immediate post-independence era continue to be influential. Suharto and his associates have made economic growth a key policy objective not because they necessarily approve of capitalism as a form of economic organisation; it has already been pointed out that a deep ambivalence about liberal market capitalism persists in contemporary Indonesia at many different levels of society. Nor is it obvious that the Suharto regime has sought to facilitate private asset accumulation through strengthening property rights. While successive cabinets have had their share of economic technocrats who see the appropriate role of the state as an even-handed facilitator of market-led development, many senior policy-makers, including Suharto himself, have interpreted their mandate to develop the private sector mainly in terms of granting favours to their immediate families and close business associates.

The main reason why economic growth has been broadly supported as a policy goal since 1966 is that all sections of the policy-making elite in Indonesia realise that rapid economic growth is occurring throughout the Asian region and that if Indonesia falls behind it will become more vulnerable to external threats and to internal insurrections. Economic growth is thus desired not as an end in itself, but as the means of achieving the pre-eminent policy objective of preserving the territorial integrity of the nation. This in itself is not surprising; a similar view of economic growth as an instrument of national self-preservation, was influential in other authoritarian developmental states, from Meiji Japan to Franco's Spain and South Korea under Park Chung Hee. But the history of these three countries would suggest that the forces of economic growth, once unleashed, will inevitably lead to demands for a stronger legal and constitutional framework which guarantees a broad range of civil liberties, including a stronger regime of property rights. In Indonesia, too, it is inevitable that economic growth will create such demands, which the political system will then have to accommodate. At the end of the 1990s, Indonesia is rapidly reaching the stage where 'apathy and acceptance of the state's rules, no matter how repressive' (North 1981: 32) are giving way to challenges from new economic forces demanding the removal of the final vestiges of the predatory state. How the government responds to these challenges will determine not just Indonesia's economic future in the new millenium, but its very survival as a nation.

Bibliography

Abramovitz, Moses (1986), 'Catching Up, Forging Ahead and Falling Behind', *Journal of Economic History*, 46(2), pp. 385–406.

Alexander, Jennifer and Paul Alexander (1979), 'Labour Demand and "Involution" of Javanese Agriculture', *Social Analysis*, No. 3, December, pp. 22–44.

Alexander, Jennifer and Paul Alexander (1991), 'Protecting the Peasants from Capitalism: The Subordination of Javanese Traders by the Colonial State', *Comparative Studies in Society and History*, Vol 33, pp. 370–94.

Amsden, Alice H. (1989), *Asia's Next Giant: South Korea's Late Industrialisation*, New York: Oxford University Press.

Amsden, Alice H. and Takashi Hikino (1994), 'Project Execution Capability, Organisational Know-how and Conglomerate Corporate Growth in Late Industrialisation', *Industrial and Corporate Change*, Vol 3(1), pp. 111–47.

Anderson, B.R.O'G. (1983), 'Old State, New Society: Indonesia's New Order in Comparative Perspective, *Journal of Asian Studies*, Vol 42(3), pp. 477–96.

Angoulvant, Gabriel (1926), *Les Indes Neerlandaises: Leur Role dans l'Economie Internationale*, Paris: Le Monde Nouveau.

Anon. (1969), 'The Five Year Plan', *Bulletin of Indonesian Economic Studies*, vol. 5(2), July, pp. 70–9.

Anspach, Ralph (1960), 'Monetary Aspects of Indonesia's Economic Reorganisation in 1959', *Ekonomi dan Keuangan Indonesia*, Vol XIII (1 and 2), January–February, pp. 2–47.

Anspach, Ralph (1969), 'Indonesia' in R. Anspach *et al.*, *Underdevelopment and Economic Nationalism in Southeast Asia*, Ithaca: Cornell University Press.

Anwar, Rosihan (1995), *Soebadio Sastrosatomo: Pengemban Misi Politik*, Jakarta: Grafiti.

Ark, Bart van (1986), 'Indonesian Export Growth and Economic Development: 117 Years of Empirical Evidence, 1823 to 1940', *Research Memorandum 189*, Institute of Economic Research, Faculty of Economics, University of Groningen.

Arndt, H.W. (1966), 'Survey of Recent Developments', *Bulletin of Indonesian Economic Studies*, No 5, October, pp. 1–21.

Arndt, H.W. (1967), 'Survey of Recent Developments', *Bulletin of Indonesian Economic Studies*, No 8, October, pp. 1–34.

Arndt, H.W. (1968), 'Survey of Recent Developments', *Bulletin of Indonesian Economic Studies*, No 11, October, pp. 1–28.

Arndt, H.W. (1971), 'Banking in Hyperinflation and Stabilization' in Bruce Glassburner (ed.) *The Economy of Indonesian': Selected Readings*, Ithaca: Cornell University.

Arndt, H.W. (1978), 'Survey of Recent Developments', *Bulletin of Indonesian Economic Studies*, Vol 14(3), pp. 1–23.

Arndt, H.W. (1983), 'Oil and the Indonesian Economy', *Southeast Asian Affairs 1983*, Aldershot: Gower Publishing Company for the Institute of Southeast Asian Studies.

Arndt, H.W (1983a), 'Survey of Recent Developments', *Bulletin of Indonesian Economic Studies*, Vol 19(2), pp. 1–26.

Arndt, H.W. (1983b), 'Financial Development in Asia', *Asian Development Review*, Vol 1(1), pp. 86–100.

Arndt, H.W. (1991), 'Japan as a Creditor: Macroeconomic Issues', *Pacific Economic Papers* No. 190, Australia-Japan Research Centre, Australian National University, Canberra.

Arndt, H.W. and R.M. Sundrum (1975), 'Regional Price Disparities', *Bulletin of Indonesian Economic Studies*, Vol 11 (2), pp. 30–68.

Arndt, H.W. and R.M. Sundrum (1984), 'Devaluation and Inflation: The 1978 Experience', *Bulletin of Indonesian Economic Studies*, Vol 20 (1), pp. 83–97.

Asher, Mukul G. and Anne Booth (1992), 'Fiscal Policy' in Anne Booth (ed.), *The Oil Boom and After: Economic Performance and Policy-making in the Soeharto Era*, Singapore: Oxford University Press.

Asian Development Bank (1994), *Asian Development Report*, Manila: Asian Development Bank.

Asra, Abuzar (1989), 'Inequality Trends in Indonesia 1969–1981: A Re-examination', *Bulletin of Indonesian Economic Studies*, Vol 25(2), pp. 100–10.

Azis, Iwan J. (1994), 'Indonesia' in John Williamson (ed.), *The Political Economy of Policy Reform*, Washington: Institute for International Economics.

Bairoch, Paul (1975), *The Economic Development of the Third World since 1900*, London: Methuen.

Bairoch, Paul (1991), 'How and Not Why; Economic Inequalities Between 1800 and 1913: Some Background Figures' in Jean Batou (ed.), *Between Development and Underdevelopment: The Precocious Attempts at Industrialization of the Periphery*, Geneva: Librairie Droz.

Bairoch, Paul and Bouda Etemad (1985), *Commodity Structure of Third World Exports, 1830–1937*, Geneva: Librairie Droz.

Bank Indonesia (1968), *Report for the Years 1960–1965*, Jakarta: Bank Indonesia.

Bank Indonesia (1994), *Annual Report for the Year 1993/4*, Jakarta: Bank Indonesia.

Barber, Alvin (1939), 'Six Years of Economic Planning in Netherlands India', *Far Eastern Survey*, Vol VIII, (17), pp. 195–203.

Bastin, John (1954), *Raffles' Ideas on the Land Rent System in Java and the Mackenzie Land Tenure Commission*, The Hague: M. Nijhoff.

Bauer, P.T. (1948), *The Rubber Industry: A Study in Monopoly and Competition*, London: Longmans, Green.

Bauer, P.T. and B.S. Yamey (1957), *The Economics of Underdeveloped Countries*, Cambridge: Cambridge University Press.

Beeby, C.E. (1979), *Assessment of Indonesian Education: A Guide in Planning*, Wellington: New Zealand Council for Educational Research in association with Oxford University Press.

Benda, Harry (1966), 'The Pattern of Administrative Reforms in the Closing Years of Dutch Rule in Indonesia,, *Journal of Asian Studies*, Vol 25, pp. 589–605.

Berg, N.P. van den (1895), *The Financial and Economic Condition of Nether-lands India Since 1870* (third edition), Singapore: Institute of Southeast Asian Studies (reprint).

Bernstein, E. (1953), 'Some Economic Aspects of Multiple Exchange Rates', *Ekonomi dan Keuangan Indonesia*, Vol VI (5), May, pp. 219–27.

Bijlmer, Joep (1986), 'Developments in Household Incomes and Expenditures on Java: A Comparative and Critical Review of Budget Studies' in Peter J.M. Nas (ed.), *The Indonesian City*, Dordrecht: Foris Publications.

Birnberg, Thomas A. and Stephen A. Resnick (1975), *Colonial Development: An Econometric Study*, New Haven: Yale University Press.

Blusse, Leonard (1984), 'Labour Takes Root: Mobilisation and Immobilisa-tion of Javanese Rural Socety under the Cultivation System', *Itinerario*, Vol VIII (1), pp. 77–117.

Boeke, J.H. (1927), 'Objective and Personal Elements in Colonial Welfare Policy' as translated and reprinted in *Indonesian Economics: The Concept of Dualism in Theory and Practice*, The Hague: W. van Hoeve (second edition, 1966).

Boeke, J.H. (1953), *Economics and Economic Policy of Dual Societies: As Exemplified by Indonesia*, Haarlem: H.D. Tjeenk Willink & Zoon.

Boomgaard, Peter (1981), 'Female Labour and Population Growth on Nine-teenth Century Java', *Review of Indonesian and Malayan Affairs*, Vol 15(2), pp. 1–31.

Boomgaard, Peter (1986), 'The Welfare Services in Indonesia' *Itinerario*, Vol X (1), pp. 57–82.

Boomgaard, Peter (1987), 'Morbidity and Mortality in Java, 1820–1880: Changing Patterns of Disease and Death' in Norman G. Owen (ed.), *Death and Disease in Southeast Asia: Explorations in Social, Medical and Demo-graphic History*, Singapore: Oxford University Press.

Boomgaard, Peter (1989), *Children of the Colonial State: Population Growth and Economic Development in Java, 1795–1880*, CASA Monograph, No 1, Amsterdam: Free University Press.

Boomgaard, Peter (1989a), 'Java's Agricultural Production, 1775–1875' in Angus Maddison and Ge Prince, *Economic Growth in Indonesia, 1820–1940*, Dordrecht: Foris Publications.

Boomgaard, Peter (1991), 'The Non-agricultural Side of an Agricultural Economy: Java, 1500–1900' in Paul Alexander, Peter Boomgaard and Ben White, *In the Shadow of Agriculture: Non-farm Activities in the Javanese Economy, Past and Present*, Amsterdam: Royal Tropical Institute.

Boomgaard, Peter (1993), 'Economic Growth in Indonesia, 1500–1990' in A. Szirmai, B. van Ark and D. Pilat (eds), *Explaining Economic Growth: Essays in Honour of Angus Maddison*, Amsterdam: Elsevier Science Publish-ers.

Booth, Anne (1980), 'The Burden of Taxation in Colonial Indonesia in the Twentieth Century', *Journal of Southeast Asian Studies*, Vol XI (1), pp. 91–109.

Booth, Anne (1986), 'The Colonial Legacy and its Impact on Post-indepen-dence Planning in India and Indonesia', *Itinerario*, Vol X (1), pp. 1–30.

Booth, Anne (1988), *Agricultural Development in Indonesia*, Sydney: Allen & Unwin for the Asian Studies Association of Australia.

Booth, Anne (1988a), 'Living Standards and the Distribution of Income in Colonial Indonesia: A Review of the Evidence', *Journal of Southeast Asian Studies*, XIX (2), 310–34.

Booth, Anne (1988b), 'Survey of Recent Developments', *Bulletin of Indonesian Economic Studies*, Vol 24 (1), pp. 3–35.

Booth, Anne (1989), 'Exports and Growth in the Colonial Economy', in Angus Maddison and Ge Prince (eds), *Economic Growth in Indonesia, 1820–1959*, Dordrecht: Foris Publications for KITLV.

Booth, Anne (1990), 'The Evolution of Fiscal Policy and the Role of Government in the Colonial Economy', in Anne Booth, W.J. O'Malley and Anna Weidemann (eds), *Indonesian Economic History in the Dutch Colonial Era*, Monograph Series 35, New Haven: Yale University Southeast Asian Studies.

Booth, Anne (1991), 'The Economic Development of Southest Asia: 1870–1985', *Australian Economic History Review*, Vol XXXI (1), 20–52.

Booth Anne (1992), 'Income Distribution and Poverty' in Anne Booth (ed.), *The Oil Boom and After*, Kuala Lumpur: Oxford University Press.

Booth, Anne (1993), 'Counting the Poor in Indonesia', *Bulletin of Indonesian Economic Studies*, Vol 29 (1), April, pp. 53–83.

Booth, Anne (1994), 'Japanese Import Penetration and Dutch Response: Some Aspects of Economic Policy Making in Colonial Indonesia' in Shinya Sugiyama and M.C. Guerrero (eds), *International Commercial Rivalry in Southeast Asia in the Interwar Period*, Monograph 39, Yale Southeast Asia Studies, New Haven: Yale Center for International and Area Studies.

Booth, Anne (1994a), 'Repelita VI and the Second Long-term Development Plan', *Bulletin of Indonesian Economic Studies*, Vol 30(3), pp.3–40.

Booth, Anne (1995), 'Real Domestic Income of Indonesia, 1880–1989: A Comment', *Explorations in Economic History*, Vol 32, pp. 350–64.

Booth, Anne and Peter McCawley (1981), 'Fiscal Policy' in Anne Booth and Peter McCawley (eds), *The Indonesian Economy During the Soeharto Era*, Kuala Lumpur: Oxford University Press.

Booth, Anne and R.M. Sundrum (1976), 'The 1973 Agricultural Census', *Bulletin of Indonesian Economic Studies*, Vol 12 (2), pp. 90–105.

Booth, Anne and R.M. Sundrum (1981), 'Income Distribution' in Anne Booth and Peter McCawley (eds), *The Indonesian Economy During the Soeharto Era*, Kula Lumpur: Oxford University Press.

Booth, Anne and R. M. Sundrum (1984), *Labour Absorption in Agriculture*, Delhi: Oxford University Press.

Booth, Anne, W.J. O'Malley and Anna Weidemann (eds) (1990), *Indonesian Economic History in the Dutch Colonial Era*, Monograph Series 35, New Haven: Yale University Southeast Asian Studies.

Boserup, Ester (1981), *Population and Technology*, Oxford: Basil Blackwell.

Bousquet, G.H. (1940), *A French View of the Netherlands Indies*, London: Oxford University Press.

Braadbaart, Okke (1995), 'Acquisition, Loss, and Recovery of Technological Capabilities in Bandung's Engineering Industries, 1920–1990', Paper presented to the First Euroseas Conference, Leiden, 29 June to 1 July.

Braadbaart, Okke (1995a), 'Sources of ethnic advantage: A comparison of Chinese and pribumi-managed engineering firms in Indonesia' in Rajeswary A. Brown (ed.), *Chinese Business Enterprise in Asia*, London: Routledge.

Breman, Jan (1980), *The Village on Java and the Early Colonial State*, Rotterdam: Erasmus University Comparative Asian Studies Programme.

Breman, Jan (1989), *Taming the Coolie Beast: Plantation Society and the Colonial Order in Southeast Asia*, Delhi: Oxford University Press.

Broek, Jan O.M. (1942), *Economic Development of the Netherlands Indies*, New York: Institute of Pacific Relations.

Brown, Ian (1993), 'Imperialism, Trade and Investment in the Late Nineteenth and Early Twentieth Centuries' in John Butcher and Howard Dick (eds), *The Rise and Fall of Revenue Farming: Business Elites and the Emergence of the Modern State in South East Asia*, London: Macmillan.

Bruno, Michael (1994), 'Development Issues in a Changing World: New Lessons, Old Debates, Open Questions', *Proceedings of the World Bank Annual Conference on Development Economics, Supplement to the World Bank Economic Review and the World Bank Research Observer*, pp. 9–20.

Bruton, Henry (1984), 'Economic Development with Unlimited Supplies of Foreign Exchange' in G. Ranis *et al.*, *Comparative Development Perspectives: Essays in Honour of Lloyd G. Reynolds*, Boulder: Westview Press.

Bulbeck, David, Anthony Reid, Tan Lay-cheng, and Wu Yiqi (forthcoming), *Southeast Asian Exports in the Long Term: Cloves, Pepper, Coffee and Sugar*, Singapore: Institute of Southeast Asian Studies.

Burger, D.H. (1939), 'The Government's Native Economic Policy', as translated and reprinted in *Indonesian Economics: The Concept of Dualism in Theory and Practice*, The Hague: W. van Hoeve (second edition, 1966).

Callis, H.G. (1941), *Foreign Capital in Southeast Asia*, New York: Institute of Pacific Relations.

Campo, J.N.F.M. a (1994), 'The Rise of Corporate Enterprise in Colonial Indonesia, 1893–1913', Paper presented at the Colloquium on Historical Foundations of a National Economy in Indonesia, 1890s-1990s, Amsterdam: Royal Netherlands Academy of Arts and Sciences. Published in Lindblad (1996).

Carey, Peter (1976), 'The Origins of the Java War (1825–30)', *English Historical Review*, Vol 90, pp. 52–78.

Carey, Peter (1979), 'Aspects of Javanese History in the Nineteenth Century' in Harry Aveling (ed.), *The Development of Indonesian Society: From the Coming of Islam to the Present Day*, St. Lucia: University of Queensland Press.

Castles, Lance (1965), 'Socialism and Private Business: The Latest Phase', *Bulletin of Indonesian Economic Studies*, No 1, June, pp. 13–46.

Castles, Lance (1967), *Religion, Politics and Economic Behaviour in Java: The Kudus Cigarette Industry*, Yale University Southeast Asia Studies Cultural Report Series No. 15.

Cator, W.J. (1936), *The Economic Position of the Chinese in the Netherlands Indies*, Oxford: Basil Blackwell for the Institute of Pacific Relations.

CEI, Volume 1 *Changing Economy in Indonesia: A Selection of Statistical Source Material from the Early 19th Century up to 1940, Volume 1 Indonesia's Export Crops 1816–1940* (Initiated by W.M.F. Mansvelt. Re-edited and continued by P. Creutzberg), The Hague: Martinus Nijhoff 1975.

CEI, Volume 2 *Changing Economy in Indonesia: A Selection of Statistical Source Material from the Early 19th Century up to 1940, Volume 2 Public Finance 1816–1940* (Initiated by W.M.F. Mansvelt. Re-edited and continued by P. Creutzberg), The Hague: Martinus Nijhoff 1976.

CEI, Volume 3 *Changing Economy in Indonesia: A Selection of Statistical Source Material from the Early 19th Century up to 1940, Volume 3 Expenditures on Fixed Assets* (Initiated by W.M.F. Mansvelt. Re-edited and continued by P. Creutzberg), The Hague: Martinus Nijhoff 1977.

CEI, Volume 4 *Changing Economy in Indonesia: A Selection of Statistical Source Material from the Early 19th Century up to 1940, Volume 4 Rice Prices* (Initiated by W.M.F. Mansvelt. Re-edited and continued by P. Creutzberg), The Hague: Martinus Nijhoff 1978.

CEI, Volume 5 *Changing Economy in Indonesia: A Selection of Statistical Source Material from the Early 19th Century up to 1940, Volume 5 National Income* (Initiated by W.M.F. Mansvelt. Re-edited and continued by P. Creutzberg), The Hague: Martinus Nijhoff 1979.

CEI, Volume 6 *Changing Economy in Indonesia: A Selection of Statistical Source Material from the Early 19th Century up to 1940, Volume 6 Money and Banking 1816–1940* (Edited by P. Creutzberg and J.T.M. van Laanen), The Hague: Martinus Nijhoff 1980.

CEI, Volume 7, *Changing Economy in Indonesia: A Selection of Statistical Source Material from the Early 19th Century up to 1940, Volume 7, Balance of Payments 1822–1939* (Edited by P. Boomgaard. Prepared by W.L. Korthals Altes) Amsterdam: Royal Tropical Institute 1987.

CEI, Volume 8, *Changing Economy in Indonesia: A Selection of Statistical Source Material from the Early 19th Century up to 1940, Volume 8, Manufacturing Industry 1870–1942* (Edited by P. Boomgaard. Prepared by W.A.I.M. Segers) Amsterdam: Royal Tropical Institute 1987.

CEI, Volume 9 *Changing Economy in Indonesia: A Selection of Statistical Source Material from the Early 19th Century up to 1940, Volume 9, Transport 1819–1940* (Edited by P. Boomgaard.) (Prepared by Gerrit J. Knapp) Amsterdam: Royal Tropical Institute 1989.

CEI, Volume 10, *Changing Economy in Indonesia: A Selection of Statistical Source Material from the Early 19th Century up to 1940, Volume 10, Food Crops and Arable Lands, Java 1815–1942,* (Edited by P. Boomgaard. Prepared by P. Boomgaard and J.L. van Zanden) Amsterdam: Royal Tropical Institute 1990.

CEI, Volume 11, *Changing Economy in Indonesia: A Selection of Statistical Source Material from the Early 19th Century up to 1940, Volume 11, Populataion Trends 1795–1942* (Edited by P. Boomgaard. Prepared by P. Boomgaard and A.J. Gooszen) Amsterdam: Royal Tropical Institute 1991.

CEI, Volume 12a, *Changing Economy in Indonesia: A Selection of Statistical Source Material from the Early 19th Century up to 1940, Volume 12a, General Trade Statistics 1822–1940* (Edited by P. Boomgaard. Prepared by W.L. Korthals Altes) Amsterdam: Royal Tropical Institute 1991.

CEI, Volume 12b, *Changing Economy in Indonesia: A Selection of Statistical Source Material from the Early 19th Century up to 1940, Volume 12b, Regional Patterns in Foreign Trade 1911–1940* (Edited by P. Boomgaard.

Prepared by Adrian Clemens, J. Thomas Lindblad and Jeroen Touwen) Amsterdam: Royal Tropical Institute 1992.

CEI, Volume 13, *Changing Economy in Indonesia: A Selection of Statistical Source Material from the Early 19th Century up to 1940, Volume 13, Wages 1820–1940* (Edited by P. Boomgaard. Prepared by Nico Dros) Amsterdam: Royal Tropical Institute 1992.

CEI, Volume 14, *Changing Economy in Indonesia: A Selection of Statistical Source Material from the Early 19th Century up to 1940, Volume 14, The Cultivation System, Java, 1834–80* (Edited by P. Boomgaard. Prepared by Frans van Baardewijk) Amsterdam: Royal Tropical Institute 1993.

CEI, Volume 15, *Changing Economy in Indonesia: A Selection of Statistical Source Material from the Early 19th Century up to 1940, Volume 15 Non-rice Prices* (Edited by P. Boomgaard. Prepared by W.L. Korthals Altes) Amsterdam: Royal Tropical Institute 1994.

Central Bureau of Statistics (1938), 'Prices, Price Indexes and Exchange Rates in Java, 1913–37', *Bulletin of the Central Bureau of Statistics 146*, Batavia: Department of Economic Affairs.

Central Bureau of Statistics (1939), 'The Living Conditions of Municipally Employed Coolies in Batavia in 1937' as translated and reprinted in *The Indonesian Town: Studies in Urban Sociology*, The Hague: W. van Hoeve 1958.

Central Bureau of Statistics (1970), *Pendapatan Nasional Indonesia 1960–8 (National Income of Indonesia)*, Jakarta: Central Bureau of Statistics.

Central Bureau of Statistics (1987), *Sensus Pertanian 1983 Seri I Sampel Pendapatan Petani*, Jakarta: Central Bureau of Statistics, August.

Central Bureau of Statistics (1990), *Survei Biaya Hidup 1989, Buku 2, Ibukota Propinsi di Jawa*, Jakarta: Central Bureau of Statistics, November .

Central Bureau of Statistics (1992), *Kemiskinan dan Pemerataan Pendapatan di Indonesia, 1976–1990*, Jakarta: Central Bureau of Statistics, February .

Central Bureau of Statistics (1994), *Sistem Neraca Sosial-Ekonomi Indonesia, 1990*, Jakarta: Central Bureau of Statistics.

Chailley-Bert, Joseph (1900), *Java et ses Habitants*, Paris: Armand Colin.

Chant, John and Mari Pangestu (1994), 'An Assessment of Financial Reform in Indonesia, 1983–1990' in Gerard Caprio, Izak Atiyas and James Hanson (eds), *Financial Reforms: Theory and Experience*, Cambridge: Cambridge University Press.

Chou, Ji (1995), 'Old and New Development Models: The Taiwanese Experience' in T. Ito and A. Krueger (eds), *Growth Theories in the Light of the East Asian Experience*, Chicago: University of Chicago Press.

Clarence-Smith, W.G. (1994), 'The Impact of Forced Coffee Cultivation on Java, 1805–1917', *Indonesia Circle*, No. 64, November, pp. 241–64.

Clark, Grover (1936), *The Balance Sheets of Imperialism: Facts and Figures on Colonies*, New York: Columbia University Press.

Cnossen, S. (1971), *The Indonesian Sales Tax*, Deventer: Kluwer.

Cole, David C. and Betty F. Slade (1996), *Building a Modern Financial System: The Indonesian Experience*, Cambridge: Cambridge University Press.

Corden, W.M. and J.A.C. Mackie (1962), 'Development of the Indonesian Exchange Rate System', *Malayan Economic Review*, Vol 7, April, pp. 37–60.

Corden, W.M. and Peter Warr (1982), 'The Petroleum Boom and Exchange Rate Policy in Indonesia, *Ekonomi dan Keuangan Indonesia*, Vol 29 (3), pp. 335–59.

Crawfurd, John (1820), *History of the Indonesian Archipelago in Three Volumes*, Edinburgh: Archibold Constable.

Creutzberg, P. (1972), *Het Ekonomisch Beleid in Nederlandsch-Indie, Eerste Stuk, (Economic Policy in the Netherlands-Indies: Selected Subjects with a Preface, Introduction and Survey of the Documents in English, First Volume)*, Groningen: Wolters-Noordhoff NV.

Creutzberg, P. (1975), *Het Ekonomisch Beleid in Nederlandsch-Indie, Derde Stuk, (Economic Policy in the Netherlands-Indies: Selected Subjects with a Preface, Introduction and Survey of the Documents in English, Third Volume)*, Groningen: Wolters-Noordhoff NV.

Cribb, Robert (1993), 'Development Policy in the Early 20th Century' in Jean-Paul Dirkse, Frans Husken and Mario Rutten (eds), *Development and Social Welfare: Indonesia's Experience under the New Order*, Leiden: KITLV Press.

Daroesman, Ruth (1971), 'Finance of Education, Part I', *Bulletin of Indonesian Economic Studies*, Vol 7 (3), pp. 61–95.

Daroesman, Ruth (1972), 'Finance of Education, Part II', *Bulletin of Indonesian Economic Studies*, Vol 8 (1), pp. 32–68.

Davis, Lance E. and Robert A. Huttenback (1986), *Mammon and the Pursuit of Empire: The Political Economy of British Imperialism, 1860–1912*, Cambridge: Cambridge University Press.

Day, Clive (1900), 'The Dutch Colonial Fiscal System' in *Essays in Colonial Finance: Publications of the American Economics Association, Third Series*, Vol 1(3), August.

Day, Clive (1904), *The Policy and Administration of the Dutch in Java*, New York: The Macmillan Company.

Department of Economic Affairs (1949) 'Economic Data on Indonesia to the end of 1948', *Economic Review of Indonesia*, Vol III (I), January–March, pp. 5–22.

Department of Information (1969), *The Five Year Development Plan, 1969–74*, Jakarta: Department of Information.

Department of Information (1993), *Lampiran Pidato Pertanggungjawaban Presiden/Mandataris MPR*, Jakarta: Department of Information.

Department of Information (1995), *Lampiran Pidato Kenegaraan 1994/95*, Jakarta: Department of Information.

Derksen, J.B.D. and J. Tinbergen (1980), 'Berekeningen over de economische betekenis van Nederlandsch-Indie voor Nederland' in C. Fasseur (ed.), *Geld en Geweten*, The Hague: M. Nijhoff.

Dick, H.W. (1979), 'Survey of Recent Developments', *Bulletin of Indonesian Economic Studies*, Vol 15 (1), pp. 1–44.

Dick, H.W. (1985), 'Survey of Recent Developments', *Bulletin of Indonesian Economic Studies*, Vol 21(3), December, pp. 1–29.

Dick, H.W. (1985a) 'The Rise of the Middle Class and the Changing Concept of Equity in Indonesia: An Interpretation', *Indonesia*, No 39, April, pp. 71–92.

Dick, H.W. (1993), 'Nineteenth-century Industrialisation: A Missed Opportunity' in J. Thomas Lindblad (ed.), *New Challenges in the Modern Economic History of Indonesia*, Leiden: Programme of Indonesian Studies.

Dick, H.W. (1993a), 'Oei Tiong Ham' in John Butcher and Howard Dick (eds), *The Rise and Fall of Revenue Farming: Business Elites and the Emergence of the Modern State in South East Asia*, London: Macmillan.

Dick, H.W. (1996), 'The Emergence of a National Economy, 1808–1990s', in J. Th. Lindblad (ed.), *The Historical Foundations of a National Economy in Indonesia, 1890s-1990s*, Amsterdam: North-Holland for the Royal Netherlands Academy of Arts and Sciences.

Dick, Howard and Dean Forbes (1992), 'Transport and Communications: A Quiet Revolution' in Anne Booth (ed.) (1992), *The Oil Boom and After: Economic Performance and Policy-making in the Soeharto Era*, Singapore: Oxford University Press.

Diehl, F. (1993), 'Revenue Farming and Colonial Finances in the Netherlands East Indies, 1816–1925' in John Butcher and Howard Dick (eds), *The Rise and Fall of Revenue Farming: Business Elites and the Emergence of the Modern State in South East Asia*, London: Macmillan.

Dixon, John (1984), 'Consumption' in Walter P. Falcon *et al.*, *The Cassava Economy of Java*, Stanford: Stanford University Press.

Dobbin, Christine (1980), 'Islam and Economic Change in Indonesia circa 1750–1930' in James J. Fox, *Indonesia: The Making of a Culture*, Canberra: Research School of Pacific Studies, Australian National University.

Dobbin, Christine (1983), *Islamic Revivalism in a Changing Peasant Economy: Central Sumatra, 1784-1847*, London: Curzon Press.

Dobbin, Christine (1994), 'Accounting for the Failure of the Muslim Javanese Business Class: Examples from Ponorogo and Tulungagung (c. 1880–1940), *Archipel*, Vol 48 pp. 87–101.

Doorn, J. van (1982), *Engineers and the Colonial System: Technocratic Tendencies in the Dutch East Indies*, Rotterdam: Comparative Asian Studies Programme, Erasmus University.

Doorn, J, van (1994), *De Laaste Eeuw van Indie: Ontwikkeling en Ondergang van een Koloniaal Project*, Amsterdam: Uitgeverij Bert Bakker.

Dowrick, S. (1992), 'Technological Catch Up and Diverging Incomes: Patterns of Economic Growth 1960–88', *Economic Journal*, Vol 102. pp. 600–10.

Drake, Peter (1972). 'Natural Resources and Foreign Borrowing in Economic Development' *Economic Journal*, Vol 82, pp. 951–62.

ECAFE (1961), *Economic Survey of Asia and the Far East, 1961*, Bangkok: United Nations Economic Commission for Asia and the Far East.

Edelstein, Michael (1982), *Overseas Investment in the Age of High Imperialism: the United Kingdom, 1850–1914*, London: Methuen.

Eeghen, Geertrui M. van (1937), 'The Beginnings of Industrialization in Netherlands India', *Far Eastern Survey*, Vol VI (12), pp. 129–33.

Eichengreen, Barry (1995), 'Financing Infrastructure in Developing Countries: Lessons from the Railway Age', *The World Bank Research Observer*, Vol 10 (1), February, pp. 75–92.

Elson, R.E. (1984), *Javanese Peasants and the Colonial Sugar Industry: Impact and Change in an East Java Residency, 1830–1940*, Singapore: Oxford University Press.

Elson, R.E. (1985), 'The Famine in Demak and Grobogan in 1849–50: Its Causes and Consequences', *Review of Indonesian and Malay Studies*, Vol 19 (1), pp. 39–85.

Elson, R.E. (1994), *Village Java under the Cultivation System: 1830–1870*, Sydney: Allen and Unwin for the ASAA.

Eng, Pierre van der (1991), 'An Observer of 65 Years of Socio-Economic Change in Indonesia: Egbert de Vries', *Bulletin of Indonesian Economic Studies*, Vol 27 (1), pp. 39–56.

Eng, Pierre van der (1992), 'The Real Domestic Product of Indonesia, 1880–1989', *Explorations in Economic History*, Vol 29, pp. 343–73.

Eng, Pierre van der (1993), *Agricultural Growth in Indonesia since 1880*, PhD dissertation, University of Groningen.

Eng, Pierre van der (1993a), 'Food Consumption and the Standard of Living in Indonesia, 1880–1990', *Economics Division Working Paper, 93/1*, Canberra: Research School of Pacific Studies, Australian National University.

Eng, Pierre van der (1993b), 'The 'Colonial Drain' from Indonesia, 1823–1990', *Economics Division Working Paper, 93/2*, Canberra: Research School of Pacific Studies, Australian National University.

Eng, Pierre van der (1994), *Food Supply in Java during the War and Decolonisation, 1940–1950*, Hull: Centre for South East Asian Studies.

Eng, Pierre van der (1994a), 'A Revolution in Indonesian Agriculture? A Long-term View on Agricultural Labour Productivity', Paper presented to the Colloquium on the Historical Foundations of a National Economy in Indonesia, 1890s–1990s, Amsterdam: Royal Netherlands Academy of Science, September. Published in Lindblad (1996).

Eng, Pierre van der (1996), 'Introduction' to N.P. van den Berg, *Currency and the Economy of Netherlands India, 1870–98*, Data Paper 5, Sources for the Economic History of Indonesia, Singapore: Institute of Southeast Asian Studies.

Eng, Pierre van der (1996a), *Agricultural Growth in Indonesia: Productivity Change and Policy Impact since 1880*, London: Macmillan Press.

Esmara, Hendra (1975), 'Regional Income Disparities', *Bulletin of Indonesian Economic Studies*, Vol 11 (1), pp. 41–57.

Esmara, Hendra (1986), *Perencanaan dan Pembangunan di Indonesia* (Planning and Development in Indonesia), Jakarta: Gramedia.

Fane, George and Chris Phillips (1991), 'Effective Protection in Indonesia in 1987', *Bulletin of Indonesian Economic Studies*, Vol 27 (1), April pp.105–26.

Fasseur, Cees (1978), 'Some Remarks on the Cultivation System in Java' *Acta Historiae Neerlandicae*, Vol 10, pp.130–62 .

Fasseur, Cees (1986), 'The Cultivation System and its Impact on the Dutch Colonial Economy and the Indigenous Society in Nineteenth-Century Java' in C.A. Bayly and D.H.A. Kolff (eds), *Two Colonial Empires*, Dordrecht: Martinus Nijhoff.

Fasseur, Cees (1991), 'Purse or Principle: Dutch Colonial Policy in the 1860s and the Decline of the Cultivation System', *Modern Asian Studies*, Vol 25 (1), pp. 33–52.

Fasseur, Cees (1992), *The Politics of Colonial Exploitation: Java, the Dutch and the Cultivation System* (Edited by R.E.Elson), Ithaca: Cornell University Southeast Asia Program.

Feinstein, Charles (1988), 'National Statistics 1760–1920' in Charles H. Feinstein and Sydney Pollard (eds), *Studies in Capital Formation in the United Kingdom, 1750–1920*, Oxford: Clarendon Press.

Feith, Herbert (1962), *The Decline of Constitutional Democracy in Indonesia*, Ithaca: Cornell University Press.

Fernando, M.R. (1996), 'Growth of Non-agricultural Economic Activities in Java in the Middle Decades of the Nineteenth Century', *Modern Asian Studies*, Vol 30 (1), February, pp. 77–119.

Fernando, M.R. and David Bulbeck (1992), *Chinese Economic Activity in Netherlands India: Selected Translations from the Dutch*, Data Paper Series no. 2, Sources for the Economic History of Southeast Asia, Singapore: Institute of Southeast Asian Studies.

Fowler, John A. (1923), *Netherlands East Indies and British Malaya: A Commercial and Industrial Handbook*, Washington: Government Printing Office for the Department of Commerce.

Fruin, Th. A. (1938), 'Popular and Rural Credit in the Netherlands Indies', *Bulletin of the Colonial Institute of Amsterdam*, Vol 1, pp. 106–7, 161–75.

Furnivall, J.S. (1934a), 'State and Private Money Lending in Netherlands India', *Studies in the Economic and Social Development of the Netherlands East Indies, IIIb*, Rangoon: Burma Book Club.

Furnivall, J.S. (1934b), 'State Pawnshops in Netherlands India', *Studies in the Economic and Social Development of the Netherlands East Indies, IIIc*, Rangoon: Burma Book Club.

Furnivall, J.S. (1943), *Educational Progress in Southeast Asia*, New York: International Secretariat, Institute of Pacific Relations.

Furnivall, J.S. (1944), *Netherlands India, A Study of Plural Economy*, Cambridge: Cambridge University Press.

Furnivall, J.S. (1948), *Colonial Policy and Practice: A Comparative Study of Burma and Netherlands India*, Cambridge: University Press.

Gardiner, Peter and Mayling Oey (1987), 'Morbidity and Mortality in Java, 1880–1940: The Evidence of the Colonial Reports' in Norman G. Owen (ed.), *Death and Disease in Southeast Asia: Explorations in Social, Medical and Demographic History*, Singapore: Oxford University Press .

Geertz, Clifford (1965), *The Social History of an Indonesian Town*: Cambridge: The MIT Press.

Gelderen, J. van (1927), 'The Economics of the Tropical Colony' as translated and reprinted in *Indonesian Economics: The Concept of Dualism in Theory and Practice*, The Hague: W. van Hoeve (second edition, 1966).

Gelderen, J. van (1929), 'Western Enterprises and the Density of the Population in the Netherlands Indies' in B. Schrieke (ed.), *The Effect of Western Influence on Native Civilisations in the Malay Archipelago*, Batavia: Kolff.

Gelderen, J. van (1939), *The Recent Development of Economic Foreign Policy in the Netherlands East Indies*, London: Longmans, Green.

Glamann, K. (1958), *Dutch-Asiatic Trade, 1620–1740*, The Hague: M. Nijhoff.

Glassburner, Bruce (1962), 'Economic Policy-Making in Indonesia, 1950–1957' as reprinted in Glassburner (1971) (*op. cit.*).

Glassburner, Bruce (ed.) (1971), *The Economy of Indonesia: Selected Readings*, Ithaca: Cornell University Press.

Glassburner, Bruce (1973), 'The January 1973 Tariff Revision', *Bulletin of Indonesian Economic Studies*, Vol 9(3), November, pp.103–8.

Glassburner, Bruce (1976), 'In the Wake of General Ibnu: Crisis in the Indonesian Oil Industry', *Asian Survey*, XVI (12), pp. 1099–112.

Glassburner, Bruce (1986), 'Survey of Recent Developments', *Bulletin of Indonesian Economic Studies*, Vol 22(1), pp. 1–33.

Goh, Taro (1986), 'Review of the Nineteenth and Early Twentieth Century Debate on the Origin of Communal Landownership with Special Reference to Java', *Masyarakat Indonesia*, Vol XIII (3), pp. 243–76.

Golay, Frank (1976), 'Southeast Asia: The 'Colonial Drain' Revisited' in C.D. Cowan and O.W. Wolters (eds), *Southeast Asian History and Historiography*, Ithaca: Cornell University Press.

Gonggrijp, G. (1931), 'Repartition des Activities Economiques entre les Colonies et la Metropole', Proceedings of the Institut Colonial International, XXI Session, Paris, May.

Gore, W.G.A. Ormsby (1928), *Report by the Right Honourable W.G.A. Ormsby Gore MP (Under-Secretary of State for the Colonies) on his visit to Malaysia, Ceylon and Java during the Year 1928*, London: HMSO (Cmd 3235).

Gotz, J.F.F. (1939), 'Railways in the Netherlands Indies', *Bulletin of the Colonial Institute of Amsterdam*, Vol 2(4), pp. 267–90.

Gotzen, L. (1933), 'Volksinkomen en Belasting', *Koloniale Studien*, Vol 17, pp. 449–84.

Gray, Clive (1982), 'Survey of Recent Developments', *Bulletin of Indonesian Economic Studies*, Vol XVIII (3), November, pp. 1–51.

Grenville, Stephen (1979), 'The Price of Rice and Inflation', *Ekonomi dan Keuangan Indonesia*, Vol XXVII (3), September, pp. 317–29.

Griffiths, Richard T. (1979), *Industrial Retardation in the Netherlands, 1830–50*, The Hague: M. Nijhoff.

Gurley, J. and E.S. Shaw (1960), *Money in a Theory of Finance*, Washington: Brookings Institution.

Halevi, Nadav (1971), 'An Empirical Test of the 'Balance of Payments Stages' Hypothesis', *Journal of International Economics*, Vol 1(1), pp. 103–17.

Hanson, John R. (1975), 'Exchange Rate Movements and Economic Development in the Late Nineteenth Century: A Critique', *Journal of Political Economy*, Vol 83, August, pp. 859–62.

Hanson, John R. (1980), *Trade in Transition: Exports from the Third World*, New York: Academic Press.

Hardjono, Joan (1977), *Transmigration in Indonesia*, Kuala Lumpur: Oxford University Press.

Hardon, H.J. (1948), 'Industrial Recovery in Indonesia', *Economic Review of Indonesia*, Vol 2(10), October-December, pp. 161–70.

Hasselman, C.J. (1914), *Algemeen Overzicht van de Uitkomsten van het Welvaart-Onderzoek, Gehouden op Java en Madoera in 1904–1905*, s'Gravenhage: Nijhoff.

Headrick, Daniel R. (1981), *The Tools of Empire: Technology and European Imperialism in the Nineteenth Century*, New York: Oxford University Press.

Heneveld, Ward (1978), 'The Distribution of Development Funds: New School Building in East Java', *Bulletin of Indonesian Economic Studies*, Vol 14 (1), pp. 63–79.

Henry, Yves (1926) 'Le Credit Populaire Agricole et Commercial aux Indes Neerlandaises', *Bulletin Economique de l'Indochine*, Vol 29, pp. 69–124.

Hicks, George (1966), 'The Indonesian Inflation', *Philippine Economic Journal*, Vol 6(2), pp. 210–24.

Higgins, Benjamin (1953), 'The Rationale of Import Surcharges', *Ekonomi dan Keuangan Indonesia*, Vol VI (5), May, pp. 228–36.

Higgins, Benjamin (1956), 'The Dualistic Theory of Underdeveloped Areas', *Economic Development and Cultural Change*, January, pp. 99–112.

Higgins, Benjamin (1957), *Indonesia's Economic Stabilization and Development*, New York: Institute of Pacific Relations.

Higgins, Benjamin (1968), 'Indonesia: The Chronic Dropout' in *Economic Development: Principles, Problems and Policies*, London: Constable.

Higgins, Benjamin (1984), 'Jan Boeke and the Doctrine of 'The Little Push', *Bulletin of Indonesian Economic Studies*, Vol 20 (3), pp. 55–69.

Hill, Hal (1980), 'Dualism, Technology and Small-scale Enterprise in the Indonesian Weaving Industry' in R.G. Garnaut and P.T. McCawley (eds), *Indonesia: Dualism, Growth and Poverty*, Canberra: Research School of Pacific Studies, Australian National University.

Hill, Hal (1983), 'Choice of Technique in the Indonesian Weaving Industry', *Economic Development and Cultural Change*, Vol 31(2), pp. 337–54.

Hill, Hal (1988), *Foreign Investment and Industrialization in Indonesia*, Singapore: Oxford University Press.

Hill, Hal (1990), 'Ownership in Indonesia' in Hal Hill and Terry Hull (eds), *Indonesia Assessment 1990, Political and Social Change Monograph 11*, Canberra: Department of Political and Social Change, Australian National University.

Hill, Hal (1992), 'Manufacturing Industry' in Anne Booth (ed.), *The Oil Boom and After: Indonesian Economic Policy and Performance in the Soeharto Era*, Singapore: Oxford University Press.

Hill, Hal (1995), 'Indonesia's Great Leap Forward? Technology Development and Policy Issues', *Bulletin of Indonesian Economic Studies*, Vol 31(2), pp. 83–123.

Hill, Hal (1996), 'Indonesia's Industrial Policy and Performance: 'Orthodoxy' Vindicated', *Economic Development and Cultural Change*, Vol 45(1), pp. 147–74.

Houben, Vincent (1994), 'Profit versus Ethics: Government Enterprises in the Late Colonial State' in Robert Cribb (ed.), *The Late Colonial State in Indonesia: Political and Economic Foundations of the Netherlands Indies, 1880–1942*, Leiden: KITLV Press.

Huff, W.G. (1994), *The Economic Growth of Singapore: Trade and Development in the 20th Century*, Cambridge University Press.

Hughenholtz, W.R. (1986) 'Famine and Food Supply in Java, 1830–1914', in C.A. Bayly and D.H.A. Kolff (eds), *Two Colonial Empires*, Dordrecht: Martinus Nijhoff.

Hugo, Graeme J. (1980), 'Population Movements in Indonesia During the Colonial Period' in James J. Fox, *Indonesia: The Making of a Culture*, Canberra: Research School of Pacific Studies, Australian National University.

Huizer, Gerrit (1980), *Peasant Movements and Their Counterforces in South East Asia*, New Delhi: Marwah Publications.

Hull, Terence H. and Valerie J. Hull (1992), 'Population and Health Policies' in Anne Booth (ed.), *The Oil Boom and After: Indonesian Economic Policy and Performance in the Soeharto Era*, Singapore: Oxford University Press.

Hunter, Alex (1966), 'The Indonesian Oil Industry', *Australian Economic Papers*, Vol 5(1), June, pp. 59–106.

Husken, Frans (1994), 'Declining Welfare in Java: Government and Private Inquiries, 1903–1914' in Robert Cribb (ed.), *The Late Colonial State in Indonesia: Political and Economic Foundations of the Netherlands Indies, 1880–1942*, Leiden: KITLV Press.

Hutasoit, M. (1954), *Compulsory Education in Indonesia*, Paris: UNESCO.

Imlah, Albert Henry (1958), *Economic Elements in the Pax Britannica: Studies in British Foreign Trade in the Nineteenth Century*, New York: Russell and Russell.

Indisch Verslag: see under *Jaarcijfers*.

Ingleson, John (1988), 'Urban Java during the Depression', *Journal of Southeast Asian Studies*, Vol XIX (2), pp. 292–309.

Ingram, James C. (1971), *Economic Change in Thailand, 1850–1970*, Kuala Lumpur: Oxford University Press.

International Customs Tariffs Bureau (1937), *Bulletin International des Douanes/International Customs Journal: Netherlands East Indies*, Brussels: International Customs Tariffs Bureau, March.

International Monetary Fund (1980), *Government Finance Statistics Yearbook, 1980*, Washington: International Monetary Fund.

International Monetary Fund (1995), *Government Finance Statistics Yearbook, 1995*, Washington: International Monetary Fund.

Ismael, J. (1980), 'Money and Credit Policy in Indonesia, 1966 to 1979', *Ekonomi dan Keuangan Indonesia*, Vol 28(1), pp. 97–107.

Jaarcijfers voor het Koninkrijk der Nederlanden: Kolonien (*Annual Statistics for the Kingdom of the Netherlands: Colonies*), A series of statistical yearbooks first published in 1887; after 1897 they were compiled by the Central Bureau of Statistics in the Netherlands. The part dealing with the colonies contained many data series derived from the annual *Koloniale Verslag* (Colonial Report). After 1922 it was replaced by the *Statistisch Jaaroverzicht van Nederlandsch-Indie* (SJO), which was in turn replaced by the second part of the *Indisch Verslag* in 1931. These publications form a continual statistical record for the last five decades of the Dutch colonial era. A series of *Statistisch Zakboekje* (Statistical Pocketbooks) were published by the Central Bureau of Statistics in Batavia in the 1930s, and in 1947. This series was continued after independence, and since 1975 a *Statistical Yearbook of Indonesia* has also been published annually by the Central Bureau of Statistics in Jakarta.

Java Bank (1953), *Report for the Financial Year 1952–1953*, Jakarta: G. Kolff.

Johnson, Chalmers (1982), *MITI and the Japanese Miracle: The Growth of Industrial Policy, 1925–1975*, Stanford: Stanford University Press.

Jones, G.W. (1966), 'The Growth and Changing Structure of the Indonesian Labour Force', *Bulletin of Indonesian Economic Studies*, Number 4, June, pp. 50–74.

Jones, Russell (1994), 'George Windsor Earl and 'Indonesia'', *Indonesia Circle*, No. 64, November, pp. 265–78.

Kahin, George Mc Turnan (1952), *Nationalism and Revolution in Indonesia*, Ithaca: Cornell University Press.

KAMI (1966), *Jalur Baru Sesudah Runtuhnya Ekonomi Terpimpin (The Leader, the Man and the Gun)*, Seminar KAMI Fakultas Ekonomi, Universitas Indonesia, January 1966, Jakarta: Sinar Harapan, 1984 (reprint).

Kano, H. (1977), *Land Tenure System and the Desa Community in Nineteenth Century Java*, Tokyo: Institute of Developing Economies.

Kano, H. (1989), 'Indonesian Business Groups and their Leaders', *East Asian Cultural Studies*, Vol 28, March, pp. 145–72.

Kensington, A. (1892), 'Note on the Present Working of the Gold Standard in Java', in van den Berg (1895).

Keuning, Steven J. (1991), 'Allocation and Composition of Fixed Capital Stock in Indonesia: An Indirect Estimate Using Incremental Capital Value Added Ratios', *Bulletin of Indonesian Economic Studies*, Vol 27 (2), pp. 91–120.

Keyfitz, Nathan (1989), 'Putting Trained Labour Power to Work: The Dilemma of Education and Employment' *Bulletin of Indonesian Economic Studies*, Vol 25 (3), pp. 35–55.

Kidron, M (1965), *Foreign Investment in India*, Cambridge University Press.

Kiernan, V.G. (1995), *Imperialism and its Contradictions* (ed. Harvey J. Kaye), New York: Routledge.

King, Dwight and Peter Weldon (1977), 'Income Distribution and Levels of Living in Java, 1963–70', *Economic Development and Cultural Change*, Vol 25(4), July, pp. 699–711.

Klasing, H. (1948), 'The Recovery of the Java Sugar Industry', *The Economic Review of Indonesia*, Vol II (2), February, pp. 17–23.

Knight, G.R. (1985), ' 'The People's own Cultivations': Rice and Second Crops in Pekalongan Residency, North Java, in the Mid-Nineteenth Century', *Review of Indonesian and Malaysian Affairs*, Vol 19(1), Winter, pp. 1–38.

Knight, G.R. (1988), 'Peasant Labour and Capitalist Production in Late Colonial Indonesia: The 'Campaign' at a North Java Sugar Factory, 1840–70', *Journal of Southeast Asian Studies*, Vol XIX (2), pp. 245–65.

Kolff, G.H. van der (1941), 'Brown and White Economy: Unity in Diversity' as translated and reprinted in *Indonesian Economics: The Concept of Dualism in Theory and Practice*, The Hague: W. van Hoeve (second edition, 1966).

Kolff, G.H. van der (1956), 'An Economic Case Study: Sugar and Welfare in Java' in Phillips Ruoff (ed.), *Approaches to Community Development*, The Hague: W. van Hoeve.

Kraan, Alfons van der (1993), 'Bali and Lombok in the World Economy, 1830–50', *Review of Indonesian and Malaysian Affairs*, Vol 27 (1 and 2), pp. 91–105.

Kraan, Alfons van der (1994), 'Bali 1848', *Indonesia Circle*, No. 62, March, pp. 1–57.

Kraan, Alfons van der (1996), 'Anglo-Dutch Rivalry in the Java Cotton Trade', *Indonesia Circle*, No. 68, March, pp. 35–64.

Kristov, Lorenzo (1995), 'The Price of Electricity in Indonesia', *Bulletin of Indonesian Economic Studies*, Vol 31 (3), pp. 73–101.

Kroef, van der Justus M. (1958), 'Disunited Indonesia', *Far Eastern Survey*, Vol XXVII (4), April, pp. 49–63.

Krueger, Anne O. (1968), 'Factor Endowments and Per Capita Income Differences Among Countries', *Economic Journal*, Vol 78, pp. 641–59.

Kuitenbrouwer, Maarten (1991), *The Netherlands and the Rise of Modern Imperialism: Colonies and Foreign Policy 1870–1902*, New York and Oxford: Berg.

Kumar, Ann (1980), 'The Peasantry and the State on Java: Changes of Relationship, Seventeenth to Nineteenth Centuries' in J.A.C. Mackie (ed.), *Indonesia: The Making of a Nation*, Canberra: Research School of Pacific Studies, Australian National University.

Laanen, Jan T.M. van (1979), 'Het Bestedingspakket van de 'Inheemse' Bevolking op Java (1921–1939)' in F. van Anrooij *et al.* (eds), *Between People and Statistics: Essays on Modern Indonesian History presented to P. Creutzberg*, The Hague: Martinus Nijhoff.

Laanen, Jan T.M. van (1982), *The World Depression (1929–1935) and the Indigenous Economy in Netherlands India*, Occasional Paper No 13, Centre for Southeast Asian Studies, James Cook University of North Queensland.

Laanen, Jan T.M. van (1989), 'Per Capita Income Growth in Indonesia, 1850–1940' in Angus Maddison and Ge Prince (eds), *Economic Growth in Indonesia, 1820–1940*, Dordrecht : Foris Publications.

Laanen, Jan T.M. van (1990), 'Between the Java Bank and the Chinese Moneylender: Banking and Credit in Colonial Indonesia', in Anne Booth, W.J. O'Malley and Anna Weidemann (eds), *Indonesian Economic History in the Dutch Colonial Era*, Monograph Series 35, New Haven: Yale University Southeast Asian Studies.

Ladejinsky, Wolf (1977), *Agrarian Reform as Unfinished Business: Selected Papers of Wolf Ladejinsky*, New York: Oxford University Press.

Lakdawala, D.T. (1946), *Justice in Taxation in India*, Bombay: Popular Book Depot.

Lal, Deepak (1988), *The Hindu Equilibrium: Volume 1, Cultural Stability and Economic Stagnation*, Oxford: Clarendon Press.

Leff, Nathaniel (1979), ' 'Monopoly Capitalism' and Public Policy in Developing Countries', *Kyklos* Vol 32(4), pp. 718–38.

Leff, Nathaniel (1982), *Underdevelopment and Development in Brazil Vol 2 Reassessing the Obstacles to Development*, London: George Allen and Unwin.

Legge, J.D. (1961), *Central Authority and Regional Autonomy in Indonesia: A Study of Local Administration 1950–60*, Ithaca: Cornell University Press.

Legge, J.D. (1990), 'Review: Indonesia's Diversity Revisited', *Indonesia*, April, pp.127–31.

LEKNAS (1965), *Masalah-Masalah Ekonomi dan Faktor Ipolsos (Ideologi, Politik, Sosial)*, Jakarta: Lembaga Ekonomi dan Kemasjarakatan Nasional.

Lewis, W.A. (1969), *Aspects of Tropical Trade, 1883–1965*, Stockholm: Almqvist and Wiksell.

Lewis, W.A. (ed.) (1970), *Tropical Development 1880–1913: Studies in Economic Progress*, London: George Allen and Unwin.

Lewis, W.A. (1972) 'Reflections on Unlimited Labour' in L. di Marco (ed.) *International Economics and Development*, New York: Academic Press.

Lewis, W.A. (1978), *Growth and Fluctuations: 1870–1913*, London: Allen and Unwin.

Lindblad, J. Thomas (1988), *Between Dayak and Dutch: The Economic History of Southeast Kalimantan, 1880–1942*, Dordrecht: Foris Publications.

Lindblad, J. Thomas (1989), 'Economic Aspects of the Dutch Expansion in Indonesia, 1870–1914', *Modern Asian Studies*, Vol 23(1), 1–24.

Lindblad, J. Thomas (1990), 'The Process of Economic Development in the Outer Provinces of the Dutch East Indies', *Journal of the Japan–Netherlands Institute*, Vol II, pp. 208–34.

Lindblad, J. Thomas (1991), 'Foreign Investment in Late-Colonial and Post-Colonial Indonesia', *Economic and Social History in the Netherlands*, 3, pp. 183–208.

Lindblad, J. Thomas (ed.) (1996) *The Historical Foundations of a National Economy in Indonesia, 1890s–1990s*, Amsterdam: North-Holland for the Royal Netherlands Academy of Arts and Sciences.

Lindsay, Holly (1989), 'The Indonesian Log Export Ban: An Estimation of Foregone Export Earnings', *Bulletin of Indonesian Economic Studies*, Vol 25(2), pp. 111–23.

Little, Ian M.D. (1982), *Economic Development: Theory, Policy and International Relations*, New York: Basic Books.

Locher-Scholten, Elsbeth (1994), 'Dutch Expansion in the Indonesian Archipelago around 1900 and the Imperialism Debate', *Journal of Southeast Asian Studies*, Vol 25(1), 91–111.

Lucas, Robert (1990), 'Why Doesn't Capital Flow from Rich to Poor Countries?', *American Economic Review*, Vol 80 (2), pp. 92–6.

Mackie, J.A.C (1961), 'Indonesia's Government Estates and Their Masters', *Pacific Affairs*, Vol 34(4), pp. 337–60.

Mackie, J.A.C. (1964), 'The Indonesian Economy: 1950–63' as reprinted in Bruce Glassburner (ed.), *The Economy of Indonesia: Selected Readings*, Ithaca: Cornell University Press 1971.

Mackie, J.A.C. (1967), *Problems of the Indonesian Inflation*, Ithaca: Cornell University Southeast Asia Program, Modern Indonesia Project Monograph Series.

Mackie, J.A.C. (1980), 'Integrating and centrifugal factors in Indonesian politics since 1945' in J.A.C. Mackie (ed.), *Indonesia: The Making of a Nation*, Canberra: Research School of Pacific Studies, Australian National University.

Mackie, J.A.C. (1985), 'The Changing Political Economy of an Export Crop: The Case of Jember's Tobacco Industry', *Bulletin of Indonesian Economic Studies*, Vol XXI (1), pp. 113–39.

Mackie, J.A.C. (1991), 'Towkays and Tycoons: The Chinese in Indonesian Economic Life in the 1920s and the 1980s', *Indonesia, Special Issue: The Role of the Chinese in Shaping Modern Indonesian Life*, Ithaca: Cornell University Modern Indonesia Project.

Mackie, J.A.C. and Sjahrir (1989), 'Survey of Recent Developments', *Bulletin of Indonesian Economic Studies*, Vol 25 (3), pp. 3–34.

Maddison, Angus (1989), 'Dutch Income in and from Indonesia, 1700–1938', in Angus Maddison and Ge Prince (eds), *Economic Growth in Indonesia, 1820–1940*, Dordrecht: Foris Publications.

Maddison, Angus (1990), 'The Colonial Burden: A Comparative Perspective' in M. Scott and D. Lal, *Public Policy and Economic Development; Essays in Honour of Ian Little*, Oxford: Clarendon Press.

Maddison, Angus (1991), 'Dutch Income in and from Indonesia, 1700–1938', *Modern Asian Studies*, Vol 23(4), October, pp. 645–70.

Maddison, Angus (1995), *Monitoring the World Economy, 1820–1992*, Paris: OECD.

Manning, Chris (1994), 'What has Happened to Wages in the New Order?', *Bulletin of Indonesian Economic Studies*, Vol 30(3), pp. 73–114.

Mathews, R.C.O. (1986), 'The Economics of Institutions and the Sources of Growth', *Economic Journal*, 96, pp. 903–18.

McCawley, Peter (1978), 'Some Consequences of the Pertamina Crisis in Indonesia', *Journal of Southeast Asian Studies*, Vol IX (1), March, pp. 1–27.

McCawley, Peter (1979), 'Industrialisation in Indonesia: Developments and Prospects', *Development Studies Centre Occasional Paper 13*, Canberra: Australian National University.

McCawley, Peter (1980), 'Indonesia's New Balance of Payments Problem; A Surplus to Get Rid Of', *Ekonomi dan Keuangan Indonesia*, Vol 28 (1), pp. 39–58.

McCawley, Peter (1981), 'The Growth of the Industrial Sector' in Anne Booth and Peter McCawley (eds), *The Indonesian Economy During the Soeharto Era*, Kuala Lumpur: Oxford University Press.

McCawley, Peter (1982), 'The Economics of Ekonomi Pancasila', *Bulletin of Indonesian Economic Studies*, Vol XVIII (1), March, 102–9.

McKendrick, David (1992), 'Obstacles to Catch-Up: The Case of the Indonesian Aircraft Industry', *Bulletin of Indonesian Economic Studies*, 28(1), pp. 39–66.

McVey, Ruth (1982), 'The *Beamtenstaat* in Indonesia' in Ben Anderson and Audrey Kahin (eds), *Interpreting Indonesian Politics: Thirteen Contributions to the Debate*, Ithaca: Cornell Modern Indonesia Project, pp. 84–92.

Mears, Leon (1981), *The New Rice Economy of Indonesia*, Yogyakarta: Gadjah Mada University Press.

Mears, Leon (1984), 'Rice and Food Self-sufficiency in Indonesia', *Bulletin of Indonesian Economic Studies*, Vol 20 (2), pp. 122–38.

Mears, Leon A. and Saleh Affif (1968), 'A New Look at the Bimas Program and Rice Production', *Bulletin of Indonesian Economic Studies*, No 10, pp. 29–47.

Meel, H. de (1950), 'Planning in Indonesia', *Economic Review of Indonesia*, Vol IV (4), pp. 127–9.

Meier, Gerald M. (1975), 'External Trade and Internal Development' in Peter Duigan and L.H. Gann (eds), *Colonialism in Africa 1870–1960, Vol 4, The Economics of Colonialism*, Cambridge: Cambridge University Press.

Meijer Ranneft, J.W. and W. Huender (1926), *Onderzoek Naar den Belastingdruk op de Inlandsche Bevolking*, Weltevreden: Lands Drukkerij.

Meilink-Roelofsz, M.A.P. (1962), *Asian Trade and European Influence in the Indonesian Archipelago between 1500 and about 1630*, The Hague: M. Nijhoff.

Mertens, Walter (1978), 'Population Census Data on Agricultural Activities in Indonesia', *Majalah Demografi Indonesia*, No. 9, June, pp. 9–53.

Metcalf, John E. (1952), *The Agricultural Economy of Indonesia*, Washington: US Department of Agriculture.

Metzelaar, J. Th. (1946), 'Irrgatie' in C.J.J. van Hall and C. van der Koppel (eds), *De Landbouw in den Indischen Archipel*, The Hague: Van Hoeve.

Meulen, W.A. van der (1940), 'Irrigation in the Netherlands Indies', *Bulletin of the Colonial Institute of Amsterdam*, Vol 3, pp. 142–59.

Miller, Robert R. and Mariusz Sumlinski (1994), 'Trends in Private Investment in Developing Countries 1994: Statistics for 1970–92', *Discussion Paper 20*, Washington: International Finance Corporation.

Minami, Ryoshin (1986), *The Economic Development of Japan: A Quantitative Study*, London: Macmillan Press.

Mitchell, B. (1982), *International Historical Statistics: Africa and Asia*, London: Macmillan.

Mokyr, Joel (1984), 'Disparities, Gaps and Abysses' *Economic Development and Cultural Change*, Vol 33(1), pp. 173–8.

Money, J.W.B. (1861), *Java or How to Manage a Colony*, London: Hurst and Blackett.

Mortimer, Rex (1974), *Indonesian Communism under Soekarno: Ideology and Politics*, Ithaca: Cornell University Press.

Muir, Ross (1986), 'Survey of Recent Developments', *Bulletin of Indonesian Economic Studies*, Vol XXII (2), August, pp. 1–27.

Muljatno (1960), 'Perhitungan Pendapatan Nasional Indonesia untuk Tahun 1953 dan 1954', *Ekonomi dan Keuangan Indonesia*, Vol 13, pp. 162–211.

Myint, Hla (1971), *Economic Theory and Underdeveloped Countries*, New York: Oxford University Press.

Myint, Hla (1973), *The Economics of the Developing Countries*, London: Hutchinson (fourth edition).

Myint, Hla (1984), 'Inward and Outward-looking Countries Revisited: The Case of Indonesia', *Bulletin of Indonesian Economic Studies*, Vol XX(2), pp. 39–52.

Napitupulu, B. (1968), 'Hunger in Indonesia', *Bulletin of Indonesian Economic Studies*, No. 9, pp. 60–70.

Nasution, Adnan Buyung (1992), *The Aspiration for Constitutional Government in Indonesia*, Jakarta: Pustaka Sinar Harapan.

Nasution, Anwar (1993), 'Reforms of the Financial Sector in Indonesia, 1983–91' *The Indonesian Quarterly*, Vol XXI(3), pp. 284–310.

Natsir, M. (1950), 'Government Statement: Economic and Financial Sections', *Economic Review of Indonesia (Supplement)*, Vol 4(3), July–September, pp. 1–6.

Natsir, Mohammad (1951), 'A Review of Indonesia's Reconstruction' *Indonesian Review*, Vol 1(1), January, pp. 49–59.

Naval Intelligence Division (1944), *Netherlands East Indies, Vol II*, Cambridge: Naval Intelligence Division Geographical Handbook Series.

Niel, Robert van (1956), *Living Conditions of Plantation Workers in 1939–1940: Final Report of the Coolie Budget Commission*, Translation Series, Modern Indonesia Project, Ithaca: Cornell University .

Niel, Robert van (1992), *Java under the Cultivation System*, Leiden: KITLV Press.

Nishijima, Shigetada and Kishi Koicho (eds) (1963), *Japanese Military Administration in Indonesia*, Washington: U.S. Department of Commerce Office of Technical Services.

North, Douglass C. (1981), *Structure and Change in Economic History*, New York: W.W. Norton.

North, Douglass C. (1990), *Institutions, Institutional Change and Economic Performance*, Cambridge: Cambridge University Press.

Nugent, J. (1973), 'Exchange-Rate Movements and Economic Development in the Late Nineteenth Century', *Journal of Political Economy*, Vol 81, September pp. 1110–35.

Nugroho (1967), *Indonesia: Facts and Figures*, Jakarta: Central Bureau of Statistics.

Ochse, J.J and G.J.A. Terra (1934), 'The Agricultural and Economic Conditions of the Natives and their Food Consumption', in *The Function of Money and Products in Relation to Native Diet and Physical Condition in Koetowinangoen (Java)*, Bogor: Department of Economic Affairs.

Oey, Beng To (1991), *Sejarah Kebijakan Moneter Indonesia (A History of Monetary Policy in Indonesia)*, Vol 1, Jakarta: Lembaga Pengembangan Perbankan Indonesia.

Ohkawa, K. and H. Kohama (1989), *Lectures on Developing Economies: Japan's Experience and its Relevance*, Tokyo: University of Tokyo Press.

Ohkawa, K. and M. Shinohara with L. Meissner (eds) (1979), *Patterns of Japanese Economic Development: A Quantitative Appraisal*, New Haven: Yale University Press.

O'Malley, W.J. (1979), 'The Bengkalis Hunger Riots of 1935' in F. van Anrooij *et al.* (eds), *Between People and Statistics: Essays on Modern Indonesian History presented to P. Creutzberg*, The Hague: Martinus Nijhoff.

O'Malley, W.J. (1990) 'Introduction' in Anne Booth, W.J. O'Malley and Anna Weidemann (eds), *Indonesian Economic History in the Dutch Colonial Era*, Monograph Series 35, New Haven: Yale University Southeast Asian Studies.

Oorschot, H.J. van (1956), *De Ontwikkeling van de Nijverheid in Indonesie*, The Hague: W. van Hoeve.

Paauw, Douglas S. (1960), *Financing Economic Development: The Indonesian Case*, Glencoe: The Free Press.

Paauw, Douglas S. (1963), 'From Colonial to Guided Economy' in Ruth McVey (ed.), *Indonesia*, New Haven: HRAF Press.

Paauw, Douglas S. (1969), 'Economic Progress in Southeast Asia', in Robert O. Tilman (ed.), *Man, State and Society in Contemporary Southeast Asia*, London: Pall Mall Press.

Paauw, Douglas (1978), 'Exchange Rate Policy and Non-Extractive Exports' *Ekonomi dan Keuangan Indonesia*, Vol XXVI (2), June, pp. 205–20.

Paauw, Douglas (1981), 'Frustrated Labour-Intensive Development: The Case of Indonesia' in Eddy Lee (ed.), *Export-led Industrialisation and Development*, Bangkok: ILO-ARTEP.

Palmer, Ingrid (1972), *Textiles in Indonesia: Problems of Import Substitution*, New York: Praeger Publishers.

Palmer, Ingrid (1977), *The New Rice in Indonesia*, Geneva: United Nations Research Institute for Social Development.

Pangestu, Mari (1987), 'Survey of Recent Developments', *Bulletin of Indonesian Economic Studies*, Vol 23(1), pp. 1–39.

Pangestu, Mari (1993), 'The Role of the State and Economic Development in Indonesia', *The Indonesian Quarterly*, Vol XXI (3), pp. 253–83.

Pangestu, Mari (1996), *Economic Reform, Deregulation and Privatization: The Indonesian Experience*, Jakarta: Centre for Strategic and International Studies.

Pangestu, Mari and Boediono (1986), 'Indonesia: The Structure and Causes of Manufacturing Sector Protection', in Christopher Findlay and Ross Garnaut (eds), *The Political Economy of Manufacturing Protection: Experiences of ASEAN and Australia*, Sydney: Allen and Unwin.

Panglaykim, J. (1960), *Beberapa Fakta dan Angka Produksi Tekstil dalam Negeri (Some Facts and Figures about Domestic Textile Production)*, Jakarta: University of Indonesia.

Panglaykim, J. (1968), 'Marketing Organisation in Transition' *Bulletin of Indonesian Economic Studies*, No 9, February, pp. 35–59.

Panglaykim, J. and H.W. Arndt (1966), 'Survey of Recent Developments', *Bulletin of Indonesian Economic Studies*, No 4, June, pp. 1–35.

Panglaykim, J. and Ingrid Palmer (1969), *State Trading Corporations in Developing Countries: With special reference to Indonesia and selected Asian Countries*, Rotterdam: Rotterdam University Press.

Panglaykim, J. and I. Palmer (1989), 'Study of Entrepreneurship in Developing Countries: The Development of One Chinese Concern in Indonesia' in Yoshihara Kunio (ed.), *Oei Tiong Ham Concern: The First Business Empire of Southeast Asia*, Kyoto: Center for Southeast Asian Studies, Kyoto University.

Panglaykim, J. and Mari Pangestu (1983), *Japanese Direct Investment in ASEAN: The Indonesian Experience*, Singapore: Maruzen Asia.

Papanek, Gustav (1980), 'The Effects of Economic Growth and Inflation on Workers' Income', in Gustav Papanek (ed.), *The Indonesian Economy*, New York: Praeger.

Parkin, M. and D. King (1991), *Economics* (First Edition), Wokingham: Addison-Wesley.

Pauker, Guy (1961), 'Indonesia's Eight-year Development Plan', *Pacific Affairs*, Vol. xxxiv (2), Summer, pp. 15–30.

Paulus, J. (1909), 'Finance' in Arnold Wright (ed.), *Twentieth Century Impressions of Netherlands India*, London: Lloyd's Greater Britain Publishing Company.

Pelzer, Karl (1945), *Pioneer Settlement in the Asiatic Tropics*, New York: American Geographical Society.

Pelzer, Karl (1978), *Planter and Peasant: Colonial Policy and the Agrarian Struggle in East Sumatra 1863–1947*, s'Gravenhage: M Nijhoff.

Penders, Chr. L.M. (ed.) (1977), *Indonesia: Selected Documents on Colonialism and Nationalism, 1830–1942*, St Lucia: University of Queensland Press.

Pick (1956), *Pick's Currency Yearbook 1956*, New York: Pick's Publishing Corporation.

Pick (1965), *Pick's Currency Yearbook 1964/5*, New York: Pick's Publishing Corporation.

Pitt, Mark (1981), 'Alternative Trade Strategies and Employment in Indonesia', in Anne O. Krueger *et al.* (eds), *Trade and Employment in Developing Countries: Vol 1, Individual Studies*, Chicago: University of Chicago Press.

Pitt, Mark (1991), 'Indonesia' in D. Papageorgiu, A.M. Choksi and M. Bruno (eds), *Liberalising Foreign Trade: Volume 5: The Experience of Indonesia, Pakistan and Sri Lanka*, Oxford: Basil Blackwell.

Poelinggomang, Edward L. (1993), 'The Dutch Trade Policy and its Impact on Makassar's Trade', *Review of Indonesian and Malaysian Affairs*, Vol 27(1 and 2), 61–76.

Polak, J.J. (1943), *The National Income of the Netherlands Indies, 1921–39*, as reprinted in P. Creutzberg (ed.), *Changing Economy of Indonesia, Vol Five, National Income*, The Hague: M. Nijhoff.

Pond, Donald H. (1964), 'Development Investment in Indonesia 1956–63', *Malayan Economic Review*, Vol IX(2), pp. 92–105.

Post, Peter (1993), 'Chinese business networks and Japanese capital in South East Asia, 1880–1940' in Rajeswary A. Brown (ed.), *Chinese Business Enterprise in Asia*, London: Routledge.

Posthumus, N.W. (1972), 'The Inter-governmental Group on Indonesia' *Bulletin of Indonesian Economic Studies*, Vol 8 (2), pp. 55–66.

Prince, Ge (1993), 'Economic Policy in Indonesia, 1900–1942' in J. Thomas Lindblad (ed.), *New Challenges in the Modern Economic History of Indonesia*, Leiden: Programme of Indonesian Studies.

Prince, G.H.A. (1996), 'Monetary policies in colonial Indonesia and the position of the Java Bank' in J. Th. Lindblad (ed.), *The Historical Foundations of a National Economy in Indonesia, 1890s–1990s*, Amsterdam: North-Holland for the Royal Netherlands Academy of Arts and Sciences.

Raffles, Thomas Stamford (1817), *The History of Java in Two Volumes*, London: Black, Parbury and Allen (Reprinted by Oxford University Press, Petaling Jaya).

Raj, K.N. (1969), 'Investment in Livestock in Agrarian Economies', *Indian Economic Review*, Vol 4(1), New Series, pp. 53–85.

Ramage, Douglas E. (1995), *Politics in Indonesia: Democracy, Islam and the Ideology of Tolerance*, London: Routledge.

Ray, Rajat Kanta (1995), 'Asian Capital in the Age of European Domination: The Rise of the Bazaar, 1800–1914', *Modern Asian Studies*, Vol 29 (3), pp. 449–554.

Reddy, K.N. (1972), *The Growth of Public Expenditure in India, 1872–1968*, New Delhi: Sterling Publishers.

Reid, Anthony (1969), *The Contest for North Sumatra: Atjeh, the Netherlands and Britain, 1858–1898*, Kuala Lumpur: Oxford University Press.

Reid, Anthony (1980), 'Indonesia: From Briefcase to Samurai Sword' in Alfred W. McCoy (ed.), *Southeast Asia under Japanese Occupation*, New Haven: Yale University Southeast Asia Studies, Monograph Series 22.

Reid, Anthony (1993), *Southeast Asia in the Age of Commerce, 1450–1680, Volume Two: Expansion and Crisis*, New Haven: Yale University Press.

Reynolds, Lloyd G. (1985), *Economic Growth in the Third World, 1850–1980*, New Haven: Yale University Press.

Ricklefs, Merle (1993), *A History of Modern Indonesia since c 1300*, (second edition), London: Macmillan.

Robison, Richard (1986), *Indonesia: The Rise of Capital*, Sydney: Allen & Unwin.

Rosendale, Phyllis (1975), 'The Indonesian Terms of Trade, 1950–73', *Bulletin of Indonesian Economic Studies*, Vol XI(3), pp.50–80.

Rosendale, Phyllis (1978), 'The Indonesian Balance of Payments: Some New Estimates', PhD Dissertation, Australian National University, Canberra.

Rosovsky, Henry (1972), 'What are the Lessons of Japanese Economic History' in A.J. Youngson (ed.), *Economic Development in the Long Run*, London: Allen and Unwin.

Rush, James (1991), 'Placing the Chinese in Java on the Eve of the Twentieth Century', *Indonesia*, Special Issue: 'The Role of the Chinese in Shaping Modern Indonesian Life', Ithaca: Cornell University Modern Indonesia Project.

Sachs, Jeffrey D. and Felipe Larrain (1993), *Macroeconomics in the Global Economy*, New York: Harvester Wheatsheaf.

Sadli, Mohammad (1971), 'Reflections on Boeke's Theory of Dualistic Economies' in Bruce Glassburner (ed.), *The Economy of Indonesia: Selected Readings*, Ithaca: Cornell University Press.

Sajogyo (1975). *Usaha Perbaikan Gizi Keluarga (ANP Evaluation Study, 1973)*, Bogor: Bogor Agricultural Institute.

Sandee, Henry (1995), 'Innovation Adoption in Rural Industry: Technological Change in Roof Tile Clusters in Central Java, Indonesia', PhD Thesis, Free University, Amsterdam.

Sandee, Henry, Piet Rietveld, Hendrawan Supratikno and Prapto Yuwono (1994), 'Promoting Small Scale and Cottage Industries in Indonesia: An Impact Analysis for Central Java', *Bulletin of Indonesian Economic Studies*, Vol 30(3), pp. 115–42.

Sartono Kartodirjo (1984), 'Social Stratification in Colonial Society' in *Modern Indonesia: Tradition and Transformation*, Yogyakarta: Gadjah Mada University Press.

Sato, Shigeru (1994), *War, Nationalism and Peasants: Java under the Japanese Occupation, 1942–5*, Sydney: Allen and Unwin for the Asian Studies Association of Australia.

Scheltema, A.M.P.A. (1936), *The Food Consumption of the Native Inhabitants of Java and Madura*, Batavia: Institute of Pacific Relations.

Schmitt, Hans O. (1962), 'Foreign Capital and Social Conflict in Indonesia, 1950–1958', *Economic Development and Cultural Change*, Vol 10 (3), April, pp. 284–93.

Schoffer, Ivo (1978), 'Dutch 'Expansion' and Indonesian Reactions: Some Dilemmas of Modern Colonial Rule (1900–1942)', in H.L. Wesseling (ed.), *Expansion and Reaction*, Leiden: Leiden University Press.

Schouten, Mieke (1995), 'Eras and Areas: Export Crops and Subsistence in Minahasa, 1817–1985', paper presented at the First European Association of South-east Asian Studies Conference, Leiden, 29 June to 1 July 1995.

Schrieke, B.J.O (1938), 'The Educational System in the Netherlands Indies', *Bulletin of the Colonial Institute of Amsterdam*, Vol 2(1), November pp. 14–24.

Setten van der Meer, N.C. van (1979), *Sawah Cultivation in Ancient Java: Aspects of Development during the Indo-Javanese Period, 5th to 15th Century*, Oriental Monograph Series 22, Canberra: Australian National University Press .

Shepherd, Jack (1941), *Industry in Southeast Asia*, New York: Institute of Pacific Relations.

Siahaan, Bisuk (1996), *Industrialisasi de Indonesia Sejak Hutang Kehormatan sampai Banting Stir [Industrialisation in Indonesia: From Debt of Honour to a Change of Direction]*, Jakarta: Pustaka Data.

Sie Kwat Soon (1968), *Prospects for Agricultural Development in Indonesia, with Special Reference to Java*, Wageningen: Centre for Agricultural Publishing and Documentation.

Sitsen, Peter H.W. (c1943), 'Industrial Development of the Netherlands Indies', *Bulletin 2 of the Netherlands and Netherlands Indies Council of the Institute of Pacific Relations*.

SJO: see under *Jaarcifers*.

Skinner, G. William (1960), 'Change and Persistance in Chinese Culture Overseas', *Journal of the South Seas Society*, Vol 16, pp. 86–100.

Soedarpo Sastrosatomo (1994), 'Recollections of my Career', *Bulletin of Indonesian Economic Studies*, Vol 30(1), pp. 39–58.

Soegijanto Padmo (1994), *The Cultivation of Vorstenlands Tobacco in Surakarta Residency and Besuki Tobacco in Besuki Residency and its Impact on the Peasant Economy and Society: 1860–1960*, Yogyakarta: Aditya Media.

Soeksmono B. Martokoesoema (1994), 'Small-scale Finance: Lessons from Indonesia' in Ross McLeod (ed.), *Indonesian Assessment 1994: Finance as a Key Sector in Indonesia's Development*, Singapore: Institute of Southeast Asian Studies.

Statistical Pocketbook of Indonesia 1941, Batavia: Department of Economic Affairs Central Bureau of Statistics, 1947.

Statistical Yearbook of Indonesia 1994, Jakarta: Central Bureau of Statistics.

Stoler, Ann (1985), *Capitalism and Confrontation in Sumatra's Plantation Belt*, New Haven: Yale University Press.

Sugiyama, Shinya, 'The Expansion of Japan's Cotton Textile Exports into Southeast Asia' (1994) in Shinya Sugiyama and M.C. Guerrero (eds), *International Commercial Rivalry in Southeast Asia in the Interwar Period*, Monograph 39, Yale Southeast Asia Studies, New Haven: Yale Center for International and Area Studies.

Sumitro Djojohadikusumo (1953), 'The Budget and its Implications', *Ekonomi dan Keuangan Indonesia*, Vol 6(1), pp. 3–30.

Sumitro Djojohadikusumo (1953a), *Persoalan Ekonomi Indonesia*, Jakarta: Toko Buku Indira.

Sumitro Djojohadikusumo (1986), 'Recollections of my Career', *Bulletin of Indonesian Economic Studies*, Vol 22(3), pp. 27–39.

Sumitro Djojohadikusumo (1989), *Kredit Rakyat di Masa Depressi*, Jakarta: LP3ES.

Sundrum, R.M. (1973), 'Money Supply and Prices: A Reinterpretation', *Bulletin of Indonesian Economic Studies*, Vol IX (3), November, pp. 73–86.

Sundrum, R.M. (1973a) 'Consumer Expenditure Patterns: An Analysis of the Socioeconomic Surveys' *Bulletin of Indonesian Economic Studies*, Vol IX (1), March, pp. 86–106.

Sundrum, R.M. (1986), 'Indonesia's Rapid Economic Growth, 1968–81', *Bulletin of Indonesian Economic Studies*, Vol 22 (3), December, pp. 40–69.

Sundrum, R.M. (1988), 'Indonesia's Slow Economic Growth, 1981–86', *Bulletin of Indonesian Economic Studies*, Vol 24 (1), April, pp. 37–72.

Sundrum, R.M. and Anne Booth (1980), 'Income Distribution: Trends and Determinants' in in R.G. Garnaut and P.T. McCawley (eds), *Indonesia: Dualism, Growth and Poverty*, Canberra: Research School of Pacific Studies, Australian National University.

Suryadinata, Leo (1972), 'Indonesian Chinese Education: Past and Present', *Indonesia*, October, pp. 49–71.

Sutton, Mary (1984), 'Indonesia, 1966–70' in Tony Killick (ed.), *The IMF and Stabilisation: Developing Country Experience*, London: Heinemann .

Svedberg, Peter (1978), 'The Portfolio-Direct Comparison of Private Foreign Investment in 1914 Revisited', *Economic Journal* 88, pp. 763–77.

Svedberg, Peter (1981). 'Colonial Enforcement of Foreign Direct Investment', *The Manchester School*, Vol 49(1), March, pp. 21–33.

Tabor, Steven R. (1992), 'Agriculture in Transition' in Anne Booth (ed.), *The Oil Boom and After: Indonesian Economic Policy and Performance in the Soeharto Era*, Singapore: Oxford University Press.

Tan, F.J.E. (1965), 'Aspects of Indonesian Economic Historiography' in Soedjatmoko *et al.* (eds), *An Introduction to Indonesian Historiography*, Ithaca: Cornell University Press.

Tandjung, I. and F. Nazar (1973), 'Prospek Keuangan Negara 1973' in Suhadi Mangkusuwondo, S.B. Joedono and Dorojatun Kuntjoro Jakti (eds), *Prospek Perekonomian Indonesia 1973*, Jakarta: LPEM, Faculty of Economics, Universty of Indonesia.

Thee, Kian-Wie (1977), *Plantation Agriculture and Export Growth: An Economic History of East Sumatra, 1863–1942*, Jakarta: National Institute for Economic and Social Research.

Thee, Kian-Wie (1991) 'The Surge of Asian NIC Investment into Indonesia', *Bulletin of Indonesian Economic Studies*, Vol 27(3), pp. 55–88.

Thee, Kian-Wie (1992) 'Technology Transfer from Japan to Indonesia', paper given at the Second Conference on the Transfer of Science and Technology between Europe and Asia since Vasco da Gama (1498–1998), Kyoto and Osaka, November. (Proceedings edited by Keiji Yamada for the International Research Center for Japanese Studies.)

Thieme, C. (1909), 'Roads and Bridges' in Arnold Wright (ed.), *Twentieth Century Impressions of Netherlands India*, London: Lloyd's Greater Britain Publishing Company.

Thomas, Ken and Peter Drysdale (1964) 'Indonesian Inflation, 1951–60', *Economic Record*, Vol 40, pp. 535–53.

Thompson, Virginia (1947), 'Aspects of Planning in Indonesia' *Pacific Affairs*, Vol 20, pp. 178–83.

Timmer, C. Peter (1973), 'Choice of Technique in Rice Milling in Java' *Bulletin of Indonesian Economic Studies*, Vol 9(2), pp. 57–76.

Timmer, C. Peter (1996), 'Does Bulog Stabilise Rice Prices in Indonesia? Should it Try?', *Bulletin of Indonesian Economic Studies*, Vol 32(2), pp. 45–73.

Twang, Peck-Yang (1987), 'Indonesian Chinese Communities in Transformation, 194–50', PhD Dissertation, Australian National University, Canberra.

UNDP (1995), *Human Development Report 1995*, New York: Oxford University Press for the United Nations Development Programme.

United Nations (1960), *Yearbook of National Income Accounts*, New York: United Nations.

United Nations (1964), *Review of Long-term Economic Projections for Selected Countries in the Ecafe Region, Development Programming Techniques*, Series, No 5, Bangkok: United Nations Economic Commission for Asia and the Far East.

Utrecht, Ernst (1969), 'Land Reform in Indonesia', *Bulletin of Indonesian Economic Studies*, Vol. 5 (3), July, pp. 71–88.

Vaidyanathan, A. (1983), 'The Indian Economy since Independence (1947–70)', in *The Cambridge Economic History of India, Vol 2, c1757–c1970*, Cambridge: Cambridge University Press.

Vandenbosch, A. (1941), *The Dutch East Indies: Its Government, Problems and Politics*, Berkeley: University of California Press.

Veur, Paul van der (1969), 'Education and Social Change in Colonial Indonesia (1)', *Papers in International Studies, Southeast Asia Series No 12*, Athens: Ohio University Center for International Studies.

Wade, Robert (1990), *Governing the Market*, Princeton: Princeton University Press.

Wal, S. van der (1961), *Some Information on Education in Indonesia up to 1942*, Amsterdam: Netherlands Universities Foundation for International Cooperation.

Wal, S. L. van der (1963), *Het Onderwijsbeleid in Nederlands-Indie 1900–1940: Een Bronnenpublikatie*, Groningen: Wolters.

Wallace, Alfred Russel (1869), *The Malay Archipelago*, London: Macmillan (Reprinted by Dover Publications, New York).

Wander, Hilde (1965), *Die Beziehungen Zwischen Bevolkerung und Wirtshaftsent-wicklung, Dargestellt am Beispiel Indonesiens*, Tubingen: J.C.B. Mohr .

Warmelo, W. van (1946), 'De Indische Industrie gedurende de Japansche Bezitting', *Economische Statistiche Berichten*, 27 March.

Warr, Peter G. (1984), 'Exchange Rate Protection in Indonesia', *Bulletin of Indonesian Economic Studies*, Vol XX (2), pp. 53–89.

Warr, Peter (1992), 'Exchange Rate Policy, Petroleum Prices and the Balance of Payments' in Anne Booth (ed.) (1992), *op cit.*

Waswo, Ann (1996), *Modern Japanese Society 1868–1994*, Oxford: Oxford University Press.

Weckstein, Richard S. (1959), 'Banking and development in a central Java city', *Ekonomi dan Keuangan Indonesia*, Vol XII (5/6), pp. 189–203.

Weinreb, F. and Madjid Ibrahim (1957), 'Penjelidikan Biaja Hidup di Djakarta', *Ekonomi dan Keuangan Indonesia*, Vol X (11 and 12), pp. 738–95.

Weinstein, Franklin B. (1976), *Indonesian Foreign Policy and the Dilemma of Dependence: from Sukarno to Soeharto*, Ithaca: Cornell University Press.

Wellenstein, E. (1909), 'Railways and Tramways' in Arnold Wright (ed.), *Twentieth Century Impressions of Netherlands India*, London: Lloyd's Greater Britain Publishing Company.

Wertheim, W.F. (1956), *Indonesian Society in Transition: A Study of Social Change*, The Hague: W. van Hoeve.

Wertheim, W.F. (1964), 'Betting on the Strong' in *East–west Parallels: Sociological Approaches to Modern Asia*, The Hague: W. van Hoeve.

Wesseling, H.L. (1978), 'Expansion and Reaction: Some Reflections on a Symposium and a Theme' in H.L. Wesseling (ed.), *Expansion and Reaction*, Leiden: Leiden University Press.

Wesseling, H.L., (1988), 'The Giant that was a Dwarf, or the Strange History of Dutch Imperialism' in Andrew Porter and Robert Holland (eds), *Theory and Practice in the History of European Expansion Overseas: Essays in Honour of Ronald Robinson*, London: Frank Cass.

White, Ben (1973), 'Demand for Labour and Population Growth in Colonial Java', *Human Ecology*, Vol 1 (3), pp. 217–36.

White, Ben (1979), 'Political Aspects of Poverty, Income Distribution and their Measurement: Some Examples from Rural Java', *Development and Change*, Vol 10, pp. 91–114.

White, Ben (1991), 'Economic Diversification and Agrarian Change in Rural Java, 1900–1990' in Paul Alexander, Peter Boomgaard and Ben White (eds), *In the Shadow of Agriculture: Non-farm Activities in the Javanese Economy, Past and Present*, Amsterdam: Royal Tropical Institute.

Widyahartono, Bob (1993), 'Konglomerat: Antara Teori dan Realitas' in Kwik Kian Gie *et al.*, *Konglomerat Indonesia: Permasalahan dan Sepak Terjangnya (Conglomerates in Indonesia: Problems and Conduct)*, Jakarta: Pustaka Sinar Harapan.

Wilde, A.N. de and J. Th. Moll (1936), *The Netherlands Indies during the Depression: A Brief Economic Survey*, Amsterdam: J.M. Meulenhoff.

Williams, Lea (1952), 'Chinese Entrepreneurs in Indonesia', *Explorations in Entrepreneurial History*, Vol 5 (1), pp. 34–60.

Williamson, John (1994), 'In Search of a Manual for Technopols' in John Williamson (ed.), *The Political Economy of Policy Reform*, Washington: Institute for International Economics.

Willner, Ann Ruth (1981),'Repetition in Change: Cyclical Movement and Indonesian "Development"', *Economic Development and Cultural Change*, Vol. 29 (2), January, pp. 409–17.

Wit, Ynto de (1973), 'The Kabupaten Programme', *Bulletin of Indonesian Economic Studies*, Vol IX (1), March, pp. 65–85.

Woo, Wing-Thye, Bruce Glassburner and Anwar Nasution (1994), *Macroeconomic Policies, Crises and Long-term Growth in Indonesia, 1965–90*, Washington: World Bank.

World Bank (1976), *World Tables*, Washington: World Bank.

World Bank (1982), *Commodity Trade and Price Trends*, Washington: World Bank.

World Bank (1983), *World Development Report, 1983*, New York: Oxford University Press.

World Bank (1993), *The East Asian Miracle: Economic Growth and Public Policy*, New York: Oxford University Press.

World Bank (1995), *World Debt Tables Vol 2*, Washington: World Bank.

Wright, Arnold (1909), 'History' in Arnold Wright (ed.), *Twentieth Century Impressions of Netherlands India*, London: Lloyd's Greater Britain Publishing Company.

Wymenga, Paul S.J. (1991), 'The Structure of Protection in Indonesia in 1989', *Bulletin of Indonesian Economic Studies*, Vol 27(1), pp. 127–53.

Yamashita, Shoichi (ed.) (1990), *Transfer of Japanese* Technology and Management to the ASEAN Countries, Tokyy: University of Tokyo Press.

Yates, P. Lamartine (1959), Forty Years of Foreign Trade, London: George Allen and Unwin.

Yoshida, Masami, Ichiro Akimune, Masayuki Nohara and Kimitoshi Sato (1994), 'Regional Economic Integration in East Asia: Special Features and Policy Implications' in Vincent Cable and David Henderson (eds), *Trade Blocs? The Future of Regional Integration*, London: Royal Institute of International Affairs.

Yoshihara Kunio (1989), 'Introduction' in Yoshihara Kunio (ed.), *Oei Tiong Ham Concern: The First Business Empire of Southeast Asia*, Kyoto: Center for Southeast Asian Studies, Kyoto University.

Yoshihara, Kunio (1994), *The Nation and Economic Growth: The Philippines and Thailand*, Kuala Lumpur: Oxford University Press.

Zanden, J.L. van (1993), *The Rise and Decline of Holland's Economy: Merchant Capitalism and the Labour Market*, Manchester: Manchester University Press.

Index